Understanding IFRS for SMEs

General Editor: Jade Jansen

Authors: Mohamed Karodia, Rashied Small

JUTA

Understanding IFRS for SMEs

First published 2020
First reprint 2021

Juta and Company (Pty) Ltd
PO Box 14373, Lansdowne, 7779, Cape Town, South Africa
1st Floor, Sunclare Building, 21 Dreyer Street, Claremont 7708
www.juta.co.za

© Juta and Company (Pty) Ltd 2021

ISBN 9781 48512 525 9

Production Specialist: Mmakasa Ramoshaba
Proofreader: Lee-Ann Ashcroft
Typesetter: Wouter Reinders
Cover designer: Adam Rumball

Typeset in Times New Roman 11pt

CONTENTS

PREFACE   x

ABOUT THE AUTHORS   xi

CHAPTER 1 – THE FRAMEWORK   **1**

1.1   INTRODUCTION   1
1.2   LEARNING OUTCOMES   1
1.3   SCOPE AND OBJECTIVES   2
1.4   CONCEPTS AND PERVASIVE PRINCIPLES   2
1.5   ELEMENTS OF FINANCIAL STATEMENTS   5
1.6   RECOGNITION CRITERIA   8
1.7   OFFSETTING   8
SELF-ASSESSMENT   9

CHAPTER 2 – FINANCIAL STATEMENT PRESENTATION   **13**

2.1   INTRODUCTION   13
2.2   LEARNING OUTCOMES   13
2.3   DEFINITIONS   14
2.4   SCOPE AND OBJECTIVES   14
2.5   FAIR PRESENTATION   14
2.6   COMPLIANCE WITH THE IFRS FOR SMEs   15
2.7   PREPARING FINANCIAL STATEMENTS   15
2.8   COMPLETE SET OF FINANCIAL STATEMENTS   18
SELF-ASSESSMENT   31

**CHAPTER 3 – ACCOUNTING FOR TAXATION AND
VALUE-ADDED TAX**   **36**

3.1   INTRODUCTION   38
3.2   LEARNING OUTCOMES   39
3.3   VAT CHARGE   39
3.4   OUTPUT VAT   41
3.5   INPUT VAT   42
3.6   INCOME TAXES   44
SELF-ASSESSMENT   63

CHAPTER – 4 PROPERTY, PLANT AND EQUIPMENT   **68**

4.1   INTRODUCTION   69
4.2   LEARNING OUTCOMES   70

4.3	DEFINITIONS	70
4.4	SCOPE AND OBJECTIVES	71
4.5	BASIC TRANSACTIONS	72
4.6	LAND AND BUILDINGS	89
4.7	SPARE PARTS	91
4.8	DISMANTLING AND REHABILITATION COSTS	94
4.9	IMPAIRMENT	98
4.10	REVALUATION	101
4.11	EFFECTS OF TAXATION	103
4.12	DISCLOSURE	105
	SELF-ASSESSMENT	106

CHAPTER 5 – INVESTMENT PROPERTY — **115**

5.1	INTRODUCTION	116
5.2	LEARNING OUTCOMES	116
5.3	DEFINITIONS	116
5.4	SCOPE AND OBJECTIVES	117
5.5	BASIC TRANSACTIONS	117
5.6	RECLASSIFICATION	125
5.7	INTEREST IN PROPERTY LEASED IN TERMS OF AN OPERATING LEASE	127
5.8	EFFECTS OF TAXATION	129
5.9	DISCLOSURE	130
	SELF-ASSESSMENT	132

CHAPTER 6 – INVENTORIES — **137**

6.1	INTRODUCTION	137
6.2	LEARNING OUTCOMES	138
6.3	SCOPE AND OBJECTIVES	138
6.4	COST OF INVENTORIES	140
6.5	MANUFACTURED GOODS	150
6.6	COST OF INVENTORIES OF A SERVICE PROVIDER	155
6.7	METHODS USED FOR MEASURING COST	157
6.8	COST FORMULAS	157
6.9	INVENTORY CONTROL SYSTEMS	158
6.10	MEASURE OF INVENTORIES	161
6.11	SPECIAL ISSUES	163
6.12	DISCLOSURE	166
6.13	PHYSICAL INVENTORY COUNT	166
	SELF-ASSESSMENT	168

CHAPTER 7 – INTANGIBLE ASSETS OTHER THAN GOODWILL   **174**

7.1   INTRODUCTION   176
7.2   LEARNING OUTCOMES   176
7.3   DEFINITIONS   176
7.4   SCOPE AND OBJECTIVES   177
7.5   CLASSIFICATION   177
7.6   INITIAL RECOGNTION   178
7.7   SUBSEQUENT MEASUREMENT   180
7.8   PRESENTATION AND DISCLOSURE   182
SELF-ASSESSMENT   184

CHAPTER 8 – IMPAIRMENT OF ASSETS   **190**

8.1   INTRODUCTION   190
8.2   LEARNING OUTCOMES   190
8.3   DEFINITIONS   191
8.4   SCOPE AND OBJECTIVES   191
8.5   IMPAIRMENT OF ASSETS   192
8.6   GUIDANCE FOR SPECIFIC ASSETS   199
8.7   CASH-GENERATING UNITS   201
8.8   DEFERRED TAXATION   206
8.9   DISCLOSURE   206
SELF-ASSESSMENT   212

CHAPTER 9 – BASIC FINANCIAL INSTRUMENTS   **218**

9.1   INTRODUCTION   229
9.2   DEFINITIONS   229
9.3   SCOPE AND OBJECTIVES   220
9.4   CLASSIFICATION   221
9.5   INITIAL RECOGNITION   223
9.6   SUBSEQUENT MEASUREMENT   224
9.7   IMPAIRMENT OF A FINANCIAL ASSET MEASURED AT
       COST OR AMORTISED COST   227
9.8   REVERSAL OF IMPAIRMENT OF A FINANCIAL ASSET
       AT COST OR AMORTISED COST   228
9.9   FAIR VALUE   239
9.10   PRESENTATION AND DISCLOSURE   239
SELF-ASSESSMENT   231

CHAPTER 10 – PROVISIONS AND CONTIGENCIES   **236**

10.1   INTRODUCTION   237
10.2   LEARNING OUTCOMES   237
10.3   DEFINITIONS   238

10.4 SCOPE AND OBJECTIVES   39
10.5 CLASSIFICATION OF FINANCIAL OBLIGATIONS   239
10.6 PROVISIONS   241
10.7 CONTINGENT LIABILITIES   250
10.8 RECOGNITION OF CONTINGENT ASSETS   251
10.9 PREJUDICIAL DISCLOSURES   252
SELF-ASSESSMENT   253

CHAPTER 11 – LEASES   **260**

11.1 INTRODUCTION   263
11.2 LEARNING OUTCOMES   263
11.3 DEFINITIONS   264
11.4 SCOPE AND OBJECTIVES   266
11.5 LESSEE   268
11.6 LESSOR   272
11.7 MANUFACTURER OR DEALER LESSORS   276
11.8 SALE AND LEASEBACK   277
11.9 PRESENTATION AND DISCLOSURE   281
SELF-ASSESSMENT   284

CHAPTER 12 – REVENUE   **290**

12.1 INTRODUCTION   291
12.2 LEARNING OUTCOMES   291
12.3 DEFINITIONS   291
12.4 SCOPE AND OBJECTIVES   292
12.5 RECOGNITION   292
12.6 GENERAL   299
12.7 PRESENTATION AND DISCLOSURE   304
SELF-ASSESSMENT   306

CHAPTER 13 – GOVERNMENT GRANTS   **312**

13.1 INTRODUCTION   313
13.2 LEARNING OUTCOMES   313
13.3 DEFINITIONS   313
13.4 SCOPE AND OBJECTIVES   314
13.5 RECOGNITION & MEASUREMENT   315
13.6 DISCLOSURE   316
13.7 REQUIREMENTS IN FULL IFRS   316
SELF-ASSESSMENT   318

CHAPTER 14 – ACCOUNTING POLICIES, ESTIMATES AND ERRORS, AND EVENTS AFTER THE END OF THE REPORTING PERIOD   **322**

14.1 INTRODUCTION   324

14.2   LEARNING OUTCOMES   324
14.3   DEFINITIONS   325
14.4   SCOPE AND OBJECTIVES   325
14.5   ACCOUNTING POLICIES   326
14.6   CORRECTIONS OF PRIOR PERIOD ERRORS   332
14.7   DISCLOSURE   334
14.8   EVENTS AFTER THE END OF THE REPORTING PERIOD   334
SELF-ASSESSMENT   340

CHAPTER 15 – FOREIGN CURRENCY TRANSLATION   346

15.1   INTRODUCTION   346
15.2   LEARNING OUTCOMES   346
15.3   DEFINITIONS   357
15.4   SCOPE AND OBJECTIVES   357
15.5   IDENTIFYING THE FUNCTIONAL CURRENCY OF THE
       ENTITY   357
15.6   REPORTING FOREIGN CURRENCY TRANSACTIONS IN THE
       FUNCTIONAL CURRENCY   350
15.7   DISCLOSURE   354
SELF-ASSESSMENT   355

CHAPTER 16 – STATEMENT OF CASH FLOWS   360

16.1   INTRODUCTION   361
16.2   LEARNING OUTCOMES   361
16.3   DEFINITIONS   362
16.4   SCOPE AND OBJECTIVES   362
16.5   CLASSIFICATION   362
16.6   REPORTING   365
16.7   PRESENTATION AND DISCLOSURE   371
SELF-ASSESSMENT   375

**CHAPTER 17 – EMPLOYEE BENEFITS AND RELATED PARTY
DISCLOSURES   382**

17.1   INTRODUCTION   384
17.2   LEARNING OUTCOMES   385
17.3   DEFINITIONS   385
17.4   SCOPE AND OBJECTIVES   396
17.5   EMPLOYEE BENEFITS   396
17.6   RELATED PARTY DISCLOSURES   400
SELF-ASSESSMENT   405

CHAPTER 18 – OTHER FINANCIAL INSTRUMENT ISSUES   **411**

18.1 INTRODUCTION   412
18.2 LEARNING OUTCOMES   413
18.3 DEFINITIONS   413
18.4 SCOPE AND OBJECTIVES   414
18.5 CLASSIFICATION   414
18.6 INITIAL RECOGNITION   416
18.7 SUBSEQUENT MEASUREMENT   418
18.8 IMPAIRMENT AND REVERSAL OF IMPAIRMENT OF A
FINANCIAL ASSET MEASURED AT COST LESS IMPAIRMENT   419
18.9 HEDGE ACCOUNTING   419
18.10 PRESENTATION AND DISCLOSURE   426
SELF-ASSESSMENT   429

CHAPTER 19 – INVESTMENTS IN ASSOCIATES   **435**

19.1 INTRODUCTION   435
19.2 LEARNING OUTCOMES   436
19.3 DEFINITIONS   436
19.4 SCOPE AND OBJECTIVES   436
19.5 CLASSIFICATION AS INVESTOR–ASSOCIATE
RELATIONSHIP   436
19.6 INITIAL RECOGNITION   437
19.7 MEASUREMENT SUBSEQUENT TO INITIAL RECOGNITION   438
19.8 PRESENTATION AND DISCLOSURE   450
SELF-ASSESSMENT   451

**CHAPTER 20 – CONSOLIDATED AND SEPARATE FINANCIAL
STATEMENTS**   **456**

20.1 INTRODUCTION   458
20.2 LEARNING OUTCOMES   458
20.3 DEFINITIONS   458
20.4 SCOPE AND OBJECTIVES   459
20.5 CLASSIFICATION AS A PARENT–SUBSIDIARY
RELATIONSHIP   459
20.6 PREPARING THE FINANCIAL STATEMENTS   460
20.7 DISCLOSURE   475
SELF-ASSESSMENT   477

CHAPTER 21 – SHARE-BASED PAYMENT   **483**

21.1 INTRODUCTION   484
21.2 LEARNING OUTCOMES   484

21.3   DEFINITIONS   495
21.4   SCOPE AND OBJECTIVES   496
21.5   CLASSIFICATION AS EQUITY SETTLED OR CASH SETTLED   496
SELF-ASSESSMENT   493

CHAPTER 22 – ANALYSIS AND INTERPRETATION OF
FINANCIAL STATEMENTS   **498**

22.1   INTRODUCTION   500
22.2   LEARNING OUTCOMES   500
22.3   LIQUIDITY RATIOS   502
22.4   WORKING CAPITAL RATIOS   503
22.5   DEBT MANAGEMENT RATIOS   505
22.6   PROFITABILITY RATIOS   508
SELF-ASSESSMENT   511

PREFACE

The literature uses an easy to understand conceptual approach to explaining the requirements for preparing financial statements in accordance with IFRS for SMEs. The logical explanations of the requirements of the standard are supported with source references to the standard, so that readers are able to reference the conceptual understanding to the direct text as written in the standard and vice-versa. In addition, illustrative examples show how the underlying concepts are operationalised into the practice of accounting. Lastly, while the text is designed to provide guidance to those wishing to understand IFRS for SMEs, reference to the (full) IFRS standards are made where appropriate, so that those readers who want to compare the requirements in the two IFRS standards are able to do so.

KEY FEATURES
Illustrative disclosure
Most chapters start with illustrative disclosure so that readers can contextualise the information presented in each chapter.

Learning objectives
Learning objectives are included at the beginning of each chapter so that readers can assess what topics and concepts will be covered in each chapter.

Illustrative diagrams
Where appropriate, illustrative visual aids such as diagrams, flowcharts etc. are included in the chapters to serve as a learning aid by visually reinforcing the main text and illustrating the articulation between related concepts.

Illustrative examples
Illustrative examples are designed to show readers how the concepts are operationalised into the practice of accounting. Various approaches are used to achieve this objective, with some illustrative examples being discussion based while others focus on calculations, the preparation of journal entries etc.

End-of-Chapter Question
Each chapter concludes with:
(i)   multiple choice questions designed to give reader high level efficient feedback on their understanding of certain key concepts in each chapter; and
(ii) comprehensive self-study questions designed to test readers' more in depth understanding and practical implications of the concepts in each chapter.

Support Material
A set of Powerpoint slides have been provided as support material for lecturers and facilitators. Each set of slides includes the learning objectives for each chapter, the main concepts that students need to understand as well as activities to assist the students in understanding the main concepts of the chapter. The slides also includes the answers to the long questions in each chapter.

ABOUT THE AUTHORS

Jade Jansen

Jade Jansen is an associate professor at the University of the Western Cape where he serves as the Deputy Head of the Department of Accounting and the Subject Head of Financial Accounting. He is a Chartered Accountant with a master's degree in accounting sciences from the University of Pretoria. He has been extensively involved with the training of various programmes, preparation of students for the examinations of and facilitating on CPD events for various professional bodies. He has trained accounting and its related subjects at all levels including to local and foreign government agencies, accounting professional bodies, audit and accounting firms. In addition, Jade has and currently serves on various committees and sub-committees of various professional accounting bodies.

Mohamed Karodia

Mohamed Karodia is currently the Head of the Faculty of Commerce at Rosebank College which is a brand of the Independent Institute of Education. He has previously lectured at the University of Johannesburg as well as the University of South Africa. He also moderates and reviews content and assessments for various institutions such as Boston Media House, Independent Colleges Group and Pearson International. Mohamed has a B. Com, B.Com Honours, Post graduate Diploma in Tertiary Education and a Master's in Education.

Rashied Small

Rashied Small is the Executive Thought Leadership at the South African Institute of Professional Accountants (SAIPA) and chairman of the Pan-African Education Committee (PAEC) and Interim Academic Advisory Committee (IAAC) responsible for the development and implementation of curricula in the accounting and auditing sectors across Africa. He is a holder of PHD in finance and education and introduced alternative education models such as competency-based education, problem-based learning and rubric grading in the accountancy profession. He has been extensively involved with the accountancy education and training both locally and internationally including the development of professional accountancy qualifications. training of various programmes including setting of professional competency-based assessments. He has trained accounting and its related subjects at all levels including to local and foreign government agencies, accounting professional bodies, audit and accounting firms. In addition, Rashied has developed digital learning platforms that promotes competencies for professionals in the accountancy profession.

CHAPTER 1
THE FRAMEWORK

1.1 INTRODUCTION

The expectations of users of financial statements together with the regulatory requirements placed on business entities to comply have resulted in significant changes in the accounting standards. There has been a major shift over many years to harmonise the accounting standards used globally, which has resulted in the development of International Financial Reporting Standards (IFRS) by the International Accounting Standards Board (IASB). The development of accounting standards, such as full IFRS, has resulted in an onerous responsibility of businesses and auditors to ensure that the transactions reported in financial statements comply with their requirements.

There are two standards of IFRS as issued by the IASB, namely IFRS and IFRS for Small and Medium Entities (SMEs).

IFRS for SMEs was developed by the IASB specifically to address the needs of the users of the financial statements of SMEs and for cost–benefit considerations (Preface to the IFRS for SMEs, p9).

1.2 LEARNING OUTCOMES

Upon completion of this chapter you should be able to:
(a) identify the characteristics of SMEs and which entities can apply IFRS for SMEs;
(b) explain the usefulness of the accounting concepts and pervasive principles;
(c) list the objectives of financial reporting;
(d) identify the qualitative characteristics of accounting information and financial statements;
(e) define the basic elements of financial statements (assets, liabilities, equity, income and expenses);
(f) apply the basic assumptions for preparing financial statements; and
(g) explain the basic application of the accounting concepts and pervasive principles.

1.3   SCOPE AND OBJECTIVES

IFRS for SMEs was not designed with the intention of replacing what we commonly refer to as full IFRS. For this reason, only those entities within the scope of IFRS for SMEs may use the standard. These are those that (s1.2):

(a)   do not have public accountability; and
(b)   publish general purpose financial statements for external users.

An entity is considered to have public accountability if (s1.3):

(a)   its debt or equity instruments are traded in a public market or it is in the process of issuing such instruments for trading in a public market (whether domestic or international market); or
(b)   it holds assets in a fiduciary capacity for a broad group of outsiders as one of its primary businesses (such as banks).

1.4   CONCEPTS AND PERVASIVE PRINCIPLES

1.4.1   Objective of financial statements of SMEs

The objective of the financial statements of SMEs is to provide information about the **financial position**, **performance** and **cash flows** of the entity that are useful for decision-making by a broad range of users (for instance, investors, lenders and other creditors) who are not in a position to demand reports tailored to meet their needs (s2.2).[1]

What decisions do users want to make? They want to make economic decisions such as lending, investing and extending credit to the entity. Financial statements which are prepared on the basis of IFRS for SMEs are therefore general purpose financial statements. For instance, financial statements prepared based on tax rules might be relevant to SARS, but they are not general purpose financial statements.

1.4.2   Qualitative characteristics

What qualities does information have that will result in useful information to users so that they can make economic decisions about the entity? Useful information, in the context of IFRS for SMEs has the following qualitative characteristics:[2]

---

[1] *The objective of financial statements in IFRS is to provide financial information about the reporting entity that is useful to existing and potential investors, lenders and other creditors in making decisions about providing resources to the entity (Conceptual Framework (CF) 1.1).*

[2] *Full IFRS has two tiers of qualitative characteristics. The first tier is the fundamental qualitative characteristics of relevance and faithful representation. The second tier, called the enhancing qualitative characteristics, includes comparability, verifiability, timeliness and understandability. These are not discussed in this book.*

1.4.2.1 Understandability

Any information presented should ideally be understandable by users who have a reasonable knowledge of business, economic activities and accounting, and who are willing to study the information with reasonable diligence (s2.4). Information cannot, however, be omitted on the grounds that it is difficult for some users to understand.

1.4.2.2 Relevance

As the provision of information is for economic decision-making, all information in the financial statements should be relevant to the decision-making of its users (s2.5). Information will be considered to be relevant if it can influence decision-making.

1.4.2.3 Materiality

Information is material if its misstatement or omission influences the economic decisions of users (s2.6). Therefore, material information is relevant information. Materiality is not only impacted by the size of the information but also its nature. For instance, information related to the tax expense of an entity might not be quantitatively material (because it is small in number) but might be qualitatively material (because tax evasion (as an example) might impact a user's decision about whether to invest in the entity).

1.4.2.4 Reliability

It is accepted that estimates are used in the preparation of financial statements. For instance, when you sell something on credit, there is no guarantee that the debtor will repay its debt. However, at the time of sale (and subsequently) the entity makes assumptions and uses estimates to determine the probability of the amount that the debtor will pay. The use of estimates can still result in reliable information. Information is considered reliable when it is free from material error and bias, and represents faithfully that which it purports to represent or can reasonably be expected to represent (s2.7). Therefore, as long as the information takes into account all of the facts and circumstances needed to make an estimate, the estimate is considered to be reliable.

1.4.2.5 Substance over form

Information presented should reflect the substance of a transaction and not merely its form (s2.8). For instance, when an entity leases an asset and obtains substantially all of the future economic benefits associated with the asset but never owns the asset (yet nevertheless controls the asset), the entity should recognise the asset in its accounting records. Even though the entity legally never owns the asset, the substance of the relationship reveals that it controls the asset.

3

1.4.2.6 Prudence

Prudence is reflected by the level of caution exercised in making judgements used in the information presented (s2.9). It involves ensuring that assets and income are not overstated and liabilities and expenses are not understated. However, prudence does not result in the deliberate understatement of assets and income, or the overstatement of liabilities and expenses.

1.4.2.7 Completeness

Information should be complete within the bounds of materiality and cost (s2.10).

1.4.2.8 Comparability

One could ask whether a profit of CU1 billion is reflective of good performance. The answer is that it depends, as all information is relative. For instance, the profit of CU1 billion will be considered good performance if all other similar-sized companies are generating profits of CU500 million. The performance might also be considered good if it reflects that profits have gone up over time or are a greater portion of the revenue than usual. All of these decisions involve comparing information (for instance, between companies, over time and between different amounts in the financial statements). For this reason, information must be comparable. Comparable information results from similar transactions, events and positions being reflected in a consistent manner within the entity, over time and across different entities (s2.11).

1.4.2.9 Timeliness

Information is only relevant if it is available in time to affect the decision by the user. For instance, it might take many months to interrogate information to ensure that it is as reliable as it can be, by which time the information may be outdated and irrelevant (s2.12).

1.4.2.10 Balance between benefit and cost

There is constantly a need to assess that the cost of producing information does not outweigh the benefits expected from it (s2.13). This ensures that all information provided have a positive value to add.

1.4.2.11 Undue cost or effort

Information is often exempt for being used in IFRS for SMEs if it will require undue cost or effort to obtain (s2.14). In order to make the evaluation of undue cost or effort, the entity considers the balance between benefit and cost of providing the information.

1.5   ELEMENTS OF FINANCIAL STATEMENTS

1.5.1   Assets

An asset is (s2.17):
(a)   a resource: something that can be used;
(b)   controlled by the entity: which means that the entity can direct the use of the item and restrict access to the future economic benefits associated with the asset;
(c)   a result of a past event: something must have given rise to the control by the entity; and
(d)   something from which future economic benefits are expected to flow: all assets have to result in a benefit to the entity.

Illustrative Example 1.1: Assets

A company purchases a machine which it can use to produce inventory.

You are required to:
Discuss whether the machine can be classified as an asset.

Suggested solution:
The machine will be classified as an asset since it is a resource (the machine can be used by the entity) which is controlled by the entity (the entity can direct its use and restrict other people from using it) as a result of a past event (the entity purchased the machinery) and from which future economic benefits are expected to emanate (the entity will be able to produce saleable inventory from the machine).

The definitions of the elements of the financial statements are different in IFRS for SMEs and full IFRS. Full IFRS defines an asset as a present economic resource controlled by the entity as a result of past events. It states that an economic resource is a right that has the potential to produce economic benefits (CF p.4.3–4.4).

1.5.2   Liabilities

A liability is (s2.20):
(a)   a present obligation: the entity has no alternative to avoid the obligation;
(b)   as a result of a past event: the obligation arose from something that happened; and
(c)   is expected to result in the outflow of economic benefits from the entity: generally such an obligation will result in the entity losing resources.

Illustrative Example 1.2: Liabilities

A company owes its creditor CU100 for inventory which it purchased but never paid for.

You are required to:
Discuss whether the amount payable by the entity to its creditor is a liability.

Suggested solution:
The inventory is clearly an asset (consider the definition of an asset above). The amount payable to the creditor is a liability as it represents a present obligation of the entity (the entity cannot avoid the obligation and is locked into paying the creditor) as a result of a past event (the purchase of the inventory is the event that locked then entity into the present obligation) and is expected to result in an outflow of economic benefits from the entity (the entity will lose resources when it settles the obligation).

Full IFRS defines a liability as a present obligation of the entity to transfer an economic resource as a result of past events (CF p.4.26)

1.5.3   Equity

Equity is the residual interest in the assets of the entity after deducting all of its liabilities (Appendix B and CF p.4.63).

This is clearly illustrated in the accounting equation:

ASSETS = EQUITY + LIABILITIES

1.5.4   Income

Income is defined as (s2.23):
(a)   the increase in economic benefits;
(b)   during the accounting period;
(c)   in the form of increases or enhancements of assets; OR
(d)   decreases of liabilities;
(e)   that result in increase in equity;
(f)   other than those resulting from contributions from owners.

Illustrative Example 1.3: Income

A company sells inventory which cost CU150 for CU180 to a customer for cash.

You are required to:
Discuss whether the sale of inventory and results in income.

Suggested solution:
The increase in cash represents an increase in assets. The increase in assets represents an increase in economic benefits during the accounting period (the sale took place in the current period) that results in increases in equity (profit is for the benefit of the shareholders) and the increase in assets is not due to contributions of owners. Therefore, the sale of inventory is classified as income.

Revenue is a special category of income. Revenue is income, but only the income that arises in the course of the ordinary activities of an entity. Therefore, not all income is revenue, but all revenue meets the definition of income. Refer to the chapter on revenue for a further discussion on the topic.

IFRS defines income as increases in assets, or decreases in liabilities, that result in increases in equity, other than those relating to contributions from holders of equity claims (CF p.4.68).

1.5.5   Expense

An expense is defined as (s2.23):
(a)   a decrease in economic benefits;
(b)   during the accounting period;
(c)   in the form of outflows or depletions of assets; OR
(d)   incurrences of liabilities;
(e)   that result in decreases in equity;
(f)   other than those relating to distributions to owners.

Illustrative Example 1.4: Expense

A company pays CU400 for advertising services.

You are required to:
Discuss whether the amount spent on advertising represents an expense.

Suggested solution:
The advertising service results in an outflow of economic benefits (use of assets to settle the advertising expense) during the accounting period (the benefit of the accounting service was consumed during the accounting period), in the form of outflows or depletions of assets (the cash payment) or incurrences of liabilities (the requirement is that either there is an outflow of assets OR an incurrence of liabilities) that result in decreases in equity (the loss is borne by the shareholder), other than those relating to distributions to owners (the cash outflow was not a distribution to shareholders). The advertising is therefore an expense.

IFRS defines expenses as decreases in assets, or increases in liabilities, that result in decreases in equity, other than those relating to distributions to holders of equity claims (CF p.4.69).

1.6   RECOGNITION CRITERIA

Just because an item meets the definition of an element of accounting, it does not mean that the item should be incorporated into the financial statements. Recognition, in the context of accounting, means to incorporate within the financial statements. There are two recognition criteria, probability and measurability.

Although full IFRS incorporates probability and measurability into its decision-making process when considering whether to recognise an item, they are merely inputs into the decision and not criteria to be met when considering the recognition of an item. The recognition criteria in full IFRS is that recognition of the transaction or event must result in information that is useful, ie relevant information that is a faithful representation of the economic phenomena it is reporting on.

1.6.1   Probability

The element in question can only be recognised if it is (in addition to being measurable) probable that the economic benefits associated with the element will flow into the entity (in the case of an asset and income) or out of the entity (in the case of a liability or expense) (s2.27(a)).

1.6.2   Measurability

The element in question can only be recognised if it is (in addition to being probable) measurable. Measurability means that a cost or value that can be reliably measured can be allocated to the item (s2.27(b)). The most common measurement bases are historical cost and fair value measurement (s2.34). Each section in the standard will determine how to measure the item in question both initially and subsequent to initial recognition (s2.46).

1.7   OFFSETTING

Assets, liabilities, income and expenses shall not be offset in the financial statements unless required or permitted by this standard. Offsetting refers to presenting a net amount for an asset and liability instead of presenting them separately (s2.52 and IAS 1 p.32).

SELF-ASSESSMENT
Multiple-choice questions: Testing principles of the Framework

1. An asset is defined as:

(a) a resource controlled by the entity as a result of a past event from which future economic benefits are expected to flow to the entity	
(b) a resource owned by the entity as a result of a past event from which future economic benefits are expected to flow to the entity	
(c) a resource accessible by all entities as a result of a past event from which future economic benefits are expected to flow to the entity	
(d) a resource controlled by the entity as a result of a past event from which future economic benefits are expected to flow to somebody	

2. A liability is defined as:

(a) a present obligation as a result of past events which is expected to result in the outflow from the entity of resources embodying economic benefits	
(b) a present asset as a result of a past event which is expected to result in the outflow from the entity of resources embodying economic benefits	
(c) a present obligation as a result of a past event which is expected to result in the inflow to the entity of resources embodying economic benefits	
(d) a present obligation as a result of a past event which is expected to result in the outflow from the entity of other obligations	

3. Which of the following items meets the definition of income:

(a) receipt of cash in a loan agreement	
(b) the purchase of property for cash	
(c) the sale of inventory to customers on credit	
(d) rent owing by the entity to the landlord	

9

4. Items should only be recognised in the financial statements if they are:

(a) probable	
(b) measurable	
(c) none of the above	
(d) both (a) and (b)	

5. Financial statements prepared in terms of IFRS for SMEs are:

(a) prepared specifically for the tax authority in the country	
(b) prepared for the needs of a specific lender	
(c) prepared for regulatory bodies	
(d) prepared for general users	

6. The following companies are included in the scope of IFRS for SMEs:

(a) all public companies	
(b) all private companies	
(c) public companies which do not hold assets in a fiduciary capacity for users	
(d) private companies which do not have public accountability and publish general purpose financial statements	

7. The following is a qualitative characteristic in IFRS for SMEs:

(a) understandability	
(b) trust	
(c) accuracy	
(d) none of the above	

8. Prudence refers to acts of:

(a) deliberately overstating assets and understating liabilities	
(b) deliberately understating assets and overstating liabilities	
(c) applying caution in making judgements about estimates used in accounting	
(d) none of the above	

9.   Information is relevant if it is:

(a) capable of influencing economic decisions of users	
(b) not understandable	
(c) immaterial	
(d) achieved without undue cost or effort	

10.   The following will be found in the statement of profit or loss and other comprehensive income:

(a) assets	
(b) liabilities	
(c) income	
(d) dividends	

Practical questions: Application of principles to business scenarios

QUESTION 1

HSJ (Pty) Ltd was sued by a customer for an injury incurred while using the company's products. The court has determined that the company is guilty of selling defective products and has to pay damages to the customer. The court is yet to decide what the amount of the damages is going to be. The company's attorneys are unable to reliably estimate the amount of damages that will be payable at year-end.

You are required to:
Discuss whether HSJ (Pty) Ltd should recognise a liability in terms of the damages payable at year-end.

QUESTION 2

You have two clients who asked you whether they are allowed to use IFRS for SMEs when preparing their financial statements. The first client is a public school which also collects school fees from its students and the second client is a bank.

You are required to:
Advise each client (the school and the bank) on whether the scope of IFRS for SMEs (s1.2) allows them to use IFRS for SMEs as the basis of preparation of their financial statements by supporting your answer with a discussion.

QUESTION 3

OMW (Pty) Ltd is a transport company operating in Cape Town. The company specialises in long-distance transport and has recently purchased a battery-powered truck which is designed to save the company a significant amount of money. The recently appointed general manager asks you, the company's accountant, how the truck can be classified as an asset when the company just spent millions on the acquisition.

You are required to:
Discuss whether the truck meets the definition of an asset of OMW (Pty) Ltd.

CHAPTER 2
FINANCIAL STATEMENT PRESENTATION

2.1 INTRODUCTION

The objective of IFRS for SMEs is to provide information about the entity's activities that is useful for decision-making by a broad range of users who are not in a position to demand reports tailored to meet the particular information needs, namely, financial reporting for external users (s2.2).[1]

As accounting is a language, the way in which we communicate and present the information has to be codified to ensure that what we communicate is received by the user as intended.

2.2 LEARNING OUTCOMES

Upon completion of this unit you should know the general requirements for the presentation of financial statements in accordance with the IFRS for SMEs.

In particular you should:
(a) know the components of a complete set of financial statements;
(b) understand how those components are identified and distinguished from other information presented in the same published document;
(c) understand the general requirements for financial statements to present fairly an entity's financial position, financial performance and cash flows;
(d) know how to assess an entity's ability to continue as a going concern;
(e) understand the accounting and financial reporting required when material uncertainties cast significant doubt on the entity's ability to continue as a going concern;
(f) understand the requirements for consistency of presentation and comparative information in financial statements; and
(g) be able to demonstrate an understanding of the significant judgements that are required in presenting financial statements, such as assessing materiality and going concern.

---

[1] *The objective of financial statements in IFRS is to provide financial information about the reporting entity that is useful to existing and potential investors, lenders and other creditors in making decisions about providing resources to the entity 'CF p. 1.2'.*

2.3   DEFINITIONS

The definitions for the important concepts and terms used in IFRS for SMEs are found in Appendix B – *Glossary of terms* in IFRS for SMEs. Some of those relating to the presentation of financial statements include the following:

- **Going concern:** An entity is a going concern unless management either intends to liquidate the entity or to cease trading, or has no realistic alternative but to do so.

- **General purpose financial statements:** General purpose financial statements are those directed to the general financial information needs of a wide range of users who are not in a position to demand reports tailored to meet their particular information needs.

- **Fair presentation:** Fair presentation is defined as the faithful representation of the effects of transactions, other events and conditions in accordance with the definitions and recognition criteria of assets, liabilities, income and expenses.

2.4   SCOPE AND OBJECTIVES

This chapter prescribes the basis for the presentation of general purpose financial statements and sets out the overall requirements for the presentation of financial statements and guidelines for their structure.

2.5   FAIR PRESENTATION

Financial statements shall present fairly the financial position, financial performance and cash flows of the entity (s3.2). Fair presentation is defined as the faithful representation of the effects of transactions, other events and conditions in accordance with the definitions and recognition criteria of assets, liabilities, income and expenses (s3.2 and IAS 2 p.15). Faithful presentation refers to that characteristic of financial statements that provides users with reasonable assurance that they can rely on the information presented in the financial statements to represent faithfully the economic circumstances and events of the entity. The application of IFRS for SMEs by an entity with public accountability does not result in a fair presentation in accordance with this IFRS [s1.5 – *Small and Medium-sized Entities*].

Compliance with IFRS for SMEs may not be sufficient to result in fair presentation in exceptional circumstances. In such circumstances, additional disclosures may be necessary to improve fair presentation and the usefulness of the financial statements.

2.6 COMPLIANCE WITH IFRS FOR SMEs

An entity must explicitly state whether its financial statements comply with IFRS for SMEs and if this fact is stated, it implies that the entity adheres to all the sections and requirements of this IFRS (s3.3).

In rare circumstances, an entity may depart from the provisions of IFRS for SMEs, such as where management is of the opinion that compliance with the IFRS for SMEs would be so misleading that it would conflict with the objective of financial statements and reduce fair presentation (s3.4).

When an entity departs from a requirement of IFRS for SMEs, the following shall be disclosed (s3.5):
(a)   the fact that management has concluded that the financial statements are now fairly presented;
(b)   that it has complied with IFRS for SMEs except for the particular departure; and
(c)   disclose:
    (i)   the nature of the departure (relating to the item of transaction);
    (ii)   the required treatment in terms of IFRS for SMEs (effect of the treatment shall be quantified); and
    (iii)   the reason why compliance with IFRS for SMEs would be so misleading that it would conflict with fair presentation and the objectives of the financial statements.

2.7 PREPARING FINANCIAL STATEMENTS

The following should be taken into consideration when preparing financial statements with the specific objective of improving the quality and integrity of financial information which will be useful and relevant for economic decision-making purposes:

2.7.1 Going concern

An entity is a going concern if management does not intend (or is not required) to liquidate or otherwise cease operations and is normally assessed over (but not limited to) a period of twelve months from reporting date.

If there are material uncertainties related to events or conditions that cast significant doubt upon an entity's ability to continue as a going concern, that entity must disclose those uncertainties. When the financial statements are not prepared on a going concern basis, the entity must disclose that fact and the basis on which the financial statements were prepared, and the reason why the entity is not considered to be a going concern (s3.9 and CF p.4.1).

2.7.2 Frequency of reporting

An entity shall present a complete set of financial statements including comparative information at least annually (s3.10 and IAS 1 p.36).

When the entity changes its reporting period ended, the entity shall disclose the following in order to provide users with useful information that may be critical for economic decision-making (s3.10 and IAS 1 p.36):
(a)   the fact that the reporting period has changed;
(b)   the reason for changing the reporting period end; and
(c)   the fact that comparative amounts presented in the financial statements are not entirely comparable.

2.7.3 Consistency of presentation

An entity shall apply its accounting policies and classification of items, transactions and events consistently from one period to the next, unless (s3.11 and IAS 1 p.45)):
(a)   IFRS for SMEs requires a change; and
(b)   the operations of the entity changed significantly and another presentation or classification is more appropriate to present the financial position and performance of the entity in a manner that is the most useful and relevant to users.

An entity changes the presentation of its financial statements only if the changed presentation provides information that is reliable and more relevant to users of the financial statements and the revised structure is likely to continue, so that comparability over time is not impaired (s3.11 and IAS 1 p.46). For example, a significant acquisition or disposal or a review of the presentation of the financial statements might suggest that the financial statements need to be presented differently.[2]

---

[2] *IASC Foundation: Training Material for the* IFRS® for SMEs *(version 2010-1)*

When the presentation or classification of items in the financial statements changes, the entity must reclassify the comparative amounts unless it is impracticable to do so (s3.12 and IAS 1 p.46). The following must be disclosed:

(a)   reason for the reclassification;
(b)   nature of the reclassification; and
(c)   amount of each item that is reclassified

If it is impracticable to reclassify comparative amounts, an entity shall disclose the reason why re-classification was not practicable (s3.13 and IAS 1 p.42).

2.7.4   Comparative information

An entity shall disclose comparative information in respect of the previous comparable period for all amounts presented in the financial statements of the current period. This generally applies to items disclosed as well where it is relevant to users in understanding the financial statements for the current period (s3.14 and IAS 1 p.38). (IFRS requires a third set of the statement of financial position to be presented at the beginning of the preceding period if (a) it applies an accounting policy retrospectively, makes a retrospective restatement of items in the statement of financial position or reclassifies items in its financial statements; and (b) the adjustment has a material impact on the information in statement of financial position at the beginning of the preceding period (IAS 1 p.40A)).

2.7.5   Materiality and aggregation

Materiality is defined as the situation where the omissions or misstatements of items, individually or collectively, influence the economic decisions of users taken on the basis of financial statements. An entity shall present categories of material items separately. Materiality is considered by nature and amount.

Illustrative Example 2.1: Materiality and aggregating

A single event which results in a major write-down of the value of an asset.

You are required to:
Discuss whether an event which causes a major write-down of the value of an asset should be disclosed separately in the annual financial statements.

Suggested solution:
A single event which results in a major write-down of the value of an asset should be disclosed separately as it may influence the decisions of users of the financial statements [abnormal items].

It is important to be careful when aggregating transactions and events that this will not result in offsetting, which is prohibited in terms of IFRS for SMEs (s2.52 and IAS 1 p.32).

2.8   COMPLETE SET OF FINANCIAL STATEMENTS

The following is a diagrammatic illustration of a complete set of financial statements:

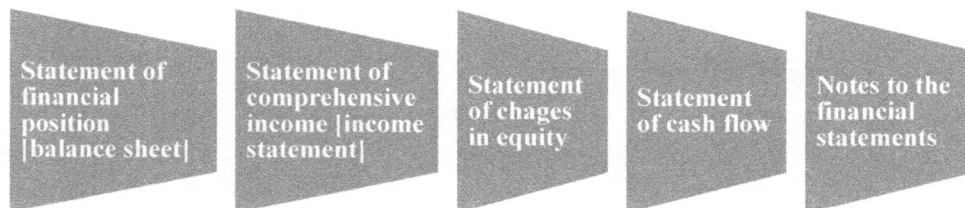

| Statement of financial position [balance sheet] | Statement of comprehensive income [income statement] | Statement of chages in equity | Statement of cash flow | Notes to the financial statements |

A complete set of financial statements of an entity shall include all of the following (s3.17 and IAS 1 p.10):

(a)   a statement of financial position (balance sheet) at the reporting date – schedule of the carrying amounts of assets, liabilities and equity;

(b)   a statement of comprehensive income (income statement) for the reporting period, either using the single-statement approach (profit or loss and other comprehensive income as a single statement) or two-statement approach (separate profit or loss statement and other comprehensive income statement) – a report on the profit for the period which is represented by income less expenses;

(c)   a statement of changes in equity for the reporting period – a statement reporting on the transactions with equity holders (can produce statement combined with income statement in certain circumstances (statement of income and retained earnings));

(d)   a statement of cash flow for the reporting period; and

(e)   notes to the financial statements for the reporting period, comprising a summary of significant accounting policies and other explanatory information.

2.8.1   General information to be displayed on financial statements

The entity has to identify clearly each of the financial statements and the notes, and distinguish these from the rest of the document in which the financial statements are presented (s3.23 and IAS 1 p.49). For instance, the financial statements are often presented together with the directors' report and other information. This other information, including the directors' report, does not fall within the scope of IFRS or IFRS for SMEs.

In addition, the following has to be displayed:
(a)   the name of the reporting entity and any change in its name since the end of the preceding reporting period;
(b)   whether the financial statements cover the individual entity or a group of entities;
(c)   the date of the end of the reporting period and the period covered by the financial statements; and
(d)   the presentation currency and the level of rounding, if any, used in presenting amounts in the financial statements.

The following must also be disclosed in the notes (s3.24 and IAS 1 p.138):
(a)   the domicile and legal form of the entity, its country of incorporation and the address of its registered office (or principal place of business, if different from the registered office); and
(b)   a description of the nature cf the entity's operations and its principal activities.

And for IFRS, the following additional information must be disclosed:
(a)   the name of the parent and the ultimate parent of the group; and
(b)   if it is a limited life entity, information regarding the length of its life.

2.8.2   Statement of financial position

2.8.2.1   Information to be presented on the face of the statement of financial position

The following is the minimum line items that have balances that must be presented on the face of the statement of financial position:
(a)   cash and cash equivalents;
(b)   trade and other receivables;
(c)   financial assets (excluding amounts shown under (a), (b), (j) and (k));
(d)   inventories;
(e)   property, plant and equipment;
(f)   investment property carried at cost less accumulated depreciation and impairment;
(g)   investment property carried at fair value through profit or loss;
(h)   intangible assets;
(i)   biological assets carried at cost less accumulated depreciation and impairment;
(j)   biological assets carried at fair value through profit or loss;

(k)   investments in associates;

(l)   investments in jointly controlled entities;

(m)   trade and other payables;

(n)   financial liabilities (excluding amounts shown under (l) and (p));

(o)   liabilities and assets for current tax;

(p)   deferred tax liabilities and deferred tax assets (these shall always be classified as non-current);

(q)   provisions;

(r)   non-controlling interest, presented within equity separately from the equity attributable to the owners of the parent; and

(s)   equity attributable to the owners of the parent.

2.8.2.2 Current vs non-current assets & liabilities

An entity should present its assets and liabilities as being either current or non-current on the face of the statement of financial position, except when a presentation based on liquidity provides information that is more reliable and more relevant. In this case, all assets and liabilities must be presented in order of approximate liquidity (either ascending or descending) (s4.4 and IAS 1 p.60).

The following criteria are used by an entity to determine whether an asset or liability is current:

(a)   The entity expects to realise the asset or settle the liability in the entity's normal operating cycle;

(b)   It holds the asset or liability primarily for purposes of trading;

(c)   It expects to realise the asset or settle the liability within twelve months after the reporting date; or

(d)   **(for an asset)** the asset is cash or a cash equivalent, unless it is restricted from being exchanged or used to settle a liability for at least twelve months after the reporting date;

(e)   **(for a liability)** the entity does not have an unconditional right to defer settlement of the liability for at least twelve months after reporting date.

COMPANY A GROUP	
Consolidated statement of financial position as at 31 December 20X8	
	20X8
	CU
ASSETS	
Non-current assets	
Property, plant and equipment	500,000
Investment property	200,000
Intangible assets	100,000
Current assets	
Inventory	80,000
Accounts receivable	70,000
Cash	50,000
TOTAL ASSETS	**1,000,000**
EQUITY	
Ordinary shares	250,000
Retained earnings	350,000
Revaluation surplus	100,000
Non-controlling interest	50,000
LIABILIITIES	
Non-current liabilities	
Loan payable	200,000

Current liabilities	
Trade payables	50,000
TOTAL EQUITY & LIABILITIES	**1,000,000**

2.8.2.3 Additional disclosure

An entity should disclose, either in the statement of financial position or in the notes, the following subclassifications of the line items presented (s4.11 and IAS 1 p.78):
(a)   property, plant and equipment in classifications appropriate to the entity;
(b)   trade and other receivables showing separately amounts due from related parties, amounts due from other parties and receivables arising from accrued **income** not yet billed;
(c)   inventories, showing separately amounts of inventories:
    (i)   held for sale in the ordinary course of business;
    (ii)   in the process of production for such sale; and
    (iii)   in the form of materials or supplies to be consumed in the production process or in the rendering of services;
(d)   trade and other payables, showing separately amounts payable to trade suppliers, payable to related parties, deferred income and accruals;
(e)   provisions for **employee benefits** and other provisions; and
(f)   classes of equity, such as paid-in capital, share premium, retained earnings and items of income and **expense** that, as required by this standard, are recognised in **other comprehensive income** and presented separately in equity.

An entity with share capital should disclose the following, either in the statement of financial position or in the notes (s4.12 and IAS 1 p.79):
(a)   for each class of share capital:
    (i)   the number of shares authorised;
    (ii)   the number of shares issued and fully paid, and issued but not fully paid;
    (iii)   par value per share or that the shares have no par value;
    (iv)   a reconciliation of the number of shares outstanding at the beginning and at the end of the period. This reconciliation need not be presented for prior periods;
    (v)   the rights, preferences and restrictions attaching to that class including restrictions on the distribution of dividends and the repayment of capital;

    (vi)   shares in the entity held by the entity or by its **subsidiaries** or associates; and

    (vii)   shares reserved for issue under options and contracts for the sale of shares, including the terms and amounts;

(b)   a description of each reserve within equity.

An entity without share capital, such as a partnership or trust, shall disclose information equivalent to that required by paragraph 4.12(a) and IAS 1 p.79(a), showing changes during the period in each category of equity, and the rights, preferences and restrictions attaching to each category of equity (s4.13 and IAS 1 p.80).

If, at the reporting date, an entity has a binding sale agreement for a major disposal of assets, or a group of assets and liabilities, the entity shall disclose the following information (s4.14):

(a)   a description of the asset(s) or the group of assets and liabilities;

(b)   a description of the facts and circumstances of the sale or plan; and

(c)   the **carrying amount** of the assets or, if the disposal involves a group of assets and liabilities, the carrying amounts of those assets and liabilities.

In addition, IFRS requires the following disclosure related to the statement of financial position (IAS 1 p.80A):

If an entity has reclassified:

a)   a puttable financial instrument classified as an equity instrument, or

b)   an instrument that imposes on the entity an obligation to deliver to another party a pro rata share of the net assets of the entity only on liquidation and is classified as an equity instrument between financial liabilities and equity, it shall disclose the amount reclassified into and out of each category (financial liabilities or equity), and the timing and reason for that reclassification.

2.8.3   Statement of comprehensive income and income statement

2.8.3.1   General

In the case where a single statement of comprehensive income and retained earnings is not presented, the entity must prepare a statement of comprehensive income and a statement of changes in equity separately. The entity may either prepare a single statement of comprehensive income or split the statement into two statements, one being the income statement and one consisting of other comprehensive income (s5.2 and IAS 1 p.10A).

Irrespective of whether the entity presents a single or separate statement of profit or loss and other comprehensive income or a single statement of profit or loss and retained earnings, the following are the minimum line items to be presented in the statement of comprehensive income (or statement of profit or loss and retained earnings) (s5.5 and IAS 1 p.82 and 81(a)):

(a)   revenue;

(b)   finance costs;

(c)   share of the profit or loss of investments in associates and jointly controlled entities *Investments in Joint Ventures*), accounted for using the equity method;

(d)   tax expense excluding tax allocated to items (e), (g) and (h);

(e)   a single amount comprising the total of:
    (i)   the post-tax profit or loss of a discontinued operation; and
    (ii)   the post-tax gain or loss attributable to an impairment, or
    (iii)   reversal of an impairment, of the assets in the discontinued operation, both at the time and subsequent to being classified as a discontinued operation and to the disposal of the net assets constituting the discontinued operation;

(f)   profit or loss (if an entity has no items of other comprehensive income, this line need not be presented);

(g)   each item of other comprehensive income classified by nature (excluding amounts in (h)). Such items shall be grouped into those that, in accordance with this standard:
    (i)   will not be reclassified subsequently to profit or loss–ie those in paragraph 5.4(b)(i)—(ii) and (iv); and
    (ii)   will be reclassified subsequently to profit or loss when specific conditions are met–ie those in paragraph 5.4(b)(iii);

(h)   share of the other comprehensive income of associates and jointly controlled entities accounted for by the equity method; and

(i)   total comprehensive income (if an entity has no items of other comprehensive income, it may use another term for this line such as profit or loss).

In addition, IAS 1 p.82 requires the following line items to be presented in the statement of comprehensive income:

(a)   gains and losses arising from the derecognition of financial assets measured at amortised cost;

(b)   impairment losses (including reversals of impairment losses or impairment gains) determined in accordance with section 5.5 of IFRS 9;

(c) *if a financial asset is reclassified out of the amortised cost measurement category so that it is measured at fair value through profit or loss, any gain or loss arising from a difference between the previous amortised cost of the financial asset and its fair value at the reclassification date (as defined in IFRS 9);*

(d) *(cb) if a financial asset is reclassified out of the fair value through other comprehensive income measurement category so that it is measured at fair value through profit or loss, any cumulative gain or loss previously recognised in other comprehensive income that is reclassified to profit or loss; and*

(e) *a single amount for the total of discontinued operations (see IFRS 5).*

In addition, an entity should present the following line items, when appropriate (s5.6 and IAS 1 p.81B):
(a)   profit or loss for the period attributable to:
     (i)   non-controlling interest; and
     (ii)   owners of the parent.
(b)   total comprehensive income for the period attributable to:
     (i)   non-controlling interest; and
     (ii)   owners of the parent.

If the entity chooses to present its statement of comprehensive income using a two-statement approach, the first statement should end with 'profit or loss' as the last line item. The second statement should then start with the line item 'profit or loss'.

COMPANY A GROUP **Consolidated statement of profit or loss and other comprehensive income for the year ended 31 December 20X8**	
	20X8
	CU
Revenue	615,000
Cost of sales	(300,000)
Gross profit	**315,000**
Other income	25,000
Administration expenses	(100,000)
Selling and distribution expenses	(30,000)

Profit before tax	**210,000**
Tax expense	(60,000)
Profit for the period	**150,000**
Other comprehensive income	
Items that will subsequently be reclassified to profit or loss:	
Cash flow hedge reserve	10,000
Tax expense	(2,800)
Items that will not subsequently be reclassified to profit or loss:	
Revaluation surplus	20,000
Tax expense	(4,480)
Total other comprehensive income	**22,720**
Total comprehensive income	**172,720**
Profit attributable to:	
The parent entity	130,000
Non-controlling interest	20,000
Total comprehensive income attributable to:	
The parent entity	17,750
Non-controlling interest	5,000

2.8.3.2 Presenting expenses by nature vs function

When presenting expenses in the statement of comprehensive income (whether using the single-statement or two-statement approach) or statement of profit or loss and retained earnings, the entity should present the expenses classified either in the nature of the expense or the function of the expense in the business (s5.11 and IAS 1 p.99). For instance, depreciation on property, plant and equipment could be presented as depreciation expense (the nature of the expense is that it is depreciation expense) or the function of the business in which the expense arose (such as under administration expenses if the depreciation relates to the administration building or accountant's computer, and selling and distribution if the depreciation relates to the entity's delivery vehicles).

Illustrative Example 2.2: Expenses classified by nature and by function

	CU
Revenue	1,990,000
Other income	300,000
Change in inventories of finished goods and work in progress	590,000
Raw materials and consumables used	130,000
Employee benefits expense	200,000
Depreciation and amortisation expense	250,000
Other expenses	150,000
Total expenses	1 320,000
Profit for the period	970,000

Expenses classified by function:

	CU
Revenue	1,990,000
Cost of sales	920,000
Gross profit	1,170,000
Other income	300,000
Administration expense	250,000
Selling and distribution expense	150,000
Profit for the period	970,000

2.8.3.3 Statement of profit or loss and retained earnings

Where the only change in equity during the period affects only retained earnings in the statement of changes in equity (ie profit for the period, dividends paid, correction of prior-period errors and/or changes in accounting policies) then the entity can prepare and present a single statement of income and retained earnings (s3.18 – there is no such concession in IFRS).

The following information should be presented in the statement of income and retained earnings (s6.5):
(a)   retained earnings at the beginning of the reporting period;
(b)   dividends declared and paid or payable during the period;
(c)   restatements of retained earnings for corrections of prior-period errors;
(d)   restatements of retained earnings for changes in accounting policy; and
(e)   retained earnings at the end of the reporting period.

Illustrative Example 2.3: Statement of income and retained earnings

	CU
Profit before taxation	990,000
Income tax expenses	300,000
Dividends paid	280,000
Retained earnings at the beginning of the period	530,000

Suggested solution:

Statement of income and retained earnings for the period ·······	CU
Profit before taxation	990,000
Income tax expenses	300,000
Profit for the period	**690,000**
Dividends paid	280,000
Retained earnings for the period	410,000
Retained earnings at the beginning of the period	530,000
Retained earnings at the end of the period	940,000

2.8.4   Statement of changes in equity

A statement of changes in equity provides the user with information on all of the changes in items of equity during the year which is used to reconcile the opening balance of the earliest period presented with the closing balance for each period presented.

The statement of changes in equity should include the following line items:

(a)   total comprehensive income for the period, showing separately the total amounts attributable to owners of the parent company and to non-controlling interests;

(b)   for each component of equity, the effects of retrospective application or retrospective restatement;

(c)   for each component of equity, a reconciliation between the carrying amount at the beginning and the end of the period, separately disclosing changes resulting from:

(i)   profit or loss;

(ii)   other comprehensive income; and

(iii)   the amounts of investments by, and dividends and other distributions to, owners in their capacity as owners, showing separately issues of shares, treasury share transactions, dividends and other distributions to owners and changes in ownership interests in subsidiaries that do not result in a loss of control.

Illustrative Example 2.4: Statement of changes in equity

	CU
Profit for the period	1,200,000
Revaluation gain during the period	300,000
Revaluation surplus at the beginning of the period	140,000
Dividends paid	280,000
Retained earnings at the beginning of the period	530,000
Ordinary shares issued at the beginning and the end of the period	100,000

Suggested solution:

Statement changes in equity for the period …….	Ordinary shares	Retained earnings	Revaluation surplus	Total equity
	CU	CU	CU	CU
Balance at 1 January 20X8	100,000	530,000	140,000	770,000
Total comprehensive income for the period:[1]		1,200,000	1,300,000	1,300,000
Profit for the period		1,200,000		1,200,000
Revaluation gain			300,000	300,000
Dividends paid		(280,000)		(280,000)
Balance at 31 December 20X8	100,000	1,450,000	440,000	1,990,000

[1]Note that this is the sum of the profit for the period and the revaluation below; be careful not to double count the amounts when working through the example.

SELF-ASSESSMENT
Multiple choice questions: Testing principles of accounting for the presentation of financial statements

1. The following is the definition of going concern:

(a) an entity is a going concern when it plans to liquidate its business after one year	
(b) an entity is a going concern when it changes directors	
(c) an entity is a going concern unless management either intends to liquidate the entity or to cease trading, or has no realistic alternative but to do so	
(d) an entity is a going concern when it sells its inventory for lower than normal prices	

2. A complete set of financial statements includes:

(a) a statement of financial position, statement of comprehensive income, statement of changes in equity, cash flow statement and notes to the financial statements	
(b) a statement of financial position, statement of comprehensive income, value added statement, cash flow statement and notes to the financial statements	
(c) a statement of financial position, statement of comprehensive income, statement of changes in equity, directors' statement and notes to the financial statements	
(d) a statement of financial position, statement of comprehensive income, statement of changes in equity, cash flow statement and audit statement	

3. An asset is a current asset if:

(a) it is expected to be realised within 12 months	
(b) it is expected to be realised within the normal operating cycle of the entity	
(c) it holds the asset for purposes of trading	
(d) all of the above	

4. An item is a current liability if:

(a) it is expected to be settled within 24 months	
(b) the entity has no unconditional right to defer payment beyond 12 months	
(c) none of the above	
(d) both of the above	

5. The following information must be displayed in the financial statements:

(a) the directors of the company	
(b) the location of the company	
(c) the presentation currency	
(d) the shareholders of the company	

6. When the movement of equity consists entirely of movements in retained earnings only, the entity may present a statement of:

(a) financial position	
(b) income and retained earnings	
(c) changes in equity	
(d) comprehensive income	

7. When expenses are classified by function, you would expect to see the following line item:

(a) depreciation expense	
(b) employee costs	
(c) raw materials utilised	
(d) cost of sales	

8. You would expect to see the following line item in the statement of changes in equity:

(a) revenue	
(b) dividends declared	
(c) property, plant and equipment	
(d) cash generated from operating activities	

9. To comply with IFRS for SMEs, you must:

(a) comply with all of the requirements of IFRS for SMEs	
(b) comply with all of the requirements of IFRS for SMEs and IFRS	
(c) comply with IFRS for SMEs and generally accepted accounting practices	
(d) none of the above	

10. Items of other comprehensive income must be:

(a) presented based on function	
(b) presented separately for items to be subsequently reclassified to profit or loss and those not to subsequently be classified to profit or loss	
(c) presented before the profit or loss section	
(d) none of the above	

Practical questions: Application of principles to business scenarios

QUESTION 1

You are the accountant of BAJ (Pty) Ltd. You were presented with the following information which was extracted from the trial balance of BAJ (Pty) Ltd for the year ended 31 December 20X8:

	Note	CU
Revenue		1,000,000
Purchases of raw material		400,000
Opening inventory		100,000
Closing inventory		150,000
Depreciation expense	1	180,000
Salaries and wages	2	200,000
Tax expense		75,600

1. Of the depreciation expense, 40% relates to items in the administration department and 60% relates to the delivery vehicles in the selling and distribution department;
2. Half of the salaries and wages relates to the administration department, 30% relates to the production department and 20% relates to the selling and distribution department.

You are required to:
Prepare the statement of profit or loss of BAJ (Pty) Ltd for the year ended 31 December 20X8, by classifying expenses according to the function of the business that it relates to.

QUESTION 2

You are the accountant of Snoekie (Pty) Ltd. You were presented with the following information which was extracted from the trial balance of Snoekie (Pty) Ltd for the year ended 31 December 20X8:

	CU
Profit for the period	500,000
Dividends declared	(100,000)
Revaluation gain	150,000
Opening retained earnings for the period	1,000,000
Opening revaluation surplus for the period	400,000
Opening balance of ordinary shares issues	140,000

You are required to:
Prepare the statement changes in equity of Snoekie (Pty) Ltd for the year ended 31 December 20X8.

QUESTION 3

You are the accountant of Worldwide Travel (Pty) Ltd. You were presented with the following information which was extracted from the trial balance of Worldwide Travel (Pty) Ltd for the year ended 31 December 20X8:

	CU
Profit for the period	1 500,000
Revaluation gain[1]	200,000
Fair value gain on cash flow hedge[2]	140,000

[1]The revaluation gain will not be reclassified to profit or loss on realisation.
[2]The fair value gain on the cash flow hedge will be reclassified to profit or loss on realisation.

You are required to:
Prepare the statement of other comprehensive income only (ie you do not have to prepare the statement of profit or loss) of Worldwide Travel (Pty) Ltd for the year ended 31 December 20X8. You may assume that Worldwide Travel (Pty) Ltd elects to present the statement of comprehensive income separately from the statement of profit or loss (two-statement approach).

CHAPTER 3
ACCOUNTING FOR TAXATION AND VALUE-ADDED TAX

ILLUSTRATIVE DISCLOSURE

Statement of Profit or Loss for the period ended					
IFRS ref		**Notes**	**20X2**	**20X1**	
			R'000	**R'000**	
	Profit before tax		6,000	5,000	
S29 & IAS12	Tax expense	4	(1,300)	(1,250)	
	Profit after tax		**4,700**	**3,750**	
Statement of Financial Position at					
S4.2 (n&o) & IAS 1 p.54 (n&o)		**Notes**	**20X2**	**20X1**	**Ch. ref**
			CU'000	**CU'000**	
	ASSETS				
	Current assets				
S29 & IAS 12	Current tax receivable		2,500	2,400	
	VAT receivable		1,500	800	
	Non-current assets				
S29 & IAS 12	Deferred tax asset	8	4,000	3,900	
	LIABILITIES				
	Current liabilities				
S29 & IAS 12	Current tax payable		2,500	2,000	
	VAT payable		1,800	1,000	
	Non-current liabilities				
S29 & IAS 12	Deferred tax liability	8	5,000	4,000	

Notes to the financial statements for the period ended					
S29.39 & IAS 12 p.79	4	TAX EXPENSE			
		Tax expense consist of the following:	20X2	20X1	
			CU'000	CU'000	
S29.39(a) & IAS 12 p.80(a)		Current tax	395	1,050	
S29.39(b) & IAS 12 p.80(b)		Correction to current tax for 20X0	5	0	
		Deferred tax:			
S29.39(c) & IAS 12 p.80(c)		- Movement in temporary differences	800	200	
S29.39(d) & IAS 12 p.80(d)		- Effect of change in tax rate	100	0	
		Tax expense recognised in profit for the period	1,300	1,250	
S29.40(c) & IAS 12 p.81(c)		Tax rate reconciliation:			
			20X2	20X1	
			CU'000	CU'000	
		Accounting profit multiplied by tax rate (20X2: 28%; 20X1: 27%)	1,680	1,350	
		Adjusted for:			
		Tax on exempt portion of capital gain on sale of property	(480)	(100)	
		Tax related to change in tax rate	100	0	
		Tax expense	1,300	1,250	
S29.40(d) & IAS 12 p.81(d)		On 28 February 20X2, the Minister of Finance in the entity's resident country announced an increase in the company tax rate from 27% to 28% effective from 01 July 20X2. The effect of the change resulted in the entity recognising an increase in its deferred tax liability of CU100,000.			

S29.40(e) & IAS 12 p.81(g)		Deferred tax in statement of financial position:					
			20X2	20X2	20X1	20X1	
			CU'000	CU'000	CU'000	CU'000	
			Assessed loss	Accelerated wear & tear	Assessed loss	Accelerated wear & tear	
		01 January	(3,900)	4,000	(3,850)	3,750	
		Increase in assessed losses	(100)		(50)		
		Increase from change in tax rate		100			
		Increase in differences between wear & tear and depreciation		900		250	
		31 December	(4,000)	5,000	(3,900)	4,000	
S29.41		The entity has not offset its current tax assets and liabilities or its deferred tax assets and liabilities, as these arise from rights and obligations with different governments in different jurisdictions. As such, the entity does not have the legally enforceable right to set off the amounts.					

3.1 INTRODUCTION

There are various taxes levied on taxpayers by governments around the world. Some of these are direct taxes (such as company tax) and some are indirect taxes (such as value-added tax (VAT)). Indirect tax, such as VAT, is not taxed directly on the organisation (although it is paid by the organisation), but rather on the goods or services produced and/or sold by the organisation. The VAT is levied directly by government on the value added (ie on the consideration received in the transaction) and collected, as part of the amount received, by the VAT vendor on behalf of the tax authority. Therefore, the portion of the amount received by the VAT vendor that represents the VAT that it has collected on behalf of government, is not for the benefit of the VAT vendor, but for the benefit of government. Therefore, the VAT vendor acts as an agent for government when collecting the VAT.

VAT collected by the tax authority on behalf of government is called output VAT, as it is levied on the output of the organisation (the goods or services which it sells).

Similarly, the amount which the entity in turn pays to a VAT vendor also typically includes VAT. The entity may claim back the VAT that it pays to its suppliers from the tax authority. This VAT is referred to as input VAT as it is levied on the inputs of the organisation (the goods or services which it purchases).

You will notice from the above discussion that the entity pays the tax authority output VAT but can claim back input VAT. Therefore, the entity sets the input VAT off against the output VAT and pays the net amount to the tax authority.

Illustrative Example 3.1: VAT payable

Company A collects CU150,000 from customers as output VAT. Company A also paid its suppliers CU15,000 as input VAT on its purchases.

You are required to:
Calculate the net output vat payable.

Suggested solution:

VAT payable	CU
Output VAT	150,000
Input VAT	(15,000)
Net output VAT payable	**135,000**

3.2   LEARNING OUTCOMES

Upon completion of this unit you should be able to:
(a)   calculate the amount of VAT included in a transaction; and
(b)   be able to account for both input and output VAT.

3.3   VAT CHARGE

VAT is:
(a)   charged at the normal VAT rate; or
(b)   charged at 0%; or
(c)   not charged at all (items or services which are exempt from VAT).

The different VAT rates (normal- and zero-rated items) and the exemption of certain items have various implications. The reporting entity may only claim the input VAT on items on which it in turn charges output VAT. Therefore, if a final product is exempt from output VAT, the reporting entity may not claim input VAT on the goods or services it purchased to produce that product.

Output VAT is collected by the reporting entity as part of the amount payable by its customers for the goods and services the reporting entity provides. The VAT is calculated by applying a rate to the pre-VAT amount. The pre-VAT amount together with the VAT is the consideration (payment) to be received from the customer or payable to the supplier. For the remainder of this chapter, we will consider the VAT rate to be 15%.

The calculation used to obtain the VAT included in a consideration is therefore $15/115 \times$ the consideration.

Illustrative Example 3.2: Calculation of VAT

Company A sells (or purchases) a product for CU230,000 (including VAT).

You are required to:
Calculate the portion of the consideration (payment) that represent VAT.

Suggested solution:

Calculation of VAT:	CU
$15/115 \times$ CU230,000	30,000

It follows, therefore, that the amount of the consideration collected by the entity for its benefit is therefore calculated as $100/115 \times$ the consideration.

Illustrative Example 3.3: Calculation of VAT

Company A sells (or purchases) a product for CU345,000 (including VAT).

You are required to:
Calculate the portion of the consideration (payment) representing the amount collected (paid) for the selling entity's own benefit.

Suggested solution:

Calculation of VAT:	CU
$100/115 \times$ CU345,000	300,000

3.4   OUTPUT VAT

Output VAT is charged on the output of the goods or services produced by the entity. As the output of the firm is sold to customers, the general journal entry that would result from the sale is as follows:

Recognising revenue in cash:		CU	
Dr:	Bank	100	
Cr:	Revenue		100
[Recognising revenue and the related cash received]			

OR:

Recognising revenue in cash:		CU	
Dr:	Accounts receivable	100	
Cr:	Revenue [SFP]		100
[Recognising revenue from a sale on credit]			

If the entity is a VAT vendor (and assuming that the goods sold or the services rendered attract VAT), then the entity should also include VAT collected on behalf of the tax authorities in the consideration it receives from customers. This means that the entity should sell the goods or render the services for a VAT inclusive amount of CU115 (R100 (VAT exclusive) × 15%). It cannot be denied that the entity collected cash (if a cash sale) of, or increased its receivables (if the sale is on credit) by, CU115. However, the VAT portion of CU14 was collected on behalf of the tax authority and not for the benefit of the entity. Therefore, the entity has a present obligation to pay over the VAT to the tax authority and the CU15 payable therefore represents a liability. The remaining portion of the consideration (CU100) is collected by the entity for its own benefit and this represents the amount of income earned by the entity on the sale of the goods or the rendering of the services. The general journal entry that would result from the sale is as follows:

Recognising revenue in cash		CU	
Dr	Bank	115	
Cr	Output VAT payable (liability) [SFP]		15
Cr	Revenue [P/L]		100
[Recognising revenue and the related cash received]			

OR:

Recognising revenue in cash		CU	
Dr	Accounts receivable	115	
Cr	Output VAT payable (liability) [SFP]		15
Cr	Revenue [P/L]		100
[Recognising revenue from a sale on credit]			

You will notice that the amount earned by the entity has not changed, only the amount collected on behalf of the tax authority (represented by the liability of CU15 and by the increase in cash and accounts receivable, as applicable, of CU15).

3.5   INPUT VAT

Input VAT is the portion of the amount paid by the VAT vendor (as part of the purchase of a good or service) to another VAT vendor which represents VAT. The input VAT can in turn be collected back from SARS (or used to reduce the total VAT payable). Therefore, the input VAT paid or payable represents an asset.

The general journal entry required to record a transaction, such as the purchase of an asset, without VAT is as follows:

Purchase of an asset for cash		CU	
Dr	Asset	100	
Cr	Bank		100
[Recognising the purchase of an asset for cash]			

OR:

Purchase of an asset on credit	CU	
Dr	Asset	100	
Cr	Payable		100
[Recognising an asset purchased on credit]		

The same principles would be applied to the incurrence of an expense as follows:

Incurrence of an expense which is paid for in cash	CU	
Dr	Expense (P/L)	100	
Cr	Bank		100
Recognising an expense paid in cash.		

OR:

Incurrence of an expense which is not paid immediately	CU	
Dr	Expense (P/L)	100	
Cr	Revenue		100
[Recognising an expense incurred but not paid]		

The supplier, if a VAT vendor, will include the VAT in the amount it collects from the entity and so the entity pays an amount inclusive of VAT. When the entity and its supplier are VAT vendors, the entity will pay (or incur a liability on) the input VAT on the goods and services it purchases and be able to collect the input VAT from or use it to reduce any VAT payable to the tax authority. Therefore, if the entity and the supplier are VAT vendors, the supplier should collect CU15 (15% × CU100) on behalf of SARS from the entity. The entity either pays or incurs a liability for the full amount of CU115. The entity in turn classifies the portion of the amount paid or payable, representing input VAT, as an asset recoverable from the tax authority. The remaining CU100 (CU115 – CU15) should be classified as an expense or asset (depending on whether the entity purchased an asset or incurred an expense). The following general journal entry will then be processed:

Recognising an asset purchased paid or unpaid		CU	
Dr	Asset [SFP]	100	
Dr	Input VAT payable [SFP]	15	
Cr	Bank/payable		115
[Recognising revenue and the related cash received]			

OR:

Recognising an expense paid or unpaid		CU	
Dr	Expense [P/L]	100	
Dr	Input VAT payable [SFP]	15	
Cr	Bank/payable		115
[Recognising revenue and the related cash received]			

3.6 INCOME TAXES

3.6.1 Company tax

The tax authority taxes companies based on the amount of taxable income it made during the tax year. The taxable income earned by the company is determined by the tax authority by taking into account only those items which meet the definition of income, including the taxable portion of any capital gains and deducting the allowances granted and any assessed loss from prior periods.

The tax authority, being part of government, implements the financial planning of government to strategically incentivise citizens to undertake certain activities over others through tax incentives. Additionally, the allowance granted by the tax authority is often a fixed rate based on an amount such as the cost of the asset. The rate of the allowance granted is often fixed irrespective of how well the entity takes care of the asset to which the allowance relates. For instance, the tax authority might grant an allowance on an item of equipment of 50% in the year in which the item is brought into use, 30% in the second year of use and 20% in the third year of use. This allowance will often be constant across entities. Therefore, if an entity estimates that it will be able to use the asset evenly over a five year period to a nil residual value, the entity-specific use is not considered in determining the tax allowance granted and therefore the taxable income.

Illustrative Example 3.4: Company tax

Company A earns taxable income before considering the impact of capital gains and any assessed loss brought forward from prior years of CU1,000,000. Company A also earns a capital gain of CU250,000 during the year. In addition, the company has an aggregate assessed loss from prior years of CU140,000 which it can use to reduce the current tax payable. The capital gains tax inclusion rate is 40% while the company tax rate is 28%.

You are required to:
Calculate the current tax payable.

Suggested solution:

Company tax	CU
Taxable income	1,000,000
Capital gain included in taxable income [CU250,000 × 40%]	100,00
Taxable income before assessed loss	**1,100,000**
Assessed loss carried forward	(140,000)
Taxable income	**960,000**
Tax rate	28%
Current tax	**268,800**

3.6.1.1 Payment of income tax

All entities registered for provisional tax make three payments during the year. The first two payments are made during the course of the year of assessment and are therefore prepayments of tax for what the company estimates the tax liability will be for that year of assessment. The first payment is made halfway through the year and is based on half of what the entity estimates the tax liability to be. The second payment is made at the end of the year and is based on the amount that the entity estimates the tax liability to be less the payment made for the first provisional payment. During the course of the second year, the tax authority will assess the entity and provide the entity with the amount of tax which is due. Should this amount differ to the total paid in the first and second provisional payment, a third payment (a top-up payment) will be made or a refund issued to the entity.

3.6.2 Accounting and income taxation

3.6.2.1 Introduction

Accounting standards have their own requirements for the recognition and measurement of assets and liabilities. Often, these requirements result in different amounts being included in profit or loss, other comprehensive income and the statement of changes in equity than those recognised for the same transactions in the entity's taxable income. The result is that the carrying amounts of assets and liabilities often differ to the equivalent amounts for the tax authorities.

Illustrative Example 3.5: Accounting vs tax

Company A purchases a machine on 1 January 20X8 for CU1,000,000. Company A depreciates the machine over an estimated useful life of 10 years to a nil residual value. The tax authorities allow for wear and tear as follows: 50% of the cost of the asset in year 1, 30% of the cost of the asset in year 2 and 20% of the cost of the asset in year 3.

You are required to:
Calculate the carrying amount and tax base of the machine at 31 December 20x8.

Suggested solution:

	1. Accounting	2. Tax
	CU	CU
Cost of machine	1,000,000	1,000,000
Depreciation (P/L)/wear and tear (taxable income) [CU1,000,000/10 years = CU100,000 per annum; CU1,000,000 × 50% = CU500,000 in year 1]	(100,000)	(500,000)
Carrying amount and tax base at 31 December 20X8	**900,000**	**500,000**

In order to reconcile the tax framework to which the entity is subjected to the accounting framework of the entity, the entity applies the standard s29 (IAS 12) – Income Taxes. The standard uses the statement of financial position approach and the deferred tax is calculated using the following working:

	CA (carrying amount)	TB (tax base)	TD (temporary difference)	DT (deferred tax)
Asset	xx	xx	xx	xx
Liability	xx	xx	xx	xx

3.6.2.2 Carrying amount

The carrying amount of the asset or liability is the easiest part of determining the deferred tax related to an item. The carrying amount of the asset or liability is the amount that the item is carried at in the statement of financial position. In other words, it is determined by the application of the other chapters in the IFRS for SMEs (standards in the IFRS).

3.6.2.3 Tax base of an asset

The tax base of an asset is dependent on whether (s29.9 and IAS 12 p.7:
(a)   the recovery of the future economic benefits will result taxable; or
(b)   whether the future economic benefits will not be taxed when recovered.

Tax base of an asset where the future economic benefits of the asset are taxable
When the recovery of the future economic benefits of the asset is taxable, the tax base is the future deduction that will be allowed for tax against the taxable future economic benefits (s29.9 and IAS 12 p.7).

Illustrative Example 3.6: Tax base of an asset

Company A purchases a machine for CU100,000 from which it will produce pens for sale to customers. The tax authority allows for the full amount of the asset to be deducted as wear and tear over 4 years. The machine was purchased on 01 January 20X8. Company A depreciates the machine over an estimated life of 5 years to an estimated nil residual value using the straight-line method.

You are required to:
Explain and quantify what the tax base of the machine is on:
(i)   The date of purchase; and
(ii)   31 December 20x8.

Suggested solution:

1. What is the tax base of the machine on the date of purchase?

The following questions need to be asked before we can correctly quantify the tax base of the machinery:

(b) *Question*: Will the economic benefits embodied in the asset (CU100,000) be taxable when it is recovered?
Answer: Yes. The entity recovers the future economic benefits of the asset (at least CU100,000) through use as it produces pens. The pens are sold to customers who pay the entity. When the pens are sold, the proceeds are included in taxable income and as such are taxed.

(c) The tax base of an asset which has future economic benefits that will be taxed on recovery of the asset is the future deductions that will be allowed against those taxable economic benefits.
Question: What are the future deductions against the taxable income of the machine allowed by the tax authority?
Answer: The tax authority will allow the full CU100,000 as a deduction in the future and therefore the tax base of the machine on the date of purchase is CU100,000.

2. What is the tax base of the machine on 31 December 20X8?

The following questions need to be asked before we can correctly quantify the tax base of the machinery:

(a) *Question*: Will the economic benefits embodied in the asset (CU80,000 (CU100,000/5 years × 4 years)) be taxable when it is recovered?
Answer: Yes. The entity recovers the future economic benefits of the asset (at least CU80,000) through use as it produces pens. The pens are sold to customers who pay the entity. When the pens are sold, the proceeds are included in taxable income and as such are taxed.

(b) The tax base of an asset which has future economic benefits that will be taxed on recovery of the asset is the future deductions that will be allowed against those taxable economic benefits.

Question: What are the future deductions against the taxable income of the machine allowed by the tax authority?

Answer: The tax authority will allow CU75,000 (CU100,000 – (CU100,000/4 years)) as a deduction in the future and therefore the tax base of the machine on the date of purchase is CU75,000.

Tax base of an asset with future economic benefits that are not taxable

When the recovery of the asset results in future economic benefits which are not taxable then the tax base of the asset is equal to its carrying amount.

Illustrative Example 3.7: Tax base of an asset

Company A sells pens to its customer for CU140,000 on credit on 31 December 20X8. The customer is scheduled to pay Company A on 31 January 20X9.

You are required to:

Explain and quantify what the tax base of the accounts receivable is on 31 December 20x8.

Suggested solution:

The following questions need to be asked before we can correctly quantify the tax base of the machinery:

(a) *Question*: Will the economic benefits embodied in the asset (CU140,000) be taxable when it is recovered?

Answer: No. When the customer pays company A on 31 January 20X8, company A will not be taxed on that date. In most jurisdictions, an entity is taxed on the earlier of the cash received or the amount accruing to the entity. The amount accrued to company A on 31 December 20X8. The amount will not be taxed again when the cash related to the accounts receivable is received on 31 January 20X9.

(b) The tax base of an asset which has future economic benefits that will not be taxed on recovery of the asset is the equivalent to its carrying amount.
Question: What is the carrying amount of the accounts receivable?
Answer: The carrying amount of the accounts receivable is whatever the IFRS for SMEs chapter (IFRS standard) is that deals with that asset. The carrying amount of the accounts receivable is CU140,000 and its tax base is CU140,000.

3.6.2.4 Tax base of a liability

The tax base of a liability is dependent on whether (s29.10 and IAS 12 p.):
(a) it is a liability other than revenue received in advance; or
(b) the revenue is received in advance.

Tax base of a liability other than revenue received in advance
The tax base of a liability other than revenue received in advance is the carrying amount less the deductions that will be allowed in the future for tax purposes in respect of that liability.

Illustrative Example 3.8: Tax base of a liability
Company A purchases raw materials from its supplier for CU70,000 on credit on 31 December 20X8. Company A is scheduled to pay its creditor on 31 January 20X9.

You are required to:
Explain and quantify what the tax base of the liability is on 31 December 20x9.

Suggested solution:
The following questions need to be asked before we correctly quantify the tax base of the machinery:

(a) *Question*: Is the liability revenue received in advance?
Answer: No. The liability arises from credit purchases and not revenue received in advance.

(b) *Question*: What is the carrying amount of the asset less future deductions as a result of the liability?
Answer: In most jurisdictions, the tax authority allows an expense as a tax deduction in whichever is earlier, the period it was paid or that it accrued. As the creditor has been recognised, the expense must have accrued in 20X8. This means that the tax deduction is taken in 20X8. When the liability is settled in the future (31 January 20X9), the tax authority will not

allow the amount as a deduction again. Therefore, the future deduction allowed on the settlement of the liability is zero. The tax base is the carrying amount less the future deductions (of zero).

Carrying amount	-	Future deductions	=	Tax base
CU70,000		CU70,000		0

Therefore, the tax base is CU0.

Tax base of a liability that is revenue received in advance

The tax base of a liability that is revenue received in advance is the carrying amount less the amount of that revenue received in advance liability that **will not** be taxable in future periods.

Illustrative Example 3.9: Tax base of a liability

Company A receives CU140,000 from its customer on 31 December 20X8 for inventory that will be delivered on 31 January 20X9.

You are required to:
Explain and quantify what the tax base of the liability is on 31 December 20x8.

Suggested solution:
The following questions need to be asked before we can correctly quantify the tax base of the machinery:

(a) *Question*: Is the liability revenue received in advance?
Answer: Yes. The liability arises from a customer who prepaid for goods.

(b) *Question*: What is the carrying amount of the asset less the amount of the revenue received in advance liability that **will not** be taxable in future periods?
Answer: In most jurisdictions, the tax authority includes income in its tax assessment on the earlier of the cash being received and the amount accruing to the entity. As the amount of cash was received in 20X8, the amount will not be taxed again in 20X9 when the inventory is delivered to the customer and the revenue is recognised in the accounting statements. Therefore, the amount of the revenue received in advance that **will not** be taxed again is the full CU140,000. As the tax base of the liability that is revenue received in advance is the carrying amount less the amount of the revenue received in advance that will not be taxed in the future, the tax base is determined as:

Carrying amount	-	Will not be taxed again (taxed already)	=	Tax base
CU140,000		CU140,000		0

Therefore, the tax base is CU0.

3.6.3 Exempt temporary differences

In terms of s29.14 (and IAS 12 p.15), deferred tax should be recognised on all taxable temporary differences except to the extent that it arises from:
(a) The initial recognition of goodwill; or
(b) The initial recognition of an asset or a liability in a transaction that:
    (i)   is not a business combination; and
    (ii)   at the time of the transaction, affects neither accounting profit nor taxable profit (tax loss).

Illustrative Example 3.10: Deferred tax balance

Company A has the following assets in its consolidated trial balance:

Asset	CU	Date of initial recognition
Goodwill	400,000	1 January 20X5
Equipment	300,000	1 January 20X6
Property	500,000	1 January 20X7

(a) The tax authorities provide no wear and tear allowances on goodwill. Company A amortises goodwill over an estimated useful life of 8 years to an estimated nil residual value.
(b) The tax authorities allow a wear-and-tear deduction of 20% of the cost of the equipment per annum. Company A depreciates the equipment over an estimated useful life of 6 years to an estimated nil residual value.
(c) The property consists of land and buildings that are used as the entity's administrative head office. The cost of the land is considered negligible. The tax authorities provide no wear-and-tear allowance in respect of the land and building. Company A depreciates the building over an estimated useful life of 20 years to an estimated nil residual value.

You are required to:
Calculate the deferred tax balance to be recognised in company A's consolidated statement of financial position as at 31 December 20X8.

Suggested solution:

	CA	TB	TD	DT
Goodwill	200,000	0	200,000	Exempt
Equipment	150,000	120,000	30,000	8,400
Property	450,000	0	450,000	Exempt
Deferred tax balance				**8,400**

Notes:

1. Carrying amount of goodwill: CU400,000/8 years × 4 years left = CU200,000
   The recognition of deferred tax related to goodwill is exempt in terms of s29.14 (IAS 12 p.15).

2. Carrying amount of equipment: CU300,000/6 years × 3 years left = CU150,000.

3. Tax base of equipment: CU300,000 × 20% × 2 years left = CU120,000.

4. Admin building: CU500,000/20 years × 18 years left = CU450,000.
   You will notice that the temporary difference related to the administration building arose on initial recognition as the carrying amount of the administration building on initial recognition was its cost of CU400,000 but the tax base has been CU0 since initial recognition. Therefore, the temporary difference arising on initial recognition is CU400,000, but the initial recognition does not affect accounting profit nor taxable profit. Therefore, in terms of s29.14 (IAS 12 p.15), the temporary difference is exempt from deferred tax recognition. An interesting point to note is that if, for instance, the building is revalued after initial recognition to CU600,000, any temporary difference caused by the revaluation is not exempt from deferred tax as it did not arise on initial recognition:

	CA	TB	TD	DT
Property	600,000	0	600,000	28,000

The portion of the CU600,000 temporary difference that arose on initial recognition is CU500,000 and is exempt. The remaining CU100,000 arose as a result of a revaluation after initial recognition and is therefore not exempt.

The same would apply to deductible temporary differences. In terms of s29.16 (IAS 12 p.24), a deferred tax asset shall be recognised for all deductible temporary differences (that it is probable that sufficient taxable profits will be available against which the deductible temporary differences can be utilised – see the next section) except if the difference arose from the initial recognition of an asset or liability in a transaction that:
(a) is not a business combination; and
(b) at the time of the transaction, affects neither accounting profit nor taxable profit (tax loss).

3.6.4 Deductible temporary differences

In terms of s29.16 (IAS 12 p.24), deferred tax assets should be recognised for all temporary differences that do not arise from transactions that are business combinations or at the time do not affect accounting profit or taxable profit (or loss) **and** are limited to the extent that it is probable that sufficient taxable profits will be available against which the deductible temporary differences can be utilised.

3.6.4.1 Assessed losses

An assessed loss arises when the entity being assessed ends up with a negative taxable income. This results in the entity paying no tax. The tax authorities in most, if not all, jurisdictions do not refund the entity an amount calculated by multiplying the negative taxable income by the tax rate. Instead, the tax authority will normally allow the entity to take the assessed loss of one period and net it off against any tax due for the next period that has a taxable income. In other words, the assessed loss can be presented to the tax authority in the next period to reduce the tax due.

Illustrative Example 3.11: Calculation and recovery of assessed loss (tax perspective)

Company A earns a profit before tax of CU100,000 for the year ended 31 December 20X7. The only difference between accounting profit and taxable income is that company A recognised depreciation of CU50,000, while the tax authority allows wear and tear on the same asset of CU175,000.

Company A earns a profit before tax of CU250,000 for the year ended 31 December 20X8. The depreciation and wear and tear recognised for accounting and tax is the same as in 20X7.

You are required to:
Calculate the amount of tax due by company A for the year ended 31 December 20X8.

Suggested solution:
Calculation of tax due:

	20X7	20X8
Profit before tax	100,000	250,000
Depreciation reversed	50,000	50,000
Wear & tear	(175,000)	(175,000)
Taxable income ignoring assessed loss	**(25,000)**	**125,000**
Assessed loss carried forward	0	(25,000)
Taxable income	**(25,000)**	**100,000**
Tax rate	28%	28%
Tax due[1]	**0**	**28,000**

Note:
[1]The tax authority will not refund the amount due, so the tax due is limited to zero.

You will notice that the assessed loss of CU25 000 in 20X7 is used to reduce the tax payable in 20X8. One could therefore think of the assessed loss as a voucher to reduce tax in the future. The ability to use that assessed loss is dependent on whether or not the entity will make sufficient taxable profits in the future against which the assessed loss can be offset. The assessed loss represents an asset of the entity as it is a resource (something that the entity can use in the future), controlled by the entity (the assessed loss is in the name of the entity), as a result of a past event (the entity was assessed as having a tax loss) and from which future economic benefits are expected to flow (the entity will save cash in the future when it reduces its tax payable with the assessed loss (tax payable would have been based on the assessment of taxable income of CU125,000, but the assessed loss reduces the tax payable to an amount based on taxable income of CU100,000)).

You will remember from Chapter 1 – *The framework* that even if an item meets the definition of an element of the financial statements, it can only be recognised in the financial statements if it meets the recognition criteria of probability and measurability. Therefore, the assessed loss, like any other asset, may only be recognised if it is probable that the economic benefits associated with the asset will be received. To this end, s29.16 (IAS 12 p.24) requires that deferred tax assets (including assessed losses) only be recognised to the extent that it will be probable that future taxable profits will be available against which the deferred tax asset (such as the assessed loss) can be offset.

In terms of s29.18 (IAS 12 p.28), it is probable that sufficient profits will be available in the future against which the deferred tax asset can be offset, when there are sufficient taxable temporary differences (these result in deferred tax liabilities) relating to the same tax authority and the same taxable entity and are expected to reverse:
(a) in the same period of the deductible temporary difference; or
(b) in periods into which a tax loss arising from the deferred tax asset can be carried back or forward.

It is evident that if an asset is recognised as a debit entry, it results in a credit to tax expense as the recognition of the asset does not result in the simultaneous recognition of a liability or reduction of another asset.

Illustrative Example 3.12: Recognition of deferred tax assets

Use the same information as in Illustrative Example 3.11. The entity estimates that it:
(a) will make sufficient profit in the future against which it can offset the assessed loss; and
(b) will not make sufficient profits in the future against which it can offset the assessed loss.

Company A also has taxable temporary differences of CU15,000 before considering the implications of the assessed loss.

You are required to:
Prepare the journal entries necessary to account for the assessed loss as at 31 December 20X7.

Suggested solution:
(i) Company A considers it probable that sufficient profits will exist in the future:

Dr	Deferred tax [SFP] (25,000 × 28%)	7,000	
Cr	Tax expense [P/L]		7,000
[Recognising the deferred tax asset as a result of the assessed loss]			

(ii) Company A does not consider it probable that sufficient profits will exist in the future:

Dr:	Deferred tax [SFP] (15,000[1] × 28%)	4,200	
Cr:	Tax expense [P/L]		4,200
[Recognising the deferred tax asset as a result of the assessed loss]			

Notes:

[1]The amount of the deferred tax asset that can be recognised is limited to the taxable temporary differences as the entity does not consider it probable that any further benefits related to the assessed loss will be received in the future. This journal entry will reduce the deferred tax liability that existed before its recognition, to nil but create no deferred tax asset either.

3.6.5   Tax rate

An entity should measure the deferred tax balance using the tax rate that is expected to be applied when the deferred tax reverses or is realised. It is not always possible for an entity to know what rates the government will use in the future periods when the deferred tax is expected to reverse. However, in order to estimate the deferred tax liability (asset) at year-end, the entity must use the tax rate that has been substantively enacted by the reporting date (s29.27 and IAS 12 p.46). Tax rates are considered substantively enacted when the remaining steps in the enactment process have not affected the outcome in the past and are unlikely to do so (s29.27 and IAS 12 p.48). For instance, tax rates are often considered to be substantively enacted once the Minister of Finance has announced the rate as it is often a formality for the president of a country to authorise the change.

Illustrative Example 3.13: Calculation of deferred tax

Company A has taxable temporary differences of CU100,000 on 1 January 20X8. Taxable temporary differences arising during the year ended 31 December20X8 amount to CU75,000. The tax rate in the jurisdiction in which Company A operates has remained constant at 29% for all years of assessment up to and including the year of assessment ending 31 December 20X7. On 1 March 20x8, the Minister of Finance of the jurisdiction announced a reduction in the tax rate 28% for all years of assessment ending on 31 December 20X8.

You are required to:
Prepare the journal entries necessary to account for deferred tax as at 31 December 20X8.

Suggested solution:

Date	CA	TB	TD	DT
31 December 20X7			100,000	30,000
Effect of rate change				(2,000)
31 December 20X7			**100,000**	**28,000**
New temporary differences			75,000	21,000
31 December 20X8			**175,000**	**49,000**

Dr	Deferred tax [SFP]	2,000	
Cr	Tax expense [P/L]		2,000
[Recognising the reduction in the deferred tax liability due to the change in the tax rate]			

Dr	Tax expense [P/L]	21,000	
Cr	Deferred tax [SFP]		21,000
[Recognising the increase in the deferred tax liability as a result of an increase in temporary differences]			

3.6.6 Manner of recovery or settlement

The deferred tax related to an asset or liability should reflect the tax consequences that would follow from the manner in which the entity expects to recover or settle the carrying amount (s29.29 and IAS 12 p.51). In some jurisdictions, recovery of an asset through sale and recovery of that same asset through use would result in different tax consequences. For instance, recovery through use would result in all of the economic benefits of that asset being taxed at the normal income tax rate while recovery through sale might result in a portion taxed at the normal income tax rate (the portion considered to be a recoupment) and a portion taxed at the capital gains tax rate (the portion above the base cost).

Illustrative Example 3.14: Change in expected manner of recovery of an asset (change of intention)

Company A purchased a building for CU5,000,000 on 01 January 20X6. Company A depreciates the building over an estimated useful life of 50 years to an estimated nil residual value. The tax authority allows wear and tear to be deducted calculated as 5% of the cost of the building per annum. Company A uses the revaluation model to account for buildings and considers its fair value to be CU5,390,000 and CU5,280,000 on 01 January 20X7 and 20X8 respectively. Company A intended to use the machine over its useful life in all periods up to and including 31 December 20X7, but changed its intention to recover the future economic benefits embodied in the building through sale from 01 January 20X8.

The building did not meet the criteria to be classified as a non-current asset held for sale at any point in the 20X8 financial year. The building was still on hand at 31 December 20X8. The income tax rate was 28% while the capital gains tax inclusion rate was 80% for all years of assessment.

You are required to:
Prepare the journal entries necessary to account for the deferred tax as at 31 December 20X8.

Suggested solution:

Date	CA	TB	TD	DT
1 January 20X6	5,000,000	5,000,000	0	0
Depreciation/wear & tear	(100,000)	(250,000)	150,000	42,000
31 December 20X6	**4,900,000**	**4,750,000**	**150,000**	**42,000**
Revaluation gain	490,000	0	490,000	137,200
1 January 20X7	**5,390,000**	**4,750,000**	**640,000**	**179,200**
Depreciation/wear & tear	(110,000)[1]	(250,000)	140,000	39,200
31 December 20X7	**5,280,000**	**4,500,000**	**780,000**	**218,400**[2]
Change in intention	0	0	0	(15,680)
1 January 20X8	**5,280,000**	**4,500,000**	**780,000**	**202,720**[3]
Depreciation/wear & tear	(110,000)	(250,000)	140,000	45,360
31 December 20X8	**5,170,000**[5]	**4,250,000**	**275,000**	**248,080**[7]

Notes:

[1] Revalued on 1 January 20X7: CU5,390,000/49 years = CU5,280,000

[2] Recovery through use: all future economic benefits will be taxed at 28%: CU780,000 × 28%
= CU218,400

[3] Recovery through sale will trigger capital gains tax on the portion above the base cost [(CU5,280,000 – CU5,000,000) × 80% × 28%] and a recoupment for the portion represented by the difference of the base cost and the tax base [(CU5,000,000 – CU4,500,000) × 28%] = CU202,720

[5] CU5,280,000/48 years × 47 years = CU5,170,000

[6] Portion above cost (CU170,000 × 80% × 28%) + Recoupment [(CU5,000,000 – CU4,250,000) × 28%]

Dr	Deferred tax [SFP]	15,680	
Cr	Tax expense [OCI]		15,680
[Recognising the reduction in the deferred tax liability due to the change in intention]			

Dr	Tax expense [OCI]	45,360	
Cr	Deferred tax [SFP]		45,360
[Recognising the increase in the deferred tax liability as a result of an increase in temporary differences]			

3.6.7 Presentation and disclosure

3.6.7.1 Presentation

An entity shall recognise tax expense in the same component of equity where the transaction or other event that resulted in the tax expense is presented (s29.35 and IAS 12 p.77 & 61A).

Deferred tax may never be classified as current assets or liabilities (s29.36). In addition, an entity may only offset current tax assets and current tax liabilities and deferred tax assets and deferred tax liabilities if:
(a)   it has a legally enforceable right to set off the amounts; and
(b)   the entity plans to settle on a net basis.

3.6.7.2 Disclosure

An entity shall disclose separately the major components of tax income or expense. Such components of tax expense (income) may include (s29.39 and IAS 12 p.80):
(a)   current tax expense (income);
(b)   any adjustments recognised in the period for current tax of prior periods;
(c)   the amount of deferred tax expense (income) relating to the origination and reversal of temporary differences;
(d)   the amount of deferred tax expense (income) relating to changes in tax rates or the imposition of new taxes;
(e)   the amount of the benefit arising from a previously unrecognised tax loss, tax credit or temporary difference of a prior period that is used to reduce tax expense;
(f)   adjustments to deferred tax expense (income) arising from a change in the tax status of the entity or its shareholders;
(g)   deferred tax expense (income) arising from the write-down, or reversal of a previous write-down, of a deferred tax asset; and
(h)   the amount of tax expense (income) relating to those changes in accounting policies and errors that are included in profit or loss because they cannot be accounted for retrospectively.

An entity shall disclose the following separately (s29.40 and IAS 12 p.81):

(a) the aggregate current and deferred tax relating to items that are recognised as items of other comprehensive income;

(b) the aggregate current and deferred tax relating to items that are charged or credited directly to equity;

(c) an explanation of any significant differences between the tax expense (income) and accounting profit multiplied by the applicable tax rate. For example, such differences may arise from transactions such as revenue that are exempt from taxation or expenses that are not deductible in determining taxable profit (tax loss) (*full IFRS requires the same, but in the format of a reconciliation reconciling the actual tax and the accounting profit before tax multiplied by the applicable tax rates or between the effective tax rate and the applicable tax rate.*)

(d) an explanation of changes in the applicable tax rate(s) compared with the previous reporting period;

(e) for each type of temporary difference and for each type of unused tax losses and tax credits:

  (i) the amount of deferred tax liabilities and deferred tax assets at the end of the reporting period; and

  (ii) an analysis of the change in deferred tax liabilities and deferred tax assets during the period.

(f) the amount (and expiry date, if any) of deductible temporary differences, unused tax losses and unused tax credits for which no deferred tax asset is recognised in the statement of financial position; and

(g) an explanation of the nature of the potential income tax consequences that would result from the payment of dividends to its shareholders.

In addition, full IFRS also requires the following disclosure (IAS 12 p.81):

(a) the amount of income tax consequences of dividends to shareholders of the entity that were proposed or declared before the financial statements were authorised for issue, but are not recognised as a liability in the financial statements;

(b) if a business combination in which the entity is the acquirer causes a change in the amount recognised for its pre-acquisition deferred tax asset (see paragraph 67), the amount of that change; and

(c) if the deferred tax benefits acquired in a business combination are not recognised at the acquisition date but are recognised after the acquisition date (see paragraph 68), a description of the event or change in circumstances that caused the deferred tax benefits to be recognised.

If an entity does not offset tax assets and liabilities in accordance with paragraph because it is unable to demonstrate without undue cost or effort that it plans to settle them on a net basis or realise them simultaneously, the entity shall disclose the amounts that have not been offset and the reasons why applying the requirement would involve undue cost or effort (s29.37).

SELF-ASSESSMENT
Multiple choice questions: Testing principles of accounting for the taxation and value-added tax

1. The VAT on a transaction with consideration of CU115 (inclusive of VAT) when the VAT rate is 15% is:

(a) CU115	
(b) CU100	
(c) CU15	
(d) CU150	

2. A VAT vendor providing zero-rated supplies:

(a) may not deduct expenditure incurred to provide the zero-rated supplies	
(b) must consider the supply as an exempt supply	
(c) may deduct the expenditure incurred to provide the zero-rated supply	
(d) may not classify itself as a VAT vendor	

3. Deferred tax assets must be:

(a) presented as current assets	
(b) presented in the statement of cash flows	
(c) disclosed instead of presented in the financial statements	
(d) presented as non-current assets	

4. The tax rate to be used to account for current tax is:

(a) the substantively enacted rate	
(b) the current tax rate	
(c) the proposed tax rate	
(d) the prior period tax rate	

5. Tax expense is presented in the financial statements:

(a) in profit or loss only	
(b) wherever the transaction that gave rise to the tax expense is recognized	
(c) in other comprehensive income	
(d) in the statement of changes in equity	

6. A deferred tax asset is recognised:

(a) if it is probable that there will be sufficient future taxable profits against which the deferred tax asset can be realised	
(b) if the entity expects users to prefer a statement of financial position with a tax loss recognised	
(c) if the deferred tax asset was purchased from an external party	
(d) if the deferred tax asset is larger than the amount recognised as a deferred tax liability	

7. When the tax rate applicable to the calculation of deferred tax changes:

(a) the prior period's deferred tax balance is adjusted in the prior period financial statements to reflect a correction of a prior period error	
(b) the current period's deferred tax balance is adjusted in the current period financial statements	
(c) the change is ignored in all financial statements	
(d) none of the above	

8. Deferred tax is recognised on:

(a) all differences between tax rules and accounting principles/rules	
(b) all temporary differences	
(c) those temporary differences which are not exempt from deferred tax	
(d) none of the above	

9. If the future economic benefits of an asset are not expected to be taxed on recovery, then:

(a) the tax base of the asset is nil	
(b) the tax base of the asset is equal to the future deductions allowed by the tax authority	
(c) the tax base is equal to the carrying amount	
(d) the tax base is less than the carrying amount	

10. A deductible temporary difference results in:

(a) a credit to profit or loss and other comprehensive income or equity	
(b) a debit to profit or loss and other comprehensive income or equity	
(c) a deduction from cash and cash equivalents in the current period	
(d) an addition to cash and cash equivalents in the current period	

Practical questions:
Application of principles to business scenarios

QUESTION 1

You are the accountant of HSJ (Pty) Ltd. You were presented with the following information which was extracted from the trial balance of Cotton (Pty) Ltd for the year ended 31 December 20X8:

	Note	CU
Revenue	1	2,300,000
Purchases of raw material	2	400,000
Opening inventory	2	100,000
Closing inventory	2	150,000
Depreciation expense	3	180,000
Salaries and wages	3	450,000
Other expenses	2	200,000
Tax expense	3	75,600

Notes:
1. Erroneously included in the trial balance inclusive of VAT.
2. VAT is paid/payable on these items but is stated here excluding VAT.
3. VAT is not paid/payable on these items.

You are required to:
Calculate the net amount of VAT payable at 31 December 20X8, assuming that the opening balance of VAT payable on 1 January 20X8 was CU40,000 and the VAT paid during the year 31 December 20X8 was CU60,000.

QUESTION 2

You are the accountant of TPJ (Pty) Ltd. TPJ (Pty) Ltd earned a profit of CU1,500,000 the year ended 31 December 20x8. TPJ (Pty) Ltd purchased machinery for CU450,000 on 1 January 20x7. TPJ (Pty) Ltd depreciates the machinery over an estimated useful life of five years to an estimated nil residual value. The tax authority allows a deduction of 33.3% of the cost of the machinery per annum. There are no other differences between accounting profit and taxable income.

You are required to:
Prepare the extract of the statement of profit or loss, together with the note showing the breakdown of the tax expense, for the year ended 31 December 20x8 for TPJ (Pty) Ltd, beginning with profit before tax.

QUESTION 3

You are the accountant of BAJ (Pty) Ltd. BAJ (Pty) Ltd earned a profit of CU2,200,000 the year ended 31 December 20X8. BAJ (Pty) Ltd purchased equipment for CU500,000 on 01 January 20X7. BAJ (Pty) Ltd depreciates the equipment over an estimated useful life of 4 years to an estimated nil residual value. The tax authority allows a deduction of 25% of the cost of the equipment per annum. BAJ (Pty) Ltd also received dividends of CU100,000 during the year which was included in the profit for the year above. The dividends are not subject to any form of tax in the jurisdiction in which BAJ (Pty) Ltd operates. BAJ (Pty) Ltd had an assessed loss of CU400,000 from the prior period which is recognised as a deferred tax asset in that prior period. There are no other differences between accounting profit and taxable income.

You are required to:
Prepare the journal entries to account for the tax expense related to the profit or loss for the year ended 31 December 20X8 for BAJ (Pty) Ltd.

CHAPTER 4
PROPERTY, PLANT AND EQUIPMENT

Property, plant and equipment are part of the value drivers of the business.

ILLUSTRATIVE DISCLOSURE

S4.2(e) & IAS 1 p.54(a)			Notes	20X2	20X1	Ch. ref
				CU'000	CU'000	
		ASSETS				
		Non-current assets				
S17 & IAS 16		Property, plant & equipment	6	2,550	2,401	
S17.31 (e) & IAS 16 p.73(e)	6	PROPERTY, PLANT & EQUIPMENT				
				Machinery	Equipment	Total
		Carrying amount at beginning of the period		1,570	831	2,401
		Cost		1,960	1,102	3,062
		Accumulated depreciation and impairment loss		(390)	(271)	(661)
		Acquisitions during the period		-	485	485
		Carrying amount of assets disposed of during period		-	(36)	(36)
		Depreciation		(30)	(240)	(270)
		Impairment loss		-	(30)	(30)
		Transferred to/(from) other assets		-	-	-
		Carrying amount at the end of the period		1,540	1,010	2,550
		Cost		1,960	1,346	3,306
		Accumulated depreciation and impairment loss		(420)	(336)	(756)

		ALTERNATIVE:			
			Machinery	**Equipment**	**Total**
		Cost:			
		Balance at beginning of the period	1,960	1,102	3,062
		Acquisitions during the period	-	485	485
		Disposals during the period	-	(241)	(241)
		Balance at the end of the period	1,960	1,346	3,306
		Accumulated depreciation and impairment loss			
		Balance at beginning of the period	(390)	(271)	(661)
		Annual depreciation	(30)	(240)	(270)
		Impairment loss for the period	-	(30)	(30)
		Accumulated depreciation on assets disposed of	-	205	205
		Balance at the end of the period	(420)	(336)	(756)
		Carrying amount at the end of the period	1,540	1,010	2,550

4.1 INTRODUCTION

Property, plant and equipment (PPE) are important components of the entity's statement of financial position and provide an indication of the investment in resources to sustain its operations for achieving its strategic objective. In general and especially in capital intensive businesses, the value of a business is based on its non-current assets, as these assets represent the income earning capacity of the entity.

The primary responsibility of management is to achieve the goals of the business and its shareholders/members, namely profit maximisation and the maximisation of shareholders' wealth and to improve the cost effectiveness of the business operations. The level of competiveness in many industries coupled with globalisation forced management to place greater emphasis on the effective allocation of its resources, especially items of property, plant and equipment, to the value creation activities of the business. Management often opt for outsourcing of capital-intensive activities which results in the shedding of items of property, plant and equipment as a means of controlling capital investment requirements. However, this type of decision-making in respect of items of property, plant and equipment often leads to the downward spiraling of the business operations and may result in the closure of the business.

Furthermore, the carrying amounts of property, plant and equipment are also affected by the accounting policies adopted by entities, in particular the depreciation policies and measurement of its carrying amount. Numerous financial statements of SMEs often reflect items of property, plant and equipment with zero carrying amounts which are continuing to be used in the operations to generate revenue.

4.2   LEARNING OUTCOMES

Upon completion of this unit you should know the financial reporting requirements for property, plant and equipment in accordance with the IFRS for SMEs. In particular, you should be able to:

(a)   distinguish items of property, plant and equipment from other assets of an entity;

(b)   identify when items of property, plant and equipment qualify for recognition in financial statements;

(c)   measure the cost of items of property, plant and equipment on initial recognition and subsequent to initial recognition;

(d)   measure the cost of self-constructed items of property, plant and equipment;

(e)   measure the cost of items of property, plant and equipment in an exchange of non-monetary assets;

(f)   recognise the impairment of items of property, plant and equipment;

(g)   identify when an item of property, plant and equipment is to be de-recognised or transferred to another classification of asset; and

(h)   present and disclose property, plant and equipment in financial statements.

4.3   DEFINITIONS

The definitions for the important concepts and terms used in IFRS for SMEs are found in Appendix B – *Glossary of terms* in IFRS for SMEs. Some important definitions relating to property, plant and equipment include the following:

- **Asset:** A resource controlled by the entity as a result of past events and from which future economic benefits are expected to flow to the entity

- **Property, plant & equipment:** Tangible assets that are:
  (a) held for use in the production or supply of goods or services, for rental to others, or for administrative purposes; and
  (b) expected to be used during more than one period.

- **Residual value:** The estimated amount that an entity would currently obtain from disposal of an asset, after deducting the estimated costs of disposal, if the asset were already of the age and in the condition expected at the end of its useful life

- **Useful life:** The period over which an asset is expected to be available for use by an entity or the number of production or similar units expected to be obtained from the asset by the entity

- **Depreciable amount:** The cost of an asset, or other amount substituted for cost (in the financial statements), less the residual value

- **Depreciation:** The systematic allocation of the depreciable amount of an asset over its useful life

- **Impairment loss:** Occurs when the carrying amount of an asset exceeds its recoverable amount

- **Recoverable amount:** The higher of an asset's fair value less cost to sell and its value in use

- **Fair value less cost to sell (fair value less cost of disposal for IFRS):** The amount obtainable from the sale of an asset in an arm's length transaction between knowledgeable and willing parties, less the cost of disposal (for IFRS, the fair value is measured with reference to IFRS 13 – *Fair value measurement*)

- **Value in use:** The present value of the future cash flows expected to be derived from the asset

4.4 SCOPE AND OBJECTIVES

This section applies to all items which satisfy the definition of property, plant and equipment, as well as those items which meet the definition for classification as investment property, but whose fair value cannot be determined without undue cost and effort on an ongoing basis (s17.1)

It is interesting to note that even though IFRS for SMEs scopes investment property measured on the cost model into s17 – Property, plant & equipment, IFRS does not have this requirement of scoping Investment Property into IAS 16. IAS 16 p.5 does not scope investment property into the standard, but indicates that investment property measured on the cost model (in IAS 40 – Investment property) shall use the cost model in IAS 16.

4.5   BASIC TRANSACTIONS

4.5.1   Classification

For any item to be classified as property, plant and equipment, it must first satisfy the definition of an asset as per the standard on *Concepts and pervasive principles* and the Conceptual Framework (s2.15(a) and Conceptual Framework (CF) 4.4(a)):

(a)   emphasis on the economic phenomenon and the purpose and intention of the transaction;

(b)   resource with future economic benefits; and

(c)   control over the item.

The specific requirements for items to be classified as property, plant and equipment focuses on the intended purpose for which the item was acquired – purpose of use. Items of property, plant and equipment are defined as tangible assets that (s17.2 and IAS 16 p.6):

(a)   are held for use in the production or supply of goods or services, for rental to others (this makes them directly linked to the revenue generating activities of the business), or

(b)   are held for administrative purposes (used to support the business in furthering its operating objective); and

(c)   are expected to be used during more than one period (which means that they are long-term investments to sustain the business activities).

The characteristics of assets which are classified as property, plant and equipment are as follows:

•   **Operating assets:** the assets must be acquired with the intended purpose of being used in the normal business operations of the entity and not for resale, ie acquired for production or administrative purposes. *For example, when an entity purchases heavy duty machinery for resale purposes, then it will be classified as inventory (s13 and IAS2), but when the heavy duty machinery is acquired to be used in the manufacturing process, then it will be classified as property, plant and equipment (s17 and IAS16).*

•   **Long-term in nature:** property, plant and equipment must yield economic benefits which exceed the operating cycle of the entity or one year, ie have enduring future economic benefits. *For example, if the operating cycle of the entity is 2 years (such as in the case of a winery) then the materials purchased cannot be classified as property, plant and equipment based on the fact that the economic benefits exceed one year; they will be classified as inventory (s13 and IAS2).*

•   **Physical substance:** property, plant and equipment are tangible assets characterised by the existence of physical substance. *For example, the* *formula used to produce Coca-Cola might satisfy the definition of an asset and some of the criteria for classification as property, plant and equipment, but it does not represent a tangible asset and must therefore be classified as an intangible asset (s18 and IAS 38).*

4.5.1.1 Specific inclusions

Furthermore, IFRS for SMEs requires that property which meets the definition of investment property (ie its intended purpose is to generate rental income or capital appreciation (s16)), but for which fair value cannot be determined without undue costs and effort (s1 – *Concepts and pervasive principles*) must be classified as property, plant and equipment (s16 p.8). *For example, an entity owns a building which was acquired for the purpose of generating rental income – ie it satisfies the criteria for classification as investment property. However, due to the specialisation of the building, there is no active market for such properties resulting in the fair value not being readily available (valuation can be performed to determine the fair value but it is too costly). As the fair value cannot be determined on an ongoing basis, the property must be classified as property, plant and equipment and measured using the cost model.*

4.5.1.2 Specific exclusions

The following items are specifically *excluded* from being classified as property, plant and equipment: (s17.3 and IAS 16 p.3):
(a) biological assets related to agricultural activity (s34 – *Specialised activities*); or
(b) mineral rights and mineral reserves, such as oil, natural gas and similar non-regenerative resources.

In addition, IAS16 p.3 also excludes the following from the scope of IAS16 (which is not in the scope of exclusion for IFRS for SMEs):
(a) property, plant and equipment classified as held for sale in accordance with IFRS 5 – *Non-current assets held for sale & discontinued operations;* and
(b) the recognition and measurement of exploration and evaluation assets.

4.5.2 Recognition

4.5.2.1 Recognition criteria

Items of property, plant and equipment can only be recognised and recorded in the accounting records if they have economic and commercial substance, ie future economic benefits must be associated with the asset and the value of such benefits must be measureable and quantifiable in monetary terms. *For example, in many instances, other than for professional sports, human resources are not recognised as an asset of the entity for various reasons, one of which is because their value cannot be measured reliably and the period of their employment is uncertain.*

Illustrative Example 4.1: Recognition of property, plant and equipment

On 12 January 20X8, the business purchased a machine at a cost of CU2,500,000 and paid cash immediately. The machine was only delivered to the premises of the business on 26 February 20X8.

You are required to:

Prepare the journal entries related to the acquisition and settlement of the amount due for the machine for the year ended 29 February 20X8.

Suggested solution:

Although the cash was paid on 12 January 20X8, the business only gained control over the machine on 26 February 20X8 when it was delivered. The recognition date will therefore be 26 February 20X8.

12/02/x8	DR: Prepaid asset	2,500,000	
	CR: Bank		2,500,000
26/02/X8	DR: Machinery	2,500,000	
	CR: Prepaid asset		2,500,000
	[Recognition of the purchase of machine]		

4.5.2.2 Component assets

If an item of property, plant and equipment consists of components with significant costs in relation to the total cost of the item and which have significantly different patterns of consumption of economic benefits or useful lives, the initial costs of the major components shall be recognised separately and depreciated separately (s17.21 and IAS 16 p.43).

4.5.2.3 De-recognition criteria

De-recognition of items of property, plant and equipment occurs when the cost of the items together with the associated accumulated depreciation and accumulated impairment losses are removed from the accounting records. Items of property, plant and equipment are de-recognised either when they are (s17.27 and IAS 16 p.67):

(a) disposed of – items is de-recognised and the profit or loss on disposal is recognised via the profit and loss; or

(b) there are no future economic benefits associated with the item – the item has no future value to the business or the carrying amount is zero.

When the item of property, plant and equipment is disposed of, depreciation must be recognised up to the date the asset was used and/or sold. The profit/loss represents the difference between the net selling price, ie selling price less costs to selling, and the carrying amount at the date of disposal (s27.30 and IAS 16.68).

Illustrative Example 4.2: Derecognition of property, plant and equipment

At 01 January 20X8, the accounting records reflected machinery with a cost of CU560 000 and accumulated depreciation of CU300 000. On 30 June 20X8 the machinery was sold at a selling price of CU270 000. Costs of CU20 000 were incurred to dismantle the machine. The machinery was depreciated on a straight-line basis to a residual value of CU60 000 at a rate of 20%.

You are required to:
Prepare the journal entries necessary to account for all aspects of the machine for the year ended 30 June 20X8.

Suggested solution:

	CU
Cost of machine	560,000
Accumulated depreciation at 01 January 20X8	300,000
Depreciation to the date of sale [(560,000 – 60,000) × 20% × 6/12]	50,000
Carrying amount at 30 June 20X8	210,000
Net selling price [270,000 – 20,000]	250,000
Profit on disposal	40,000

30/06/X8	DR: Depreciation	50,000	
	CR: Accumulated depreciation		50,000
	[Depreciation for the period to the date of sale]		
30/06/X8	DR: Bank	270,000	
	CR: Asset disposal account		270,000
	[Receipt for the sale of the machine]		
30/06/X8	DR: Asset disposal account	20,000	
	CR: Bank		20,000
	[Payment for the dismantling of the machine]		
30/06/X8	DR: Accumulated depreciation	350,000	
	DR: Disposal account	210,000	
	CR: Machine account		560,000
	[De-recognition of the machine sold]		

It is important to note that the discontinuation or de-commissioning of items of property, plant and equipment does not necessary imply that they should be de-recognised. *For example, if the use of a particular machine (property, plant and equipment) was discontinued because it violated certain regulations but it may be used in future, it is not required to be de-recognised.*

Before an item of property, plant and equipment with a zero carrying amount can be de-recognised, management must assess whether it holds future economic benefits for the business, ie whether it is still being used in business operations. If it is still used in the business operations, then the item has future economic benefits and management must consider whether the item must be revalued and its residual value and useful life re-estimated.

4.5.3   Measurement

4.5.3.1   Measurement

At initial recognition property, plant and equipment shall be measured at the cash equivalent of the consideration paid or incurred for the acquisition of the item to bring it (s17.9 and IAS 16.16(b)):
(a)   to its location – the location where management intends using it in the manner in which it intended to; and
(b)   into a condition ready for its intended purpose, ie ready to be used.

Expenditure included in cost
The expenditure to be included in the cost of an item of property, plant and equipment consists of the following :

(a) Price paid
The cash consideration transferred to the supplier of the item of property, plant and equipment:
(i)   includes the purchase price, including legal and brokerage fees which are necessary to complete the purchase of the item – the legal fees and brokerage expenses must be directly associated with the purchase transaction. *For example, the purchase of a factory plant will include the attorney's fees, transfer duties and agent's commissions;*
(ii)   includes import duties and non-refundable taxes, but excludes VAT where the VAT can be claimed back by the purchaser – the cost must represent the net cash consideration transferred. *For example, when purchasing a machine from a registered VAT vendor, the VAT paid cannot be included in the cost of the machine;* but
(iii) excludes any trade discounts and rebates – the cost must represent the net cash consideration transferred or paid.

(b) Direct costs

The direct costs to be included in the initial cost of the item of property, plant and equipment are:

(i)   the expenses incurred to bring the item to its present location, but not relocation costs. For example, if the machinery is delivered to its premises for testing but is then relocated to a factory other than that where the testing occurred, the only the costs incurred to transport the item to its first location (where testing occurred) can be included in the cost of the item while the costs to relocate it to the factory must be recognised as an expense;

(ii) the expenses incurred to bring the item to a condition necessary for it to be used for its intended purpose – these include all expenses incurred to ensure that the item meets the operating specifications and regulations. For example, the costs incurred to install as well as test the machine, ie required to ensure the machine can be used for its intended purposes, must be capitalised as part of the cost of the machine. However, any income generated from the disposal of the products produced during testing must be set off against the expenses incurred during testing, limited to the actual expenses incurred – a company cannot capitalise a net income to the cost of the asset (the net income must be recognised as revenue).

(c) Dismantling costs

(i)   The initial estimate of the costs of dismantling, removing the item and restoring the site on which it is located (rehabilitation) must be capitalised as part of the cost of the item of property, plant and equipment – see section 9 in this chapter.

Capitalised to property, plant and equipment	Explanation
Purchase price	Necessary to get the item
Direct costs	If incurred to bring the item into a condition or location available for use as intended by management
Dismantling costs	If incurred to bring the item into a condition or location available for use as intended by management

Expenses excluded from costs

The following expenses are *excluded* from the initial cost of property, plant and equipment:

Expenses excluded	Explanation
Costs of opening a new facility	Expenses incurred does not form part the expenses incurred to bring the item into the location and condition ready for its intended use
Costs of introducing a new product or service, such as advertising expenses	Expenses relate to the product and its promotion and marketing – represents an operating expense
Cost of conducting business in a new location or with a new class of customer, including staff training expenses and re-locating costs	Expenses are not incurred to acquire control of the item at initial recognition
Administrative and other general overhead costs	Expenses incurred represent general operating expenses and are not directly associated with the item acquired
Borrowing costs which are not permitted to be capitalised [s25 – *Borrowing costs]*	S25 – *Borrowing costs* requires that borrowing costs be expensed in the period in which they are incurred

Income or expenses incidental to or not necessary to bring the item of property, plant and equipment to its intended location and operating condition do not form part of its cost (s17.12 and IAS 16 p.21).

NB: It is interesting to note that in terms of IAS 23 (full IFRS), borrowing costs may be capitalised to the cost of an asset (the asset has to be a qualifying asset) under certain conditions.

Illustrative Example 4.3: Cost of property, plant and equipment

The following details are provided referring to expenditure incurred in relation to a machine:

Details	Cost
	CU
Purchase price	1,500,000
Transport costs to location intended for use	40,000
Installation costs	120,000
Cost for testing machine	65,000
Sale of the products produced during testing	-35,000

Staff training costs	20,000
Cost of launching the new products produced	50,000
Total cost	**1,690,000**

You are required to:

Prepare a schedule detailing which expenditure is capitalised or not and for each item of expenditure, include an explanation of why the expenditure is or is not capitalised.

Suggested solution:

Details	Cost	Expensed	Explanation
	CU	**CU**	
Purchase price	1,500,000		Initial costs excluding VAT and discounts
Transport costs to location intended for use	40,000		Expenses incurred to bring to location – from supplier to business premises and excludes re-location costs
Installation costs	120,000		Expenses incurred to make ready for its intended use – necessary to use the item to generate revenue
Cost for testing machine	65,000		Expenses incurred to make ready for its intended use – ensure the item meets the production and operating specifications
Sale of the products produced during testing	−35,000		Recovery of expenses incurred during testing – set off against expenses limited to the actual expense incurred
Staff training costs		20,000	Expenses incurred as part of the operating expense
Cost of launching the new products produced		50,000	Expenses incurred as part of general business expense – only capitalise expenses until the item is ready for its intended use
Total cost	**1,690,000**		

4.5.3.2 Measurement on initial recognition

Deferred payments – extended credit terms

The cost of an item of property, plant and equipment is represented by the cash consideration paid or payable as determined at the date of initial recognition. If the payment for the purchase of the item of property, plant and equipment is deferred beyond normal credit terms granted by the supplier, the cost of the item at initial recognition is measured at the present value of all future cash payments discounted at the effective interest rate (s17.13 and IAS 16.23). The interest component included in the cash payable is deferred at the transaction date (initial recognition) and expensed equally over the period of the credit agreement, ie expensed periodically.

Illustrative Example 4.4: Deferred payments

On 01March 20X8, an entity purchased a machine from a supplier at a total cost of CU1,800,000 in terms of an agreement which required an initial payment of CU1,000,000 and the balance to be paid on 28 February 20X9. The normal credit term granted by the supplier is 90 days. The effective interest rate is considered to be 13%. The reporting date of the entity is 30 June 20X8.

You are required to:
Prepare the journal entries necessary to account for the purchase of the machine and any amount payable to the supplier for the year ended 30 June 20X8.
Suggested Solution:
The transactions represent a deferred payment agreement, thus the cost of the machine must be measured at the present value of the future cash flows discounted at the effective interest rate, and the interest must be expensed periodically.

	CU
Initial payment	1,000,000
Add: Present value of settlement amount [800,000 @ 13% after 1 year]	707,965
Present value of cash flows – cost	1,707,965
Total price paid	1,800,000
Interest element – for the full year [CU707 965 × 13%]	92,035
Interest expensed at 30 June 20X8 [CU92,035 × 4/12]	30,678

01/03/X8	DR: Machinery	1,707,965	
	CR: Bank		1,000,000
	CR: Accounts payable		707,965

[Recognition of machine acquired in terms of a deferred payment agreement]

30/06/X8 DR: Interest expense	30,678	
CR: Accounts payable		30,678
[Interest expense for the period]		

The interest element can be calculated from the transaction date (full period of the agreement) or only for the extended period of the agreement (period after the normal credit terms to the settlement date). In illustrative example 4.4 interest was calculated for the entire period.

Low interest charged transactions

Similarly, if the interest rate charged by the supplier is significantly lower than that charged under normal circumstances and the risk of the buyer has been taken into account, then the excess interest charged must be excluded from the initial cost of the item of property, plant and equipment and recognised as interest expense over the period of the agreement. The cost of the item must be measured at initial recognition based on the present value of the future cash flows discounted at the fair interest rate.

Illustrative Example 4.5: Deferred payment with low interest

On 01 March 20X8, an entity purchased a machine from a supplier at a cost of CU2,000,000 in terms of an agreement which required settlement on 31 August 20X8 and charges interest at a rate of 11%. The normal interest rate charged by the supplier is 15%. The reporting date of the entity is 30 June 20X8.

You are required to:

Prepare the journal entries related to the purchase of the machine and any amount payable to the supplier for the year ended 30 June 20x8.

Suggested solution:

The transactions represent a low interest charged agreement, thus the cost of the machine must be measured at the present value of future cash flows discounted at the fair interest rate and the interest must be expensed periodically.

	CU
Initial payment	2,000,000
Add: Interest charged [2,000,000 @ 11% × 6/12]	110,000
Total cash flow – Settlement amount	2,110,000
Cash value – Cost [2,110,000 @ 15% after 6 months]	1,962,791
Interest element – Deferred expense	147,209
Interest expensed at 30 June 20X8 [147,209 × 4/12]	49,070

01/03/X8	DR: Machinery	1,962,791	
	CR: Accounts payable		1,962,791
	[Recognition of machine acquired in terms of a deferred payment agreement]		
30/06/X8	DR: Interest expense	49,070	
	CR: Accounts payable		49,070
	[Interest expense for the period]		

Exchange of items of property, plant and equipment – barter transactions

Items of property, plant and equipment acquired through and exchanged for a non-monetary asset are only recognised as a business transaction for recording purposes if the transaction has commercial substance, has economic benefits for the parties concerned (s17.14 and IAS 16 p.24). An exchange of assets, ie a barter transaction, is only considered to have economic/commercial substance if the assets exchanged are dissimilar in nature and condition. However, if the items exchanged are similar in nature and condition, then the transaction is deemed to have no economic/commercial substance and thus no transaction is recognised in the accounting records other than a change in description of the items received and transferred. *For example, if a business exchanges its scanning machine for a machine with similar functions and nature, then such a transaction will not be considered to have economic substance and thus no transaction is recognised.*

The cost of the asset acquired through and exchanged for an item for a consideration other than cash and which transaction has commercial substance must be measured based on the following conditions:

Fair value of items	Cost determinant
Fair value of the item transferred by the entity is known	The cost of the item received is measured at the fair value of the item transferred (given up)
Fair value of the item transferred is known but cannot be measured reliably and the fair value of the item received is known	The cost of the item received is measured at its fair value
The fair value of both items transferred and received cannot be measured reliably	The cost of the item received shall be measured at the carrying amount of the item transferred

The recognition of the item of property, plant and equipment received must be accompanied by de-recognising the item transferred (disposal of the item) to the counterparty.

Illustrative Example 4.6: Exchange of assets

The following information is provided to you related to the exchange of two dissimilar item of property, plant and equipment:

	Fair value of existing item	Fair value of item received	No fair value is available
	CU	CU	CU
Cost – existing item	520,000	520,000	520,000
Accumulated depreciation – existing item	360,000	360,000	360,000
Carrying amount of item received	280,000	280,000	280,000
Fair value of existing item	410,000	N/A	N/A
Fair value of item received	Unknown	370,000	N/A

You are required to:

In each scenario, calculate the profit on disposal resulting from the exchange transaction.

Suggested solution:

	Fair value of existing item	Fair value of item received	No fair value is available
Profit on disposal	250,000[1]	210,000[2]	Nil[3]

Note:
1. *The cost of the item received is measured at the fair value of the asset given, and the profit on disposal amounts to (CU410,000 – CU160,000)*
2. *The cost of the item received is measured at the fair value of the item received, and the profit on disposal amounts to (CU370,000 – CU160,000)*
3. *The cost of the item received is measured at the carrying value of the existing item, the profit on disposal is zero*

4.5.3.3 Measurement after initial recognition

Property, plant and equipment shall be measured after initial recognition at cost less accumulated depreciation and any accumulated impairment loss (s17.15 and IAS 16 p.29) or shall be measured in accordance with the revaluation model.

Depreciation
(a) Classification
Depreciation is defined as the systematic allocation of the depreciable amount of an item of property, plant and equipment over its estimated useful life. Depreciation can be considered to be an estimate of the amount by which the carrying amount of an item of property, plant and equipment diminishes as a result of it being used by the entity in carrying out its operating activities, ie the consumption of the economic benefits. Certain items of property, plant and equipment such as land have an unlimited useful life and shall not be depreciated (s17.16 and IAS 16 p.58).

(b) Recognition
Depreciation for each reporting period shall be recognised as an expense in the profit or loss (s17.17 and IAS 16 p.48). However, if depreciation is recognised as part of the conversion costs in manufacturing finished goods, the depreciation shall be included in the cost of those finished goods (s13 and IAS 2). *For example, depreciation relating to machinery used in the production process becomes part of conversion costs (manufacturing overheads), while the depreciation relating to office equipment is recognised as an operating expense.*

If major components of items of property, plant and equipment have significantly different patterns of consumption of economic benefits, an entity shall allocate the initial cost to its major components, ie recognise the components separately, and depreciate each component over its useful life (s17.16 and IAS 16 p.43).

Depreciation must be recognised with effect from the date that the item is available for use, ie from the date the item is in the location and condition necessary for it to be used for the purposes intended by management (s17.21 and IAS 16 p.55) and not from the date the item is actually used.

Illustrative Example 4.7: Commencement of depreciation

The following information is presented in chronological order related to the acquisition, preparation and use of an item of property, plant and equipment:

Details
01/01/X8: Received asset
28/01/X8: Completed installation and testing and approved for use
01/04/X8: Use in production process

You are required to:
Prepare a table explaining whether you would or would not depreciate the item from each of the dates provided above.

Suggested solution:

Details	Accounting treatment
01/01/X8: Received asset	Initial recognition of item – gain control over the item
28/01/X8: Completed installation and testing and approved for use	Date from which depreciation is calculated and recognised
01/04/X8: Use in production process	Irrelevant as it does not affect the depreciation calculation

Depreciation of an item of property, plant and equipment ceases when the item is de-recognised (no economic benefits expected to be left or disposed of (s17.20 and IAS 16 p.55)) or classified as a non-current asset held for sale. Depreciation does not cease when the item becomes idle or retired from active use, ie temporary interruptions in the use of the item do not result in the item not being depreciated for that period unless the asset is fully depreciated.

(c) Measurement

The depreciation of the property, plant and equipment is limited to its depreciable amount, ie the difference between the item's carrying amount and its estimated residual value. (s17.20 and IAS 16.6).

The useful life of an item of property, plant and equipment is defined as the period over which an item is expected to be available for use for its intended purpose by the entity to realise the economic benefits embedded in the item (s17.21 and IAS 16 p.56).

The following factors should be taken into account when determining the useful life of an asset or selecting a depreciation policy:
(a)   manner in which the asset will be used and its expected usage;
(b)   physical wear and tear of the asset, which is directly affected by operational factors such as maintenance and service, utilisation, etc.;
(c)   technical or commercial obsolescence and technological advances resulting from changes in the market environment; or
(d)   legal limits on the use of the asset.

It is important to note that the wear-and-tear deduction allowed in terms of the Income Tax Act should not be a primary factor in determining the useful life and depreciation policy of an entity.

(d) Depreciation method

The entity shall select a depreciation method (the basis of calculating depreciation) that reflects the pattern in which the business expects to consume the future economic benefits of the item over its remaining useful life. The following depreciation methods are available:

Straight-line method: allocate the depreciable amount of the item equally over its estimated useful life, there is a fixed depreciation amount charge per period over its useful life. This method is appropriate when the economic benefits are consumed consistently over time or when the items are used in an operating process and environment which is stable.

Diminishing balance method: the depreciation charge declines over the useful life to compensate for the increase in repair and maintenance costs, ie the base used can be a fixed rate or sum-of-the-digits. This method is appropriate when the entity expects most of the economic benefits to be consumed in the early years of the asset's useful life.

Production method: the depreciation charge is based on the output and capacity of the item. This method is used when the output generated from the use of the asset is not consistent over periods, such as tyres which may be determined based on mileage if the vehicle is not used evenly.

Illustrative Example 4.8: Depreciation methods

The following information is provided to you related to the depreciation of an item of property, plant and equipment:

	Straight-line method	Diminishing balance method	Sum-of-the-digits method	Usage
Cost	CU3,000,000	CU3,000,000	CU3,000,000	CU 3,000,000
Useful life	5 years	15%	5 years	600,000 units

You are required to:

In each of the scenarios presented, calculate the depreciation expense for the first two financial years.

Suggested solution:

	Straight-line	Reducing balance	Sum-of-the-digits	Usage
Period 1:	600,000 (CU3,000,000/5)	450,000 (CU3,000,000 x 15%)	1,000,000 (CU3,000,000 x 5/15*)	750,000 (CU3,000,000 x #150,000/600,000)
Period 2:	600,000 (CU3,000,000/5)	382,500 (CU2,550,000 x 15%)	800,000 (CU3,000,000 x 4/15*)	500,000 (CU3,000,000 x #100,000/600,000)

*The sum of the digits total is calculated by adding the number value of each year in the useful life ie. (year): $1 + 2 + 3 + 4 + 5 = 15$ digits.
#These refer to the assumed number of units (period 1: 150,000 units and Period 2: 100,000 units) produced during the year.

(e) Changes to depreciation bases – useful life and residual value
An entity is required to review the appropriateness of its depreciation policy at the end of each reporting period to determine if there are any indications that there are significant changes in the pattern in which the entity expects to consume the future economic benefits (s17.23 and IAS 16 p.51). If there are changes in either the estimated residual value and/or useful life, the entity must change the depreciation method to reflect the new pattern in which the economic benefits are consumed.

Changes in the depreciation method resulting from a revision of the estimated residual value and/or useful life shall be recognised as a change in an accounting estimate (s10.15 and IAS 8). Such a change shall be implemented prospectively with effect from the beginning of the reporting period, ie the carrying amount of the item must be depreciated over its estimated remaining useful life (s17.23 and IAS 16 p.36).

Illustrative Example 4.9: Change in depreciation bases

On 01 January 20X6, an entity purchased machinery with an aggregate cost of CU1 600 000 and a residual value of zero. The machine is depreciated on a straight-line basis to its residual value over an estimated period of 8 years. On 01 January 20X8 management revised the residual value to CU200 000 and the remaining useful life to 4 years. The reporting period ends 31 December.

You are required to:
Prepare the journal entries necessary to account for the depreciation of the machine for the year ended 31 December 20X8.

Suggested solution:

	CU
Cost	1,600,000
Accumulated depreciation $[1,600,000 \times 2/8]$	400,000
Carrying amount at 01 January 20X8	1,200,000
Depreciation $[(1,200,000 - 200,000)/4]$	250,000

31/12/X8 DR: Depreciation	250,000	
CR: Accumulated depreciation		250,000
[Depreciation for the reporting period]		

Repairs and improvements

(a) Classification

Expenses incurred as part of the day-to-day servicing and maintenance of items of property, plant and equipment must be recognised as repairs and maintenance expenses in the profit or loss account in the period in which the costs are incurred – the expenses incurred restore the future economic benefits embodied in the item. Expenditure incurred which improves future economic benefits of the entity, such as increasing efficiency and output or leading to cost savings, must be capitalised as part of the carrying amount of an item of property, plant and equipment. *For example, the repainting of a building is expensed to profit and loss (no increase in future economic benefits), while the expenses incurred to construct separating walls in an office may be capitalised as part of the cost of the building or recognised as a separate item of property, plant and equipment.*

Decision summary for classification of expenditure:

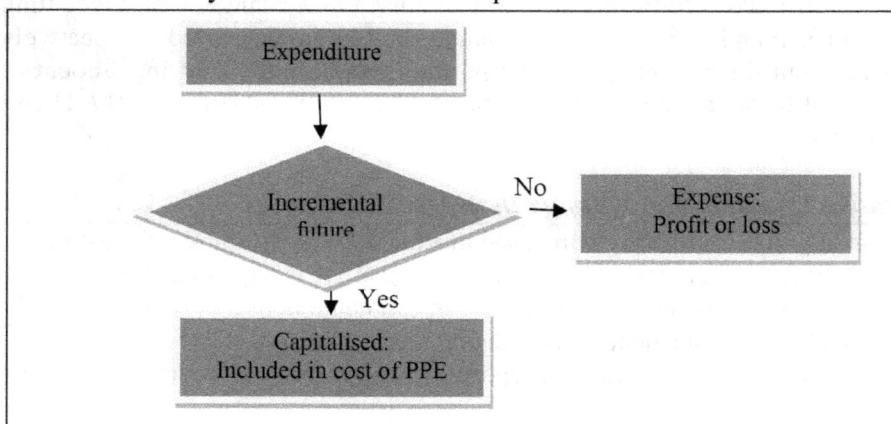

(b) Recognition

Summary guide: capitalisation versus expensing

Expenditure	Accounting treatment
Additions	If the expenses meet the definition of an asset, the amount is capitalised to the carrying amount of the asset.
Improvements and replacements	If the expenses incurred result in the incremental future economic benefits of the item, the amount is capitalised to the carrying amount of the asset and the carrying amount of the replaced item is de-recognised.

Relocation and re-installation	If the amount is material and it results in incremental future economic benefits, the amount is capitalised to the carrying amount of the asset.
Repairs	If the expenses incurred form part of the ordinary day-to-day activities of ensuring that the item can be used for its intended purpose, the amount must be expensed. However, if the amount is material and results in incremental future economic benefits (consider a major overhaul), the amount is capitalised as an improvement or replacement.

When the expenses incurred are capitalised as part of the carrying amount of the item of property, plant and equipment, the depreciation expense must be adjusted to incorporate the increase in the carrying amount of the item – the increased carrying amount will be depreciated over the remaining useful life of the item.

Illustrative Example 4.10: Subsequent expenditure

On 01 March 20X8, the carrying amount of a machine was CU270 000 (original cost of CU450 000) and had an original estimated nil residual value and a total estimated useful life of 5 years. The remaining useful life of the machine is therefore 3 years at 01 March 20X8.

At 01 March 20X8, the business incurred CU60 000 to improve the efficiency of the machine.

You are required to:
Calculate the depreciation expense before and after the expenditure related to the improvement of the machine.

Suggested solution:
Depreciation prior to the improvement amounted to CU90 000 (CU450,000/5), but after the improvement it amounts to CU110 000 [(CU270,000 + U60,000)/3].

4.6 LAND AND BUILDINGS

4.6.1 Recognition and measurement

Land and buildings which are classified as property, plant and equipment must be recognised separately in the financial records even if they were acquired as a single transaction. If the land and buildings were acquired as a single transaction and their costs were not separately identified, the cost of the land shall be estimated based on comparative market values for similar vacant land in the area – active market price. However, if the market value of the land cannot be measured reliably, then its cost will be measured as the residual of the total cost after accounting for the market value of the building, ie the estimated current cost of constructing the building.

When the vacant land of the entity is used to construct a building, then all expenses such as developing the infrastructure, excavating etc incurred to make the land available for its intended use (construction of the building) must be capitalised as part of the cost of the land. Similarly, if an existing building was demolished to construct a new building, the demolition costs form part of the land as they represent the costs to prepare the land for its intended use. However, in practice, some entities may deem the demolition costs to be part of the costs of the new building constructed.

Illustrative Example 4.11: Land vs buildings

The following information is presented to you related to the entity's land and buildings:

	CU
Cost of land	500,000
Cost of building [old]	900,000
Demolition expenses incurred – old building	250,000
Construction cost [new building]	2,800,000

You are required to:
Prepare a table detailing the cost of the land and building after the construction of the building.

Suggested solution:

	Land	*Building*
	CU	*CU*
Cost of land	*500,000*	
Cost of building [old]		*900,000*
Cost of building [old] – Re-classified	*900,000*[1]	*(900,000)*
Demolition expenses incurred – Old building	*250,000*[2]	
Construction cost [new building]		*2,800,000*
Carrying amount	*1,650,000*	*2,800,000*

Notes:
1. *Cost of the existing building forms part of the cost of the land on which the new building is constructed.*
2. *Demolition costs form part of the cost in bringing the land available for its intended use – construction of the new building.*
3. *The land needs to be tested for impairment at the end of each reporting date.*

When demolishing an existing building for the construction of a new building, the carrying amount of the existing building may be treated as follows:
(a) de-recognise the amount and treat it as a loss via the profit or loss;
(b) re-classify the amount as part of the cost of the land – the land must be tested for impairment after the reclassification; or
(c) capitalise the amount as part of the cost of the new building – the new building must be tested for impairment.

4.7 SPARE PARTS

4.7.1 General – recognition and measurement

'Sometime, it is difficult to classify spare parts and consumables as property, plant and equipment or inventory. Items such as these will be classified as property, plant and equipment when it meets the definition of property, plant and equipment, otherwise it will be classified as inventory (s17.5 and IAS 16 p.8).'

4.7.2 Major parts and replacements

4.7.2.1 Recognition

Major spare parts and stand-by equipment are recognised as property, plant and equipment only if:
(a) the entity expects to use them for more than one period; or
(b) they are used only with a specific item of property, plant and equipment.

When the spare parts are recognised as property, plant and equipment (specific asset), then the spare parts should be de-recognised when the asset is de-recognised.

4.7.2.2 Measurement

Replacement of major parts

Major parts of property, plant and equipment which are not recognised as separate items may require replacement at regular intervals during the useful life of the asset.   The costs of replacing such parts are capitalised and recognised as property, plant and equipment, and not expensed as repairs via profit or loss (s17.6 and IAS 16 p.13). The cost of the replacement part must be capitalised to the carrying amount of the asset if it is expected to provide incremental future economic benefits to the asset and is depreciated over its remaining useful life.

The carrying amount of the parts that are replaced should be de-recognised at the date they are replaced and the carrying amount must be recognised as a scrapping loss or as profit/loss on disposal (s17.27 and IAS 16 p.68). If the part being replaced was recognised as a separate item or its cost was measured reliably at the date of initial recognition of the item of property, plant and equipment, the carrying amount to be de-recognised can be determined easily. However, if the carrying amount of the parts being replaced cannot be determined, then the depreciated carrying amount of the replacement parts will be deemed to be equivalent to the depreciated cost of the replacement part.

The adjustment to the carrying amount of the item as a result of capitalising the replacement part results in the re-calculation of depreciation over the estimated remaining useful life of the item.   However, if the replacement part is recognised as a separate component which has its own useful life, the replacement part shall be depreciated separately over its estimated useful life, but cannot exceed the remaining useful life of the principle item of property, plant and equipment.

Illustrative Example 4.12: Replacement of major parts

On 01 September 20X8, an entity replaced a major part of a machine at a cost of CU300 000. The part being replaced had an estimated carrying amount of CU90 000 (cost and accumulated depreciation of CU200 000 and CU110 000 respectively). The carrying amount of the machine was CU660 000 with a remaining useful life of 3 years. The machine is depreciated on a straight-line basis to a zero residual value over its estimated useful life. The reporting period of the business is 31 August 20X9.

You are required to:
Prepare the journal entries necessary to account for the machine for the year ended 30 September 20x8.

Suggested solution:

	CU
Carrying amount of machine	660,000
Less: Carrying amount of part replaced	90,000
Add: Cost of replacement part	300,000
Carrying amount of machine at 01 September 20X8	870,000
Depreciation [CU 70,000/3]	290,000

01/09/X8	DR: Loss on scrapping	90,000	
	DR: Accumulated depreciation	110,000	
	CR: Machinery		200,000
	[De-recognition of major part being replaced]		
01/09/X8	DR: Machinery	300,000	
	CR: Bank		300,000
	[Capitalisation of replacement part]		
01/09X8	DR: Depreciation	290,000	
	CR: Accumulated depreciation		290,000
	[Depreciation for the period]		

Major inspections

An item of property, plant and equipment may require a licence or major inspections on a regular basis over its estimated useful life to ensure its continuing use regardless of whether parts of the item require replacement. If such expenses are incurred on initial recognition of the item (paid in advance), then the expenses should be capitalised as part of the carrying amount of the specific item of property, plant and equipment and amortised over its estimated useful life (s17.6 and IAS 16 p.14), and should not be recognised as a prepaid expense.

Illustrative Example 4.13: Major inspections

On 01 June 20X6, an entity acquired a factory plant and paid an amount of CU120 000 for major bi-annual monitoring and inspections which will be conducted by the anti-pollution agency over the next two years. On 01 June 20X8, the entity renewed the agreement and paid CU165 000. The reporting period of the entity is 28 February.

You are required to:

Prepare the journal entries necessary to account for the plant for the year ended 28 February 20x9.

Suggested solution:

01/06/X6	DR: Factory plant – Inspections	120,000	
	CR: Bank		120,000
	[Capitalisation of inspection costs]		

The costs will be amortised at an amount of CU60 000 over a period of 2 years.

01/06/X8	DR: Inspection costs expensed [P/L]	20,000	
	CR: Accumulated amortistion		20,000
	[Amortisation of inspection costs for the period (CU120 000/2 × 4/12]		

01/06/X8	DR: Accumulated amortisation	120,000	
	CR: Factory plant – Inspections		120,000
	[De-recognition of inspection costs]		

01/06/X8	DR: Factory plant – Inspections	165,000	
	CR: Bank		165,000
	[Capitalisation of inspection costs]		

28/02/X9	DR: Inspection costs expense	55,000	
	CR: Amortised inspection costs		55,000
	[Amortisation of inspection costs for the period (CU165 000/2 × 8/12]		

4.8   DISMANTLING AND REHABILITATION COSTS

4.8.1   Classification and recognition

If an entity has a contractual obligation in terms of an agreement or an expectation in terms of a constructive obligation for dismantling an item of property, plant and equipment or rehabilitating the site on which the item is located in future, usually the end of the useful life of the item, then a provision exists at the date the obligation is known – the date the item is acquired or the consequence of having used (or installed) the item (or damaging the area) becomes clear (s17.10 and IAS 16 p.16(c)). The expenses incurred must be:

(a)   recognised as a provision – future obligation of which the occurrence or the amount is uncertain (s21.5 and IAS 37); and

(b)   capitalised as part of the cost of the item of property, plant and equipment – represents direct cost which are necessary to realise the benefits embedded in the related asset.

4.8.2   Measurement

4.8.2.1   Initial measurement

The estimated costs of dismantling and rehabilitation at the date of initial recognition of the item of property, plant and equipment are measured at the present value of the future cash flows discounted at the effective interest rate (s21.11 and IAS 16 p.18).

4.8.2.2   Measure after initial recognition

Unwinding of provision – fair value

At the end of each reporting date, the carrying amount of the provision shall be measured at its fair value (present value at that date) through an unwinding process. The change in the carrying amount must be recognised as a finance cost in the profit or loss for the period. The unwinding of the carrying amount of the provision at the end of each reporting period does not affect the carrying amount of the item of property, plant and equipment.

Illustrative Example 4.14: Provision for dismantling

On 01 January 20X8, an entity purchased machinery at an aggregate cost of CU4,500,000 which was depreciated to a zero residual value over an estimated useful life of 10 years. The entity made a commitment to dismantle the machinery at the end of its useful life to ensure it meets the environmental regulations. The estimated cost for dismantling the machinery was CU800,000 and the effective interest rate is 10%. The financial reporting period ends 31 December.

You are required to:

Prepare the journal entries necessary to account for the machine as well as the provision for dismantling for the year ended 31 December 20X9.

Suggested solution:

	CU
Cost of machinery	4,500,000
Add: Capitalised dismantling costs [CU800,000 @ 10% after 10 years]	
	308,434
Cost of machinery	4,808,434
Depreciation per year	480,843
01/01/X8 Present value of dismantling costs	308,434
31/12/X8 Interest element	30,843
31/12/X8 Fair value	339,277
31/12/X9 Interest element	33,928
31/12/X9 Fair value	373,205

01/01/X8	DR:	Machinery	4,808,434	
	CR:	Provision for dismantling costs		308,434
	CR:	Bank		4,500,000
		[Acquisition machinery including capitalisation of dismantling costs]		
31/12/X8	DR:	Depreciation	480,843	
	CR:	Accumulated depreciation		480,843
		[Depreciation for the period]		
31/12/X8	DR:	Interest expense	30,843	
	CR:	Provision for dismantling costs		30,843
		[Fair valuing the provision for dismantling costs]		
31/12/X9	DR:	Depreciation	480,843	
	CR:	Accumulated depreciation		480,843
		[Depreciation for the period]		
31/12/X9	DR:	Interest expense	33,928	
	CR:	Provision for dismantling costs		33,928
		[Fair valuing the provision for dismantling costs]		

Change in the estimated costs

If there are changes to the estimated cost of dismantling and rehabilitation, the entity shall account for it as a change in accounting estimate in accordance with paragraphs (s10.15 – s10.18 and IAS 8 (specific guidance is given in IFRIC 1)). The change in the estimated costs of dismantling and rehabilitation must be accounted for as an adjustment to the carrying amount of the item of property, plant and equipment (s17.19–23 and IFRIC 1). The adjustment shall be made to the carrying amount at the beginning of the period and the depreciation should be calculated on the adjusted carrying amount, after taking into account the change in the provision.

Illustrative Example 4.15: Change in the cost of provision for environmental restoration

On 01 January 20X7, an entity purchased a factory plant at a cost of CU5,000,000 with a residual value of CU50,000 and useful life of 10 years. The entity must rehabilitate the environment at the end of the useful life of the factory. The estimated costs of rehabilitation were CU600,000 and CU1,000,000 on 01 January 20X7 and 20X9 respectively. The effective interest rate is 12%. The reporting period ends 31 December.

You are required to:
Prepare the journal entries necessary to account for the machine and the related provision for the environmental restoration for the years ended 31 December 20X7 and 20X9.

Suggested solution:

Provision:	CU
01/01/X7 Fair value [CU600,000 @ 12% after 10 years]	193,320
31/12/X8 Fair value [CU600,000 @ 12% after 9 years]	216,480
31/12/X8 Fair value [CU600,000 @ 12% after 8 years]	242,460
01/01/X9 Fair value [CU1,000,000 @ 12% after 8 years]	404,100
Adjustment in estimated cost	161,640
31/12/X9 Fair value [CU1,000,000 @ 125 after 7 years]	452,500

Factory plant:	CU
01/01/X7 Cost	5,000,000
Capitalisation of rehabilitation of costs	193,320
Aggregate cost	5,193,320
31/12/X8 Carrying amount [CU5,193,320 – (CU5,193,320 – CU500,000)/10 × 2]	4,254,656
01/01/X9 Capitalisation of change in rehabilitation costs	161,640
Adjusted carrying amount	4,416,296
31/12/X9 Depreciation [(CU4,416,296 – CU500,000)/8]	489,537

01/01/X7	DR: Factory plant	5,193,320	
	CR: Provision for rehabilitation costs		193,320
	CR: Bank		5,000,000
	[Recognition the acquisition of factory plant]		
31/12/X7	DR: Depreciation	469,332	
	CR: Accumulated depreciation		469,332
	[Depreciation for the period]		
31/12/X7	DR: Interest expense	23,160	
	CR: Provision for rehabilitation costs		23,160
	[Fair value of provision at reporting date]		
01/01/X9	DR: Machinery	161,640	
	CR: Provision for rehabilitation costs		161,640
	[Recognition of the change in estimated rehabilitation costs]		
31/12/X9	DR: Depreciation	489,537	
	CR: Accumulated depreciation		489,537
	[Depreciation for the period]		
31/12/X9	DR: Interest expense	48,400	
	CR: Provision for rehabilitation costs		48,400
	[Fair value of provision at reporting date]		

4.9   IMPAIRMENT

Although we cover the elementary understanding of impairment of assets here, please refer to Chapter 8 for detailed guidance on the impairment of assets.

4.9.1   Recognition

4.9.1.1   Initial recognition

An impairment loss arises when the carrying amount of an item of property, plant and equipment exceeds it recoverable amount (higher of the fair value less cost to sell or its value in use) (s27.1 and IAS 36 p.6). An asset's value in use is a quantification of the present value of the economic benefits expected from using the asset.

At each reporting date, the entity shall test whether there are any indications of impairment for the items of property, plant and equipment (s27 and IAS 36). If there are indications that an item is impaired, the impairment loss is recognised immediately in the profit or loss with a corresponding adjustment to the carrying amount of the asset through the accumulated depreciation or accumulated impairment account (s17.24 and IAS 36 p.60) unless the asset is revalued, in which case the impairment loss is recognised in other comprehensive income to the extent that there is enough revaluation surplus to which the loss can be allocated (s27.6 and IAS 16 p.61). It is important to note that the impairment test cannot be conducted on the category of property, plant and equipment as a single unit. After the recognition of the impairment loss, the recoverable amount must be depreciated over its remaining useful life.

Illustrative Example 4.16: Impairment of property, plant and equipment

At 28 February 20X8, the carrying amount of machinery was CU1,896,000 with a remaining useful life of 4 years. The selling price was CU1,800,000, the estimated cost to sell was CU200,000 and the value in use was CU1,720,000.

You are required to:
Prepare the journal entries necessary to account for the impairment of the machine for the year ended 29 February 20x8.

Suggested solution:

	CU
Recoverable amount – higher of selling price less cost to sell or value in use	1,720,000
Carrying amount	1,896,000
Impairment loss	176,000

Depreciation from 20X9 onwards [CU1,720,000/4]		430,000
29/02/X8 DR: Impairment loss [P&L]	176,000	
CR: Accumulated impairment loss [SFP]		176,000
[Recognition of impairment loss]		

4.9.1.2   Recognition subsequent to initial recognition

If at the reporting date, after the impairment loss was recognised, the recoverable amount exceeds the carrying amount, then the increase must be recognised as a reversal of the impairment loss and not as a fair value adjustment or revaluation. The reversal of the impairment loss must be recognised via the profit and loss, up to the historical cost carrying amount had the item never been impaired, with any difference recognised in other comprehensive income as a revaluation (assuming that the accounting policy relating to the item is to account for the item on the revaluation model).

Illustrative Example 4.17: Reversal of impairment of property, plant and equipment

At 28 February 20X6, the carrying amount of machinery (carried on the cost model) was CU800 000 with a remaining useful life of 4 years while the recoverable amount was CU760 000. At 28 February 20X8, the recoverable amount of the machinery was CU420 000.

You are required to:
Prepare the journal entries necessary to account for the machine for the year ended 28 February 20X8.

Suggested solution:

	Impaired CA	Historical CA
	CU	CU
Carrying amount	800,000	800,000
Impairment loss at 28 February 20X6 [CU8000000 – CU760,000]	(40,000)	0
Adjusted carrying amount	**760,000**	**800,000**
Depreciation expenxe 28 February 20X7 [CU760,000/4] & [CU800,000/4]	(190,000)	(200,000)
Depreciation expenxe 28 February 20X8 [CU760,000/4] & [CU800,000/4]	(190,000)	(200,000)
Carrying amount at 28 February 20X8	**380,000**	**400,000**
Recoverable amount at 28 February 20X8	420,000	420,000
Increase in carrying amount [CU400,000 – CU380,000]	**20,000**	**0**

28/02/X8	DR: Depreciation expense [P/L]	190,000	
	CR: Accumulated depreciation		190,000
	[Depreciation expense for the year]		
28/02/X8	DR: Accumulated depreciation & impairment	20,000	
	CR: Reversal of impairment loss [P&L]		20,000
	[Reversal of impairment loss]		

4.9.2 Compensation for impairment

When a third party compensates the business for an impairment loss relating to items of property, plant and equipment, the compensation received must be recognised in profit or loss as a gain (s17.25 and IAS 16 p.65). The gain is only recognised when the compensation becomes receivable, ie when the entity has an enforceable right to claim the compensation due. The manner in which the compensation received is recognised depends on the circumstances causing the impairment:

(a)   *the item is de-recognised:* the compensation received is recognised as part of the disposal of the item – used to calculate the profit or loss on disposal; or

(b)   *continue to use the item:* the compensation received can be set off against the impairment loss and the net amount (gain/loss) is reported via the profit or loss.

Illustrative Example 4.18: Compensation for damages

At 28 February 20X8, the carrying amount of the machine was CU900 000. The machine was damaged as a result of the negligence of the servicing company. Management estimated the recoverable amount to be CU700 000 and decided that the machine could still be used in the manufacturing process. The servicing company paid an amount of CU140 000 as compensation for the damages caused.

You are required to:
Prepare the journal entries necessary to account for the machine for the year ended 29 February 20X8.

Suggested solution:

	CU
Impairment loss [CU900,000 – CU700,000]	200,000
Compensation received	140,000

29/02/X8	DR: Impairment loss	200,000	
	CR: Accumulated impairment		200,000
	[Recognition of impairment loss]		

29/02/X8	DR: Bank/Receivable	140,000	
	CR: Gain – Compensation received		140,000
	[Compensation received for cause of impairment]		

4.10 REVALUATION

4.10.1 Recognition of revaluation

It is prudent for a business entity to revalue items of property, plant and equipment if there are significant changes to their fair values. By revaluing such items, the integrity and quality of the financial information presented in the financial statements are improved. The decision to revalue the class of items of property, plant and equipment, for the first time, represents a change in the accounting policy, namely changing the basis of measurement from historical cost to the revaluation model (s18 and IAS 8).

The surplus resulting from the revaluation of the items must be recognised as other comprehensive income and reported as a separate line item in the statement of comprehensive income.

4.10.2 Measurement

The revalued amount of an item of property, plant and equipment must represent its fair value. The fair value of the item may be measured using the following:

(a) *market value:* if there is an active market for the item and the market is easily determined then market represents its fair value. However, if the market value cannot be easily determined, then that market value of an item which is similar in nature and condition can be used as an indication of its fair value.

(b) *valuation:* if there is no active market for the item, then its fair value can be estimated using a valuation technique which is considered appropriate for the type of asset.

NB: For IFRS (full IFRS), reference is made to IFRS 13 to determine fair value.

4.10.2.1 Gross revaluation method

The gross revaluation method is based on the fair value of the item at the current date, but in a condition at initial recognition (new item). This method results in the historical cost and accumulated depreciation being adjusted based on the gross fair value of the asset. The surplus on revaluation represents the net surplus and is derived from (i) the actual surplus, based on the difference between the historical costs and the gross fair value, and (ii) the adjustment to the accumulated depreciation account for prior periods.

Illustrative example 19: Gross revaluation method

At 29 February 20X8 machinery had a carrying amount of CU600,000 (original cost of CU1,000,000) and a remaining useful life of six years. The gross replacement cost of the machine was CU1,300,000. The machine is depreciated on a straight-line basis over its useful life of 10 years. The reporting period ends 28 February.

You are required to:

Prepare the journal entries necessary to account for the machine for the year ended 29 February 20x8. You may assume that the entity uses the gross replacement method to account for the revaluation of the machine.

Suggested solution:

	Cost model CU	Revaluation CU	Surplus CU
Cost	1,000,000	1,300,000	300,000
Accumulated depreciation	400,000	520,000	(120,000)
Carrying amount at 28 February 20X8	600,000	780,000	180,000
Depreciation for 28 February 20X9		130,000	

01/03/X8	DR: Machinery	300,000	
	CR: Accumulated depreciation		120,000
	CR: Revaluation surplus (OCI)		180,000
	[Revaluation of machinery using the gross replacement model]		

28/02/X8	DR: Depreciation expense	130,000	
	CR: Accumulated depreciation		130,000
	[Depreciation for the reporting period]		

4.10.2.2 Net revaluation method

The net revaluation method is based on the fair value of the item in its current condition, viz. fair value of a used asset. The net revaluation method is implemented prospectively, resulting in the surplus being represented by the difference between the carrying amount and the fair value. In addition, the accumulated depreciation at the date of the revaluation must be written off against the cost of the item to reflect it at its carrying amount. The item will be depreciated based on the fair value over its remaining useful life. This method of presenting the information in the financial statements gives the impression that the revalued item represents one which was acquired during the current reporting period – no accumulated depreciation prior to the revaluation.

Illustrative example 20: Gross revaluation method

You are required to:

Using the same information as in illustrative example 19, prepare the journal entries necessary to account for the machine for the year ended 29 February 20X8. You may assume that the entity uses the net replacement method to account for the revaluation of the machine.

Suggested solution:

	Cost model CU	Revaluation CU	Surplus CU
Cost	1,000,000	1,300,000	300,000
Accumulated depreciation	400,000	520,000	(120,000)
Carrying amount at 28 February 20X8	600,000	780,000	180,000
Depreciation for 28 February 20X9		130,000	

01/03/X8	DR: Accumulated depreciation	400 000	
	CR: Machinery		400,000
	[Recording the elimination of the accumulated depreciation of the machine against its cost]		
1/03/X8	DR: Machinery	180,000	
	CR: Revaluation surplus (OCI)		180,000
	[Recording the revaluation of the machine using the net replacement method]		
28/02/X8	DR: Depreciation expense	130,000	
	CR: Accumulated depreciation		130,000
	[Depreciation for the reporting period]		

If the item being revalued includes the capitalisation of dismantling or rehabilitation costs, then the fair value of the asset will include the fair value of the costs capitalised. The surplus recognised must be based on the aggregate fair value of the item and there may not be a need to estimate the fair value of the dismantling or rehabilitation costs when revaluing the item.

4.11 EFFECTS OF TAXATION

4.11.1 Recognition

The cost of an item of property, plant and equipment on initial recognition is usually regarded as its tax base (must always be tested against the definition of the tax base of an asset in IFRS for SMEs and IFRS) in terms of the Income Tax Act, ie expenditure of a capital nature. Furthermore, it is important to note that the expenses included in the initial tax base of the item must represent the cash or other consideration when the item is acquired, and thus the capitalisation of future expenditure such as dismantling and rehabilitation costs are usually not included in the tax base of the item. Expenditure such as this is then treated as a deduction for income tax purposes – ie not capitalised as part of the tax base.

The depreciation for accounting purposes must be based on the accounting policy which is considered most appropriate to allocate the cost of the item systematically over its estimated useful life. The capital deduction (wear and tear) for tax purposes is prescribed by the schedule of the Income Tax Act.

4.11.2 Measurement

Deferred tax shall be provided if the carrying amount of an asset differs from its tax base (s29 and IAS 12). A temporary difference will arise if the depreciation policy differs from the capital allowance (wear and tear deduction) for Income Tax purposes – giving rise to deferred tax. The deferred tax relating to the surplus arising on revaluation must be recognised via the other comprehensive income and not through the profit and loss.

Illustrative Example 4.19: Taxation

At 298 February 20X8 machinery with a cost of CU2,000,000 had a carrying amount and tax base of CU1,200,000 and CU1,000,000 respectively. Machinery is depreciated on a straight-line basis to a nil residual value over a useful life of 5 years while the wear & tear allowance is calculated at 25% for tax purposes. On 01 March 20X8 the machinery was revalued to a gross replacement cost of CU2,800,000. The reporting period ends 28 February.

You are required to:
Prepare the journal entries necessary to account for the machine for the year ended 28 February 20x9. You must also account for any tax consequences. You may assume a company tax rate of 28%.

Suggested solution:

	CU
Surplus (CU2,800,000 – CU2,000,000)	800,000
Adjustment to accumulated depreciation (CU1,120,000 – CU800,000)	(320,000)
Net Surplus	480,000
Deferred tax on surplus (CU480,000 x 28%)	134,400
Temporary difference at 28 February 20X8	
(CU1,200,000 – CU1,000,000)	200,000
Deferred tax balance at 28 February 20X8	56,000
Temporary difference at 28 February 20X9	
(CU1,120,000 – CU500,000)	620,000
Deferred tax balance at 28 February 20X8	173,600
Deferred tax expense [(CU56,000 + CU134,400) – CU173,600]	(16,800)

01/03/X8	DR: Machinery	800,000	
	CR: Accumulated Depreciation		320 000
	CR: Revaluation Surplus (OCI)		480,000
	[Revaluation of machinery using the gross replacement cost]		
01/03/X8	DR: Taxation Expense (OCI)	134,400	
	CR: Deferred tax		134,400
	[Deferred tax provision relating to the revaluation surplus]		
28/02/X9	DR: Depreciation expense	560,000	
	CR: Accumulated depreciation		560,000
	[Depreciation for the period]		
28/02/X9	DR: Deferred tax	16,800	
	CR: Taxation expense [P&L]		16,800
	[Deferred tax provision for the period]		

4.12   DISCLOSURE

Property, plant and equipment shall be classified as non-current assets, ie assets which are not held for trading purposes or expected to be realised within 12 months after the reporting date (s4.5 and IAS 1).

The following shall be disclosed for each class of property, plant and equipment (s17.31 and IAS 16 p.73):
(a) accounting policies adopted – method applied to determine the gross carrying amount;
(b) depreciation method used;
(c) useful lives or depreciation rate;
(d) gross carrying amount and accumulated depreciation (aggregated with accumulated impairment losses) at the beginning and end of the period;
(e) Reconciliation of carrying amount:
    (i)   additions (separating additions through business combinations);
    (ii)   disposals;
    (iii)   net gains/losses on fair value adjustments;
    (iv)   transfers to and from investment properties;
    (v)   impairment losses recognised or reversed;
    (vi)   depreciation expense for the period; and
    (vii)   other changes.

The following shall also be disclosed (s17.32 and IAS 16 p.74):
(a) carrying amount to which the entity has restricted title or pledged as security for liabilities; and
(b) the amount of contractual obligations for the acquisition of property, plant and equipment.

SELF-ASSESSMENT
Multiple choice questions: Testing the conceptual framework and principles of property, plant and equipment

1. Assets acquired by an entity can only be classified as items of property, plant and equipment if:

(a) they are used by the business to generate cash inflows	
(b) they are used to further the business goals of the organisation	
(c) they are used in production and administrative activities of the organisation	
(d) they add value to the business and its owners	

2. Property acquired to generate rental income can be classified as property, plant and equipment:

(a) at the discretion of management	
(b) if management recommended that such property be depreciated	
(c) if the rental agreement contains a renewal clause for the existing tenants	
(d) if the property is specialised and there is no active market for the property	

3. The cost of an item of property, plant and equipment is measured at

(a) the purchase price of the item	
(b) all the costs incurred to acquire ownership of the item	
(c) all the costs incurred to acquire control of the item	
(d) all costs to bring the item to its present location and ready for its intended use	

4. Expenses that are directly related to an item of property, plant and equipment incurred subsequent to initial recognition must be accounted for by:

(a) recognising them as expenses via profit and loss	
(b) capitalising them as part of the cost of the item	
(c) recognising them as a prepaid expense	
(d) (a) and (b)	

5. The income generated from the sale of goods produced during the testing of an item of property, plant and equipment must be:

(a) recognised as revenue via profit and loss	
(b) written off against the cost of the asset	
(c) written off against the cost of the item, but limited to the expenses incurred	
(d) recognised as other income via profit and loss	

6. Items of property, plant and equipment acquired for no consideration, such as a donation or government grant, must:

(a) not be included in the financial statements other than as part of the notes	
(b) be recognised and measured at the agreed upon value	
(c) be recognised and measured at the market/fair value	
(d) be initially recognised at a cost of zero and can be revalued subsequently	

7. Items of property, plant and equipment acquired in terms of a barter transaction which renders commercial value to the parties must be recognised:

(a) by changing the description of the item in the asset register	
(b) at the fair value of the item received	
(c) at the fair value of the item transferred to the other party	
(d) in terms of (b) and (c)	

8. An item of property, plant and equipment must be depreciated with effect from the date the item:

(a) is used in the manufacturing process	
(b) is available to be used for its intended purpose	
(c) is brought under the control of the entity purchasing it	
(d) is considered to decrease in value	

9. Depreciation for an item of property, plant and equipment ceases from the date:

(a) it ceases to be used in the manufacturing process	
(b) its fair value becomes greater than its carrying amount	
(c) it reaches its estimated useful life	
(d) none of the above	

10. The acquisition of spare parts for items of property, plant and equipment must be recognised as:

(a) expenses when acquired	
(b) part of inventory	
(c) capitalised costs of the asset	
(d) capitalised costs of the asset only if they can be used solely for the specific asset	

11. Future costs for the decommissioning of items of property, plant and equipment must be recognised as:

(a) expenses when they are incurred	
(b) part of the cost of the asset at the estimated expenditure	
(c) part of the cost of the asset at the present value of the estimated expenditure	
(d) part of the cost of the asset only if a present obligation exists	

12. The revaluation model can be used by management as a basis for measurement of property, plant and equipment:

(a) when management is seeking to raise long-term debt financing	
(b) when the incorrect depreciation method was applied	
(c) when assets are fully depreciated but continue to be used	
(d) when the carrying amount does not reflect the future economic benefits	

13. The revaluation model for property, plant and equipment must be implemented:

(a) at the end of the reporting period	
(b) only for selected items in a category of property, plant and equipment	
(c) from the beginning of the reporting period	
(d) an effective date depending on the revaluation method adopted	

14. The surplus arising on the implementation of the revaluation model must be recognised through:

(a) changes in equity statements (statement of financial position approach)	
(b) profit and loss to improve profitability	
(c) off-balance sheet (off-statement of financial position) accounting (ie disclosed only by way of notes)	
(d) a statement of other comprehensive income	

Practical questions:
Application of principles to business scenarios

QUESTION 1

Objective: Determining the initial measurement of an item of property, plant and equipment

JAJ (Pty) Ltd provided the following information for expenditure incurred in respect of the acquisition and installation of machinery for a new factory plant (all amounts exclude VAT):

Details	Cost
	CU
Net cost as per the suppliers invoice	8,750,000
Transportation costs from the supplier to the business premises	376,000
Inspection cost to ensure the machinery meets the specification and operating licence regulations	112,000
Total product cost of testing the manufacturing process of the machinery	198,000
Revenue generated from the sale of the products manufactured during the testing phase	215,000
Estimated cost of training staff responsible for operating the machinery	75,000
Estimated loss incurred as a result of the delay in using the machine in the manufacturing process – delay was caused due to lease negotiations	243,000
Cost of transporting the machine from the business premises to the new factory plant	65,000
Cost of installing the machine in the new factory plant	125,000

You are required to:
Determine the cost of the machine on initial recognition by JAJ (Pty) Ltd.

QUESTION 2

Objective: Determining the initial measurement of an item of property, plant and equipment which was acquired in terms of a financing arrangement

On 01 January 20X5, machinery was purchased in terms of a financing agreement whereby an initial amount of CU1,000,000 was the paid at the date of concluding the agreement (01 January) and a settlement amount of CU1,400,000 was paid on 31 December 20X5. The agreement did not specify any interest element, but the fair market interest rate for the business is estimated to be 12% per annum.

You are required to:
Determine the cost of the machine which was acquired in terms of the financing arrangement.

QUESTION 3

Objective: Recognising the cost of major replacement of parts which have been incorporated in the cost of the item of property, plant and equipment

On 01 January 20X1, machinery with an aggregate cost of CU3,600,000 was acquired and installed by a business entity. The machine is depreciated on a straight-line basis to a zero residual value at a rate of 10% per annum. On 01 January 20X5, the business entity replaced a major part of the machine at a cost of CU600,000 in order to meet the manufacturing regulations of the industry. The cost of the major part was estimated to be CU400,000 at the date the machine was purchased (01 January 20X1).

You are required to:
Apply the recognition, measurement and de-recognition of major parts of property, plant and equipment.

QUESTION 4

Objective: Implementing changes in the useful life and/or residual value of an item of property, plant and equipment

On 01 January 20X3, equipment with an aggregate cost of CU3,000,000 was acquired to be used in the manufacturing processes of the business. The business adopted a policy of depreciating its equipment on a straight-line basis to a zero residual value over a useful life of 4 years, which is the allowance granted for tax purposes. At 31 December 20X5, after reviewing the accounting policies of the business, management decided that the policy for depreciating equipment should be revised. The policy hence revised the useful life of the equipment to 6 years and a residual value of CU180,000. The change in the policy must be incorporated in the financial statements for the reporting period ended 31 December 20X5.

You are required to:

Record the transactions for depreciation, taking into account the changes in the factors (residual value or useful life) affecting the depreciation policy.

QUESTION 5

Objective: Recognition of demolition and rehabilitation costs directly associated with an item of property, plant and equipment

On 01 January 20X1, a factory plant was constructed at an aggregate cost of CU12,000,000. In terms of the operating licence, the business must demolish the factory plant at the end of the licence period – 10 years from the date of commencement. At the date of commencement (01 January 20X1), management estimated that the demolition costs would amount to CU800,000. The fair market rate for the business is estimated to be 10%. At 01 January 20X4, management revised the cost of demolishing the factory plant to CU1,500,000, based on information obtained from specialist consultants in the industry.

You are required to:

Record the transactions relating to the demolition cost of the factory plant.

QUESTION 6

Objective: Recognition and measurement of the impairment loss for a depreciable item of property, plant and equipment

On 01 January 20X3, the business acquired machinery with an aggregate cost of CU2,500,000. The machine was depreciated to a zero residual value using the straight-line method over an estimated useful life of 10 years. On 31 December 20X5, the machine had a recoverable amount of CU1,610,000. On 31 December 20X7, the recoverable amount of the machine was CU1,250,000. The useful life and residual value of the machinery remained unchanged.

You are required to:

Record the transactions relating to the impairment of the machinery.

QUESTION 7

Objective: The recognition and measurement of the revaluation of an item of property, plant and equipment

On 01 January 20X4, machinery with an aggregate cost of CU3,000,000 was acquired and implemented in the production process of the business. Machinery is depreciated to a zero residual value using a straight-line basis over an estimated useful life of 6 years. On 01 January 20X6, management recommended that the machine be revalued to its gross fair value of CU3,600,000. The revaluation of the machine will be implemented using the gross revaluation method.

You are required to:
Record the transaction relating to the revaluation of the machinery.

CHAPTER 5
INVESTMENT PROPERTY

It is often claimed that the investments in properties in a volatile market are the most stable and secure investment decision.

ILLUSTRATIVE DISCLOSURE

IAS 1 p.54		Notes	20X2	20X1	Ch. ref
			CU'000	CU'000	
	ASSETS				
	Non-current assets				
S16, S17 & S27	Investment properties	7	453	378	

		Accounting policy			
	6	**Investment property** Investment property is measured at its fair value and any gain or loss is recognised via the profit & loss.			
IAS 40 p.76 & 79(d)			20X2	20X1	Ch. ref
			CU'000	CU'000	
	7	INVESTMENT PROPERTIES			
		Carrying amount at beginning of the period	378	378	
		Fair value adjustment [increase/(decrease)]	75	-	
		Impairment loss for the period	-	-	
		Transfer (to)/from property, plant and equipment	-	-	
		Carrying amount at the end of the period	453	378	

5.1   INTRODUCTION

The assumption is often that when a manufacturing or retail business entity owns property, that such property must be classified under property, plant and equipment in the financial statements. However, irrespective of the primary business of the entity, whenever property is acquired with the intention of generating rental income or for capital appreciation, it must be classified as investment property.

5.2   LEARNING OUTCOMES

Upon completion of this chapter you should know the financial reporting requirements for investment property in accordance with the accounting standards (full IFRS and IFRS for SMEs). In particular, you should be able to:
(a) distinguish investment property from other assets of an entity;
(b) measure items of investment property on initial recognition and subsequently;
(c) account for an item of investment property when the fair value cannot be reliably measured;
(d) disclose investment property in the financial statements; and
(e) account for an item of investment property which is transferred to or from another asset classification.

5.3   DEFINITIONS

The definitions for the important concepts and terms used in IFRS for SMEs are found in Appendix B – *Glossary of terms* in IFRS for SMEs. Some important definitions relating to investment property include the following:

• **Investment property:** Investment property is defined as property (land or building, or part of a building, or both) held by an entity/owner or by a lessee under a finance lease with the primary objective:
    (a) of earning rental income,
    (b) for capital appreciation; or
    (c) both: for earning rental income and capital appreciation

    Instead of for:
    (a) use in the production or supply of goods or services or for administrative purposes; or
    (b) sale in the ordinary course of business.

- **Property, plant and equipment**: Tangible assets that are:
  (a) held for use in the production or supply of goods or services, for rental to others, or for administrative purposes; and
  (b) expected to be used during more than one period.

- **Fair value:** The fair value is the amount obtainable from the sale of an asset in an arm's length transaction between knowledgeable and willing parties – fair value if there is an active market for the property (full IFRS – refer to IFRS 13 – *Fair value measurement*).

- **Valuation:** The valuation represents the value determined using appropriate valuation techniques.

- **Impairment:** An impairment loss occurs when the carrying amount of an asset exceeds its recoverable amount.

5.4   SCOPE AND OBJECTIVES

This standard is only applicable to properties that meet the definition of investment properties and provided the fair value of such properties can be measured reliably without undue cost or effort on an ongoing basis. Investment properties whose fair value cannot be measured reliably are accounted for as property, plant and equipment (s17). (*IAS 40 includes all investment properties which meet the definition of investment properties, although when investment property is accounted for on the cost model, the cost model shall be the same cost model as in IAS 16 – Property, plant & equipment. So while these items are not scoped out of IAS 40 – Investment property for full IFRS, the cost model is the same model in IAS 16 – Property, plant & equipment.*)

5.5   BASIC TRANSACTIONS

5.5.1   Classification

When property is acquired by an entity, the classification will be based on the intention for which it was purchased. The property will be classified as investment property if it is held by an entity or owner or by a lessee under a finance lease with the primary objective:
(a)   of earning rental income,
(b)   for capital appreciation; or
(c)   both: for rental income and capital appreciation (s16.2 and IAS 40 p.5).

A characteristic of investment property is that it generates cash flows largely independently of the other assets held by an entity, ie investment property has the capacity to generate rental income independently of other assets while a factory building (property, plant and equipment) generates revenue through the products which are manufactured.

5.5.1.1 Exclusions

The following properties are excluded from being classified as investment property (IAS 40 p.4):
(a) *biological assets* related to agricultural activity; and
(b) *mineral rights* and *mineral reserves*.

The definition of investment property specifically excludes:
(a) *business use* – properties which are acquired to be used by the entity for its own purposes and not to generate rental income or capital appreciation cannot be classified as investment property. Properties used in the production process (factory building) or for administrative purposes by the entity shall be classified as property, plant and equipment (s16.2 and IAS 40 p.5);
(b) *resale* – properties acquired by entities for re-sale (real estate) and/or development (property developers) must be recognised as inventory (s13 and IAS 2). If an entity acquires property for development, ie land acquired will be divided into plots which will be sold for the development of residential purposes, the property must be classified as inventory, as the intention is to re-sell the property as part of the core business of the entity.

5.5.1.2 Land

Land acquired by an entity for investment purposes, ie capital appreciation, shall be classified as investment property. Similarly, if the land is purchased at a bargain price (below its fair value), then it will be deemed to have been purchased with an intention of making a capital gain and must therefore be classified as investment property.

However, if the land is acquired with an undetermined intention, then it shall be classified as investment property based on the guidance provided by full IFRS (IAS 40.8(b)) as IFRS for SMEs does not make specific provision for such transactions. When there is a change in intention after the date of acquisition of such property, then it must be reclassified to the appropriate classification (s10, IAS 40 p.57–58 and IAS 8).

5.5.1.3 Mixed-use property

When property is used for mixed purposes, ie to earn rental income and used for administrative or other purposes by the owner, it should be classified separately between investment property and property, plant and equipment, where practicable (s16.4 and IAS 40).

The criteria used in IFRS for SMEs to classify properties separately are that they are:
(a) separately identified – the physical structures must be separately identified (eg house and a granny flat) and must be able to be sold (or leased out under a finance lease) separately; and
(b) separately measured – the fair value for each component must be reliably measured, ie each component must have a separate fair value rather than an estimated proportional allocation.

Decision summary for mixed-use properties:

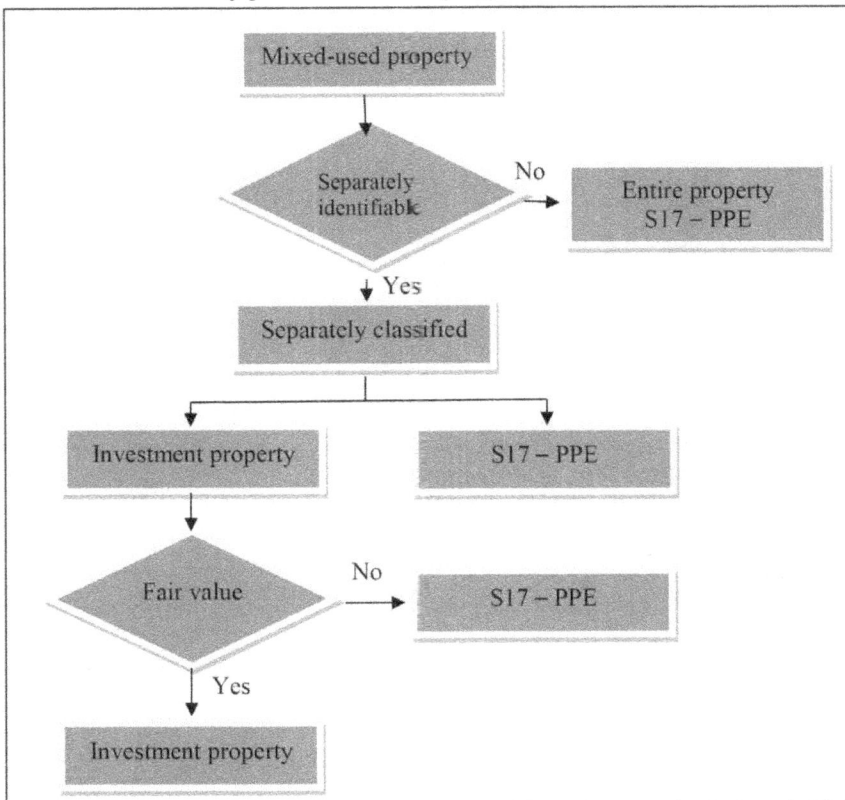

The following are illustrations of the application of the decision metrics:

(a) *property cannot be separately identified and measured* – entire property shall be recognised as property, plant and equipment (s16.2 and IAS 40);

(b) *properties can be identified and measured separately and the fair value is easily determined* – the components shall be classified separately between investment property and property, plant and equipment (s16.2 and IAS 40.8), based on the major use of the property;

(c) *properties can be identified and measured separately and the fair value is not easily determined* – the entire property shall be classified as property, plant and equipment (s16.2 and IAS 40).

Illustrative Example 5.1: Mixed-use classification

On 01 April 20X8, an entity purchased a property consisting of an office block and a factory building at an aggregate cost of CU4,500,000. The estimated costs of the office block and the factory were CU3,000,000 and CU1,5000,000 respectively. Management decided to allocate 25% of both the office block and the factory for use by the entity, with the remainder being rented to third parties. Due to the uniqueness of the nature of the factory, there was no fair value available.

You are required to:

(i) Discuss how the property should be classified in the financial statements of the entity; and

(ii) Based on you conclusion in (i), prepare the journal entries necessary to account for the property in the financial statements of the entity on 1 April 20X8.

Suggested solution:

As the sections used by the entity and third parties cannot be separately identified or measured, the classification must be based on the major use of the property. However, the fair value of the factory cannot be determined, thus it must be classified as property, plant and equipment.

01/04/X8 DR: Property, plant & equipment – factory	1,500,000	
DR: Investment property – offices	3,000,000	
CR: Accounts payable		4,500,000

The criteria used in full IFRS to classify the property separately are that the physical structures must be separately identified, meaning they must be able to be

(a) sold separately; or

(b) leased out under a finance lease separately.

Examples of these include one building representing a block of flats with individual flats that can be sold or leased out under a finance lease separately.

If the property cannot be sold, or leased out under a finance lease, separately then the building must be classified as property, plant and equipment unless an insignificant portion is used for purposes of property, plant and equipment (IAS 40 p.10).

5.5.2   Recognition

5.5.2.1   Initial recognition

In order for any transaction to be recognised in the accounting records, it must be:
(a)   probable that the transactions will be concluded – the entity will gain control over the property; and
(b)   the cost must be measured reliably.

If the property acquired meets the definition to be classified as investment property, then it must be recognised as such when all the criteria for recognition as an asset are satisfied – the date the entity gains control over the property.

5.5.2.2   Subsequent recognition – reclassification

A property can continue to be classified as investment property subsequent to initial recognition only if its fair value can be determined reliably without any undue effort. Management must apply judgement in determining whether the fair value of an investment property can be measured reliably without undue cost or effort on an ongoing basis. Although there is no specific definition of 'ongoing basis', clarity is provided in the context of 'ongoing basis' implying now and in the future; ie at present and for the foreseeable future (s16.1 and IAS 40 p.53). For example, a once-off non-binding offer does not in itself constitute an ongoing basis, while adequate guidance is provided on determining fair value (s11.27–11.32 and IFRS 13).

5.5.3   Measurement

5.5.3.1   Initial recognition

Investment property shall be measured at initial recognition at its aggregate cost, ie total costs incurred to acquire control over the property and make it ready for its intended purpose (s16.5 and IAS 40 p.20). The cost of purchased investment property consists of the purchase price plus all direct costs related to its acquisition, such as transfer fees, taxes and other transaction costs. When costs are incurred prior to the acquisition such as negotiation fees or costs to review purchase options, these costs may not be capitalised as part of the cost of the property unless the purchase transaction cannot be finalised with the pre-contract costs being incurred.

5.5.3.2 Deferred payment agreements

When investment property is acquired in terms of a deferred payment or an instalment sales agreement, the initial cost must be measured at the cash price or the present value of all future payments discounted at the effective interest rate.

Illustrative Example 5.2: Deferred payments

On 01 March 20X8, an entity purchased property which meets all the criteria to be classified as investment property in terms of an agreement that requires an initial payment of CU400,000 and two half-yearly instalments of CU500,000, the first commencing six months from the date of purchase. The effective interest rate is 14%.

You are required to:
Prepare the journal entries necessary to account for the property in the financial statements of the entity at 1 March 20X8.

Suggested solution:

Initial payment	400,000	
Instalment payments [CU500,000 @ 7% for 2 periods]	904,050	
Cost of property – present value	1,304,050	
01/03/X8 DR: Investment property	1,304,050	
CR: Accounts payable		904,050
CR: Bank		400,000

5.5.3.3 Cost of self-constructed investment property

The cost of self-constructed investment property involves aggregating the total costs incurred to bring the property to a condition and location ready for its intended purpose; all the direct costs must be capitalised.

Illustrative Example 5.3: Cost of self-constructed property

An entity constructed an office building that will be leased to tenants and which meets all the criteria to be classified as investment property. The land was acquired at an aggregate cost of CU1,100,000. The following were incurred to construct the building: (i) architects' costs of CU156,000; (ii) civil engineering costs of CU291,000; (iii) CU72,000 for clearing the land; (iv) inspection costs of CU48,000; (v) construction costs of R 3.9 million; and (vi) advertising costs of CU120,000.

You are required to:
Calculate the aggregate cost of the building.

Suggested solution:

Cost of land	1,100,000
Civil engineering costs – preparation for its intended use	291,000
Clearing costs – preparation for its intended use	72,000
Architects' costs – capitalised as designing costs	156,000
Inspection costs – capitalised as approval for use	48,000
Construction costs	3,900,000
Advertising costs – expensed (incurred after available for use	NIL
Aggregate cost of building	5,567,000

5.5.3.4 Capitalisation of borrowing costs

The construction of property is often financed by long-term debt/loans. The interest incurred on the debt financing can be capitalised as part of the cost of the property in terms of full IFRS under certain conditions (IAS 23), but must be expensed in terms of IFRS for SMEs (s20). The net interest (interest paid less interest expense) incurred from the period between when commencement of capitalisation and cessation can be capitalised. If the interest received exceeds the interest paid for the period, then the net interest received cannot be capitalised. The interest incurred prior to the commencement and after the completion of the construction must be expensed. If there is an extended suspension in the construction of the property, then the interest incurred during such a period cannot be capitalised – interest paid must be expensed.

Illustrative Example 5.4:

The following schedule was extracted from the accounting records maintained for the construction of an office block that will be rented to tenants:

	CU
Aggregate construction costs	9,150,000
Debt financing	8,000,000
Interest paid: Pre-construction	28,000
During construction	265,000
Extended suspended period of construction	68,000
Post-construction	97,000

Interest received: Pre-construction	53,000
During construction	105,000
Extended suspended period of construction	22,000

You are required to:
Calculate the cost of the investment property.

Suggested solution:

Aggregate construction costs	9,150,000
Borrowing costs capitalised:	
Interest paid: During construction	265,000
Interest received: During construction	(105,000)
Cost of investment property	9,310,000

Interest paid and interest received not capitalised as part of the cost of the property must be recognised via the profit & loss.

5.5.4   Subsequent to initial recognition

The objective of financial statements is to report on the economic substance of transactions and events, thus an entity's accounting policy for investment property is to measure it at its fair value if such a fair value is known or can be determined without undue cost or effort on an ongoing basis. The gain or loss resulting from the fair value measurement must be recognised through profit and loss (statement of financial performance) (s16.7 and IAS 40 p.35).

Illustrative Example 5.5: Subsequent cost

On 01 June 20X8, an entity acquired property (classified as investment property) at an aggregate cost of CU2,500,000. At the reporting periods ended 31 December 20X8 and 20X9, the fair value of the property was CU3,200,000 and CU2,200,000 respectively.

You are required to:
Prepare the journal entries necessary to account for the movements in fair value of the property for the years ended 31 December 20x8 and 20x9.

Suggested solution:
At 31 December 20X8, the increase in the carrying amount of the property of CU700,000 must be recognised as a gain through profit and loss, while the decrease in the carrying amount of CU1,000,000 (change in the fair value from CU3,200,000 to CU2,200,000) must be recognised as a loss in profit or loss.
31/12/X8 DR: Investment property   700,000

CR: Fair value gain [P/L]		700,000
31/12/X9 DR: Fair value loss [P/L]	1,000,000	
CR: Investment property		1,000,000

5.6 RECLASSIFICATION

5.6.1 Classification

Property can only be classified as investment property if it meets the definition (in addition, IFRS for SMEs requires that the fair value be able to be determined without any undue costs). Properties must be reclassified from investment property if there is a:

(a) *change in use:* a change in the use or intention for the property may result in the property not meeting the definition of investment property, for example a factory building that was leased to tenants is now being used by the entity in its production process – the property now meets the definition of property, plant and equipment; and the

(b) *fair value is not available:* if the fair value cannot be determined without undue costs and effort on an ongoing basis, then the item must be reclassified appropriately to another category of assets. For example, if the fair value of the property classified as investment property cannot be determined on an ongoing basis, then such property, even if it meets the definition of investment property, must be reclassified as property, plant and equipment (in terms of IFRS for SMEs).

5.6.2 Recognition and measurement

When property is reclassified from or to investment property (measured at fair value), it must be measured at its fair value at the date of reclassification, ie the property must first be revalued before the reclassification based on the appropriate provisions of the relevant standards (this is the case even if the entity applies the cost model to the property in terms of s17 and IAS 16). This implies that the fair value of the property at the date of reclassification is deemed to be its cost under the category to which it has been transferred (s16.8 and IAS 40 p.61). However, if circumstances change and a reliable measure of fair value becomes available for the property and it meets the criteria to be classified as investment property, then it should be reclassified to investment property.

Full IFRS allows for investment property to be accounted for on the cost model. Where property is transferred from to the one category to the other, and the entity accounts for property under property, plant and equipment and investment property under the cost model (not an option under IFRS for SMEs), then the entity transfers the property at its current carrying amount in terms of the previous standard without adjusting the property's carrying amount to fair value (IAS 40 p.59).

5.6.2.1 Reclassification from investment property

When the property is reclassified from investment property, the increase or decrease in the fair value must be recognised via profit and loss (s16.7 and IAS 40 p.60). After the reclassification, the property must be accounted for and measured in terms of the relevant standard. For example, if investment property is reclassified to property, plant and equipment, then the property must be measured using the cost or revaluation model applying the appropriate depreciation policy.

Illustrative Example 5.6: Reclassification from investment property

At 28 February 20X8, an office building with a fair value of CU1,870,000 million was classified as investment property. On 30 June 20X8, the property was reclassified to property, plant and equipment. The fair value at 30 June 20X8 was CU2,400,000 million. Properties are depreciated on a straight-line basis to a nil residual value over a remaining useful life of 20 years. The company has a 28 February year-end.

You are required to:
Prepare the journal entries necessary to account for the property for the year ended 30 June 20x8.

Suggested solution:

30/06/X8	DR: Investment property	530,000	
	CR: Fair value gain [P/L]		530,000
30/06/X8	DR: Property, plant & machinery	2,400,000	
	CR: Investment property		2,400,000
28/02/X8	DR: Depreciation expense	80,000	
	CR: Accumulated depreciation [CU2,400,000/20/12 × 8]		80,000

5.6.2.2 Reclassification to investment property

When an item is transferred to investment property from another category of asset, then the increase or decrease resulting from fair valuing the property at the date of reclassification must be recognised in terms the applicable accounting standard immediately prior to the reclassification. For example, if property is reclassified from property, plant and equipment to investment property, then the property must be adjusted to its fair value by applying the principles of the revaluation model – surplus must be recognised via other comprehensive income (OCI).

Illustrative Example 5.7: Reclassification to investment property

At 28 February 20X8, an office building with a carrying amount of CU800,000 (original cost of CU1,200,000 million) was classified as property, plant and equipment. On 01 March 20X8, the property was reclassified to investment property. The fair value of 01 March 20X8 was CU1,600,000 million. Properties are depreciated on a straight-line basis to a nil residual value over an estimated useful life of 20 years.

You are required to:
Prepare the journal entries necessary to account for the property on 1 March 20X8.

Suggested solution:

01/03/X8	DR: Accumulated depreciation	400,000	
	CR: Property, plant & equipment		400,000
01/03/X8	DR: Property, plant & equipment	800,000	
	CR: Revaluation surplus (OCI)		800,000
01/03/X8	DR: Investment property	1,600,000	
	CR: Property, plant & equipment		800,000

5.7 INTEREST IN PROPERTY LEASED IN TERMS OF AN OPERATING LEASE

5.7.1 Classification and recognition

Prior to the change to the accounting standards and the issue of IFRS 16 – *Leases*, a property interest that is held by a lessee under an operating lease may be classified as investment property only if (s16.3 and IAS 40 p.IN5):
(a) the property would otherwise meet the definition of investment property; and
(b) the lessee can measure the fair value of the property interest without undue cost or effort on an ongoing basis.
(c) For full IFRS, the operating lease should also be accounted for as if it were a finance lease in accordance with IAS 17.

Prior to the implementation of IFRS 16 –*Leases*, property leased under an operating lease is not recognised as an asset in the records of the lessee, but the lessee accounts for the rental payments as expenses (s20.15 and IAS 17 p.33). However, if the lessee sub-leases the property to independent third parties, the leased property meets the definition of investment property and can be accounted for in accordance with the provisions of the standard. If the rental income received from the sub-lease is greater than the rental payments to the lessor, the lessee can recognise its interest in the leased property as an investment property. In such a situation, the lessee is allowed to elect whether or not to recognise the operating lease as investment property as if it were a finance lease provided the lessee can measure the fair value of property interest reliably on a continuous basis (s16.3 and IAS 40 p.53). An entity can elect to recognise the property interest as investment property on a property-to-property basis, ie each situation shall be reviewed in isolation.

Illustrative Example 5.8: Interest in property leased in terms of an operating lease

An entity leased property in terms of an operating lease at a rental of CU240,000 per annum. Due to the penalties for termination, the entity sub-leased the property to an independent third party at a rental CU320,000 per annum for the remaining period of the lease.

You are required to:
Discuss how the entity should account for its interest in the property.

Suggested solution:
The entity [lessee] generates rental income from the property leased and can classify the property as investment property. As the rental income exceeds the rental paid, the benefit enjoyed by the entity in terms of the favourable sub-lease can be recognised as a property interest. If the fair value of the property interest can be determined, the entity can elect to recognise the property interest as investment property. If the fair value cannot be measured, the entity is prohibited from recognising the property interest as investment property.

5.7.2 Measurement

The interest in the property leased in terms of an operating lease and which is classified as investment property is measured based on the guidelines for finance leases even if it is an operating lease, namely, the lower of its fair value and present value of minimum lease payments (s20.9 and IAS 17 p.20). The rental income received will be recognised as a repayment of the lease payable – the amount received must be separated between the capital and interest components using the effective interest rate method.

Illustrative Example 5.9: Measurement of interest in property leased in terms of an operating lease

An entity sub-leased property which it leased in terms of an operating lease to an independent third party for a period of five years. The present value of the minimum lease rentals was CU1,450,000, while the fair value at the commencement of the sub-lease was CU1,900,000.

You are required to:

Prepare the journal entries necessary to account for the interest in the property in the financial statements of the entity for the year ended 30 September 20x8.

Suggested solution:

On 01 April 20X8, an entity (lessee) generates rental income from the property leased and must classify the property as investment property. The property must be measured at CU1,450,000, which is the lower of the present value and the fair value.

01/04/X8	DR: Investment property	1,450,000	
	CR: Interest in leased property liability		1,450,000
30/09/X8	DR: Interest in leased property liability	300,000	
	DR: Interest expense [assumption]	35,000	
	CR: Bank		335,000

5.7.3 Investment property with additional services

The classification of properties which meet the definition of investment property and are leased to tenants in terms of an operating lease that includes the rendering of additional services such as maintenance, security, etc. shall be based on the significance of the services rendered (s20 and IAS 40 p.12). If the additional services are considered to be insignificant, the properties shall be classified as investment properties. If the services are considered to be significant, the properties shall be classified and accounted for as property, plant and equipment.

5.8 EFFECTS OF TAXATION

Investment property is measured at its original cost or base cost (eg in South Africa, the tax base of property acquired prior to 01 October 2001 is represented by its fair value at that date) in terms of the Income Tax Act. Adjustments to the carrying amount of investment properties resulting from the application of the fair value measurement policy or the impairment test are not allowed for income tax purposes. The difference between the carrying amount and the tax base is regarded as a temporary difference which is recoverable through sale (s29.30 and IAS 12 p.51C).

Illustrative Example 5.10: Investment property and the effects of taxation

Investment property was acquired at an aggregate cost of CU2,500,000. The fair value of the property at 29 February 20X8 and 28 February 20X9 was CU3,100,000 and CU2,860,000, respectively. The capital gains inclusion rate is 80%. The tax rate for companies is 28%.

You are required to:
Prepare the journal entries necessary to account for the investment property in the entity financial statements for the year ended 29 February 20X8 and 28 February 20X9.

Suggested solution:

28/02/X8 DR: Investment property	600,000	
CR: Fair value gain [P/L]		600,000
28/02/X8 DR: Deferred tax expense [P/L]	134,400	
CR: Deferred tax liability [CU600,000 × 80% × 28%]		134,400
28/02/X9 DR: Fair value adjustment [P/L]	240,000	
CR: Investment property		240,000
28/02/X9 DR: Deferred tax liability [CU240,000 × 80% × 28%]	53,760	
CR: Deferred tax expense [P/L]		53,760

5.9   DISCLOSURE

An entity shall disclose the following for all investment property accounted for at fair value through profit or loss (s16.10 and IAS 40 p.75 & 76):
(a) accounting policies adopted: method and assumptions applied to determine the fair value;
(b) extent to which the fair value is determined by an independent valuator together with the professional qualifications and experience, if there has been no such valuation the fact should be stated;
(c) existence and amounts of restrictions on the realisability of investment property (income and proceeds on disposal);
(d) capital contractual obligations in respect of investment property (purchase, construction or repair and enhancements);

(e) reconciliation of carrying amount at the beginning and end of the reporting period:
  (i)   additions (separating additions through business combinations);
  (ii) net gains/losses on fair value adjustments;
  (iii) transfers to and from other assets resulting from reclassifications; and
  (iv) other changes.

NB: It should be noted that full IFRS (IAS 40 – Investment property) allows, as an accounting policy choice, for a class of investment property to be accounted for on the cost model. IAS 40 p.79 provides additional disclosure for those investment properties accounted for on the cost model.

An entity that holds investment property under a finance or operating lease provides lessees' disclosure for finance leases and lessors' disclosure for any operating leases (S20 and IAS 17).

SELF-ASSESSMENT
Multiple choice questions: Testing the conceptual framework and principles of investment property

1. In terms of IFRS for SMEs, a building should be classified as investment property if:

(a) management decided not to depreciate the building	
(b) the building is used to generate rental income	
(c) the fair value of the building can be determined without undue cost and effort	
(d) (b) and (c)	

2. Property that is used and occupied by the organisation as well as tenants must be classified in the financial statements:

(a) as investment property	
(b) as property, plant and equipment	
(c) as investment property or property, plant and equipment at the discretion of management	
(d) depending on the composition of the utilisation of the property	

3. In terms of IFRS for SMEs, investment property must be measured at the reporting date using:

(a) the historical cost method	
(b) the amortised cost method	
(c) the fair value method	
(d) the accounting policy adopted by management	

4. If the fair value of investment property cannot be determined, then:

(a) the fact must be stated in the notes to the financial statements	
(b) the property must be reclassified to property, plant and equipment	
(c) the carrying amount should remain unchanged	
(d) property must be reclassified as available for sale	

5. When property is reclassified from property, plant and equipment to investment property, then the increase in the fair value must be recognised:

(a) as fair value gain through profit and loss	
(b) as revaluation surplus through other comprehensive income	
(c) as a note to investment property in the financial statements	
(d) directly to the reserves through the statement of changes in equity	

6. Investment property must initially be recognised at:

(a) fair value	
(b) cost	
(c) replacement value	
(d) none of the above	

7. Machinery that is held to earn rental income is classified as:

(a) property, plant and equipment	
(b) investment property	
(c) inventory	
(d) an intangible asset	

8. Investment property is:

(a) depreciated	
(b) amortised	
(c) impaired in terms of s27 – *Impairment of assets*	
(d) none of the above	

9. Land acquired with an undetermined use is classified as:

(a) an intangible asset	
(b) property, plant and equipment	
(c) investment property	
(d) inventory	

10. If property previously classified as property, plant and equipment is transferred to investment property:

(a) the property is transferred at cost	
(b) the property is transferred at its carrying amount at the date of transfer	
(c) the property is transferred at fair value at the date of transfer	
(d) none of the above	

Practical questions:
Application of principles to business scenarios

QUESTION 1

Objective: Classification of properties which are leased to tenants in compliance with investment property

NJ (Pty) Ltd acquired an office building at an aggregate cost of CU3,500,000. The property was leased to tenants. The lease agreement included a clause specifying the additional services (security, maintenance, insurance, etc) which were to be rendered by the landlord. The average annual rental amounted to CU800,000, while the estimated additional service costs were CU490,000.

You are required to:
Determine how the office building should be classified in the financial statements of NJ (Pty) Ltd.

QUESTION 2

Objective: Classification of multi-purpose properties based on use

A factory plant with an aggregate cost of CU2,400,000 million consisting of adjoining structures was used by the business entity, while 25% of the plant was leased to a tenant. The fair value of the property at the reporting date was CU3,200,000 million. The business uses the fair value model to account for investment property, but the cost model for property, plant and equipment.

You are required to:
Determine how the factory plant should be classified in the financial statements.

QUESTION 3

Objective: Classification, recognition and measurement of property subjected to an operating lease that is sub-leased

A tenant has a 10-year operating lease agreement for a building which was sub-leased for the remaining period of the lease (8 years) as the business acquired an alternative premises as its primary operating site. The reason for entering into the sub-lease was to avoid an onerous penalty for the business on termination of the lease agreement. The fair value of the building at the date of entering into the sub-lease agreement was CU1,800,000.

You are required to:
Determine how the building should be classified in the financial statements.

QUESTION 4

Objective: Reclassification of investment property when the fair value model is applicable

On 01 January 20X2, a factory building, leased to a tenant by DG (Pty) Ltd, with an aggregate cost of CU3,500,000, was classified as investment property. On 31 December 20X3, the fair value was CU4,100,000. However, for the reporting periods 20X4 to 20X6, it was not possible to determine the fair value of the factory building. At 31 December 20X7, the fair value of the factory building was CU4,500,000 and was again considered to be determinable on an ongoing basis. Properties are depreciated on a straight-line basis over an estimated useful life of 50 years where applicable.

You are required to:
Record the transactions, relating to the reclassification of the factory building in terms of IFRS for SMEs, necessary to prepare the financial statement of DG (Pty) Ltd.

CHAPTER 6
INVENTORIES

ILLUSTRATIVE DISCLOSURE [EXTRACT]

IFRS ref		Notes	20X2	20X1	Ch. ref
			CU'000	CU'000	
	ASSETS				
	Current assets				
S13 & s27 (IAS 2)	Inventories	10	57	48	

IFRS ref			20X2	20X1	Ch. ref
			CU'000	CU'000	
S13 & s27 (IAS 2)	10	INVENTORIES			
		Inventories consist of:			
		Raw material	42	36	
		Work-in-progress	1	1	
		Finished goods	14	11	
			57	48	

6.1 INTRODUCTION

Generally, inventories provide future economic benefits to an entity in the form of potential future revenue through sales if its business model is to convert inventory (finished goods) into cash through sales activities. Many owners of small and medium-sized businesses believe the level of inventories on hand is an indication of the future growth and sustainability of the business. However, the risk which many small and medium-sized business owners tend to ignore is that inventories misrepresent the future prospects of the operating activities of the entity because of faster-changing markets, consumer behaviour, business practices such as e-commerce, and modern inventory management systems such as just-in-time (JIT).

A substantial increase in inventories may be viewed as high potential future revenue, but this substantial increase may be a leading indicator of a decline in future profits as a result of the business not having the capacity to convert inventories into sales. When inventory levels are excessively high, management needs to decrease the selling price of the goods to improve its operating cycle, namely, converting inventories into sales, which results in a decline in profits. However, when manufacturers increase their inventory levels of raw materials and work-in-progress, it is an indication that the entity is building its inventories to meet increased demands.

6.2   LEARNING OUTCOMES

Upon completing this unit, you should know the financial reporting requirements for inventories in accordance with the IFRS for SMEs. In particular, you should be able to:
(a)   distinguish items of inventory from other assets of an entity;
(b)   identify when items of inventory qualify for recognition in financial statements;
(c)   measure items of inventory at initial recognition and subsequently;
(d)   distinguish between perpetual and periodic inventories systems;
(e)   identify when an item of inventory is to be recognised as an expense;
(f)   measure valuation and inventory loss as part of subsequent measurement;
(g)   present and disclose inventories in financial statements; and
(h)   demonstrate an understanding of the significant judgements that are required in accounting for inventories.

6.3   SCOPE AND OBJECTIVES

This section is applicable to the following assets which should be recognised as inventories if they are (s13.1 and IAS 2 p.6):
(a)   held for sale in ordinary course of business – finished goods;
(b)   in the process of production – work-in-progress; or
(c)   materials or supplies to be consumed in the production process or the rendering of services.

For any item to be recognised as inventory it must satisfy the criteria to be recognised as an asset, namely, a resource controlled by the entity from which future economic benefits will flow to the entity (s2.15 and CF p.4.4(a)). An item is classified as inventory if it is converted into revenue through the operating cycle of the entity or through the ordinary business activities of the entity (s23.1 – *Revenue* and IFRS 15 – *Revenue from contract with customers*).

Illustrative Example 6.1: Classification

A real estate entity has commercial property which it purchased with the intention of selling at a profit as part of its primary business activities. Its associate company, which operates in the manufacturing industry, keeps highly specialised parts for the maintenance of some of its machinery as well as lubricants used during the operation of its machinery.

You are required to:

Advise their accountant on how to account for (i) the commercial property of the real estate company, (ii) the spare parts, and (iii) the lubricant used in servicing the machinery.

Suggested solution:

(i)   The commercial property – as the real estate company holds the property for sale in the course of its ordinary business, the property must be classified as inventory.

(ii) The spare parts – although the spare parts are consumed as part of the production process, they are expected to be used during more than one period or operating cycle and are therefore not current assets but rather non-current assets such as property, plant and equipment.

(iii) The lubricant – as the lubricant will be consumed during the production process and during the operating cycle, the lubricant is considered to be inventory.

6.3.1   Exclusions from s13 (IAS 2) – Inventories

Section 13 does not apply to the following items which may be classified as inventories as they are governed by other sections of IFRS for SMEs (IFRS) (s13.2 and IAS 2 p.2):

(a)   work-in-progress under construction contracts (s23 – *Revenue*);

(b)   financial instruments (s11 – *Basic financial instruments*; s12 – *Other financial instrument issues*; IAS 32 – *Financial instrument presentation*; IFRS 9 – *Financial instruments*); and

(c)   biological assets and agricultural products at point of harvest (s34 – *Specialised activities*; IAS 41 – *Agriculture*).

This section does not apply to the measurement of inventories held by (s13.3 and IAS 2 p.3):

(a)   producers of agricultural and forest products, agricultural produce after harvest, and mineral and mineral products, to the extent that they are measured at fair value less cost to sell through (IFRS: net realisable value) profit or loss; or

(b) commodity brokers and dealers that measure their inventories at fair value less cost to sell through profit or loss.

Items which are used in the operating activities of the business, such as stationery and spare parts, may also be classified as inventory even though they do not satisfy the definition of inventory in its entirety. Technically, these items represent a prepaid expense and their future economic benefits will be realised through use in the operating activities rather than through revenue activities.

6.4   COST OF INVENTORIES

Inventories are classified as assets and thus the basic principle of measuring the cost of an asset should apply. The cost of inventories shall be measured as the total costs incurred by the entity to acquire control and bring the inventory to its present location and condition, namely, all the costs incurred to bring the inventories to a condition ready and available for sale (s13.5 and IAS 2 p.10).

6.4.1   Costs included

The cost of inventory includes the aggregated costs incurred to acquire control over the inventory plus the direct costs incurred to bring the inventory into a saleable condition (s13.5–12 and IAS 2 p.11–15).

The cost of inventory includes the following:
(a) purchase price – the costs incurred to acquire control of the inventory;
(b) transportation or delivery costs – the costs incurred in bringing inventory to its present location; and
(c) processing or conversion costs – the costs incurred in bringing inventor to a saleable condition.

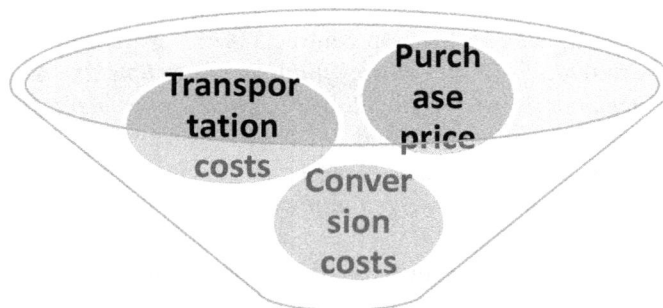

Cost of inventory

Figure 6.1 What is included in the total cost of inventory

Generally, as for measuring all assets, the costs incurred can only be capitalised as part of the cost of inventory up to and including the date the goods are ready for sale, thus any costs incurred after the date should be expensed.

Illustrative Example 6.2: Cost of inventory

Cost of inventory	CU
Purchase price of goods for resale purposes	540,000
Transportation costs – from supplier to the buyer's warehouse	38,000
Packaging material costs – designed packaging	26,500
Packaging labour cost	12,500

You are required to:
Calculate the cost of the inventory.

Suggested solution:

Purchase price of goods	540,000
Transportation costs – from supplier to warehouse	38,000
Packaging material costs – customised packaging	26,500
Packaging labour cost	12,500
Cost of inventory	617,000

6.4.2   Costs excluded

Costs and expenses incurred which are general or indirectly related to the inventory, such as administrative and distribution costs, do not form part of the cost of the inventory (s13.13 and IAS 2 p.16).

The following costs are excluded from the cost of inventories and are recognised as expenses in the period in which they are incurred:
(a)   abnormal amounts of wasted materials, labour or other production costs;
(b)   storage costs, unless those costs are necessary during the production process;
(c)   administrative overheads that do not contribute towards bringing the inventories to their present location and condition; and
(d)   selling costs.

Wastage of materials, labour and overheads which are incurred during the normal production process are regarded as normal wastage and form part of the cost of inventory as these costs, even though they appear to be indirect costs, are considered part of the production process. The proceeds realised from the sale of the normal wastage, materials or damaged products shall set-off against the cost of the inventory (s13.10 and IAS 2 p.14).

However, abnormal wastage represents costs which are incurred during the production process but are not regarded as directly associated with the normal production process. Abnormal wastage does not form part of the cost of inventory and shall be recognised as losses by the entity (s13.13(a) and IAS 2 p.16(a)).

Illustrative Example 6.3: Expenses included in the cost of inventory

An entity measured the costs of wastage incurred during the production process to be CU11,000, of which CU7,500 was regarded as being abnormal to the production process (breakdown of the machine).

You are required to:
Discuss whether or not the entity should capitalise the wastage incurred during production to the cost of the inventory.

Suggested solution:
The normal wastage cost of CU3,500 shall be included in the cost of the inventory, while the CU7,500 relating to abnormal wastage shall be expensed and recognised as a loss.

An entity incurred packaging expenses of CU15,000 for designer packaging for a major customer's goods and CU22,000 for the general packaging, such as wrapping and boxing, of goods delivered to customers after the items are already available for sale.

The CU15,000 incurred for designer packaging forms part of the cost of inventory (costs incurred to bring goods to a saleable condition – the goods cannot be sold to the customer without the special packaging), while the CU22,000 forms part of normal operating costs (cost which is incurred for the sale of the goods to all customers). The general packaging costs do not affect the condition of the goods being available for sale, so they cannot form part of the cost of inventory.

Summary of inventory costs:

Costs included	Costs excluded
Costs incurred to bring inventories to: • present location; and • a saleable condition.	Abnormal amounts of wastage
Changes in fair value of the hedging instrument – cash flow hedge	Storage costs – costs after initial recognition
	Administrative costs – not incurred to bring inventories to a saleable condition
	Selling costs

Illustrative Example 6.4:[1] Special order

Special order:	CU
Cost of raw material used in the production of the finished clothing (before discount of CU50,000)	620,000
Designing costs: Consultant's cost to design the product for the customer (based on the request of the customer)	17,000
Labour costs (in designing the garment)	9,000
Machine modification and testing costs: Raw material	24,000
Labour costs	15,000
Depreciation	6,000
Sale of samples	7,000
Production costs: Consumables (indirect materials)	45,000
Labour conversion costs	65,000
Depreciation	15,000
Loan raised to fund purchase of materials (include fee of CU5,000)	750,000

---

[1] IASC Foundation: Training Material for the IFRS® for SMEs (version 2010-1)

You are required to:
Calculate the cost of the inventory.

Suggested solution:

Special order:	CU	Ref
Cost of raw materials [CU550,000 – CU50,000][1]	570,000	s13.6 & IAS 2 p.11
Designing costs [CU17,000 + CU9,000][2]	26,000	s13.11 & IAS 2 p.15
Testing costs [CU24,000 + CU11,000 + CU6,000 – CU7,000][3]	34,000	s13.10 & IAS 2 p.14
Production costs [CU 45,000 + CU65,000 + CU15,000][4]	125,000	s13.8 & IAS 12 p.12–13
Fee charged on loan	0	S25.2 & IAS 2 p.4(b)
Cost of inventory	755,000	

Notes:
1. Purchase price shall represent the net cash flow, excluding the discount.
2. The design costs form part of the costs to bring the inventory to a saleable condition – specialised to meet the customer's specifications.
3. Modification and testing costs form part of the costs to bring inventories to a saleable condition – specialised to meet the customer's specifications.
4. Production costs form part of the conversion costs.

6.4.3   Purchase price

The purchase price should represent the net cash flows paid or payable at the date the purchaser gains control over the inventories. Thus, the purchase price is measured by (s13.6 and IAS 2 p.11–15)

- **including:** import duties and other taxes, transport, handling and other costs directly attributable to the acquisition of inventories; and
- **excluding:** any taxes recoverable from third parties such as value added tax (VAT), rebates, trade discounts and settlement discounts granted by suppliers.

Illustrative Example 6.5: VAT

VAT	CU
Purchases [1,000 units @ CU150 each]	150,000
Trade rebate	10%
VAT (included in the price above)	15%

You are required to:

Prepare the journal entries necessary to account for the purchase of the inventory in the financial statements of the entity.

Suggested solution:

Total purchase price		150,000
Less: Trade rebate [CU150,000 × 10%]		15,000
Purchase price after rebate		135,000
VAT [CU135,000/115% × 15%]		17,609
Cost of inventory		117,391

	Debit	Credit
	CU	CU
Inventory/purchases	117,391	
VAT control	17,609	
Trade payable		135,000

Settlement discount

Settlement discount is one of the situations when professional judgement should be applied as the discount will only be known when the stipulated conditions are satisfied at a date after the purchase transaction is recognised. Settlement discounts should be deducted from the purchase price in terms of s13.6 (IAS p.11) which states "… rebates and other similar items are deducted …". However, s23.3 (IFRS 15 p.51) is more explicit and states that the purchase price of the inventories is measured after the settlement discount is taken into consideration.

The settlement discount may only be set-off against the purchase price if there is certainty at the date that the transaction occurs that the discount will be claimed. If the settlement discount is set-off against the purchase price at the transaction date and the purchaser defaults on the agreement, then the settlement discount should be reversed against the cost of the inventories.

If there is uncertainty whether the discount will be claimed at the transaction date, then the settlement discount should be adjusted against the cost of the inventory (if the inventory is still on hand) (s10.17 and IAS 8 p.37) or cost of sales if it is already sold (s10.36 and IAS 8 p.16).

Illustrative Example 6.6: Settlement discount

Settlement discount	CU
Purchase price [excluding VAT of 15%]	500,000
Settlement discount	5%

You are required to:
Prepare the journal entries necessary to account for the purchase of the inventory in the financial statements of the entity.

Suggested solution:

	Certainty	Uncertainty
	CU	CU
Purchase price (including VAT at 15%)	575,000	575,000
Settlement discount [CU517,500 × 5%]	28,750	0
Cost of inventory (including VAT)	546,250	575,000
VAT included in cost of inventory [CU546,250/115% × 15%]	71,250	75,000
Cost of inventory	475,000	500,000

	Debit	Credit
	CU	CU
Inventory/purchases	475,000	
Provision for settlement discount	28,750	
VAT control account [CU500,000 × 15%]	71,250	
Trade payables		571,250
Provision for VAT control [CU25,875/115% × 15%]		3,750
The net VAT account will reflect a balance of CU67,500 (CU71,250 − CU3,750)		

Deferred payment and low-interest arrangements

Deferred purchase agreements include those arrangements where the payment is postponed to a period which exceeds the normal credit terms, and a low-interest purchase agreement occurs when the agreement is at an interest-free rate or interest is charged at an interest rate below the market rate. The difference between the purchase price under normal credit terms and the settlement amount should be recognised as finance costs. Such a purchase agreement represents a financing transaction, and the purchase price is measured by the fair value of the consideration or the present value of all future payments discounted at the imputed interest rate (s13.7 and IAS 2 p.18).

There is no clear guidance as to whether the adjustment for finance costs should be from the transaction date to the settlement date (entire period) or only for the extended period (after the normal terms). The argument for recognising finance costs for the entire period is that the deferred payment agreement is for the 'financing transaction' as a whole and thus the finance cost is charged from the transaction date. However, the argument against accounting for the finance cost for the entire period is that for normal credit terms, the transaction would have been interest-free and that the finance cost is only for the period beyond the normal terms.

Illustrative Example 6.7: Deferred payment

Deferred payment	Details
01 Jan 20X9: Purchased inventories (cost excluding VAT at 15%]	300,000
30 Jun 20X9: Settlement date	6 months
Normal terms granted	3 months
Imputed interest rate	12%

You are required to:
Prepare the journal entries necessary to account for the purchase of the inventory in the financial statements of the entity.

Suggested solution:

	Full period	*Extended*
	CU	CU
Purchase price	256,000	256,000
Financing element (cost less present value of future cash flows) [CU256,000 – CU241,509] & [CU256,000 – CU248,544]	14,491	7,456
Cost of purchases [CU256 000/1.06] & [CU256 000/1.03]	241,509	248,544
	Debit	**Credit**
	CU	CU
Inventory/purchases	241,509	
Deferred financing costs	14,491	
Trade payables		256,000
NB: the above illustration excludes VAT.		

The finance costs recognised should be expensed over the period for which the interest is charged. When the finance costs are recognised using the extended period approach, no interest will be expensed during the normal credit terms and should be expensed periodically from the end of the normal terms over the extended period.

6.4.4   Transport costs

Transport costs incurred to bring the inventory to its present location (ie from the supplier to the initial location/premises of the purchasing organisation for use in production) must be capitalised as part of the cost of inventory (s13.6 and IAS 2 p.11). Transport costs incurred to distribute inventory from its initial location to the point-of-sale outlets, however, are recognised as an operating expense and therefore cannot be included in the purchase price. For example, the cost of the distribution warehouse of a large retailing store can be capitalised as part of the cost of inventory, but the transport costs to deliver the goods to its chain stores must be recognised as an operating cost.

Illustrative Example 6.8: Expenses included in the cost of inventory

An entity incurred the following transportation costs: (i) CU13,500 for transporting building materials from the supplier to its warehouse, (ii) CU25,200 for transporting materials to the factory where it will be used to produce a finished product that is sold to customers from the factory premises, and (iii) CU8,000 for transporting the goods to its customer's retail outlets.

You are required to:

Discuss whether or not the entity should capitalise the trasnport costs to the cost of the inventory.

Suggested solution:

CU13,500 forms part of the cost of bringing the materials to their present location and shall be included in the cost of inventory (raw materials). CU25,200 forms part of the costs of bringing the materials to the location for production and shall be included in the cost of the finished goods. CU8,000 shall be expensed as the costs do not bring the finished goods into a saleable condition but deliver them to the customers.

6.5   MANUFACTURED GOODS

In a manufacturing environment, inventory may consist of the following categories:
(a)   materials to be consumed in the production process (raw materials and consumables);
(b)   goods in the process of production – work-in-progress; or
(c)   completed goods held for sale in the ordinary course of business – finished goods.

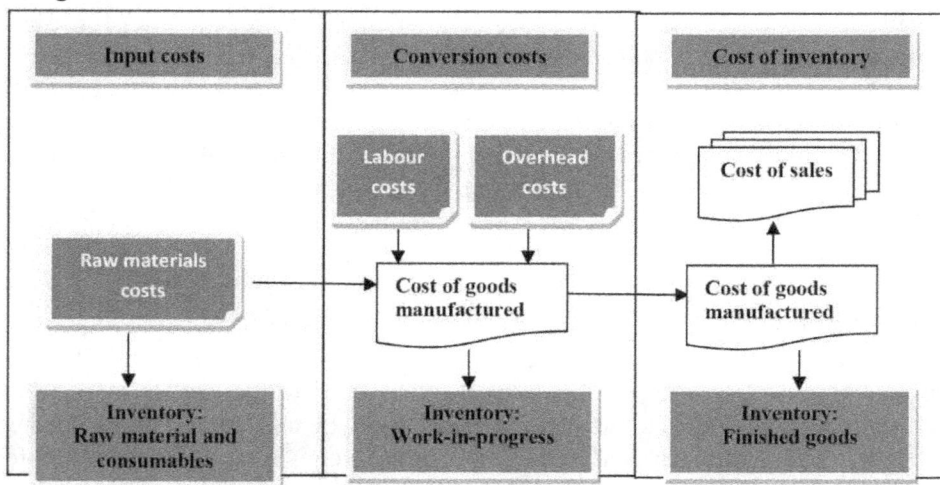

Figure 6.2 Illustration of the flow of costs in a manufacturing environment

Finished goods are the only category of inventory that has the potential of realising the future economic benefits through revenue transaction. The future economic benefits embedded in the raw materials and work-in-progress are only realised on the sale of the finished goods.

6.5.1   Conversion costs

Conversion costs to be included in the cost of inventory are determined based on the absorption costing method, namely, total direct costs associated with the manufacturing process such as indirect labour costs, plus a systematic allocation of production overheads [variable and fixed] incurred to produce the finished goods (s13.8 and IAS 2 p.12). It is important to note that even though an entity may use marginal costing techniques to determine the cost of finished goods for management accounting purposes it cannot be used to measure the cost of finished goods for financial reporting purposes.

Figure 6.3 Components of conversion costs

6.5.2 Allocation of production overheads

Fixed production overheads represent the indirect costs (costs which cannot be traced easily to the product manufactured) to the production process and include such costs as depreciation, supervisor costs, maintenance costs, etc. The fixed production costs are allocated to the cost of inventories [cost of goods manufactured – finished goods] based on the overhead absorption rate, namely, the pre-determined rate in terms of the average budgeted fixed production overhead cost per unit under normal production capacity (s13.9 and IAS 2 p.13). The normal production capacity is used to allocate the fixed production costs to the determine the inventory unit costs. The pre-determined rate is not adjusted for temporary fluctuations in the production levels unless these changes represent changes in the expected production levels in future periods.

Normal capacity is the production expected to be achieved on average over several periods under normal circumstances taking into consideration normal idle capacity such as planned maintenance activities. If the actual production level approximates the normal capacity, then the actual production level can be used to determine the overhead absorption rate.

As the product cost be unit is based on the pre-determined rate using the budgeted costs, the unallocated fixed production overhead costs [difference between the actual costs and the allocated costs based on the absorption rate] is recognised as expenses during the period they are incurred. During periods of abnormally high production levels, the unallocated fixed production costs represents a gain/saving that is recognised as other income. In such situations unallocated fixed production overhead costs is written off against the product cost per unit so that the inventories are not measured at a value above it actual cost; unlike in the management accounting system where the over absorbed fixed production overhead costs [actual costs are less than the allocated costs] is recognised as gains.

Illustrative Example 6.9: Budget costs

Budgeted costs:	
Variable direct costs [materials & labour] per unit	CU6.80
Production overheads: Direct variable costs per unit	CU1.60
Production overheads: Fixed costs (budgeted and actual)	CU850,000
Normal production capacity (units)	200,000
Actual production capacity: Scenario 1 (units) Scenario 2 (units)	180,000 230,000

You are required to:
Calculate the cost of the finished goods for each scenario.

Suggested solution:

	Scenario 1	Scenario 2
	CU	CU
Allocated fixed production cost per unit [CU850,000 / 200,000]	4.25	42.25
Variable costs [materials & labour] [180,000 x CU6.80] & [230,000 x CU6.80]	1,224,000	1,564,000
Production overheads: Variable costs [180,000 x CU1.60] & [230,000 x CU1.60]	288,000	368,000
Production overheads: Fixed costs [180,000 x CU4.25] & [230,000 x CU4.25]	765,000	977,500
Cost of inventories – finished goods [CU1,224,000 + CU288,000 + CU765,000] & [CU1,564,000 + CU368,000 + CU977,500]	2,277,000	2,909,500
Cost per unit [CU2,277,000 / 180,000] & [CU2,909,500 / 230,000]	12.65	12.65

Unallocated – expense/Over-allocated – gain [(200,000 – 180,000) x CU4.25] & [(230,000 – 200,000) x CU4.25]	85,000	(127,500)
Cost of finished goods before adjustment	2,277,000	2,909,500
Adjustment to inventories [Over-allocated]	0	(127,500)
Cost of finished goods	2,277,000	2,782,000

6.5.3 Joint products and by-products

When the production process produces more than one product or joint and by-products and the raw materials and conversion costs are not separately identifiable then the cost of goods manufactured [finished goods] consists of:
(a) an allocation of the joint costs; and
(b) further direct costs incurred to complete the specific products.

The joint costs can be allocated between the products in terms of a rational and consistent basis such as the relative sales value of the products at the stage the separate products become identifiable or on completion of the production process.

If costs attributable to the by-products are immaterial, inventory shall be measured at the selling price less costs to complete and sell the product which can be set-off against the cost of the principle product (s13.10 and IAS 2 P.14).

Illustrative Example 6.10: By-product

By-product	CU
Joint cost [Main product and by-product but by-product's cost is immaterial]	460,000
Separate conversion costs: Main product	90,000
: By-product	6,000
Selling price: Main product	980,000
: By-product	22,000

You are required to:
Determine the cost of the products.

Suggested solution:

	CU
By-product: Selling price	22,000
: Separate conversion costs	(6,000)
: Cost of inventory [Net selling price]	16,000
Joint cost	460,000
Less: Cost of by-product [net selling price]	(16,000)
Add: Separate conversion cost – main product	90,000
Cost of inventory – main product	534,000

If the joint products are material, namely, the costs are significant and products require further conversion in order to make it ready for sale, then the joint costs must be allocated based a method that is appropriate to reflect the fair value of the joint products.

Illustrative Example 6.11: Joint products

Joint products	Product A	Product B
Further/separate costs	CU290,000	CU190,000
Units produced	150,000	85,000
Selling price [completed units]	CU100.00	CU75.00
Joint costs		CU960,000

Suggested solution:

Production schedule:	Product A	Product B
	CU	CU
Sales value [150,000 x CU100] & [85,000 x CU75]	15,000,000	6,375,000
Sales value rate – considered to be the most appropriate to allocate the joint costs [CU15,000,000 / CU21,375,000] & [CU6,375,000CU /21,375,000]	70%	30%
Joint costs allocated [CU960,000 x 70%] [CU960,000 x 30%]	672,000	288,000
Separate costs	290,000	190,000
Cost of inventories	962,000	478,000

6.6   COST OF INVENTORIES OF A SERVICE PROVIDER

The cost of inventories of a service provider are measured at their costs of production and consist primarily of labour costs, overhead and other costs which a directly incurred in providing the services. All other costs such as general administrative costs that are not directly related to rendering the service should be expensed as they are incurred. The cost of inventories of service providers does not include the profit margin or non-attributable overheads that are often factored into the price charged by the service provider (s13.14).

6.7   METHODS USED FOR MEASURING COST

The following techniques can be used to measure cost of inventories provided that the results approximate their cost (s13.16 and IAS 2 p.21–22):

- **purchase price:** the most recent purchase price can be used if it results in the approximate cost of inventories – this is used when an organisation, such as a retail store, purchase finished goods for resale;
- **standard cost:** standard costs is determined based on the direct material, labour and the pre-determined overhead absorption rate taking into consideration the production efficiency and capacity utilisation. The standard costs should be reviewed regularly to determine whether they are still relevant and appropriate to estimate the product cost, and if necessary, be revised taking based on the current conditions in order to ensure that they approximate the cost of the inventories. This method is usually used in a manufacturing environment with a good management accounting system. It

is important to note that the full standard costing absorption method should be used and not marginal costing; and

- **retail method:** measures the cost by reducing the sales value by the appropriate gross margin. This method is used more commonly in the clothing retail sector where accounting systems tracking the inventories apply the selling price method.

An entity is allowed to measure the cost of inventories by applying the method most appropriate for its business, namely, the standard cost method, the retail method or most recent purchase price, provided that the difference between the cost calculated and the actual cost of inventories is not material.

Illustrative Example 6.12: Retailed method

Retail method	20X9	20X8
Constant mark-up on cost	50%	50%
Estimated selling price of inventory on hand	CU300,000	CU250,000
Latest price of goods	CU222,000	
During 20X9 the price of goods increased due to the shortage of materials. The entity did not adjust its selling price to pass on the increase to customers.		

You are required to:
Determine the cost of inventories based on the retail price method.

Suggested solution:

Retail method	20X9	20X8
Constant mark-up on cost	45%	50%
	CU	**CU**
Estimated selling price of inventory on hand	324,000	270,000
Latest price of goods	219,000	
Estimated cost [CU324,000 x 100/150] & [CU270,000 x 100/150]	216,000	180,000
Cost of inventory	219,000 [1]	180,000

1. Based on the latest price. Remember that these alternative methods can only be used if they approximate cost, if they do not, they must be revised.

6.8   COST FORMULAS

Generally, there are three cost formulas that can be used to determine the cost of inventory on hand, namely, last-in-first-out (LIFO), first-in-first-out (FIFO) and the weighted average. However, in terms of the accounting standard s13 or IAS 2) an entity shall measure the cost of inventories using either FIFO or the weighted average methods. LIFO is not permitted as a method to measure the cost of inventories. An entity shall use the same method for all inventories which are similar in nature or having similar uses. It is permitted for the entity to use a different method to measure the cost of inventories with different nature or use provided the method can be justified in providing an approximation of the cost (s13.18 and IAS 2 p.25).

Illustrative Example 6.13: Cost formulas

Cost formulas	CU
07 April: Purchased [3 000 units at CU12 per unit]	36,000
11 April: Sold [1 200 units at CU20 per unit]	24,000
14 April: Purchased [4 000 units at CU15 per unit]	60,000
16 April: Sold [2 800 units at CU20 per unit]	56,000

You are required to:
Calculate the cost of the inventory on hand using FIFO and the weighted average methods.

Suggested solution:

FIFO	Units	Price	Cost
		CU	CU
07 April: Purchased [3 000 units at CU12 per unit]	3,000	12.00	36,000
11 April: Sold [1 200 units at CU20 per unit]	(1,200)	12.00	(14,400)
11 April: Balance	1,800	12.00	21,600
14 April: Purchased [4 000 units at CU15 per unit]	4,000	15.00	60,000
14 April: Balance	5,800		81,600

16 April: Sold [2 800 units at CU20 per unit]	(1,800)	12.00	(21,600)
	(1,000)	15.00	(15,000)
16 April: Balance	3,000	15.00	45,000
Weighted Average	**Units**	**Price**	**Cost**
		CU	**CU**
07 April: Purchased [3 000 units at CU12 per unit]	3,000	12.00	36,000
11 April: Sold [1 200 units at CU20 per unit]	(1,200)	12.00	(14,400)
11 April: Balance	1,800	12.00	21,600
14 April: Purchased [4 000 units at CU15 per unit]	4,000	15.00	60,000
14 April: Balance	5,800	14.07	81,600
16 April: Sold [2 800 units at CU20 per unit]	(2,800)	14.07	(39,396)
16 April: Balance	3,000	14.07	42,204

An entity shall measure the cost of inventories that are not ordinarily inter-changeable, and goods or services produced and segregated for specific projects by using specific identification of their individual costs (s13.17 and IAS 2 p.23).

When determining whether specific identification should be used when valuing inventory, management needs to apply its professional judgment to determine whether the items of inventory are inter-changeable without making any difference. If the items of inventory are homogenous or indistinguishable from one another, the specific identification method would be inappropriate to use. The specific identification method is an appropriate treatment for items such as materials which are purchased for a specific project, i.e. the materials cannot be used for general purposes in the operating cycle.

6.9 INVENTORY CONTROL SYSTEMS

Inventory management, planning and control are important to businesses to mitigate risks especially the risk associated with misappropriation and fraud associated with inventory. Poor inventory management and systems of internal control may also result in the entity losing sales and thereby customers due to the

entity being out of stock. Furthermore, it is important for entities to monitor inventory levels as it has financing, cash flow and other cost implications.
Depending on the level of inventory and business risk coupled with the type of accounting system, the entity may use one of the following inventory methods:

- **perpetual system:** the perpetual system is often referred to as "a real-time system" of recording inventories as it tracks the movement of inventories with every transaction. The perpetual inventory system provides a continuous record of the "theoretical" balances of inventories on hand. The perpetual system for recording inventories allows for the reconciliation between the accounting records and the inventory management system. The perpetual system for recording inventories recognizes the inventories as assets at the date of purchase or produced and cost of sales as the goods are sold;
- **periodic system:** the periodic system of recording inventories does not keep track of the movement in inventories on a continuous basis. The quantity of inventories is determined periodically when physical inventory counts are conducted. The periodic system of recording inventories recognizes the inventories acquired as expenses at the transaction date via the Purchases account; and the cost of goods sold is only determined after the physical inventory count is performed. The inventories on hand are recognized as assets and depend on the physical inventory count which is used as the closing stock balance.

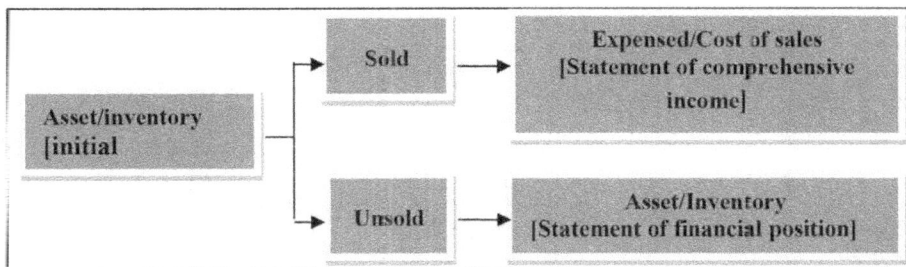

Figure 6.3 Illustration of the perpetual accounting system:

When inventories are sold the carrying amount should be recognised as expenses [cost of goods sold] at the date the revenue transaction is recognised [perpetual method] or in the end of the reporting period [periodic method]. (s23.20 and IAS 2 p.34)

Illustrative Example 6.14: Perpetual vs periodic methods

Perpetual vs periodic methods	CU
12 March: Purchased [30,000 units at CU20.00 per unit]	600,000
21 March: Sold [10,000 units at CU45.00 per unit]	450,000
25 March: Sold [8,000 units at CU50.00 per unit]	400,000

You are required to:
Record the above transactions using the (i) perpetual and (ii) periodic methods.

Suggested solution:

	Perpetual method		Periodic method	
	Debit	Credit	Debit	Credit
	CU	CU	CU	CU
12 Mar: Inventory	600,000			
Purchases			600,000	
Bank/Creditor		600,000		600,000
[Purchase of goods for resale]				
21 Mar: Bank/Debtors	450,000		450,000	
Revenue		450,000		450,000
[Recognition of revenue from sale of goods]				
21 Mar: Cost of sales [8,000 x CU15]	200,000			
Inventory		200,000		
[Recognition of the cost of the goods sold as an expense]				
25 Mar: Bank/Debtors	400,000		400,000	
Revenue		400,000		400,000
[Recognition of revenue from sale of goods]				

25 Mar: Cost of sales [7,000 x CU15]	160,000			
Inventory		160,000		
[Recognition of the cost of the goods sold as an expense]				
31 Mar: Inventory [(20,000 – 10,000 – 8,000) x CU20]			240,000	
Profit or Loss [C.O.S]				240,000
[Recognising cost of inventory on hand]				

Any differences between the physical inventory count and the accounting records under the perpetual method should be recognized as a valuation loss, viz. it represents a loss results from misappropriation or theft of goods.

6.10   MEASURE OF INVENTORIES

Inventories shall be measured at the lower of cost or the net realisable value (estimated selling price less cost to complete or sell) (s13.4 and IAS 2 p.9 (IAS 2 refers to this measurement concept as net realisable value)). This implies that the carrying amounts of inventories presented in the financial statements shall represent its future economic benefits or expected net cash inflows (its recoverable amount].

s13.4 (IAS 2 p.9) requires an entity to perform an impairment test at the end of the reporting period (s13.19 and IAS 2 p.30) and is often referred to as an "internal" impairment test requirement for inventory as the selling price is entity specific (determine by management) as opposed to fair value which is market-related.

The impairment loss in respect of inventories shall be recognized immediately in profit or loss (s13.19 and IAS 2 p.34). The impairment loss for inventories is recognised as an expense via cost of goods sold. It may be argued that by recognising the impairment loss for inventories via the costs of sales may result in the gross profit margin being distorted. Thus, for the purposes of providing more useful information to the users of financial statements the impairment loss recognised should be disclosed elsewhere in the financial statements, usually as part of the note for inventory.

Illustrative Example 6.15: Impairment of inventory

Impairment of inventory	CU
Carrying amount – cost of inventory on hand	325,000
Selling price	300,000
Estimated costs to sell	5,000

You are required to:
Prepare the journal entries necessary to account for the impairment of inventory.

Suggested solution:

	CU	
Net realizable value [CU300,000 – CU5,000]	295,000	
Impairment loss [CU325,000 – CU295,000]	30,000	
	Debit	**Credit**
	CU	CU
Cost of sales – Impairment Loss	30,000	
Inventories		30,000

6.10.1 Impairment of raw materials

Raw materials are purchased with the primary intention to be used in the manufacturing process and therefore its recovery is through the sale of the finished products. Raw materials can only be impaired if an impairment loss exists in respect to the finished product. The impairment loss recognised for the finished product should first be applied to reduce the carrying amount of raw materials to its net realisable value, and any excess should be recognised as an impairment of the finished goods.

Illustrative Example 6.16: Impairment of raw material

Impairment of raw material	Cost	Replacement cost	NRV
	CU	CU	CU
Raw material	86,000	77,000	
Finished goods: Scenario 1	345,000		376,000
: Scenario 2	345,000		310,000

You are required to:

Calculate the impairment loss for raw material and finished goods separately in each of the scenarios presented.

Suggested solution:

	Scenario 1	Scenario 2
	CU	CU
Impairment loss: Raw material	Nil	5,000
Impairment loss: Finished goods	Nil	35,000

In scenario 1, the finished goods are not impaired (net realisable value is greater than its cost), therefore the raw materials cannot be impaired as its cost will be realized through the sale of the finished goods.

In scenario 2, the finished goods are impaired by CU40,000 and because of this, the raw materials, which are going to be recovered through the sale of the finished goods in which they are incorporated, is considered impaired.

6.11   SPECIAL ISSUES

6.11.1 Transfer of inventory

Items of inventory which are allocated to other assets shall be de-recognised as inventory at its carrying amount and be re-classified to the other asset. For example, items of inventory may be used in self-constructed items of property, plant and equipment. Inventories allocated to other assets shall be accounted for subsequently in accordance with the section of IFRS for SMEs (IFRS) relevant to that type of asset (s13.21 and IAS 2 p.35).

Illustrative Example 6.17: Transfer of inventory

An entity used inventory with a carrying amount of CU200,000 in the construction of a machine that will be used in its production process. The entity depreciates is machinery on a straight-line basis over an estimated useful life of five years.

You are required to:
Discuss how the amount previously recognized as inventory should be accounted for in the financial statements of the entity.

Suggested solution:
The carrying amount of the inventory shall be de-recognised as inventory and recognised as part of the cost of the machine. The cost of the machine including the cost of inventory will be depreciated over the estimated life of the machine.

An entity acquired customised parts for its machinery that are used to manufacture inventories.

You are required to:
Discuss how the customized parts should be accounted for in the financial statements of the entity.

Suggested solution:
On initial recognition, the customised parts are classified as property, part and equipment as they have no alternate use. When the parts are consumed in the production process, the carrying amount of the parts used in the production forms part of the conversion costs which are included in the cost of inventory – usually in the form of depreciation.

6.11.2 Agricultural produce

Producers of agricultural and forest products, agricultural produce after harvest, and mineral products, to the extent that they are measured at fair value less cost to sell through profit or loss cannot apply s13 – *Inventories* (s13.3(a) and IAS 2 p.2(c)).

The cost of inventory for agricultural produce on initial recognition shall be its fair value less cost to sell (s34.5 and IAS 41 p.13). Any changes in the fair value less cost to sell shall be recognised in profit and loss with a corresponding adjustment to the carrying biological assets. Once harvested, the items are measured to its fair value less costs to sell at the point of harvest (s34.5 and IFRS 41 p.13) at which point the new fair valued carrying amount becomes the cost of the items transferred to inventory. The items will be accounted for in terms of the standard on inventories (s13 – *Inventories* and IAS 2 – *Inventories*) at its lower of cost and net realisable value.

Illustrative Example 6.18: Agricultural produce

Agricultural produce	Date of harvest	Reporting period
Date of transaction/event	31 March 20X9	31 August 20X9
	CU	CU
Fair value [estimated market value]	850,000	820,000
Selling price	900,000	840,000
Cost to sell	52,000	56,000

You are required to:
Record the journal entries for the reporting period ended.
Suggested solution:

		CU	CU
31 Mar: Inventory [CU850,000 – CU52,000]		798,000	
Biological assets			798,000
[Initial recognition of agricultural produce at fair value less cost to sell]			
31 Aug: Cost of sales [P&L] [CU798,000 - (CU840,000 – CU56,000)]		14,000	
Inventory			14,000
[Account for the change in the value of inventory from cost to net realizable value]			

6.11.3 Commodity broker/trader

Brokers/traders buy or sell commodities such as coffee, grain, crude oil, etc. on behalf of others or for themselves. Brokers/traders acquire inventories for the primary purpose of making profit through selling it in future. Commodity brokers and dealers that measure their inventories at fair value less cost to sell through profit and loss shall not apply s13 – *Inventories* (s13.3(b) and IAS 2 p.3(b)).

6.12   DISCLOSURE

In terms of s13.22 (IAS 2 p.36), an entity shall disclose the following:
(a) the accounting policy adopted in measuring inventories including the cost measurement method;
(b) the total carrying amounts of inventories and the carrying amount of each classification of inventory;
(c) the amount of inventory recognised as an expense during the reporting period, namely, cost of sales;
(d) impairment losses recognised or reversed in profit or loss; and
(e) the total carrying amounts of inventories pledged as security for liabilities.

IAS 2 p.36 requires the following disclosures in addition to those above:
(a) the carrying amounts of inventories carried at fair value less costs to sell; and
(b) the circumstances or events that lead to the reversal of a write-down of inventories.

6.13   PHYSICAL INVENTORY COUNT

The physical inventory count is an assurance test about the existence of the inventories on hand at a specific date, usually at the reporting date. Under the perpetual method (where the inventory balance is theoretically updated continuously), a physical inventory count confirms the theoretical balance and identifies discrepancies, if any, between the physical inventory on hand and the accounting records. The discrepancies usually represented by a shortfall in the physical inventory on hand and shall be recognised as an adjustment to the accounting records in the form of an inventory loss or write-off. However, under the periodic inventory system, the physical inventory count is used to identify the quantity and value of the inventory on hand (remember with this method, the inventory on hand is only identified by the inventory count as the accounting records are not updated continuously).

The following summarises which goods shall be included in the physical inventory count:

Table 6.1 Summary of physical goods included in inventory

Transaction type	Discussion
Free on Board (FOB)	Buyer assumes the risk (and pays for the transportation and insurance) of the item once it is

	placed on board the transporting vessel – this is recognized as goods in transit for which a corresponding liability must be recognized
Cost, Insurance and Freight (CIF)	Buyer assumes the risk of the item once it is placed on board the transporting vessel (but the seller pays for transportation and insurance to destination port) - this is recognized as goods in transit for which a corresponding liability must be recognized.
Delivery at Terminal (DAT)	Risk passes to buyer when the seller delivers and unloads at the identified terminal – seller cannot recognize the inventory while it is being transported, but once it is delivered at customs, it must be recognized
Sales with buyback options	Seller's inventory until the date the option expires – this implies that the goods are sold in terms of a conditional agreement and can only be recognized as inventory when the conditions are fulfilled
Sales on instalments	Buyer's inventory if the collectability of the debt can be estimated reliably – an instalment sales agreement is a financial option and does not affect the recognition of the goods are inventory
Consignment goods held on buyer's premises	Seller's inventory – the organization acts as an agent on behalf of the principal therefore the goods represents inventory to the principal

SELF-ASSESSMENT
Multiple choice questions: Testing the principles of accounting for inventories

1.   Inventory includes:

(a) raw material	
(b) property held for rental income	
(c) investment in a company	
(d) all of the above	

2.   Inventory is purchased for 114,000 (including VAT). The inventory should be initially recognized at:

(a) 114,000	
(b) 98,040	
(c) 100,000	
(d) 14,000	

3. Which of the following are _not_ appropriate cost formulas?:

(a) First-in-first-out (FIFO)	
(b) Weighted average	
(c) Retail method	
(d) Last-in-first-out (LIFO)	

4. Raw material has a historical cost of 100,000 and a replacement cost of 90,000 while finished goods have a historical cost of 250,000 and a selling price less costs to complete and sell of 300,000. The raw material must be adjusted by:

(a) 0	
(b) 10,000	
(c) 50,000	
(d) None of the above.	

5. Inventories must be recognized at the:

(a) Lower of cost and estimated selling price less costs to complete and sell	
(b) Higher of cost and estimated selling price less costs to complete and sell	
(c) Always at cost	
(d) Always at estimated selling price less costs to complete and sell	

6.   Car Ltd purchased inventories for 100,000 (excluding VAT and transport costs). The transport costs from the supplier to the place where it is available for sale amounted to 10,000. Transport costs from Car Ltd to its customer (the person to whom Car Limited was going to sell the inventory to) amounted to 5,000. The cost of inventory is:

(a) 100,000	
(b) 105,000	
(c) 110,000	
(d) 115,000	

7.   Fixed production overheads amount to 100,000. Actual production was 100,000 units while budgeted production was 80,000. The fixed production overhead allocated each unit produced amounted to:

(a) 1.25	
(b) 1.00	
(c) 0.80	
(d) None of the above	

8.   IFRS for SMEs requires you to allocate the following costs to inventory:

(a) Fixed production costs only	
(b) Variable costs only	
(c) (a) and (b)	
(d) None of the above	

9.   Fixed production overheads amount to 100,000. Actual production was 100,000 units while budgeted production was 125,000. The fixed production overhead allocated each unit produced amounted to:

(a) 1.25	
(b) 1.00	
(c) 0.80	
(d) None of the above	

10.   The following properties will be considered inventory:

(a) Building used as a warehouse by the entity	
(b) Building used as a production facility by the entity	
(c) Building held for sale by a property dealer	
(d) None of the above	

Practical questions:
Application of principles to business scenarios

QUESTION 1

Objective: Initial recognition of inventory with discounts and VAT implications

CAPER (PTY) LTD purchased a consignment of inventory for delivery on 1 March 20x7. The inventory had a cost of CU1,150,000 (including VAT). CAPER (PTY) LTD paid CU50,000 (to a non-VAT vendor) on transporting the inventory to its premises and CU20,000 on advertising the inventory for sale to its customers. The supplier granted CAPER (PTY) LTD a trade discount of 5% of the cost of the goods sold and offered CAPER (PTY) LTD a further 2% discount if the outstanding balance due after the trade discount is settled within ten days from the date of purchase. CAPER (PTY) LTD considers it probable that they will settle the amount due within the ten day period and thereby qualify to receive the settlement discount as well.

You are required to:
Prepare the journal entry necessary to account for the purchase of the inventory and the related amounts provided in the scenario on 1 March 20X7.

QUESTION 2

Objective: Recognition, measurement and valuation of inventory transactions in terms of the provisions of the accounting standards relating to inventory

The manufacturing department of KABAAL (PTY) LTD uses marginal costing methods in determining the unit costs of the products. The accounting department prepares the inventory records using a costing method based on materials purchased and disregards manufacturing overhead costs in the calculations.

The following was an extract from the drafted financial statements prepared by Mr. Mehmood:
"Accounting Policies: Inventory – inventory consists of raw materials, work-in-progress and finished goods which are measured at the marginal costing method and cost excluding production overheads using the Last-in-first-out method."

You are required to:

(a) Provide a critique of the accounting policy for inventory included in the financial statements by Mr. Mehmood in terms of the IFRS for SMEs.

(b) Discuss whether the company can adopt marginal costing as a basis of measurement of inventory in the financial statements in order to comply with the accounting standards.

(c) Discuss the consequences and financial implications of using the marginal costing method of valuing inventory on the financial performance and financial position of the business.

QUESTION 3

Objective: Recognition and measurement of impairment of inventory in terms of the provisions of the accounting standards relating to inventory

CHADRIN (PTY) LTD is a business entity engaged in the manufacture of commercial and household health food products which are distributed nationally through a number of retail outlets.

At 28 February 20X6 100,000 units of raw materials had a cost and carrying amount of CU220,000 while its recoverable amount was estimated to be CU180,000. At the same date the finished goods had a total cost and carrying amount of CU1,350,000. 100,000 Units of raw material were used to produce the finished goods.

Due to the increased level of competition in the market, management estimated that the goods can be sold for CU1,200,000 with associated selling costs of CU12,000. However, market conditions changed during the year ended 28 February 20X7 so that the finished goods were expected to be sold for CU1,580,000. None of the inventory on hand at 28 February 20X6 were sold at 28 February 20X7.

The accountant recognised an impairment loss for raw materials of CU40,000 and zero for finished goods at 28 February 20X6.

You are required to:

(a) Discuss whether the accountant treated the impairment of materials and finished goods in compliance with IFRS for SMEs at 28 February 20X6.

(b) Record the journal entries to correctly recognise the transactions relating to impairments for the reporting period ended 28 February 20X6 and 28 February 20X7 in compliance with IFRS for SMEs.

CHAPTER 7
INTANGIBLE ASSETS OTHER THAN GOODWILL

ILLUSTRATIVE DISCLOSURE [EXTRACT]

IFRS ref		Notes	20X2	20X1	
			CU'000	CU'000	
	Non-current assets				
S4.2(g) & IAS 1 p.54	Intangible assets	14	240,000	190,000	

IFRS ref			20X2	20X1	
			CU'000	CU'000	
S5.11 & IAS 1 p.99	**Operating expenses**		24,000	19,000	

S18.27 & IAS 38 p.121	1	**Accounting policies**			
		The entity has the following intangible assets:		**Useful life**	**Amortisation method**
		- Software		3 years	Straight-line
		- Licences		5 years	Reducing balance
		- Other rights		4 years	Units of production

S18.27(d) & IAS 1 p.104	5	Other operating expenses		20X2	20X1
		Other operating expenses include the following:		CU	CU
		- Amortisation of intangible assets		12,000	11,000
S18.29 & IAS 38 p.126		- Expenditure on research and development which was recognised in profit or loss		2,400	1,200
S18.27(c) & (e) IAS 38 p.118	14	**Intangible assets:**		**20X2**	
				CU	
		Gross carrying amount at beginning of year		200,000	
		Accumulated amortisation		(10,000)	
		Carrying amount		**190,000**	
		Additions		90,000	
		Disposals		(20,000)	
		Acquisitions through business combinations		30,000	
		Amortisation		(50,000)	
		Gross carrying amount at end of year		300,000	
		Accumulated amortistation		(60,000)	
		Carrying amount		**240,000**	
S18.28 & IAS 38 p.122		Included in the carrying amount of intangible assets at year-end is the company's software which has a carrying amount of CU180,000 and an estimated remaining useful life of two years.			

7.1 INTRODUCTION

An asset is defined, in the framework, as a resource which is controlled by the entity as a result of a past event and from which future economic benefits are expected to flow. It is interesting to note that the definition is not limited to physical or tangible assets. For instance, rights in a contract might be intangible (not tangible), but might well meet the definition of an asset. The challenge is that intangible assets are often difficult to identify as standalone assets as they cannot always be easily separated from the entity. For example, it is plain to see that the administration building is a separate asset as it stands on its own, but it is not always easy to identify the right to operate in a certain area from the rest of the operations of the entity. For this reason, IFRS for SMEs addresses these concerns with direct guidance.

7.2 LEARNING OUTCOMES

Upon completion of this unit you should know the financial reporting requirements for accounting for intangible assets other than goodwill in accordance with the IFRS for SMEs. In particular, you should be able to:
(a) identify intangible assets that qualify for recognition under this section;
(b) recognise and measure intangible assets other than goodwill at initial recognition;
(c) account for the subsequent measurement of intangible assets other than goodwill; and
(d) present and disclose intangible assets other than goodwill in the financial statements.

7.3 DEFINITIONS

The definitions for the important concepts and terms used in IFRS for SMEs are found in Appendix B – *Glossary of terms* in IFRS for SMEs. Some important definitions relating to intangible assets, over which we need to gain a thorough command before we can understand the accounting for intangible assets, include the following:

- **Intangible asset:** An identifiable non-monetary asset without physical substance

- **Goodwill:** Future economic benefits arising from assets that are not capable of being individually identified and separately recognised

- **Inventory:** Assets:
  (a) held for sale in the ordinary course of business;
  (b) in the process of production for such sale; or
  (c) in the form of material or supplies to be consumed in the production process or in the rendering of services.

7.4 SCOPE AND OBJECTIVES

Section 18 – *Intangible assets other than goodwill* must be applied to accounting for all intangible assets other than goodwill and those intangible assets held for sale in the ordinary course of business, which should be classified as inventory, financial assets, mineral rights and mineral reserves (s18.1).

7.5 CLASSIFICATION

As the definition states, an intangible asset is:
(a) identifiable: which means that it can be separately identified as an asset, separate from other assets and separate from the rest of the operations of the entity. In order for an intangible asset to be identifiable and separable, the asset must be able to be sold, transferred, licensed, rented or exchanged, individually or together with a related contract, asset or liability, or arises from contractual or other legal rights.
(b) non-monetary: which implies that it is not receivable in a fixed or determinable amount of money;
(c) an asset: which implies that all intangible assets are firstly assets and therefore have to meet the definition of asset in the framework;
(d) without physical substance: which means that intangible assets are assets other than those with physical substance, such as property, plant and equipment.

Illustrative Example 7.1: Classification of intangible assets

The entity has the following balances in its trial balance: accounts receivable, licence agreement, patent, accounts payable, cash, land, machinery.

Item:	Intangible asset?
Accounts receivable	
License agreement	
Patent	
Accounts payable	
Cash	
Land	
Machinery	

You are required to:
Using the template below, indicate whether or not each item is an intangible asset.

Suggested solution:

Item	Intangible asset?
Accounts receivable	No (it represents a monetary asset)
Licence agreement	Yes
Patent	Yes
Accounts payable	No (it is not an asset)
Cash	No (it represents a monetary asset)
Land	No (it is tangible)
Machinery	No (it is tangible)

7.6 INITIAL RECOGNTION

7.6.1 Recognition criteria

The entity must apply the recognition criteria in s18.4 (IAS 38 p.21) (which are aligned to the recognition criteria in the framework) to determine whether an intangible asset should be recognised. The entity should recognise an intangible asset if:

(a) it is probable that the future economic benefits associated with the asset will flow to the entity – which is always considered satisfied for an intangible asset which is separately acquired (s18.7);

(b) the cost or value of the asset can be measured reliably; and

(c) the asset does not result from expenditure incurred internally on an intangible item, unless it forms part of the cost of another asset that meets the criteria to be recognised (*not included as a requirement in IAS 38 p.21*).

The past expenditure on an intangible asset that was expensed must never be capitalised.

Full IFRS requirements
The requirements in IFRS for SMEs for internally generated intangible assets differ substantially to full IFRS. Full IFRS also emphasises that any intangible asset must be separable from the business. For this reason, an entity may never recognise internally generated goodwill. Once the internally generated asset that is to be produced is considered separable, IAS 38 splits the expenditure on internally generated intangible assets into two categories (IAS 38 p.52):
(a) a research phase; and
(b) a development phase. →

Important definitions (IAS 38 p.8):

Research: *This is original and planned investigation undertaken with the prospect of gaining new scientific or technical knowledge and understanding.*
Development: *This is the application of research findings or other knowledge to a plan or design for the production of new or substantially improved materials, devices, products, processes, systems or services before the start of commercial production or use.*

Research is the phase wherein the knowledge regarding the intangible asset and the related markets in which its output can be used or sold is gathered. Development, on the other hand, refers to the application of knowledge to a plan or design to produce the intangible asset.

All expenditure in the research phase must be expensed. Expenditure in the development phase can be capitalised if the entity can show (IAS 38 p.57):
(a) the technical feasibility of completing the financial asset so that it will be available for use or sale;
(b) its intention to complete the financial asset and use or sell it;
(c) how the intangible asset will generate future economic benefits. Among other things, the entity can demonstrate the existence of a market for the output of the intangible asset or the intangible asset itself or, if it is to be used internally, the usefulness of the intangible asset;
(d) the availability of adequate technical, financial and other resources to complete the development and to use or sell the intangible assets; and
its ability to measure reliably the expenditure attributable to the intangible asset during its development.

7.6.2 Initial measurment

The entity should initially measure an intangible asset at cost (s18.9 and IAS 38 p.). Cost is considered to be comprised of all expenditure necessarily occurred in order to get the intangible asset into a condition available for its intended use (s18.10). If the intangible asset is acquired as part of a barter transaction, the cost of the intangible asset acquired is determined in the following order:
(a) the fair value of the asset given up in exchange for the intangible asset acquired;
(b) if the fair value of the asset given up in exchange for the intangible asset acquired cannot be determined, then the intangible asset acquired is measured at its fair value; and
(c) if the fair value of neither asset can be determined, then the intangible asset is measured at the carrying amount of the asset given up.

7.7   SUBSEQUENT MEASUREMENT

After initial recognition, an entity should measure an intangible asset at cost less accumulated amortisation and impairment (s18.18 and IAS 38 p.24).

IAS 38 p.72 also allows the entity to make an accounting policy decision to account for its intangible assets under the revaluation model if the fair value of the intangible asset can be referenced to an active market only.

An entity has to systematically allocate the depreciable amount of the intangible asset over its estimated useful life to its estimated residual value (s18.19 and IAS 38 p.72) and recognise the amortisation in profit or loss unless IFRS for SMEs allows it to be capitalised to another asset (s18.21 and IAS 38 p.68). Amortisation starts when the intangible asset is available for use and stops on derecognition only (s18.22). IFRS for SMEs requires an entity to consider all intangible assets to have finite useful lives. This is different to full IFRS, where IAS 38 – *Intangible assets* allows an entity to consider an intangible asset to have an indefinite useful life. A finite useful life means that the intangible asset has a foreseeable limit over which the intangible asset will produce economic benefits. An entity shall attribute a useful life of a maximum of 10 years to an intangible asset which useful life cannot be determined reliably (s18.20 (*IFRS has no such requirement)*). The useful life of such an intangible asset can be shorter, but should be based on management's estimate.

An intangible asset which is established by contract or law cannot have a useful life that is longer than the contract or period that the legal rights were granted for (including a renewal period, if the entity can show that it can renew without significant cost). If, however, the entity estimates that it will use the asset for a shorter period, the shorter period should be used (s18.19 and IAS 38 p.94).

Illustrative Example 7.2: Subsequent measurement

The company purchased a transferable licence to fish in a particular area for a period of four years. The company only plans to use the licence for three years after which it plans to sell the licence.

You are required to:
Discuss the period over which the entity will amortize the license.

Suggested solution:
The useful life of the licence is the period that the entity expects to use the asset, which in this case is three years. Even though the licence is for a four-year period, this would indicate the maximum but not actual amortisation period. The licence will therefore be amortised over a period of three years (the shorter period).

The entity should choose an amortisation method that reflects the pattern of consumption of economic benefits related to the intangible asset, but default to the straight-line method if the entity cannot determine such a method (s18.22 and IAS 38 p.97). Possible methods include the straight-line method, the reducing balance method, the sum of the digits method or the units of production method.

The intangible asset is amortised to its residual value, which should be reviewed together with its estimated useful life if indicators suggest. Any change in the estimated residual value and estimated useful life should be treated as a change in accounting estimate (s18.24 and IAS 38 p.104 *IFRS requires this review annually*). The residual value is assumed to be zero (as a default) unless (s18.23 and IAS p.100):
(a) a third party is committed to purchase the intangible asset at the end of its useful life;
(b) there is an active market for the asset and:
  (i) residual value can be determined with reference to that market; and
  (ii) it is probable that such a market will exist at the end of the asset's useful life.

Illustrative Example 7.3: Subsequent measurement

The company purchased software which it plans to use for three years. The software can be used for a longer period, but will no longer suit the needs of the company after three years. There is no active market for the software and it is unlikely that a third party will purchase the software as it will be considered outdated after the three years.

You are required to:
Discuss, giving reasons, what the residual value of the software is.

Suggested solution:
The software is considered to have a nil residual value as there is *no* evidence that:
(a) a third party is committed to purchase the intangible asset at the end of its useful life;

(b) there is an active market for the asset and:
   (i) residual value can be determined with reference to that market; and
   (ii) it is probable that such a market will exist at the end of the asset's useful life.

7.8   PRESENTATION AND DISCLOSURE

7.8.1   Presentation

The presentation requirements for intangible assets follow the general presentation requirements for assets. In particular, s4.2(g) requires that the entity include a line item for intangible assets in its statement of financial position (if the entity has intangible assets). The related amortisation expense recognised should be recognised in the statement of profit or loss and guided by whether the entity prepares its income statement (or statement of comprehensive income) based on the analysis of expenses by their nature or function (s5.11).

7.8.2   Disclosure

7.8.2.1   General disclosures

It should be noted that IFRS has additional disclosure requirements, not listed here, for intangible assets with indefinite useful lives and accounted for under the revaluation model.

The entity should disclose the following for each class of intangible asset (s18.27 and IAS 38 p.118):
(a) the useful lives or amortisation rates used;
(b) the amortisation methods used;
(c) the gross carrying amount and any accumulated amortisation at the beginning and the end of the reporting period;
(d) the line items in the statement of comprehensive income (income statement) where the line items are included;
(e) a reconciliation at the beginning and end of the reporting period showing separately:
   (i)   additions;
   (ii)   disposals;
   (iii)   acquisitions through business combinations;
   (iv)   amortisation;
   (v)   impairment losses; and
   (vi)   other changes.

An entity must also disclose (s18.28 and IAS 38 p.122):

(a) a description of the carrying amount and remaining amortisation period of any individual intangible asset that is material to the entity's financial statements;

(b) for intangible assets acquired by way of a government grant and initially recognised at fair value:
    (i)   the fair value initially recognised for these assets; and
    (ii) their carrying amounts.

(c) the existence and carrying amounts of intangible assets to which the entity has restricted title or that are pledged as security for liabilities; and

(d) the amount of contractual commitments for the acquisition of intangible assets.

An entity shall disclose the aggregate amount of research and development expenditure recognised as an expense during the period (ie the amount of expenditure incurred internally on research and development that has not been capitalised) (s18.29 and IAS 38 p.126).

1. The following item is classified as an intangible asset:

(a) loans payable	
(b) loans receivable	
(c) trademark	
(d) building	

2. The following is necessary in considering whether an intangible asset is identifiable:

(a) it is internally generated	
(b) it is separable	
(c) it is tangible	
(d) it has value	

3. The following is the definition of an intangible asset:

(a) a non-monetary asset without physical substance	
(b) an identifiable asset that cannot be seen	
(c) a non-monetary asset with physical substance	
(d) an identifiable non-monetary asset without physical substance	

4. The following recognition criteria must be present (among others) in order to recognise an intangible asset:

(a) it must have a cost or value that is measurable	
(b) it must be valuable	
(c) it must be possible to generate economic benefits with the asset	
(d) it must be held in good faith	

5. An intangible asset obtained in a barter transaction is recognised at an amount equal to:

(a) the fair value of the asset given up in exchange for the intangible asset	
(b) the original cost of the asset given up	
(c) the fair value of the intangible asset acquired at all times	
(d) the carrying amount of the asset given up in exchange for the intangible asset	

6. Intangible assets are initially recognised at:

(a) replacement cost	
(b) historical cost including transaction costs	
(c) fair value	
(d) net realisable value	

7. An intangible asset is purchased for CU50,000 (excluding VAT), on which the entity paid an additional CU7,500 in VAT and CU2,500 in other transaction costs. The initial cost of the intangible is:

(a) CU60,000	
(b) CU57,500	
(c) CU50,000	
(d) CU52,500	

8. The residual value of an intangible asset is considered to be which default amount:

(a) CU100	
(b) CU250	
(c) CU50	
(d) CU0	

9. An intangible asset which is created from legal rights for a set period of time will have the following useful life:

(a) always the period over which the legal rights are granted	
(b) the shorter of the period over which the legal rights have been granted or the period that the entity intends using the intangible asset	
(c) always the period over which the entity intends using the intangible asset	
(d) none of the above	

10. Where the entity cannot determine the intangible asset's useful life without undue cost, the following will be deemed to be its maximum useful life:

(a) 0 years	
(b) 1 year	
(c) 10 years	
(d) 5 years	

Practical questions:
Application of principles to business scenarios

QUESTION 1

The following assets have been identified in the accounting records of TTG (Pty) Ltd:

Asset
Equipment
Inventory
Patent
Vehicles
Software
Hardware
Rights to broadcast sports events

You are required to:
Indicate which of the listed assets are classified as intangible assets or not. If you conclude that an asset should *NOT* be classified as an intangible asset, provide a reason.

QUESTION 2

Procurement (Pty) Ltd purchased a fishing licence on 01 January 20X7 which allows it to fish in the coastal waters of the country in which the entity is domiciled for a period of five years. The licence allows the entity to catch an unlimited amount of fish in that period. The licence was immediately available for use, but the entity only commenced using the licence from 01 February 20X7. The entity paid CU100,000 for the licence after incurring legal costs of CU10,000 in obtaining the licence. The company only expects to use the licence for four of the five years, after which it plans on selling the licence for CU40,000. The entity has not yet found a buyer for the licence who is willing to purchase the licence at the end of the four-year period. The company uses the straight-line method to amortise the licence.

You are required to:
Calculate the amortisation expense for the licence for the year ended 31 December 20X7.

QUESTION 3

Rafael (Pty) Ltd purchased the exclusive rights to broadcast tennis matches for an international tennis tournament in its student village only. The acquisition involved Rafael (Pty) Ltd exchanging a plant which it owned for the broadcasting rights. The plant had a cost of CU250,000 and a carrying amount of CU160,000. The plant had a fair value of CU100,000. The exclusive broadcasting rights had a fair value of CU120,000.

You are required to:
Record the journal entries to account for the exchange transaction and the acquisition of the broadcasting rights.

CHAPTER 8
IMPAIRMENT OF ASSETS

The choice between fair value and historical cost accounting reflects the possible conflict between relevance and reliability of financial statements; is the recognition of impairment losses the compromise position?

8.1 INTRODUCTION

The carrying amount of assets must represent the future economic benefits that the assets have the potential to contribute, directly or indirectly, to the cash flows of the entity through use or disposal (s2.17 and Conceptual Framework (CF) p.4.8). As IFRS for SMEs incorporates the concept of prudence, the carrying amount of assets should represent, at most, the future economic benefits expected from their use, disposal or a combination of use and disposal. This implies that the carrying amount of an asset must be measured at the most at the asset's estimated future economic benefits that are considered probable to flow to the entity – the accountant must apply professional scepticism to determine such values.

To improve the quality and reliability of the financial statements, the carrying amount of the assets presented in the statements of financial position should represent the probable future economic benefits that will flow to an entity through their use/disposal, based on the current economic conditions.

8.2 LEARNING OUTCOMES

Upon completion of this unit, you should know the financial reporting requirements for intangible assets other than goodwill in accordance with the IFRS for SMEs. In particular, you should be able to:
(a) explain the concept of impairment of assets;
(b) identify the circumstances that may result in the impairment of assets;
(c) determine the recoverable amount of an asset;
(d) recognise, measure and account for impairment losses in the financial statements;
(e) recognise, measure and account for the reversal of impairment losses in the financial statements; and
(f) account for the effects that impairment losses have on the depreciation charge of assets.

8.3 DEFINITIONS

The definitions for the important concepts and terms used in IFRS for SMEs, are found in Appendix B – Glossary of terms in IFRS for SMEs. Some important definitions relating to impairment of assets include the following:

- **Impairment loss:** Occurs when the carrying amount of an asset exceeds its recoverable amount

- **Recoverable amount:** The higher of an asset's fair value less cost to sell and its value in use (full IFRS: costs of disposal)

- **Fair value less cost to sell:** The amount obtainable from the sale of an asset in an arm's length transaction between knowledgeable and willing parties, less the cost to sell (full IFRS: reference should be made to IFRS 13 to determine an asset's fair value)

- **Value in use:** The present value of the future cash flows expected to be derived from the asset

- **Cash generating unit:** The smallest identifiable group of assets that generates cash inflows that are largely independent of the cash inflows from other assets or group of assets

8.4 SCOPE AND OBJECTIVE

The objective of this section of the standard is to prescribe procedures for the recognition and measurement of the impairment of all assets other than (s27.1 & IAS 36 p.2):
(a) deferred tax assets (s29 and IAS 12);
(b) assets arising from employee benefits (s28 and IAS 19);
(c) financial assets (s11 or s12 and IFRS 9);
(d) investment property measured at fair value (s16 and IAS 40);
(e) biological assets related to agricultural activities at fair value less estimated cost to sell (s34 and IAS 41); and
(f) full IFRS scopes out IAS 2 – *Inventories* from IAS 36, while IFRS for SMEs includes inventories within its scope, but has a separate section dedicated to the impairment of inventories (s27.2–3).

The impairment standard excludes the items listed above not because they are not subject to impairment testing of one kind or another, but primarily because the concept of impairment is incorporated into the relevant standard. For example, for investment property measured at fair value, if the carrying amount is greater than the recoverable amount or fair value, then the loss is recognised as a fair value loss rather than as an impairment loss.

8.5   IMPAIRMENT OF ASSETS

8.5.1   Classification

Impairment testing and the recognition of impairment losses applies to all assets, but the standard is only applicable to those assets which are measured using the historical cost or a variation thereof. Assets which are measured using a model other than the historical cost model, such as the fair value model (eg investment property) and assets which have their own impairment model, such as inventories (lower of cost or selling price less costs to complete and sell), incorporate the impairment through their valuation.

8.5.1.1   Assessing the assets for impairment

An entity shall assess at each reporting date whether there is any indication that an asset may be impaired (s21.7 and IAS 36 p.9). If any such indication exists, then management must apply their minds to determine if there is an impairment loss based on the estimated recoverable amount. If there is no indication of impairment, it is not necessary to estimate the recoverable amount.

However, for purposes of full IFRS, an entity has to conduct annual impairment tests on intangible assets with an indefinite useful life or that are not yet available for use, but may test these intangible assets for impairment any time during the reporting period, provided the tests are performed at the same time every reporting period. Furthermore, different intangible assets may be tested for impairment at different times.

8.5.1.2   Indicators of impairment

In assessing whether there is any indication that an asset is impaired, an entity shall consider, as a minimum, the following indicators (s27.0 and IAS 36 p.12):

External sources of information
The following are external factors that indicate that the asset may be impaired:
(a)   the market value has declined more than expected as a result of the passage of time or normal use (usually cause by obsolescence);
(b)   significant changes in technology, market, economic or legal environment have occurred or will occur in future which have had or may have an adverse effect on the entity, or the market to which the asset is dedicated (usually a decline in the economic use to the business);

(c) market interest rates or market rates of return on investments have increased, and those increases are likely to have a material effect on the discount rate used in calculating an asset's value in use and decrease the asset's fair value less cost to sell (decrease in the estimated value of the asset); and

(d) the carrying amount of the net assets of the entity is more than the estimated fair value of the entity as a whole (net asset value of the business is inflated).

Internal sources of information

The following are internal factors that indicate that the asset may be impaired:

(a) evidence is available of obsolescence or physical damage of an asset;

(b) significant changes to the extent to which or the manner in which an asset is used or expected to be used or which are expected to occur in future which had or may in future have an adverse effect on the entity. These changes include the asset becoming idle, plans to discontinue or restructure the operations to which an asset belongs, plans to dispose of an asset before the previously expected date, and re-assessing the useful life of an asset as finite rather than indefinite; and

(c) evidence is available from internal reports that indicates that the economic performance of an asset is, or will be, worse than expected.

8.5.2   Measurement

8.5.2.1   Measuring the recoverable amount

The recoverable amount of an asset or cash-generating unit is measured at the higher of the fair value less cost to sell (full IFRS: costs of disposal) and the value in use (s27.11 and IAS 36 p.6). If there is no indication that the value in use materially exceeds the fair value less cost to sell, the asset's fair value less cost to sell (full IFRS: costs of disposal) may be used as the recoverable amount, and there is no need to estimate the value in use (s27.13 and IAS 36 p.13).

Fair value less cost to sell

The fair value less cost to sell is the amount obtainable from the sale of an asset in an arm's length transaction between knowledgeable and willing parties less the costs of disposal (s27.14 and IAS 36 p.28). The fair value less cost to sell of an asset is represented by the price in a binding sale agreement in an arm's length transaction or a market price in an active market.

The price in a sale agreement between related parties may not provide the true fair value less cost to sell of the asset. If there is no binding sale agreement or active market for the asset, the fair value less cost to sell is determined based on the best information available to reflect the amount that an entity can obtain at the reporting date from the disposal of the asset in an arm's length transaction. The outcome of recent transactions for similar assets within the same industry may be used as a guide when determining the fair value less cost to sell.

For purposes of full IFRS, you have to refer to IFRS 13 – Fair value measurement *to determine fair value.*

Value in use

The value in use can be determined by using valuation techniques which are appropriate for the nature and type of assets, such as the net present value of the future cash flows expected to be derived from the use of the asset in its intended purpose (s27.15 and IAS 36 p.31).

The following elements shall be reflected in the calculation of the asset's value in use (s27.16 and IAS 36 p.30):
(a) an estimate of future net cash flows from the use of the asset;
(b) expectations about possible variations in the amounts or timing of those future cash flows – probability of cash flows (expected value of cash flows);
(c) the time value of money, represented by the current market risk-free rate of interest;
(d) the price for bearing uncertainty inherent in the asset – business/financial risks; and
(e) other factors, such as illiquidity, that market participants would reflect in pricing the future cash flows the entity expects to derive from the asset.

The discount rate used in the present value calculation shall be the pre-tax rate that reflects current market assessment of (i) the time value of money (effects of inflation), and (ii) the risk specific to the asset for which the future cash flow estimates have not been adjusted (s27.10 and IAS 36 p.55).

Estimating cash flows

The estimated future cash flows should include (s27.17 and IAS 36 p.39):
(a) projections of cash inflows from the continuing use of the asset;
(b) projections of cash outflows that are necessarily incurred to generate the inflows from continuing use of the asset, and can be directly attributed, or allocated on a reasonable and consistent basis, to the asset; and
(c) the net cash flows, if any, expected to be received or paid for the disposal of the asset at the end of its useful life in an arm's length transaction between knowledgeable and willing parties.

The estimates must reflect the cash flows from the use of the asset in its current condition and shall exclude (s27.19 and IAS 36 p.44 & 50):
(a) cash flows arising from future restructuring of the operations which have not yet been committed to;
(b) improvement to enhance the capacity/performance of the asset;
(c) cash flows from financing activities; and
(d) cash flows and benefits from tax regulations.

The entity may use any recent financial budgets or forecasts available to estimate the cash flows expected to be derived from the asset. To estimate cash flow projections beyond the period covered by the most recent budgets or forecasts (full IFRS defines this maximum period as five years, unless a longer period can be justified) an entity may extrapolate the projections based on the budgets or forecasts using a steady or declining growth rate for subsequent periods, unless an increasing rate can be justified (s27.17 and IAS 36 p.33).

Illustrative Example 8.1: Value in use

At 30 June 20X8, machinery with a carrying amount of CU560 000 (cost of CU900 000) had an estimated selling price of CU520 000 and at the expiry of its useful life, with an estimated selling cost of CU40 000. The estimated net cash inflow of CU120 000 per annum was expected for the remaining useful life of four years for the machinery. The expected rate of return is considered to be 12%.

You are required to:
Calculate the impairment loss to be recognized in the financial statements of the entity for the year ended 30 June 2x8.

Suggested solution:

Selling price less cost to sell (immediately: 520,000 – 40,000)	480 000
Value in use	440 750
(annuity for 4 years – 120,000 × 3.0374) + (present value on sale – 120 000 × 0.635518)	
Recoverable amount (higher value)	480 000
Carrying amount	560 000
Impairment loss	80 000

8.5.3   Recognition of impairment loss

If the recoverable amount of an asset is less than its carrying amount, the entity shall reduce the carrying amount to its recoverable amount. The reduction in the carrying amount represents an impairment loss (s27.5 and IAS 36 p.59). The impairment loss must be recognised immediately in profit or loss unless the asset is measured in accordance with the revaluation model, in which case the impairment loss shall be recognised in other comprehensive income first, to the extent that the revaluation surplus is not turned into a negative balance (s27.6 and IAS 36 p.60).

8.5.3.1 Initial recognition of an impairment loss – historical cost

If there are indications that an asset is impaired, ie the carrying amount of an asset exceeds its recoverable amount, then an impairment loss shall be recognised by reducing the carrying amount of the asset to its recoverable amount (s27.5 and IAS 36 p.59). The impairment loss is usually recognised in the profit and loss section of the statement of comprehensive income with the corresponding amount recognised as a contra asset. For example, for a trade receivable it is recognised as an allowance for credit losses (or doubtful debts), while for a depreciable asset it is recognised as accumulated depreciation and impairment losses. After adjusting the carrying amount of an asset for an impairment loss or the reversal thereof, the entity shall adjust the depreciation charge for the asset in future periods to allocate the asset's revised carrying amount on a systematic basis over its remaining life (s27.10 and IAS 36 p.63).

However, if there is indication that an asset may be impaired but no impairment loss was recognised, then the entity should review the remaining useful life, the depreciation method or the residual value of the asset and adjust it accordingly (s27.10 and IAS 36 p.17) – such an adjustment must be recognised as a change in estimate (s8 and IAS 8).

Illustrative Example 8.2: Recognition of an impairment loss

At the reporting date, an item of machinery had a carrying amount of CU560 000 (based on the historical cost model with a cost of CU800 000, an estimated useful life of 10 years and a nil residual value), but its recoverable amount was estimated to be CU480 000. The remaining useful life of the machinery is 4 years.

You are required to:
Prepare the journal entries necessary to account for the impairment loss in the financial statements of the entity in the current and subsequent periods.

Suggested solution:
Current period:
DR: Impairment loss [P/L]   80 000
CR: Accumulated impairment loss [SFP]   80 000
[Recognition of impairment loss at the reporting date]

Subsequent periods:		
DR: Depreciation	120 000	
CR: Accumulated depreciation (SFP) [480,000/4 years]		120 000
[Provision for depreciation after recognising the impairment loss]		

8.5.3.2 Recognition subsequent to initial recognition

An impairment test must be conducted at each reporting date to determine whether the carrying amount of the asset fairly reflects at least its estimated economic benefits. If an asset was impaired in prior periods and the recoverable amount exceeds the carrying amount, the entity shall increase the carrying amount to its recoverable amount subject to the asset's carrying amount had no impairment been recognised for that asset in prior periods (s27.30(a)–(c) and IAS 36 p.117). The increase in the carrying amount to its recoverable amount represents a reversal of the impairment loss previously recognised and must be recognised in the profit and loss component of the statement of comprehensive income (up to the historical cost carrying amount had the asset never been impaired).

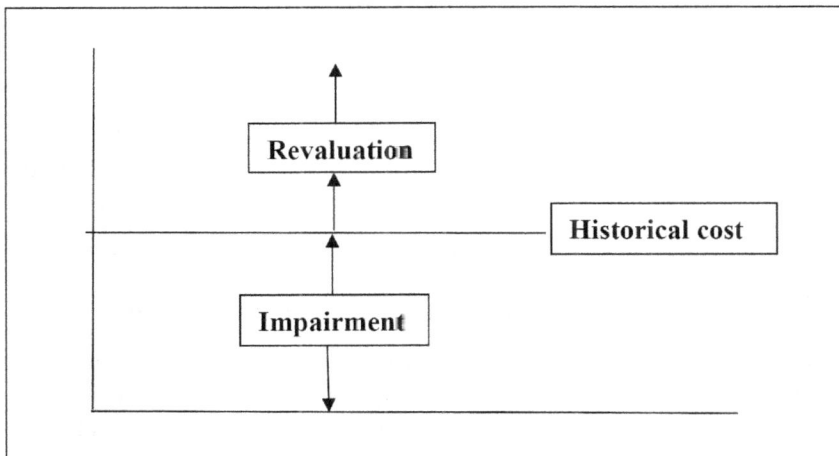

Figure 8.1 Diagrammatic illustration of an impairment and its reversal

Illustrative Example 8.2: Reversal of impairment loss

At 28 February 20X6, the carrying amount of a machine was CU450 000 with a remaining useful life of 4 years. The machine is depreciated on a straight-line basis to a zero residual value over its estimated useful life. The recoverable amounts at 28 February 20X6 and 20X8 were CU400 000 and CU240 000 respectively.

You are required to:

Prepare the journal entries necessary to account for the impairment and its reversal in the financial statement of the entity for the years ended 28 February 20x6 and 29 February 20x8.

Suggested solution:

28/02/X6	Carrying amount	450 000
	Recoverable amount	400 000
	Impairment loss	50 000

28/02/X8	Carrying amount [400,000 – (400,000 × 2/4)]	200 000
	Recoverable amount	240 000
	Increase in asset value	40 000
	Historical carrying amount [450,000 × 2/4]	225 000
	Increase to historical cost – limitation	25 000

28/02/X6	DR: Impairment loss [P/L]	50 000	
	CR: Accumulated depreciation & impairment [SFP]		50 000
	[Recognition of impairment loss on initial recognition]		

NB: Depreciation after 28 February 20X6 amounts to CU100 000 [400,000/4] over the remaining useful life.

28/02/X8	DR: Accumulated impairment loss [SFP]	25 000	
	CR: Reversal of impairment loss [P/L]		25 000
	[Reversal of impairment loss to reflect the asset at its recoverable amount]		

8.5.4   Initial recognition of impairment loss – revaluation model

When conducting an impairment test for assets measured using the revaluation model, bear in mind that an impairment loss may only be recognised in profit or loss to the extent that there is an insufficient balance on the revaluation surplus to absorb the impairment. If the asset is measured using the revaluation model, then the decrease in the carrying amount of the asset is treated as a revaluation decrease, ie recognised in other comprehensive income to the extent that the balance of the revaluation can absorb the impairment. Any additional impairment loss is then recognised in profit or loss.

Illustrative Example 8.4: Impairment loss and the revaluation model

At 30 June 20X8, the carrying amount of a machine (using the revaluation model) was CU780 000, while its historical cost carrying amount was CU690 000. The recoverable amount at the reporting date was CU630 000. The company releases the revaluation surplus to retained earnings over the remaining useful life of the machine.

You are required to:
Prepare the journal entries necessary to account for the impairment of the machine in the financial statements of the entity.

Suggested solution:

Carrying amount (revaluation model)	780,000
Recoverable amount	630,000
Decrease in the carrying amount	150,000
Impairment loss (other comprehensive income: 780,000 – 690,000)	90,000
Impairment loss (profit or loss: 690,000 – 630,000)	60,000

DR: Reversal of revaluation surplus (OCI)	90,000	
DR: Impairment loss (P/L)	60,000	
CR: Accumulated depreciation and impairment (SFP)		60,000

[Recognition of impairment loss for asset using the revaluation model]

8.6   GUIDANCE FOR SPECIFIC ASSETS

As mentioned before, the accounting standard s27 – *Impairment of assets* (and IAS 36) excludes certain assets from its scope because the standards relating to those assets have their own impairment model incorporated into them, such as the standard on investment property and inventories (it is interesting to note that IFRS for SMEs includes inventories in its scope, but has a specific section in the standard dedicated to the impairment of inventories, while in full IFRS, IAS 36 – *Impairment of assets* excludes inventories from its scope, however IAS 2 – *Inventories* includes very similar requirements for the impairment of inventories as is contained in IFRS for SMEs).

8.6.1   Inventories

The accounting standard governing the impairment of inventories stipulates that inventories shall be measured at the lower of cost and net realisable value, ie estimated selling price less costs to complete and sell (s27.2 and IAS 2 p.9).

8.6.1.1 Initial recognition

If there is evidence that inventories are impaired at the reporting date, the carrying amount should be reduced to its net realisable value by recognising the impairment loss in the profit and loss section of the statement of comprehensive income (s27.2 and IAS 2 p.34). The impairment loss for inventories shall be recognised as a direct reduction of the cost of the inventories via cost of sales – no provision such as the accumulated impairment loss is created. However, it is important to note that when performing profitability analysis, gross profit percentages will be distorted as a result of the impairment loss included within cost of sales.

8.6.1.2 Reversal of impairment loss

If the circumstances that previously caused inventories to be impaired no longer exist or there is evidence that the selling price less costs to complete and sell has increased because of changes in the economic conditions, the impairment loss previously recognised must be reversed by increasing inventories to the lower of their cost or recoverable amount. It is important to note that an impairment loss recognised in prior periods can only be reversed if the inventories which were impaired are still on hand at the reporting date when the impairment test is conducted.

8.6.1.3 Impairment of raw materials

If it is impracticable to determine the net realisable value for each item of inventory independently, the entity may group/cluster items of inventory relating to the same product line that have similar purposes when assessing impairment (s27.3 and IAS 2 p.29).

If it is difficult or impractical to estimate the net realisable value for raw materials, the impairment test should be conducted on the finished product to determine whether the raw materials should be impaired. If the finished goods are impaired, this may be an indication that the raw materials are also impaired. Even when the value of raw materials on a stand-alone basis appears to be impaired (eg the replacement cost is lower than the carrying amount), if the finished goods are not impaired, then no impairment loss will be recognised for the raw materials – the reason being that the raw materials are recovered through the sale of the finished goods. The impairment loss recognised for raw materials is limited to the impairment loss of the finished goods, for example if the impairment losses of raw materials and finished goods are CU50 000 and CU30 000 respectively, then the raw materials can only be impaired by CU30 000 (limitation).

Illustrative Example 8.5: Impairment of inventory

At 30 June 20X8, the carrying amounts of materials and finished goods were CU190 000 per unit and CU830 000 per unit respectively, while the respective replacement cost (materials) and net realisable value were CU165 000 per unit and CU790 000 per unit respectively. One unit of material is used to produce one unit of finished goods and conversion costs of CU640 000 are incurred to turn one unit of raw material into a finished good.

You are required to:
Calculate the impairment loss related to raw material and finished goods separately, that should be recognized in the financial statements of the entity.

Suggested solution:

Apparent impairment loss: Materials (190,000 – 165,000)	25,000
Impairment loss: Finished goods (830,000 – 790,000)	40,000

As the finished goods are impaired by an amount greater than the impairment for the materials, the full impairment loss of CU25 000 per unit can be allocated to the raw material. The finished goods will also be reduced to their recoverable amount.

8.6.2 Investment property

Investment property is measured at fair value, thus any change in the fair value must be recognised as a fair value gain or loss via the profit and loss account (s16.7 and IAS 40 p.35). If there is a decline in the fair value of the property, which may indicate an impairment, then it must be recognised as part of the fair value adjustment.

8.7 CASH-GENERATING UNITS

A cash-generating unit is defined as the smallest identifiable group of assets that generates cash inflows that are largely independent of the cash inflows from other assets or groups of assets (s27.8 and IAS 36 p.6).

8.7.1 Initial recognition of an impairment loss

When performing the impairment test for a cash-generating unit (CGU), it is important to determine the recoverable amount of the unit rather than the individual assets constituting the unit. However, there may be impairments of individual assets within the CGU but in aggregate, the CGU may not be impaired, resulting in no impairment loss being recognised for the CGU.

The impairment loss recognised in respect of a CGU must be allocated to reduce the carrying amounts of the component assets in the following order (s27.21 and IAS 36 p.104):

(a) reduction of the carrying amount of any goodwill to zero; and
(b) thereafter, proportionate allocation to remaining assets based on their carrying amounts.

Assets included in the CGU which are excluded from the scope of s27 and IAS 36, such as investment property (and inventory, as the s27 has specific guidance relating to the impairment of inventories and IAS 36 excludes inventories from its scope), shall be excluded from the allocation of the impairment loss of the CGU. This implies that assets such as inventory which are measured at the lower of cost or net realisable value, and receivables which are net of the allowance for credit losses (doubtful debts), cannot be included as part of the assets to which the impairment loss is allocated on a pro rata basis. However, an asset included in the CGU shall not be reduced to an amount below the highest of (s27.22 and IAS 36 p.105):
(a) its fair value less cost to sell;
(b) its value in use; and
(c) zero.

This implies that the individual assets in a CGU cannot be impaired to an amount lower than their individual recoverable amount. Any portion of the impairment loss that was not recognised as a result of the limitation shall be allocated to the remaining assets proportionately based on their carrying amount (s27.23 and IAS 36 p.105).

Illustrative Example 8.6: Impairment of cash-generating units

At 28 February 20X6 the cash generating unit consisted of the following assets measured at their carrying amounts:

Goodwill	200,000
Property, plant & equipment	760,000 (fair value less cost to sell – 680,000)
Intangible assets	180,000 (fair value less cost to sell – 100,000)
Inventories	250,000
Trade receivables	870,000
Other assets	330,000 (fair value less cost to sell – 250,000)
Cash generating unit	2,590,000 (recoverable amount – 2,200,000)
Total impairment	390,000

You are required to:
Prepare the journal entry necessary to account for the impairment of the cash-generating unit for the year ended 28 February 20x6.

Suggested solution:

First allocated to goodwill	200,000
Impairment loss: Remainder of the cash generating unit	190,000
Asset to which the impairment loss can be allocated:	
Property, plant & equipment	760,000
Intangible assets	180,000
Other assets	330,000
Carrying amount of asset to which impairment can be allocated	1,270,000

Allocation of impairment loss of CGU:	
Property, plant & equipment (760,000/1,270,000 × 190,000)	113,701
Intangible assets (180,000/1,270,000 × 190,000)	26,929
Other assets (330,000/1,270,000 × 190,000)	49,370
	190,000

The allocated impairment loss for property, plant and equipment exceeds the impairment loss for the asset, thus the excess of the allocated loss of CU33,701 (113,701 – 80,000) must be reallocated to the remaining assets.

Carrying amount of remaining assets to which the excess can be allocated:	
Intangible assets (180,000 – 26,929)	153,071
Other assets (330,000 – 49,370)	280,630
Total	433,701
Allocate the excess of the impairment loss:	
Intangible assets (153,071/433,701 × 33,701)	11,894
Other assets (280,630/433,701 × 33,701)	21,807

DR: Impairment loss (P/L)	190,000	
CR: Accumulated impairment loss – PPE (SFP)		80,000
CR: Intangible assets (SFP) [26,929 + 11,894]		38,823
CR: Other assets (SFP) [49,370 + 21,807		71,177
[Recognition of impairment loss of CGU]		

8.7.2 Recognition of impairment loss – subsequent to initial recognition

If the recoverable amount exceeds the carrying amount of the CGU subsequent to the initial recognition of the impairment loss, the increase must be recognised as a reversal of an impairment loss (s27.31(b) and IAS 36 p.114). No reversal of a previous impairment loss may be allocated to goodwill. The reversal of the impairment loss must be allocated to the assets on a pro rata basis based on their carrying amounts at that date, except for goodwill. When allocating the reversal of the impairment loss to the respective assets, it shall not increase the carrying amount of an asset above the lower of its recoverable amount, and what the carrying amount of the asset would have been had there been no prior impairment (s27.31(c) and IAS 36 p.117 & 123). Any reversal of the impairment loss which was not allocated to a specific asset because of this limitation (s27.31(c) and IAS 36 p.117 & 123) shall be re-allocated on a pro rata basis to the remaining assets. After a reversal of an impairment loss is recognised, the depreciation/amortisation of the asset in the CGU must be adjusted to allocate its carrying amount on a systematic basis over its remaining useful life (s27.31(e) and IAS 36 p.123).

Illustrative Example 8.7 Reversal of impairment of cash-generating units

Use the same information as in illustrative example 8.6.
At 29 February 20X8, the cash generating union consisted of assets at their carrying amounts:

	Excluding impairment	Including impairment
Goodwill	200,000	Nil
Property, plant & equipment	456,000	408,000 (recoverable amount – 540,000)
Intangible assets	180,000	141,500 (recoverable amount – 150,000)
Inventories	360,000	360,000
Trade receivables	980,000	980,000
Other assets	140,000	10,500 (recoverable amount – 180,000)
Cash generating unit	2,316,000	1,900,000 (recoverable amount – 2,520,000)

You are required to:
Prepare the journal entries necessary to account for the reversal of the cash-generating unit in the financial statements of the entity for the year ended 29 February 20x8.

Suggested solution:

Reversal of impairment loss: Cash generating unit [limited to historical cost]	416,000
Asset to which the reversal of the impairment loss can be allocated:	
Property, plant & equipment	408,000
Intangible assets	141,000
Other assets	10,500
Carrying amount of asset to which impairment can be allocated	559,500

Allocation of the reversal of the impairment loss of the CGU:

Property, plant & equipment [408,000/559,500 × 416,000]	303,357
Intangible assets [141,000/559,500 × 416,000]	104,836
Other assets [10,500/559,500 × 416,000]	7,807
	416,000

The allocation of the reversal of the impairment loss cannot result in the asset being re-stated at a carrying amount higher than its carrying amount had there not been a previous impairment loss. The carrying amount of the items after the allocated reversal of the impairment above would be:

PPE [408,000 + 303,357]	711,357
Intangible asset [141,000 + 104,836]	245,836
Other assets [10,500 + 7, 807]	18,307
Re-allocation of impairment loss:	
Property, plant & equipment [711,353 – 456,000]	(255,357)
Intangible assets [245,836 – 150,000]	(95,836)
Other assets [140,000 – 18,307]	121,693
Reversal of impairment unallocated	(229,500)

DR: Accumulated depreciation & impairment – PPE [SFP]	48,000
[303,357 – 255,357]	
DR: Accumulated depreciation & impairment – Intangible [SFP]	9,000
[104,836 – 95,836]	
DR: Other assets [SFP]	129,500
[7,807 + 121,693]	
CR: Reversal of impairment loss [P/L]	186,500
[Recognition of impairment loss of CGU]	

8.7.3   Goodwill

The recoverable amount of goodwill cannot be determined or measured directly but is based on the recoverable amount of the cash-generating unit to which goodwill has been allocated (s27.24 and IAS 36 p.81). Goodwill acquired in a business combination shall at the date of acquisition be allocated to each of the acquirer's CGUs that are expected to benefit from the synergies of the business combination (s27.25 and IAS 36 p.80). When performing the impairment test of the goodwill acquired in a business combination, the impairment loss must be based on the recoverable amounts of the CGUs to which the goodwill was allocated.

In a business combination, the recoverable amount of a CGU is also attributable to the non-controlling interest in goodwill (s27.26 and IAS 36 p.C1 & C4). If the non-controlling interest is measured based on its proportionate share of the net asset of the acquirer, the goodwill should be grossed up (measured at 100% to include the non-controlling interest's share) as the carrying amount of the CGU includes the non-controlling interest in goodwill. The notionally adjusted carrying amount of the CGU is compared to its recoverable amount when determining whether the CGU is impaired.

If the goodwill acquired in a business combination cannot be allocated to individual CGUs on a non-arbitrary basis, then when testing the goodwill for impairment, the entity shall determine the recoverable amount of (s27.27 and IAS 36 p.81):
(a) the acquired entity – perform a business valuation or net asset valuation if it has not been restructured or dissolved into the reporting entity; and
(b) the group of entities, excluding any entities that have not been integrated into the consolidation of the group, if the goodwill relates to an entity that has been integrated into the reporting entity.

8.8 DEFERRED TAXATION

Subsequent to initial recognition, the asset shall be measured at its carrying amount which reflects at a maximum the future economic benefits embodied in it, for example property, plant and equipment shall be measured at cost less any accumulated depreciation or revalued amount.

The Income Tax Act generally only permits deductions when they occur, and thus impairment losses which represent an allowance for reductions in the probable economic benefits expected are not recognised as deductions for income tax purposes, ie the tax base of the asset remains unchanged when the asset is impaired. The reduction in the carrying amount of the asset due to the recognition of an impairment loss results in a temporary difference which in turn results in a provision for deferred tax.

8.9 DISCLOSURE

An entity shall disclose the following for each class of assets which has been impaired (s27.32 and IAS 36 p.126):
(a) the amount of impairment losses recognised in profit and loss during the period and the line items in the statement of comprehensive income in which those impairment losses are included;
(b) the amount of reversals of impairment losses in the profit and loss during the period and the line items in the statement of comprehensive income in which those impairment losses are reversed;

(c)   the amount of impairment losses on revalued assets recognised in other comprehensive income during the period, as required by full IFRS (IAS 36 p.126); and

(d)   the amount of reversals of impairment losses on revalued assets recognised in other comprehensive income during the period.

An entity shall disclose the information required by s27.32 for each of the following classes of assets (s27.33):
(a)   inventories;
(b)   property, plant and equipment;
(c)   goodwill;
(d)   intangible assets other than goodwill;
(e)   investment in associates; and
(f)   investments in joint ventures.

NB! Note that full IFRS requires certain additional disclosures. For a complete reading of these additional disclosures, you can refer to IAS 36 p.127–137.

Comprehensive Example 8.1

On 01 March 20X5, ABC Ltd acquired machinery at cost of CU2,000,000 which was to be depreciated on a straight-line basis to its residual value of CU200,000 over an estimated useful life of six years. On 01 March 20X7, the company adopted the revaluation model (gross replacement cost) of accounting for machinery. At 01 March 20X7, the gross replacement cost was CU2,600,000, while the recoverable amounts at 28 February 20X9 and 20X10 were CU700,000 andCU600,000 respectively. The company releases the revaluation surplus to retained earnings over the remaining useful life of the asset.

You are required to:
Ignore deferred taxation.
Suggested solution:

		Cost	Revaluation	Surplus
	Cost	2,000,000	2,600,000	
	Accumulated depreciation [(2,000,000 – 200,000)/6 × 2] and [(2,600,000 – 200,000)/6 × 2]	600,000	800,000	
01-Mar-07	Carrying amount [2,000,000 – (2,000,000 – 200,000)]	1,400,000	1,800,000	400,000
28-Feb-09	Accumulated depreciation [1,400,000 – 200,000) × 2/4]	600,000	800,000	

28-Feb-09	Carrying amount	800,000	1,000,000	
	Recoverable amount		700,000	
	Decrease in carrying amount		300,000	
	Other comprehensive income		200,000	
	Profit or loss		100,000	
28-Feb-10	Depreciation	300,000	250,000	
	Carrying amount	500,000	450,000	
	Recoverable amount		600,000	
	Increase in carrying amount		150,000	
	Reversal of impairment loss [450,000 – 500,000]		50,000	
	Revaluation surplus		100 000	
			Debit	**Credit**
01-Mar-07	Machinery		600,000	
	Accumulated depreciation and impairment			200,000
	Revaluation surplus (OCI)			400,000
	[Revaluation of machinery]			
28-Feb-08	Depreciation		400,000	
	Accumulated depreciation and impairment			400,000
	[Depreciation for the period]			
28-Feb-09	Depreciation		400,000	
	Accumulated depreciation and impairment			400,000
	[Depreciation for the period]			
28-Feb-09	Impairment loss		100,000	
	Revaluation surplus (OCI)		200,000	
	Accumulated depreciation and impairment			300,000
	[Recognition of fair value adjustment]			
28-Feb-10	Depreciation		250,000	
	Accumulated depreciation and impairment			250,000
	[Depreciation for the period]			

28-Feb-10	Accumulated depreciation and impairment (SFP)	150,000	
	Reversal of impairment loss (P/L)		50,000
	Revaluation surplus (OCI)		100,000
	[Recognition of reversal of impairment loss]		

Comprehensive Example 8.2

The following information was extracted from the accounting records relating to the carrying amounts of a CGU:

	20X8		20X9		
	Carrying amount (CA)	Fair value less cost to sell	CA before impairment	CA after impairment	Fair value less cost to sell
Property, plant & equipment	960,000	900,000	720,000	705,000	750,000
Investment property	560,000	530,000			
Intangible assets	300,000	210,000	200,000	140,000	180,000
Inventory	380,000				
Other assets	450,000	350,000	360,000	320,000	400,000
Goodwill	200,000		200,000		
Cash generating unit	2,850,000		1,480,000	1,165,000	

The recoverable amount of the CGU in 20X9 is considered to be CU1,330,000 (20X8: CU2,400,000).

Suggested solution:

First adjust investment property to fair value [560,000 – 530,000]	(30,000)				
Impairment loss for CGU [(2,850,000 – 30,000) – 2,400,000]	**420,000**				
First to goodwill	(200,000)				
Remaining impairment loss to be allocated	**220,000**				
	Carrying amount	Proportion	Limit	Still to allocate	Re-allocation
Property, plant & equipment	960,000	123,509	60,000	63,509	
Intangible assets	300,000	38,596	90,000		25,404
Other assets	450,000	57 895	100,000		38,105
Cash generating unit	1,710,000	220 000		63,509	63,509

The impairment loss of the CGU must first be allocated to goodwill (written off to a zero value) and investment property (measured at fair value). Thereafter, the loss is allocated on a pro rata basis to the other assets. The allocated impairment loss is limited to the impairment loss of the individual assets; and the balance of the allocated impairment loss is re-allocated on a pro rata basis to the remaining assets – PPE has an allocated loss of CU123,509, but the impairment loss for the specific asset is CU60,000, resulting in the balance being re-allocated.

	Before impairment	**After impairment**	Impairment reversal
CA before impairment	**1,480,000**	**1,165,000**	
Cannot reverse impairment losses relating to goodwill	(200,000)	0	
Recoverable amount relating to assets for which impairment losses can be reversed	**1,280,000**	**1,165,000**	**115,000**

	Carrying amount	Reversal	Limit	Still to allocate	Re-allocate
Property, plant & equipment	705,000	69,592	15,000	54,592	
Intangible assets	140,000	13,820	16,000		2,180
Other assets	320,000	31,588	40,000		8,412
Cash generating unit	1,165,000	115,000			10,592

		Debit	Credit
28-Feb-08	Impairment loss [P/L]	420,000	
	Goodwill		200,000
	Accumulated impairment loss – PPE		60,000
	Accumulated impairment loss – Intangible assets [38,596 + 25,404]		64,000
	Accumulated impairment loss – Other assets [57,895 + 38,105]		96,000
	[Recognition of impairment loss for CGU]		
28-Feb-09	Accumulated impairment loss – PPE	15,000	
	Accumulated impairment – Intangible assets	18,180	
	Accumulated impairment loss – Other assets	48,412	
	Reversal of impairment loss [P&L]		81,592
	[Recognition of reversal of impairment loss]		

SELF-ASSESSMENT
Multiple choice questions: Testing of principles of accounting for impairment of assets

1. Impairment tests of assets should only be conducted when:

(a) management considers it appropriate	
(b) there are indications that the assets are impaired	
(c) the fair value method is used to measure assets	
(d) none of the above	

2. An impairment loss is only recognised when:

(a) management considers the amount to be material	
(b) the intention is to reduce the tax liability	
(c) the recoverable amount cannot be determined reliably	
(d) estimated future economic benefits are less than the asset's carrying amount	

3. When the recoverable amount increases subsequent to the initial recognition of an impairment loss, the carrying amount of the asset must be:

(a) increased to the recoverable amount	
(b) increased by an amount equal to the initial impairment loss	
(c) increase to the recoverable amount limited to the historical carrying amount	
(d) increased limited to the original cost of the asset	

4. The decrease in the revalued amount of the asset to its recoverable amount must be recognised in the financial statements first as:

(a) an impairment loss via the profit or loss	
(b) reversal of the revaluation surplus via other comprehensive income	
(c) a combination of a devaluation and impairment loss	
(d) revaluation adjustment as a change in estimate	

5. An impairment of inventory (finished goods) must be recognised in the financial statements as:

(a) an inventory loss against cost of sales	
(b) a valuation loss as part of operating expenses	
(c) an allowance for future losses against inventory	
(d) a valuation loss in administration expenses	

6. An impairment loss for raw materials can only be recognised in the financial statements:

(a) if the materials will not be used in the production of goods in future	
(b) as a valuation loss of raw materials	
(c) if the finished goods are impaired	
(d) limited to the impairment loss of the finished goods	

7.   The impairment loss for a CGU must be:

(a) allocated to all of the assets comprising the CGU proportionately	
(b) allocated to those assets of the CGU which are impaired individually	
(c) allocated to goodwill in full and proportionately to the other assets	
(d) allocated to goodwill in full and proportionately to the other assets, limited to their fair value less cost to sell	

8.   The reversal of the impairment loss for a CGU must be:

(a) reversed against all assets previously impaired	
(b) reversed against all assets, except for goodwill, limited to the history carrying amount	
(c) recognised as a revaluation surplus of the CGU	
(d) none of the above	

9.   The following asset is allocated a proportionate share of the impairment of the CGU:

(a) investment property	
(b) accounts receivable	
(c) intangible asset	
(d) none of the above	

10.   A CGU represents:

(a) the smallest grouping of assets that can generate independent cash flows	
(b) always a grouping of all of the assets of the entity	
(c) all of the liabilities of the entity	
(d) none of the above	

Practical questions:
Application of principles to business scenarios

QUESTION 1

Objective: Recognition of impairment loss of raw material used in the production of finished goods

At 31 December 20X5, the cost of the raw material used in the production of finished goods was CU762,000 (1,000 units) while its recoverable amount was CU700,000. The cost of finished goods at that date was CU1,984,000 (1,000 units) when the selling price was CU1,890,000 and the cost to sell the finished goods was estimated to be CU22,000. Two units of raw material produce one unit of finished good.

You are required to:
Determine how the impairment of inventory should be recognised in the financial statements.

QUESTION 2

Objective: Measurement of the effect of impairment loss on subsequent depreciation

On 01 January 20X3, machinery and equipment with an aggregate cost of CU3,000,000 and a residual value of CU300,00 was depreciated on a straight-line basis over an estimated useful life of nine years. At 31 December 20X5, the recoverable amount of the asset was estimated to be CU1,920,000.

You are required to:
Determine how the impairment loss affects the subsequent depreciation of the machinery.

QUESTION 3

Objective: Recognition and measurement of the recovery of the impairment loss in subsequent periods

On 01 January 20X2, machinery with a cost of CU2,400,000 and an estimated useful life of six years was depreciated to a zero residual value using the straight-line method. The recoverable amounts at 31 December 20X3 and 20X5 were CU1,000 and CU900,000 respectively.

You are required to:
Record the journal entries for the increase in the recoverable amount subsequent to the initial recognition of the impairment loss.

QUESTION 4

Objective: Recognising impairment losses for CGUs

At 31 December 20X8, the carrying amount of the CGU consisted of the following:

	Carrying amount
Goodwill	170,000
Machinery	560,000
Equipment	120,000
Other	150,000

The recoverable amount of the CGU was estimated to be CU760,000 and the fair value less cost to sell of the machine was considered to be CU530,000.

You are required to:
Record the impairment loss for the CGU.

CHAPTER 9
BASIC FINANCIAL INSTRUMENTS

ILLUSTRATIVE DISCLOSURE [EXTRACT]

IFRS ref		Notes	20X2	20X1	
			CU'000	CU'000	
	Non-current assets				
4.2(c)	Financial assets		100,000	80,000	
	Current assets				
4.2(c)	Financial assets		50,000	58,000	
	Non-current liabilities				
4.2(m)	Financial liabilities		25,000	20,000	
	Current liabilities				
4.2(m)	Financial liabilities		12,000	10,000	

IFRS ref		20X2	20X1	
		CU'000	CU'000	
5.11(b)	**Other income**	**4,500**	**3,000**	
5.5(b)	**Finance costs**	**5,000**	**4,000**	
	Accounting policies			
11.40	The entity has chosen to account for financial instruments using sections 11 and 12 of IFRS for SMEs. Basic financial instruments are initially measured at cost (including transaction costs), while complex financial instruments are initially measured at fair value.			
	Basic financial instruments are subsequently measured at amortised cost using the effective interest rate method. Complex financial instruments are measured at fair value with fair value gains recognised in profit or loss except for equity instruments not publicly traded and for which fair value cannot be obtained without undue cost or effort, in which case these financial instruments are measured at cost less accumulated impairment.			

11.41		12. Categories of financial instruments	Fair value through profit or loss	Amortised cost	Cost less impairment
			CU	CU	CU
		Financial assets	90,000	40,000	20,000
		Financial liabilities	20,000	17,000	0
11.48		Financial asset gains/(losses)	3,000	1,500	**0**
		Financial liability gains/(losses)	(2,000)	(3,000)	
		All financial assets and liabilities, which are measured at fair value, have fair value determined with reference to quoted prices in active markets.			

9.1 INTRODUCTION

Financial instruments are often considered the more difficult transactions and balances to account for. For this reason, IFRS for SMEs and IFRS differ significantly in the prescribed accounting treatment for items which are in the scope of the financial instrument standards. IFRS for SMEs split the accounting for financial instruments into two sections, section 11 – *Basic financial instruments* and section 12 – *Other financial instruments*.

Upon completion of this unit you should know the financial reporting requirements for accounting for basic financial instruments in accordance with the IFRS for SMEs. In particular, you should be able to:
(a) identify basic financial instruments that qualify for recognition under this section;
(b) recognise and measure basic financial instruments at initial recognition;
(c) account for the subsequent measurement of basic financial instruments; and
(d) present and disclose basic financial instruments in the financial statements.

9.2 DEFINITIONS

The definitions for the important concepts and terms used in IFRS for SMEs are found in Appendix B – *Glossary of terms* in IFRS for SMEs. Some important definitions relating to financial instruments include the following:

- **Financial instrument:** A contract that gives rise to a financial asset of one entity and a financial liability or equity instrument of another entity

- **Financial asset:** Any asset that is:
    - (a)   cash;
    - (b)   an equity instrument of another entity;
    - (c)   a contractual right:
        - (i)   to receive cash or another financial asset from another entity; or
        - (ii) to exchange financial assets or financial liabilities with another entity under conditions that are potentially favourable to the entity; or
    - (d)   a contract that will or may be settled in the entity's own equity instruments and:
        - (i)   under which the entity is or may be obliged to receive a variable number of the entity's own equity instruments; or
        - (ii) that will or may be settled other than by the exchange of a fixed amount of cash or another financial asset for a fixed number of the entity's own equity instruments. For this purpose, the entity's own equity instruments do not include instruments that are themselves contracts for the future receipt or delivery of the entity's own equity instruments.

- **Financial liability:** Any liability that is:
    - (a)   a contractual obligation:
        - (i)   to deliver cash or another financial asset to another entity; or
        - (ii) to exchange financial assets or financial liabilities with another entity under conditions that are potentially unfavourable to the entity; or
    - (b)   a contract that will or may be settled in the entity's own equity instruments and:
        - (i)   under which the entity is or may be obliged to deliver a variable number of the entity's own equity instruments; or
        - (ii) will or may be settled other than by the exchange of a fixed amount of cash or another financial asset for a fixed number of the entity's own equity instruments. For this purpose, the entity's own equity instruments do not include instruments that are themselves contracts for the future receipt or delivery of the entity's own equity instruments.

9.3   SCOPE AND OBJECTIVES

Sections 11 and 12 together deal with the accounting for all financial instruments. Section 11 applies to basic financial instruments only, while section 12 applies to financial instruments other than basic financial instruments (s11.1). Entities applying IFRS for SMEs have to make a policy choice to determine whether they will apply the requirement of both sections 11 and 12 or IFRS 9 – *Financial instruments* of full IFRS in accounting for all financial instruments (s11.2).

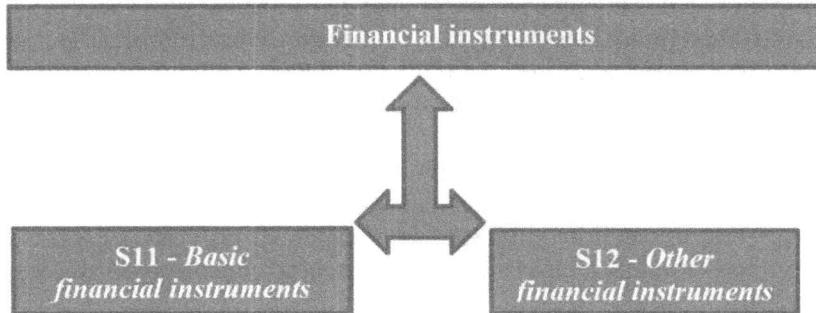

Figure 9.1 Sections that govern the accounting of financial instruments

9.4   CLASSIFICATION

Basic financial instruments are those financial instruments which are (s11.8):
(a)   cash;
(b)   debt instruments that meet the conditions below*;
(c)   commitments to receive a loan that:
      (i)   cannot be settled net in cash; and
      (ii)   when the commitment is executed, are expected to meet the conditions in explained below*
(d)   investments in non-convertible preference shares and non-puttable ordinary shares or preference shares.
*A financial instrument that satisfies all of the criteria in (a)–(d) shall be accounted for in accordance with section 11 – *Basic financial instruments* (s11.9) as follows:

(e)   returns to the holder assessed in the currency in which the debt instrument is denominated are:
      (i)   a fixed amount; or
      (ii)   a fixed rate of return over the life of the instrument; or
      (iii)   a variable return that, throughout the life of the instrument, is equal to a single referenced quoted or observable interest rate; or
      (iv)   some combination of fixed and variable rates, provided that both the fixed and variable rates are positive.
For fixed and variable rate interest returns, interest is calculated by multiplying the rate for the applicable period by the principal amount outstanding during the period;

(a)   there is no contractual provision that could, by its terms, result in the holder losing the principal amount or any interest attributable to the current period or prior periods. The fact that a debt instrument is subordinated is not an example of such a contractual provision;

(b)   contractual provisions that permit or require the practitioner to prepay a debt instrument or permit or require the holder to put it back to the issuer before maturity are not contingent on future events other than to protect:

    (i)   the holder against credit risk of the issuer or the instrument or a change in control of the issuer; or

    (ii)   the holder or issuer against changes in relevant tax or law;

(c)   there are no conditional returns or prepayment provisions except for the variable rate return described in (a) and prepayment provision described in (c).

Illustrative Example 9.1: Basic financial instruments

An entity has the following balances reflected in its statement of financial position:

	CU
Cash	100,000
(Trade) Accounts receivable	50,000
Loan receivable (interest linked to prime)	40,000
Investment in compulsorily convertible preference shares	85,000

You are required to:

State whether the above items are (or are not) classified as basic financial instruments and provide reasons.

Suggested solution:

	Classification
Cash	Basic – included in s11.8 (a)
Accounts receivable	Basic – included in s11.8 (b) & 11.9 (a) (ii)
Loan receivable	Basic – included in s11.8 (b) & 11.9 (a) (iii)
Preference shares	Other – excluded in s11.8 (d)

The following financial instruments are specifically excluded from section 11 – *Basic financial instruments* (s11.7):
(a)   investments in subsidiaries, associates and joint ventures;
(b)   compound financial instruments;
(c)   leases;
(d)   employee benefits;
(e)   share-based payment transactions; and
(f)   reimbursement assets that are accounted for in terms of section 21 – *Provisions and contingencies*.

9.5   INITIAL RECOGNITION

An entity recognises a financial asset or liability when the entity becomes a party to the contractual provisions of the instrument.

The entity should initially recognise and measure a basic financial asset or financial liability at transaction price unless the arrangement is a financing transaction for either of the contracting parties. A financing arrangement is one where payment is deferred beyond normal business terms. If the transaction constitutes a financing arrangement, the financial asset or financial liability is measured at the present value of the future payments discounted at the market interest rate for similar debt instruments as determined at initial recognition.

Transaction costs are capitalised to the cost of the financial asset or financial liability, unless the financial asset or financial liability is subsequently measured at fair value.

Illustrative Example 9.2: Initial recognition of financial instruments

An entity has the following financial instruments in its statement of financial position:
(a)   it has a loan of CU121,000 receivable in two years. The loan agreement includes that no interest will be charged;
(b)   it sells products to a customer for CU121,000 and grants the customer 30 days credit (its normal credit terms are 30 days); and
(c)   it sells products to a customer for CU121,000 and grants the customer one year's credit (its normal credit terms are 30 days).

You may consider a market related interest rate to be 10% per annum compounded annually.

You are required to:

Explain what amount the above financial instruments should be initially recognized at in the financial statements of the entity.

Suggested solution:

The entity has a loan of CU121,000 receivable in two years. The loan agreement includes that no interest will be charged. Similar loans bear interest at 10% per annum compounded annually.	Deferred credit terms mean that the amount of CU121,000 discounted using the market rate of 10% to a present value of CU100,000.
The entity sells products to a customer for CU121,000 and grants the customer 30 days credit (its normal credit terms are 30 days).	As the payment is within normal credit terms, the amount initially recognised is the transaction price of CU121,000.
The entity sells products to a customer for CU121,000 and grants the customer one year's credit (its normal credit terms are 30 days).	Deferred credit terms mean that the amount of CU121,000 discounted using the market rate of 10% to a present value of CU100,000. Notice how this is the same answer as for the loan. The entity has in effect sold products to a customer and simultaneously provided a loan for the amount due.

9.6   SUBSEQUENT MEASUREMENT

Financial instruments shall be measured as follows, at the end of each financial reporting period (s11.14):

(a) debt instruments that meet the conditions in s11.8(b) shall be measured at amortised cost using the effective interest rate method. Debt instruments that are classified as current assets or current liabilities shall be measured at the undiscounted amounts;

(b) commitments to receive a loan shall be measured at cost; and

(c) investments in non-convertible preference shares and non-puttable ordinary or preference shares shall be measured as follows:

    (i)   if the shares are publicly traded or their fair value can otherwise be measured reliably without undue cost or effort, the investment shall be measured at fair value with changes in fair value recognised in profit or loss; and

(ii)   all other such investments shall be measured at cost less accumulated impairment.

Amortised cost = principal amount + interest (at the effective interest rate) – payments – impairments.

Illustrative Example 9.3: Subsequent measurement

Following from Illustrative Example 2.
The loan will be accounted for as follows subsequent to initial recognition:

You are required to:
Calculate the amount at which the loan will be accounted for in the financial statements of the entity at the end of years 1 and 2.

Suggested solution:
Year 1:
Initial recognition: CU100,000 [CU120,000/$(1.1)^2$]
Interest = CU100,000 × 10% = CU10,000
Amortised cost balance = CU100,000 + CU10,000 = CU110,000

Year 2:
Principal (opening balance) = CU110,000
Interest = CU110,000 × 10% = CU11,000
Amortised cost balance before settlement = CU110,000 + CU11,000 = CU121,000

Amortised cost balance after settlement = CU121,000 – CU121,000 = 0

The above can also be illustrated in an amortisation table as follows:

Year	Principal	Interest	Payment	Balance
1	100,000	10,000	0	110,000
2	110,000	11,000	(121,000)	0

Illustrative Example 9.4: Use of the amortisation table (multiple payments)

Company A provides services to a customer and requires the customer to pay for the services in three instalments of CU100,000 each, with the first payment being one year after rendering the service. Company A does not normally allow credit terms on services which it renders. A market-related interest rate is considered to be 8% per annum compounded annually.

You are required to:
Prepare the amortization table for the entire period that the amount owing is outstanding.

Suggested solution:
Present value calculation:

CU100,000/1.08	92,593
CU100,000/$(1.08)^2$	85,734
CU100,000/$(1.08)^3$	79,383
	257,710

Year	Principal	Interest	Payment	Balance
1	257,710	[1]20,617	(100,000)	178,327
2	178,327	[2]14,266	(100,000)	92,593
3	92,593	[3]7,407	(100,000)	0

Notes:
[1] CU257,710 × 8% = CU20,617
[2] CU178,327 × 8% = CU14,266
[3] CU92,593 × 8% = CU7,407

NB: The amortisation table works the same for assets and liabilities. You have to consider how you recognise the amounts in the amortisation table – for instance, interest expense (on a liability) is recognised as a debit entry, but interest income (on an asset) is recognised as a credit entry.

9.7 IMPAIRMENT OF A FINANCIAL ASSET MEASURED AT COST OR AMORTISED COST

An entity shall assess whether there is objective evidence of impairment of all financial assets that are measured at cost or amortised cost at each reporting date. If a financial asset measured at cost or amortised cost is impaired, the impairment loss must be recognised in profit or loss immediately (s11.21).

Objective evidence includes observable data about the following loss events (s11.22):

(a)   significant financial difficulty of the issuer or obligor;

(b)   a breach of contract, such as a default or delinquency in interest or principal payments;

(c)   the creditor, for economical or legal reasons relating to the debtor's financial difficulty, granting to the debtor a concession that the creditor would not otherwise consider;

(d)   it has become probable that the debtor will enter bankruptcy or other financial reorganisation; or

(e)   there has been a measurable decrease in the estimated future cash flows from a group of financial assets since initial recognition of those assets, which could be a result of adverse national or local economic conditions or changes in the industry, technological market, economic or legal environment.

The following assets must be tested individually for impairment (s11.24):

(a)   equity instruments (irrespective of significance); and

(b)   other financial assets that are individually significant.

The impairment loss is calculated as the asset's carrying amount less the present value of the estimated cash flows discounted at the asset's original effective interest rate.

Illustrative Example 9.5: Interest revenue

Following Illustrative Example 9.4, assume that there is an indication of impairment at the end of year 1 (party owing to the fact that the entity money is having financial difficulty) and that evidence shows probable receipts at the end of year 2 of CU90,000 and year 3 of CU90,000. A market interest rate was considered to be 8% on initial recognition of the financial asset and 10% at the end year 1 (the date of the impairment calculation).

You are required to:

Calculate the amount that should be recognized to impair the financial asset in the financial statements of the entity at the end of year 1.

Suggested solution:
As per Illustrative Example XX.4, the carrying amount of the financial asset is CU178,327. The present value of the financial asset is:

	CU
CU90,000 / 1.08	83,333
CU90,000 / $(1.08)^2$	77,160
	160,493

An impairment loss of CU17,834 (CU178,327 − CU160,493) is therefore recognized at the end of year 1 in profit or loss.

9.8 REVERSAL OF IMPAIRMENT OF A FINANCIAL ASSET AT COST OR AMORTISED COST

When there is objective evidence of a reversal of the conditions that gave rise to the impairment loss, the entity must reverse the impairment loss up to a maximum of what the carrying amount of the asset would have been had there been no impairment.

Illustrative Example 9.6: Reversal of impairment

Following on from Illustrative Example 9.4 and 9.5, assume that the condition that gave rise to the impairment is no longer present (the party owing the entity money is no longer having financial difficulty) by the end of year 2 (before any amounts are received for year 2 and after). The entity therefore expects receipts for year 2 of CU100,000 and year 3 of CU100,000. You may assume that the fair value of the financial asset as determined by a valuator is CU250,000.

You are required to:
Calculate the amount to be recognized as the reversal of the impairment loss at the end of year 2.

Suggested solution:
The carrying amount of the financial asset before the receipt of cash for year 2 is:

Year	Principal	Interest	Payment	Balance
1	257,710	20,617	(100,000)	178,327
			Impairment	17,833
				160,494
2	160,494	12,840	0	173,333

The balance (before receipt for year 2), had there been no impairment, would have been:

Year	Principal	Interest	Payment	Balance
1	257,710	20,617	(100,000)	178,327
2	178,327	14,266	0	192,593

The impairment reversal at the end of year 2 is therefore:
CU19,260 (CU192,593 – CU173,333)

NB: Notice that the reversal is limited to what the carrying amount would have been had there been no impairment, CU192,593 and not CU250,000.

9.9   FAIR VALUE

When financial instruments are not measured at cost or amortised cost, they are measured at fair value. To determine fair value, the following hierarchy should be used (s11.27):
(a)   a quoted price or an identical asset in an active market;
(b)   if quoted prices are unavailable, the price in a binding sale agreement or recent transaction for an identical asset (or similar asset), adjusted if the entity can demonstrate that the last transaction price is not a good estimate of fair value;
(c)   failing the above, the use of a valuation technique which should:
    (i)   reasonably reflect how the market could be expected to price the asset; and
    (ii)   have inputs that reasonably represent market expectations and measures of the risk return factors inherent in the asset.

Dividends should be recognised when the shareholder's right to receive the dividend has been established.

9.10   PRESENTATION AND DISCLOSURE

9.10.1 Presentation

Section 11 does not have specific presentation requirements for basic financial instruments. The related requirements are included in sections 3 to and include the fact that the statement of financial position should have a separate line item for financial assets (s4.2(c)) and financial liabilities (s4.2(m)), and should classify financial instruments as either current or non-current in terms of sections 4.5 to 4.8. Entities should present the resultant dividend income, interest income, interest expense, impairment losses and reversals in profit or loss as appropriate in terms of section 5 (including s5.5(b)). Interest and dividends received may be presented as either operating or investing activities, and interest paid may be presented as either operating or financing activities in the statement of cash flows (ss7.14 to 7.16).

9.10.2 Disclosure

9.10.2.1 General disclosures

The entity should disclose the significant accounting policies relating to financial instruments (s11.40) together with any other information that would be useful for users to evaluate the significance of financial instruments for the entity's financial position and performance (s11.42). An entity should disclose the carrying amounts of each of the following categories in the statement of financial position or in the notes (s11.41):

(a)   financial assets measured at fair value through profit or loss;

(b)   financial assets that are debt instruments measured at amortised cost;

(c)   financial assets that are equity instruments measured at cost less accumulated impairment;

(d)   financial liabilities measured at fair value through profit or loss;

(e)   financial liabilities measured at amortised cost; and

(f)   loan commitments measured at cost less impairment.

The entity should disclose the following for financial assets pledged as collateral or security (s11.46):

(a)   the carrying amount of financial instruments pledged as collateral; and

(b)   the terms and conditions relating to its pledge.

The entity should also disclose the following relating to any breaches of loans payable which are not remedied by reporting date:

(a)   details of the breach or default;

(b)   the carrying amount of the related loans payable at the reporting date; and

(c)   whether the breach was remedied, or the terms renegotiated before the financial statements were authorised for issue.

The entity should disclose the following relating to income, expense, gains or losses:

(a)   all income, expense, gains and losses (including fair value gains and losses) for:

(i)   financial assets measured at fair value through profit or loss;

(ii)   financial liabilities measured at fair value through profit or loss;

(iii)   financial assets measured at amortised cost; and

(iv)   financial liabilities measured at amortised cost.

(b)   the total interest income and

SELF-ASSESSMENT
Multiple choice questions: Testing principles of accounting for basic financial instruments

1. A financial instrument is defined as:

(a) a contract that gives rise to a financial asset of one entity and a liability or equity instrument of another entity	
(b) a contract that gives rise to a financial asset of one entity and a financial liability of another entity	
(c) a contract that gives rise to a financial asset of one entity and an equity instrument of another entity	
(d) a contract that gives rise to a financial asset of one entity and a financial liability or equity instrument of another entity	

2. The following is included in the definition of a financial asset:

(a) cash	
(b) the contractual right to receive cash	
(c) an equity instrument of another entity	
(d) all of the above	

3. The following are classified as financial assets:

(a) accounts receivable	
(b) tax receivable (tax refund)	
(c) prepayment for inventory	
(d) none of the above	

4. The following is included in the definition of a financial liability:

(a) a contractual obligation to deliver an asset to another entity	
(b) a contractual obligation to deliver cash or another financial asset to another entity	
(c) a contractual obligation to deliver only cash to another entity	
(d) a contractual obligation to deliver inventory to another entity	

5. The following items are financial liabilities:

(a) revenue received in advance	
(b) traffic fines payable	
(c) SARS penalty	
(d) accounts payable	

6. The following is included within the scope of Section 11 – *Basic financial instruments*:

(a) leases	
(b) investments in subsidiaries	
(c) loans receivable	
(d) an entity's own equity instruments	

7. The default measurement basis for basic financial instruments is:

(a) amortised cost	
(b) historical cost	
(c) cost less accumulated depreciation	
(d) replacement cost	

8. Basic financial assets (that do not constitute a financing arrangement) are initially recognised at:

(a) fair value	
(b) transaction price	
(c) transaction price plus transaction costs	
(d) fair value plus transaction price	

9. Financial instruments that constitute a financing arrangement are initially recognised at:

(a) transaction price	
(b) present value	
(c) transaction price plus transaction costs	
(d) none of the above	

10. Interest related to basic financial instruments is calculated using:

(a) the effective interest rate method	
(b) the sum of years' digits method	
(c) reducing balance method	
(d) none of the above	

Practical questions:
Application of principles to business scenarios

QUESTION 1

GAS (Pty) Ltd used its surplus cash to invest in 1 000 government bonds on 01 January 20X7. The bonds were issued for CU45 each when they had a face value of CU50 each. The bonds have a coupon rate of 5% per annum payable on 31 December of each year. The bonds were initially issued on 01 January 20X5 and are redeemable on 31 December 20X10. The accountant correctly calculated the effective interest rate to be 8.021%.

You are required to:
Record the journal entry to account for the bonds in the financial statements of GAS (Pty) Ltd for the year ended 30 June 20X7.

QUESTION 2

SHOPPERS (Pty) Ltd sells inventory to a customer for CU250,880 on 01 January 20X7, payable after two years, while normal credit terms are six months. A market-related interest rate is considered to be 12% per annum compounded annually.

You are required to:
Record the journal entries to account for the revenue and amount receivable for the year ended 31 December 20X7.

QUESTION 3

SPECTRA (Pty) Ltd purchased inventory from its supplier for CU110,000 on 01 January 20X7, payable on 01 January 20X8. A market-related interest rate for a similar transaction is considered to be 10%.

You are required to:
Record the journal entries to account for the receipt of the inventory and the related payable for the year ended 31 December 20X7.

CHAPTER 10
PROVISIONS AND CONTINGENCIES

Provisions and contingent liabilities are separated by probabilities, but the risk attached to that fine line can mean the death of a business.

ILLUSTRATIVE DISCLOSURE [EXTRACT]

IFRS ref		Notes	20X2	20X1
			CU'000	CU '000
	Non-current liabilities			
S4 .4 & IAS 37 p.71	Long-term portion of provisions	15	96	50
	Current liabilities			
S4.4 & IAS 37 p.71	Current portion of provisions	15	34	-

IFRS ref			20X2	20X1
			CU'000	CU'000
S21.14 (IAS 37 p.84)	15	PROVISIONS……….. [Details]		
		Balance at the beginning of the period	50	29
		Additional accrual during the period	70	25
		Payment made during the period	(40)	(4)
		Balance at the end of the period	80	50
		Less: Current portion of provisions	(34)	-
		Long-term portion of provisions	46	50

S21.15 (IAS 37 p.85 & 86)	24	CONTINGENT LIABILITIES		
		During 20X2, a customer initiated proceedings against the company for a fire caused by faulty candles. The customer asserts that its total losses are CU65,000 and has initiated litigation to claim this amount. The company's [group's] counsel does not consider that the claim has merit, and the company intends to contest it. No provision has been recognised in these financial statements as the company's [group's] management does not consider it probable that a loss will arise.		
S21.16 (IAS 37 p.89)	25	CONTINGENT ASSET		
		In 20X2, the company instigated legal proceedings against a customer for damages to its property caused by negligence. The company's [group's] lawyers believe that it is probable that damages of CU60,000 will be awarded by the court. An asset is not recognised in the financial statements for this possible asset, the existence of which is dependent upon the outcome of the legal proceedings.		

10.1 INTRODUCTION

The classification of financial obligations between liabilities, provisions and contingent liabilities is separated by fine lines between the existence of present obligations and the satisfaction of the recognition criteria which is largely dependent on management's professional judgement. This depends on management's interpretation and estimation of the circumstances prevailing at the reporting date about the occurrence or non-occurrence of past and future events, and the measurement thereof. The manner in which financial obligations are recognised and presented significantly influences the integrity and quality of the financial statements, especially in terms of the solvency and liquidity of the organisation.

10.2 LEARNING OUTCOMES

Upon completion of this unit you should know the financial reporting requirements for provisions, contingent liabilities and contingent assets in accordance with the accounting standards. In particular, you should be able to:
(a) distinguish between liabilities, provisions and contingent liabilities;
(b) identify and recognise provisions and contingent liabilities for presentation in financial statements;
(c) measure provisions and contingent liabilities on initial and subsequent recognition;

(d) present and disclose provisions and contingent liabilities in financial statements; and

(e) recognise, measure and disclose contingent assets.

10.3 DEFINITIONS

The definitions for the important concepts and terms used in IFRS for SMEs are found in Appendix B – *Glossary of terms* in IFRS for SMEs. Some important definitions relating to provisions and contingencies include the following:

- **Liability**: A present obligation of the entity arising from a past event, the settlement which is expected to result in an outflow from the entity of resources embodying economic benefits

- **Provision**: A liability of uncertain timing or amount

- **Contingent liability:** Either:
  (a) a liability which is not measureable and/or probable; or
  (b) a possible obligation that arises from past events and whose existence will be confirmed only by the occurrence or non-occurrence of one or more uncertain future events not wholly within the control of the entity

- **Contingent asset**: A possible asset that arises from past events and whose existence will be confirmed by the occurrence or non-occurrence of one or more uncertain future events not wholly within the control of the entity

- **Onerous contract**: A contract in which the unavoidable costs of meeting the obligations under the contract exceed the economic benefits expected to be received under it

- **Present obligation**: Characterised by the entity having no realistic alternative but to make the sacrifice of economic benefits to settle the obligation

- **Constructive obligation**: An obligation that is implied by a set of circumstances in a particular situation (announcement, communication or action of the organisation) where the entity has created a valid expectation by the parties to whom the entity has communicated (implicitly or explicitly) that it will discharge certain responsibilities

10.4 SCOPE AND OBJECTIVES

This section is applicable to all provisions, contingent liabilities and contingent assets except the following provisions which are covered by other sections of the accounting standards:
(a) leases [s20 and IFRS 16], except for those operating leases which have become onerous;
(b) construction contracts [s23 and IFRS 15];
(c) employee benefit obligations [s28 and IAS 19]; and
(d) income tax [s29 and IAS 12].

In addition, IAS 37 p.5 includes in its list:
(a) insurance contracts [IFRS 4]; and
contingent consideration of an acquirer in a business combination [IFRS 3].

10.5 CLASSIFICATION OF FINANCIAL OBLIGATIONS

10.5.1 Categories of financial obligations

Financial obligations arise as a result of organisations utilising debt financing for both non-current assets and operating activities. Financial obligations relate to the payment of interest as well as the repayment of the capital amount borrowed. Financial obligations result from contractual/legal obligations as well as constructive obligations (legitimate expectation by third parties resulting from public announcements or actions).

Financial obligations can be classified into the three major categories:
1. **Liability:** a present obligation of the entity arising from a past event, the settlement which is expected to result in an outflow from the entity of resources embodying economic benefits (s2.15(b) and IAS 31 p.10). An essential characteristic of a liability is that the entity has a present obligation through legal or constructive agreements to act or perform in a particular way to fulfil its financial obligations (s2.20 and Conceptual Framework (CF) p.4.4). Although it is sometimes necessary to estimate the amount or timing of liabilities, the uncertainty is generally much less than for provisions;
2. **Provision:** a liability of uncertain timing or amount (s21.11 and IAS 37 p.10). A provision is recognised as a result of managements' judgement that a probability exists at the specific point in time that the organisation will have to fulfil that will result in an outflow of cash or a reduction in resources; and

3. **Contingent liability:** a possible obligation that arises from past events and whose existence will be confirmed only by the occurrence or non-occurrence of one or more uncertain future events not wholly within the control of the entity or a present obligation which is either not measurable and/or not probable (s21.12 and IAS 37 p.10).

10.5.2 Classification criteria

The process for classifying an obligation can be summarised as follows:[1]

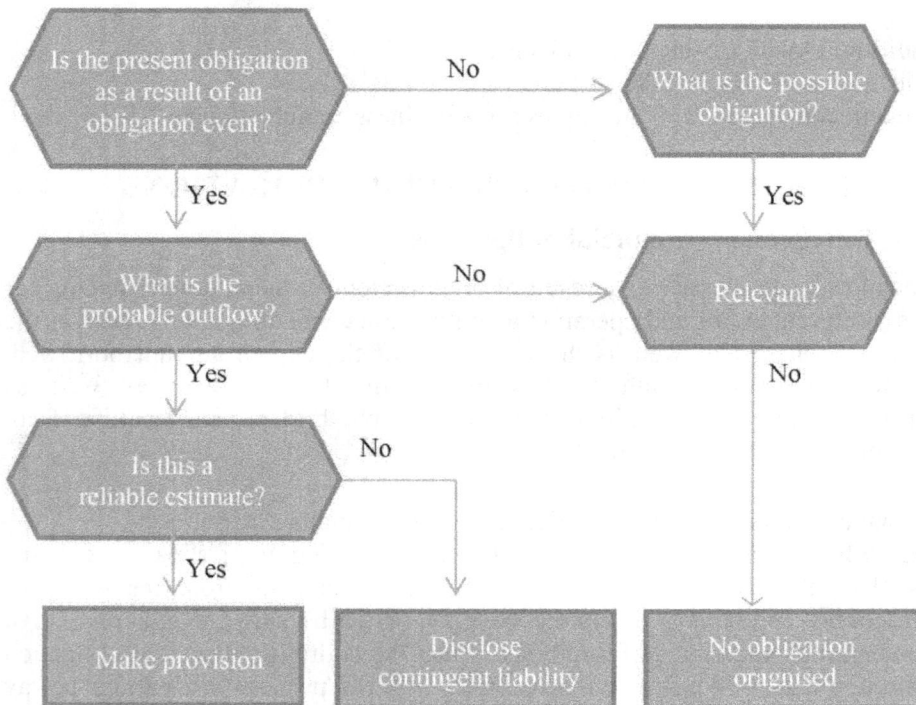

10.6 PROVISIONS

10.6.1 Classification

The term 'provision' is often used in the context of such items as depreciation, impairment losses and uncollectible receivables. These items are referred to as 'contra-assets', as they adjust the carrying amount of the assets. However, as they do not present liabilities of uncertain timing or amount, they are not covered by this section of the accounting standards (s21.3 and IAS 37 p.10).

The distinguishing characteristic of a provision is the level of uncertainty of the timing or amount of the financial obligation. A provision is often regarded as a liability whose timing and amount will only be confirmed by the occurrence or non-occurrence of a future event. For example, an entity purchased goods from a supplier which will only be settled 30 days after the buyer sells the goods and the settlement amount to be paid will be based on the market price of the goods at the settlement date. The obligation to pay the supplier is recognised as a provision because there is uncertainty as to when payment will be made (payment is dependent on the buyer's ability to sell the goods) as well the amount that will be paid (the amount to be paid depends on the market price which could fluctuate significantly).

10.6.2 Initial recognition

An entity shall only recognise a provision in the financial statements if (s21.4 and IAS 37 p.14):
(a) the entity has an obligation at the reporting date as a result of a past event, ie a present obligation exists as a result of a legal contract or constructive obligation;
(b) it is probable (more likely than not) that the entity will be required to transfer economic benefits in settlement of the financial obligation; and
(c) the amount of the obligation can be estimated reliably, ie the basis for measurement is available.

A provision shall be recognised in the accounting records as an expense, unless another section of the accounting standards requires the cost to be recognised as part of the cost of an asset such as inventory or property, plant and equipment.

10.6.2.1 Present obligation

A present obligation only results from a contractual obligation which is enforced by law, or from a constructive obligation which arises because of the past actions of the entity which creates a valid expectation in other parties that the entity will discharge the obligation (s21.6 and IAS 37 p.10). A constructive obligation is an obligation that derives from an entity's actions:

(a) by an established pattern of past practice, such as published policies, or a sufficiently specific current public statement/communication, or the entity has indicated to other parties that it will accept particular responsibilities; and

(b) when, as a result of the above, the entity has created a valid expectation on the part of those other parties that it will discharge those responsibilities.

For example, an entity contracts with the local municipality to restore the environment to its original state after a set period of operations. The entity is not certain what the restoration will cost, but can estimate. In addition, the entity has, as past practice, made donations to the local community calculated at 1% of its net profit before the donation. Management is of the opinion that the practice has created a valid expectation in the community to the extent that failure to honour the past practice by making donations in the current financial reporting period will significantly impact its reputation and therefore its customer relations and sales. The entity is able to establish the amount of the donation at year-end, but is uncertain about the timing of the settlement of the donation. In terms of the costs of restoration, the entity will recognise a provision at year-end as the restoration represents a legal obligation of uncertain amount while the donation is recognised as a provision as it represents a constructive obligation of uncertain timing (the amount is certain).

A provision can only be recognised if the present obligation existed prior to the reporting period ending. Therefore, an organisation cannot recognise a provision in respect of an obligation that arises from future actions. No matter how likely its occurrence is, it does not represent a present obligation at the reporting date. For example, say the government plans to implement environmental laws two years from the current date, resulting in offenders being fined R500 000. At the reporting date, management cannot recognise a provision as the law has not been implemented and thus does not represent a present obligation – the organisation will only have an obligation when it is found to be guilty of violating the law (future event). However, the exception is for the recognition of an onerous contract (see section 8.6.6).

10.6.2.2 Probable occurrence

A financial obligation is only considered probable if it is more likely than not (more than 50% chance) to be fulfilled. The probable occurrence of the event must be determined based on the facts and circumstances available at the reporting date and management's judgement, and the basis used to make the decision must be presented in the notes to the financial statements if the amounts involved are material in nature. For example, an organisation's operation (fracking) has the potential to contaminate underground water and legislation requires restoration of the area. Management estimates that the costs to restore the environment could be between CU10–CU60 million. The organisation has a present obligation (conducting operations which contaminate the underground water) and is required by law to restore the environment, but the timing of fulfilling the obligation and the amount is not certain, therefore the entity should recognise a provision.

10.6.2.3 Initial recognition/recording

The provision should be recognised as an expense via the profit and loss. However, if the provision is directly associated with an asset (such as rehabilitation and demolition cots), then it should be capitalised as part of the carrying amount of the asset (s17.10(c) and IAS 16 p.16(c)).

10.6.3 Initial measurement

A provision relates to uncertainty about the timing and/or amount of the present obligation, however the amount of the provision can be estimated, as reliable estimates are not considered to reduce reliability of the financial statements (s2.30 and IAS 37 p.25). The measurement of the provision should represent the best estimate of the amount that an organisation would rationally expect to pay in order to settle the obligation at the end of the reporting period or to transfer it to a third party at that time (s21.7 and IAS 37 p.36). If the provision cannot be measured reliably, then even though a present obligation exists, it cannot be recognised; such an obligation should be disclosed as a contingent liability (s21.12 and IAS 37 p.36).

When the provision involves a large range of possible outcomes, the best estimate is represented by the weighted average of all possible outcomes, taking into account the probability for each outcome, ie using the expected value to determine the estimate (s21.7(a) and IAS 37 p.39). Where there is a continuous range of possible outcomes, and each point in that range is as likely as any other, the mid-point is used as the possible outcome. If the possible outcomes are either mostly higher or mostly lower than the most likely outcome, the best estimate will be the higher or lower amount, ie the entity must apply the prudence concept (s21.7(b) and IAS 37 p.40).

Illustrative Example 10.1: Initial measurement

The following were extracted from the attorney's files:
(a)   a customer instituted a claim against the organisation for lack of performance in terms of a contract that was completed before the reporting date. The attorney estimated that there was a high probability that the court would rule in favour of the customer, with a 60% chance of

the claim being CU500,000 and a 40% chance of the claim being CU200,000; and

(b)   a customer instituted a claim against the company for negligence after the reporting date which alleged negligence also occurred after the reporting date. The attorney estimated that the courts would rule in favour of the customer for an amount of CU60,000.

You are required to:
Prepare the journal entries necessary to account for the items above in the financial statements of the entity.

Suggested solution:
(i) Claim for lack of performance

DR: Litigation expenses	380,000	
CR: Provision for litigation costs		380,000

[Recognition of provision for litigation – ((CU500,000 × 60%) + (CU200,000 × 40%))]

(ii) Claim for negligence
Provisions can only be recognized at the reporting date for present obligations which exist at the reporting date, the claim by the customer for negligence occurred after the reporting date and thus no provision can be recognized.

When determining the best estimate of the provision which is originally capitalised against the cost of an asset, the gains realised from the expected disposal of the asset shall be excluded from the measurement of the provision (s21.8 and IAS 37 p.51).

10.6.3.1 Time value of money

A provision which will be settled in a future period shall be measured at its present value if the time value of money is considered to be material (s21.7 and IAS 37p.45). The materiality of the present value is assessed by taking into account the estimated amount of the provision in relation to the other amounts on the financial statements as well as the time period until settlement of the obligation. The discounted rate use to present value the amount is the market related pre-tax discount rate.

10.6.4 Subsequent measurement

10.6.4.1 Expenses incurred in relation to the provision

When the payment related to the provision is incurred, for example the claim against the organisation is settled, then the entity should set those payments off against the provision which was previously raised (s21.10 and IAS 37 p.61). When setting off the expenditures, the following must be considered:

(a) if the expense exceeds the provision, then the amount in excess of the provision must be recognised as an expense for that particular period; or

(b) if the expense is less than the provision and the provision is no longer required, then the provision should be written off as a reversal in the profit or loss.

Illustrative Example 10.2: Subsequent measurement

At 01 March 20X7, the balance of the provision for litigation was CU100,000 and final settlement of the claim against the organisation amounted to CU165,000.

You are required to:
Prepare the journal entries necessary to account for the provision at the settlement date.

Suggested solution:

DR: Provision for litigation	100,000	
DR: Litigation expenses	65,000	
CR: Bank		165,000
[Settlement of the provision for litigation recognised in previous periods]		

10.6.4.2 Valuation at subsequent reporting dates

At the end of subsequent reporting dates after its initial recognition, management must assess whether the provision is required and at which amount. When a provision is measured at its present value, the provision's carrying amount increases in each reporting period to reflect the passage of time. The unwinding of the provision, if there is no change in the estimated amount, must be recognised as a financing cost in the profit and loss – the adjustment to the provision resulting from unwinding should not be recognised as an adjustment against the carrying amount of the asset (if the provision has been capitalised to an asset).

Illustrative Example 10.3: Subsequent measurement

At 01 January 20X7, the following provisions were recognised: (a) the provision for loss on a lawsuit of CU240,000 (due to be settled shortly after year end), and (b) the provision for demolition costs CU225,790 (cost of R 400,000 discounted at 10% with a remaining period of 6 years). At the reporting date ended 31 December 20X7, management considered that both provisions were still relevant but that the provision for the lawsuit should be CU300,000.

You are required to:
Prepare the journal entries necessary to account for the provision for the lawsuit and demolition.

Suggested solution:
31 Dec 20X7:

DR: Litigation expenses	60,000	
CR: Provision for lawsuit		60,000

[Recognition of the re-assessment of the provision for litigation – (CU300,000 – CU240,000)]

DR: Finance costs	22,579	
CR: Provision for demolition costs		22,579

[Recognition of the unwinding of the provision – (CU225,790 × 10%)]

10.6.4.3 Changes in the estimate of the provision

Any change to the provision must be treated as a change in an accounting estimate and implemented prospectively (s10.16 & 17 and IAS 8 p.36). Changes in the provision (based on prevailing conditions) must be recognised as an expense or adjustment to the carrying amount of an asset (s21.11 and IAS 8 p.37).

Illustrative Example 10.4: Change in estimate related to provisions

At 01 March 20X7, the entity purchased a machine on which it capitalized a provision for rehabilitation costs amounting to CU256,580 (CU500,000 discounted at 10% after 7 years). At 28 February 20X8, management reviewed the rehabilitation costs and considered a realistic cost to be CU750,000 with an interest rate of 11%.

You are required to:
Prepare the journal entries necessary to account for the

Suggested solution:

01 Mar 20X7: Change in estimate [*(CU750,000 @ 11% after 7 years) – CU256,580]	104,665
28 Feb 20X8: Unwinding [(CU750,000 @ 11% after 6 years) – CU361,244]	39,737

1 March 20X7:
DR: Machinery & equipment   104,665
CR: Provision for rehabilitation costs   104,665
[Recognition of the change in estimate of the rehabilitation costs]

28 Feb 20X8:
DR: Finance costs   39,737
CR: Provision for rehabilitation costs   39,737
[Recognition of unwinding of the provision for rehabilitation costs]
*If you are using a financial calculator to calculate the present value of the
rehabilitation cost, you would need to enter the following:
[PV = i: 11%; n: 6; PMT: 0; FV:CU750,000]

10.6.5 Re-imbursement for obligations

In order to mitigate against potential business risks, such as claims from
customers, competitors or employees, an entity often has insurance contracts,
indemnity clauses in agreements and/or suppliers' warranties. If an entity can
recover some or the entire amount required to settle an obligation, such as a
lawsuit by a customer against the organisation, from a third party, then such a re-
imbursement from the third party shall be recognised as a separate asset (s21.9
and IAS 37 p.53). The re-imbursement is only recognized as an asset when there
is absolute certainty that it will be received. The organisation should recognise the
provision for the obligation and the asset for the reimbursement separately – it
cannot set off the one against the other in the statement of financial position;
however, the re-imbursement can be set-off against the expense in the statement
of financial performance (s2.52 and IAS 37p.54). The amount recognized for the
re-imbursement shall not exceed the amount of the provision.

It is important to note whether the entity remains liable for the settlement of the
full obligation irrespective of re-imbursement. If the third party fails to pay for
any reason and the entity is not liable to settle the obligation, the entity has no
obligation for those costs and shall not raise a provision – such as factory
warranties being the responsibility of the supplier and not that of the organisation
selling the goods to the customer.

For example, goods sold by an entity have a manufacturer's warranty where the
manufacturer is obliged to repair or replace any defects. The customer must return
the defective goods directly to the manufacturer if there are any defects. The
entity has no obligation to repair or replace any defective goods and thus no
provision needs to be recognised.

Illustrative Example 10.5: Reimbursements related to provisions

The financial manager stated that the following provisions should be recognised at the reporting date: (a) a provision for warranty of CU350,000, and (b) a re-imbursement receivable based on the warranty above of CU500,000.

You are required to:
Prepare the journal entries necessary to account for the provision for warranty and the related reimbursement in the financial statements of the entity.

Suggested solution:
The re-imbursement is only recognised if there is certainty that the amount will be received and is limited to the value of the provision for the obligation recognised – the excess of CU150,000 of re-imbursement is not recognised.

DR: Warranty expenses	350,000	
CR: Provision for warranty obligations		350,000
[Recognition of provision for obligations in terms of warranties]		

DR: Warranty re-imbursement asset	350,000	
CR: Warranty re-imbursement income		350,000
[Recognition of re-imbursement for warranty obligations]		

10.6.6 Onerous contract

An onerous contract is one in which the unavoidable costs of meeting the obligations under the contract exceed the economic benefits. Obligations that arise from the entity's future actions do not meet the criteria of 'being a present obligation' and thus cannot be recognised as a provision (s21.6 and IAS 37 p.63).

However, this accounting standard specifically requires the entity to recognise provisions for onerous contracts. The provision for an onerous contract is measured at the estimated unavoidable costs and is represented by the lower of the cost of fulfilling the contract and any compensation or penalties arising from the failure to fulfil it.

Illustrative Example 10.6: Onerous contract

Management intends to terminate an operating lease agreement which contains a penalty clause for early termination of a year's annual rental of CU300,000 plus compensation of CU120,000. The lease agreement has 18 months before it expires. The rental property cannot be sublet and management can no longer use the property for its intended (nor any other) purpose.

You are required to:

Prepare the journal entries necessary to account for the early termination of the lease agreement.

Suggested solution:

The termination of the lease agreement represents an onerous contract (penalty exceeds the rental costs). The provision for the onerous contract is measured at the lower of the rental payment of CU450,000 (continuation of the lease – CU300 000/12 months × 18 months) and the termination costs (CU420,000 – rental plus compensation).

DR: Rental expense	420,000	
CR: Provision for rental expenses		420,000
[Recognition of a provision for onerous contract]		

10.6.7 Effects of taxation

Provisions recognised for financial reporting purposes are generally not allowed as deductions for income tax purposes during the same reporting periods – deductions are only recognised when they are actually incurred. The different treatment of provisions for accounting and tax, results in a temporary difference which gives rise to deferred tax (s29 and IAS 12).

10.6.8 Disclosure requirements

For each class of provision, an entity shall disclose all the following (s21.14 and IAS 37 p.84–86):

(a) a reconciliation showing:

    (i)   carrying amount at the beginning and end of the period;

    (ii)   additions during the period, including adjustments that result from changes in measuring the discounted amount (change in estimates and finance costs);

    (iii)   amounts charged against the provision during the period (expenses incurred); and

    (iv)   unused amounts reversed during the period (cancellation of provisions);

    (v)   a brief description of the nature of the obligation and the expected amount and timing of any resulting payments;

    (vi)   an indication of the uncertainties about the amount or timing of those outflows;

(vii)   the amount of any expected re-imbursement, stating the amount of any asset that has been recognised for that expected re-imbursement; and

(viii)   comparative information for prior periods is not required.

10.7   CONTINGENT LIABILITIES

10.7.1 Recognition of contingent liabilities

There are two types of contingent liabilities (s21.12 and IAS 37 p.10):

1. *Present obligations:* contingent liabilities that arise from past events, ie a present obligation exists, but the occurrence of the event (fulfillment of the obligation) is uncertain or the amount cannot be measured reliably; and

2. *Possible obligation:* a contingent liability that arises from past events and whose existence will be confirmed only by the occurrence or non-occurrence of one or more uncertain future events not wholly within the control of the entity. Possible obligations do not meet the criteria of the definition of liabilities (probable occurrence of the event) and thus cannot be recognised as contingent liabilities.

When, as a result of past events, there may be an outflow of resources embodying future economic benefits in settlement of (a) a present obligation, or (b) a possible obligation whose existence will be confirmed only by the occurrence or non-occurrence of one or more uncertain future events not wholly within the control of the entity and ...

Illustrative Example 10.7: Contingent liabilities

A health care organisation is suing the entity for the sale of meat which has gone bad and used in the production of processed meat products by a local manufacturer. The manufacturer uses a host of different suppliers and has not, as yet, provided any concrete evidence that the expired meat was purchased from the entity being sued by the health care organisation. As such, the entity denies selling any expired meat and is defending itself in the matter. The entity can however not be sure that it did not sell expired meat with absolute certainty. The matter is under investigation and the identity of the supplier of the expired meat will only be established after the investigation is concluded. The legal counsel considers any possible damages to be in the range of CU4 million and CU40 million.

You are required to:
Discuss whether the lawsuit brought against the entity should be classified as a provision or a contingent liability.

Suggested solution:
It appears that there is no certainty as to whether a present or possible obligation exists. The following will be considered and the relevant conclusion drawn: (i) if it is probable, on the balance of the evidence available, that the entity will lose the court case, then the entity is considered to have a present obligation of uncertain timing or amount and hence a provision should be recognised (the amount of the damages is still uncertain); and (ii) if it is probable, on the balance of the evidence available, that the entity will successfully defend the court case, then the entity is not considered to have a present obligation (it is considered to have a possible obligation) and hence a contingent liability should be disclosed (unless the possibility of the outflow of economic benefits is remote).

If an entity is jointly and severally liable for a contingent liability, the part that is expected to be settled by other parties is treated as a contingent liability, but for the portion that it is expected to settle as a provision. Except for those present obligations of an acquiree that are recognised as contingent liabilities in a business combination, a contingent liability must not be recognised (s21.12 and IFRS 3).

10.7.2 Disclosure requirements

Unless the possibility of any outflow of resources in settlement is remote, an entity shall disclose, for each class of contingent liability as at the reporting date, a brief description of the nature of the contingent liability and, when practicable (s21.15 and IAS 37 p.86):
(a) an estimate of its financial effect, measured based on the best estimate;
an indication of the uncertainties relating to the amount or timing of any outflow, and
the possibility of any re-imbursement.
If it is impracticable to make one or more of these disclosures, that fact shall be stated.

10.8   RECOGNITION OF CONTINGENT ASSETS

A contingent asset is defined as a possible asset that arises from past events and whose existence will be confirmed only by the occurrence or non-occurrence of one or more uncertain future events not wholly within the control of the entity (Appendix B and IAS 37 p.10).

Contingent assets usually arise from unplanned or other unexpected events that give rise to the possibility of an inflow of economic benefits to the entity. An entity shall not recognise a contingent asset as an asset, but shall disclose the contingent asset as a note to the financial statements when the inflow of economic benefits is probable (s21.13 and IAS 37 p.31–33). However, when the flow of future economic benefits to the entity is virtually certain, the entity shall recognise the future inflow as an asset.

10.9 PREJUDICIAL DISCLOSURES

In extremely rare cases, if disclosure of some or all of the information required by the accounting standard can be expected to prejudice seriously the position of the entity in a dispute with other parties on the subject matter of provision, contingent liability or contingent asset [s21.17 and IAS 37 p.92], there is no need to disclose the information, but the entity shall disclose the general nature of the dispute, together with the fact that, and reason why, the information has not been disclosed.

SELF-ASSESSMENT
Multiple choice questions: Testing principles of accounting for provisions and contingencies

1. Liabilities are recognised if the organisation has obligations that are:

(a) legally enforceable on both parties	
(b) to be confirmed by the occurrence of future events	
(c) present obligations at the reporting date	
(d) deemed by management to be crucial to the financial position of the entity	

2. Liabilities are only recognised in the financial statements if the obligations are:

(a) specified in terms of contracts	
(b) measured reliably in monetary terms	
(c) to result in future outflows of economic benefits	
(d) settled on fixed dates and the amount due can be measured reliably	

3.   A provision for a financial obligation should only be recognised:

(a) as a note to the financial statements	
(b) if the outcome of the event is certain or guaranteed	
(c) if management is confident that there are sufficient funds to meet the obligation	
(d) none of the above	

4.   A provision for a financial obligation is recognised:

(a) for a future obligation when the amount can be measured reliably	
(b) for a present obligation when the timing and/or amount is uncertain	
(c) for a present obligation when the timing and/or amount is certain	
(d) for a future obligation when the amount cannot be measured reliably	

5.   A provision for a financial obligation can only be recognised if it relates to:

(a) expenses and is recognised via profit and loss	
(b) assets and can be capitalised as part of the asset's cost	
(c) transactions that are allowed to reduce the tax liability	
(d) (a) and (b)	

6.   A provision for a financial obligation is measured at an amount based on:

(a) the value agreed by management	
(b) the estimate to settle the potential obligation in the future	
(c) the expected value of all possible outcomes for the obligation	
(d) (b) and (c)	

7.   The value of the provision reported in the financial statements:

(a) remains unchanged until it is settled	
(b) must be reviewed and assessed at each reporting date	
(c) must be increased at each reporting date to account for inflation	
(d) must be adjusted to satisfy the profit projections for the period	

8.   A contingent liability must be recognised if:

(a) the occurrence of the outcome of a present obligation is remote (highly unlikely)	
(b) the occurrence of the outcome of a future obligation is remote (highly unlikely)	
(c) present obligation is dependent on the outcome of a future event which is uncertain	
(d) none of the above	

9. A contingent liability is:

(a) recognised in the statement of financial position	
(b) disclosed in the accounting/auditors report	
(c) disclosed in the notes to the financial statements	
(d) (a) and (b)	

10. An onerous contract is defined as:

(a) one which does not have a present obligation	
(b) one that is too costly for the organisation to fulfil	
(c) one where the costs of not fulfilling an obligation exceed the economic benefits expected from the contract	
(d) none of the above	

11. The measurement of the onerous contract is presented by:

(a) the amount of the costs associated with the non-fulfilment of the obligation	
(b) the lower of the obligation and the cost of non-fulfilment	
(c) the amount that management is prepared to settle in future	
(d) the value of the penalties of non-fulfilment of the obligation	

12. Contingent assets should:

(a) never be recognised in the financial statements	
(b) always be recognised in the financial statements	
(c) only be recognised if there is certainty about the realisation of the benefits	
(d) only be recognised when the benefits are received	

Practical questions:
Application of principles to business scenarios

QUESTION 1

Objective: Determining the initial measurement of a provision

A customer was injured in a shopping centre and decided to institute a lawsuit against the management of the mall, owned by JLJ (Pty) Ltd, as the injury suffered required major surgery. The centre management was advised by their attorneys that the following actions were available:
(a) defend the court case: the attorneys indicated that there was a 50% possibility of successfully defending the court case; or
(b) negotiate an out-of-court settlement for a reduced compensation amount.

At the reporting date of 28 February 20X7, the attorneys estimated from experience that should the customer win the court case, the centre management had a 30% change of being ordered to pay the customer compensation of CU200,000 and a 70% chance of being ordered to pay compensation of CU500,000.

You are required to:
Discuss how the lawsuit should be recognised in the financial statements of JLJ (Pty) Ltd for the reporting period 28 February 20X7 in compliance with the accounting standards.

QUESTION 2

Objective: Initial and subsequent recognition of provisions

At the reporting date of 28 February 20X6, the company recognised a provision of CU500,000 in respect of a claim resulting from a dispute with a customer. The dispute was resolved and the company agreed to make a final payment of CU300,000 in settlement of the claim, which was paid on 30 April 20X6.

You are required to:
Record the journal entries relating to the claim by the customer for the reporting periods ended 28 February 20X6 and 20X7 in compliance with the accounting standards.

QUESTION 3

Objective: Initial and subsequent recognition and measurement of a provision

With effect from 01 June 20X5, a company implements a warranty policy of one year for certain of its high value products. In terms of the warranty, the company takes responsibility to (i) repair the product at no cost to the customer, and (ii) replace the product if it cannot be repaired. The customer relations manager estimates that only 15% of the products sold will be returned, of which 90% will require repairs while the remainder will need to be replaced. The cost of repairs is estimated at CU800 per unit, while the standard unit cost is CU12,500. The company maintains a mark-up of 50% on repairs and 25% on goods sold.

The company sold 1 200 of the products during the year, of which 10 were returned and repaired at a cost of CU8 000 and 2 were replaced at the standard cost by 31 December 20X5.

You are required to:
Record the journal entries relating to the warranty agreements for the reporting period 31 December 20X5 in compliance with the accounting standards.

QUESTION 4

Objective: Recognition and measurement of the re-imbursement for obligations/provisions

The goods sold by a retailer contain a manufacturer's warranty of one year, but the retailer includes a further one year warranty – the total warranty is for two years. The retailer estimates the value of the warranty on goods sold to be CU325,000, of which CU250,000 represents the manufacturer's warranty. The retailer is virtually certain that the manufacturer will reimburse the retailer for fulfilling the obligations of the warranty.

You are required to:
Record the journal entries relating to the warranty agreements for the reporting period 28 February 20X7 in compliance with the accounting standards.

CHAPTER 11
LEASES

Why buy assets?
True wealth does not lie in ownership of property but in the use of it – Aristotle

ILLUSTRATIVE DISCLOSURE [EXTRACT]

IFRS ref		Notes	20X2	20X1	
			CU'000	CU'000	
	Non-current assets				
S17, S16 & S27	Property, plant and equipment	6	2,550	2,401	
	Non-current liabilities				
S20 & S16	Long-term portion of finance lease	14	24	45	
	Current liabilities				
S4 & S20	Current portion of finance lease obligations	14	21	20	

IFRS ref			20X2	20X1	
			CU'000	CU'000	
	6	**PROPERTY, PLANT & EQUIPMENT**			
			Machinery	**Equipment**	**Total**
S17		**Carrying amount at beginning of the period**	**1,570**	**831**	**2,401**
		Cost	1,960	1,102	3,062
		Accumulated depreciation and impairment loss	(390)	(271)	(661)
		Acquisitions during the period	-	485	485
		Carrying amount of assets disposed of during period	-	(36)	(36)
		Depreciation	(30)	(240)	(270)

			Machinery	Equipment	Total
		Impairment loss	-	(30)	(30)
		Transferred to/(from) other assets	-	-	-
		Carrying amount at the end of the period	**1,540**	**1,010**	**2,550**
		Cost	1,960	1,346	3,306
		Accumulated depreciation and impairment loss	(420)	(336)	(756)
		ALTERNATIVE:			
			Machinery	**Equipment**	**Total**
		Cost:			
		Balance at beginning of the period	1,960	1,102	3,062
		Acquisitions during the period	-	485	485
		Disposals during the period	-	(241)	(241)
		Balance at the end of the period	1,960	1,346	3,306
		Accumulated depreciation and impairment loss			
		Balance at beginning of the period	(390)	(271)	(661)
		Annual depreciation	(30)	(240)	(270)
		Impairment loss for the period	-	(30)	(30)
		Accumulated depreciation on assets disposed of	-	205	205
		Balance at the end of the period	(420)	(336)	(756)
		Carrying amount at the end of the period	**1,540**	**1,010**	**2,550**

S20	14	**FINANCE LEASE OBLIGATIONS**			
		The finance lease obligations are measured at the amortised costs using the effective interest rate method [only if applicable]. The loan is secured over the [asset] owned by the entity with a carrying amount of Rxx [20X1 – R…]. The loan is repayable by installments of Rxx for the next … years [remaining period]. Interest is payable at a rate ………….%.	45	65	
		Less: Current portion of finance lease obligations	21	20	
		Long-term finance lease obligations	24	45	
		Obligations under finance lease – reconciliation			
			Following year	Thereafter	Total
		Lease rental payments	25	25	50
		Finance costs	4	1	5
		Repayment of finance lease obligation	21	24	45
S20	17	**COMMITMENT UNDER OPERATING LEASE**			
		Operating lease commitments under non-cancellable operating leases that fall due as follows:			
		Following year [within one year]	13	26	
		Later than one year but within five years]	-	13	
		Thereafter [later than five years]	-	-	
			13	39	

11.1 INTRODUCTION

Leasing has grown tremendously in popularity under modern economic and business environments. Leasing is favoured as a financing option because instead of investing large cash resources in assets, or borrowing money to acquire assets, leasing allows the entity to make periodic payments to lease the assets. Modern day management has concluded that Aristotle's observation that '[w]ealth is in use and not ownership' was right, resulting in many entities becoming heavily involved in leasing assets rather than buying them.

The requirements for accounting for leases differ fundamentally between IFRS for SMEs and IFRS. The focus of this chapter is on the accounting for leases in terms of IFRS for SMEs.

11.2 LEARNING OUTCOMES

Upon completion of this unit you should know the financial reporting requirements for accounting for the lease of assets in accordance with the IFRS for SMEs. In particular, you should be able to:
(a)   identify lease arrangements that qualify for recognition under this section;
(b)   explain the nature, economic substance and advantages of lease transactions;
(c)   distinguish between finance leases and operating leases;
(d)   recognise and measure finance leases at the inception of the lease in the financial statements of the lessee and those of the lessor;
(e)   recognise and measure the assets and liabilities after their initially recognising the finance lease in the financial statements of the lessee and those of the lessor;
(f)   recognise and measure operating leases in the financial statements of the lessee and those of the lessor; and
(g)   present and disclose leases in the financial statements of the lessee and those of the lessor.

Diagramatic representation of lease accounting:

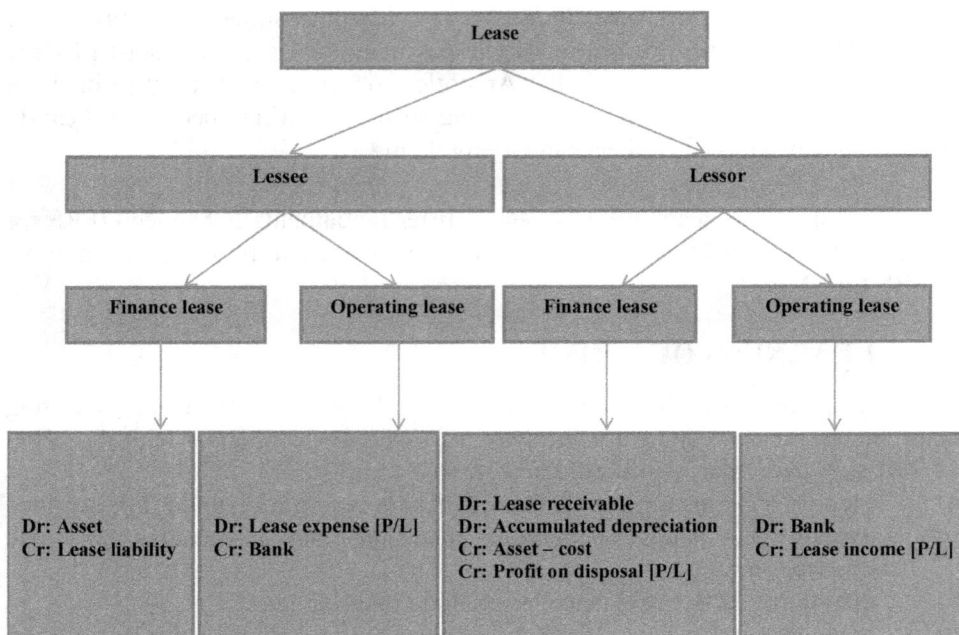

```
                          ┌─────────────────────────┐
                          │          Lease          │
                          └─────────────────────────┘
                           ╱                       ╲
              ┌──────────────────┐         ┌──────────────────┐
              │      Lessee      │         │      Lessor      │
              └──────────────────┘         └──────────────────┘
               ╱            ╲                ╱             ╲
    ┌──────────────┐ ┌──────────────┐ ┌──────────────┐ ┌──────────────┐
    │ Finance lease│ │Operating lease│ │ Finance lease│ │Operating lease│
    └──────────────┘ └──────────────┘ └──────────────┘ └──────────────┘
```

Dr: Asset	Dr: Lease expense [P/L]	Dr: Lease receivable	Dr: Bank
Cr: Lease liability	Cr: Bank	Dr: Accumulated depreciation	Cr: Lease income [P/L]
		Cr: Asset – cost	
		Cr: Profit on disposal [P/L]	

11.3 DEFINITIONS

The definitions for the important concepts and terms used in IFRS for SMEs are found in Appendix B of IFRS for SMEs. Some important definitions relating to leases include the following:

- **Finance lease:** A lease that transfers substantially all the risks and rewards of ownership of the asset. Title may or may not eventually transfer. A lease that is not a finance lease is an operating lease (s20.4).

- **Operating lease:** A lease that does not transfer substantially all the risks and rewards incidental to ownership. A lease that is not an operating lease is a finance lease (Appendix B).

- **Lease:** An agreement whereby the lessor conveys to the lessee in return for a payment or a series of payments the right to use an asset for an agreed period of time.

- **Lessee's incremental borrowing rate of interest:** The rate of interest the lessee would have to pay on a similar lease or, if that is not determinable, the rate that, at the inception of the lease, the lessee would incur to borrow over a similar term, and with similar security, the funds necessary to purchase the asset.

- **Interest rate implicit in the lease:** The discount rate that, at inception of the lease, causes the aggregate present value of (a) the minimum lease payments, and (b) the unguaranteed residual value to be equal to the sum of (i) the fair value of the leased asset, and (ii) any initial direct costs of the lessor.

- **Effective interest rate:** The rate that exactly discounts estimated future cash payments or receipts through the expected life of the financial instrument or, when appropriate, a shorter period to the net carrying amount of the financial asset of financial liability.

- **Effective interest method:** A method of calculating the amortised cost of a financial asset or financial liability (or a group of financial assets or financial liabilities) and of allocating the interest income or interest expense over the relevant period.

- **Fair value:** The amount for which an asset could be exchanged, a liability settled or an equity instrument granted, between knowledgeable, willing parties in an arm's length transaction.

- **Net investment in a lease:** The gross investment in a lease discounted at the interest rate implicit in the lease.

- **Minimum lease payments:** The payment over the lease term that the lessee is or can be required to make, excluding contingent rent, costs for services and taxes to be paid by and reimbursed to the lessor, together with:
  (a) for a lessee, any amounts guaranteed by the lessee or by a party related to the lessee; or
  (b) for the lessor, any residual value guaranteed to the lessor by:
    (i) the lessee;
    (ii) a party related to the lessee; or
    (iii) a third party unrelated to the lessor that is financially capable of discharging the obligations under the guarantee.

- **Guaranteed residual value:**
  (a) for a lessee, that part of the residual value that is guaranteed by the lessee or by a party related to the lessee (the amount of the guarantee being the minimum amount that could, in any event, become payable); and
  (b) for a lessor, that part of the residual value that is guaranteed by the lessee or by a party unrelated to the lessor that is financially capable of discharging the obligation under the guarantee.

- **Unguaranteed residual value:** That portion of the residual value of the leased asset, the realisation of which by the lessor is not assured or is guaranteed solely by a party related to the lessor.

- **Contingent rent:** That portion of the lease payment that is not fixed in amount, but is based on the future amount of a factor that changes other than with the passage of time, for example percentage of future sales, amount of future use, future price indices and future market rates of interest.

The terms lessor and lessee are not defined in Appendix B of IFRS for SMEs. The lessor refers to the party who is leasing (renting) the asset *out* and who will receive payment for the counterparty using their asset. The lessee is the party who is leasing (renting) the asset *in* and who will make payment to the lessor for using the asset.

11.4   SCOPE AND OBJECTIVES

S20.1: This section is applicable to accounting for all leases in the accounting records of both lessees and lessors and excludes the following:
(a)   leases to explore for or use minerals, oil, natural gas and similar non-regenerative resources (s34 – *Specialised activities*);
(b)   licensing agreements for such items as motion picture films, video recordings, plays, manuscripts, patents and copyrights (s18 –*Intangible assets other than goodwill*);
(c)   measure of property held by lessees that is accounted for as investment property and measurement of investment property provided by lessors under operating leases (s16 – *Investment property*);
(d)   measurement of biological assets held by lessees under finance leases and biological assets provided by lessors under operating leases (s34 – *Specialised activities*);

(e)   leases that could lead to a loss to the lessor or the lessee as a result of contractual terms that are unrelated to changes in the price of the leased asset, changes in foreign exchange rates or default by one of the counterparties (s12 – *Other financial instrument issues*); and

(f)   operating leases that are onerous (s21 – *Provisions and contingencies*).

Illustrative Example 11.1: Classification as a lease

Application of s20 – Leases

An entity owns an office building that was acquired with the intention of generating rental income by renting it to independent third parties.

You are required to:
Discuss whether the arrangement above meets the definition of a lease.

Suggested solution:
As the entity conveys the right to the tenant to use the building for a payment or series of payments for an agreed period of time, the arrangement meets the definition of a lease and the income received shall be accounted for in terms of the s20 – *Leases*.

An entity (lessee) leased property in terms of an operating lease, and rents out the property to independent third parties. The entity profits (rental income received exceeds rental expense) from its property interest in the operating lease and selected the option to recognise its property interest as investment property (s16 – *Investment property*).

You are required to:
Discuss whether the arrangements above can be classified as leases.

Suggested solution:
The entity has the right to use the lessor's property for a period of time in exchange for a payment or series of payments and therefore, the arrangement between the entity and the lessor meets the definition of a lease. In turn, the entity subleases the property by transferring to the lessee its right to use the property for a period of time for a payment or series of payments for a period of time and therefore the sublease also meets the definition of a lease in terms of s20 – *Leases*. Although the arrangement meets the definition of a lease, the fact that the entity elected to recognise its property interest from an operating lease as investment property, the requirement of s20 – *Leases* does not apply, provided the recognition criteria for investment property are satisfied (fair value can be measured reliably).

11.5   LESSEE

11.5.1 Lessee – Finance lease

11.5.1.1   Initial recognition

Under a finance lease agreement, the lessee rents the asset, but the substantial risk and rewards associated with that asset are considered to transfer to the lessee from inception of the lease. However, the lessee has not paid the full amount outstanding, which implies that the asset is no different to an asset that was acquired by the lessee and financed, either in full or partially, with a loan. For this reason, the lessee recognises the asset (as the lessee controls the substantial risks and rewards incidental to ownership) and a related liability at inception of the lease (as the lessee would not have made full, if any, payment on the lease).

The asset and related liability initially recognised is measured at the lower of the following (s20.9):
(a)   the fair value of the leased asset; or
(b)   the present value of the minimum lease payments.

The following shows the recognition of the transaction as it would appear in the general journal:

LESSEE – FINANCE LEASE		
	Debit	**Credit**
	CU	**CU**
Asset – eg. Property [SFP]	100,000	
Lease liability [SFP]		100,000
[Recognising the payment under an arrangement recognised as a finance lease]		

11.5.1.2 Subsequent measurement

Subsequently, the lessee accounts for the asset recognised on initial recognition in accordance with the section related to that standard, for example s17 – *Property, plant & equipment* (s20.12). This means that the asset should potentially be depreciated, amortised and tested for impairment. If the asset is depreciated or amortised and there is no reasonable certainty that the lessee will receive ownership at the end of the lease term, the asset will be depreciated or amortised over the shorter of its useful life and lease term (s20.12).

The related liability recognised at initial recognition shall be accounted for using the amortised cost method. This implies that interest will be charged on the lease liability at the effective interest rate and any lease payments made will be used to reduce the lease liability.

Illustrative Example 11.2: Lessee finance lease - subsequent measurement

A manufacturer leases equipment with a fair value of R120,000 and a minimum lease payment of R100,000 at inception from a supplier from 1 January 20X6. The lease is correctly classified as a finance lease at inception. The equipment has an estimated useful life of 12 years and a zero estimated residual value. The lease term is for a period of 10 years. The lessee has to return the asset to the lessor after the lease term and there is no option to renew the lease. The effective rate implicit in the lease is 8% per annum compounded annually. The lease payments are R14,903.

You are required to:

Prepare the journal entries necessary to account for the lease for the year ended 31 December 20X6 in the financial statements of the lessee.

Suggested solution:

INITIAL RECOGNITION		
1 January 20X6	**Debit**	**Credit**
	CU	**CU**
Asset – eg property [SFP]	100,000	
Lease liability [SFP]		100,000
[Recognising the payment under an arrangement recognised as a finance lease]		

SUBSEQUENT MEASUREMENT		
31 December 20X6	**Debit**	**Credit**
Interest expense [P/L] [CU100,000 × 8%]	8,000	
Lease liability [SFP]		8,000
[Recognising the interest expense related to the lease]		

SUBSEQUENT MEASUREMENT		
31 December 20X6	**Debit**	**Credit**
Lease liability [SFP]	14,903	
Bank [SFP]		14,903
[Recognising the lease payment at year-end]		

The last two journal entries can be consolidated into one comprehensive journal entry as follows:

SUBSEQUENT MEASUREMENT		
31 December 20X6	**Debit**	**Credit**
	CU	**CU**
Lease liability [SFP]	6,903	
Interest expense [SFP]	8,000	
Bank [SFP]		14,903
[Recognising the interest expense and lease payment at year-end]		

11.5.2 Lessee – Operating lease

11.5.2.1 Initial recognition

An operating lease is one in which the risks and rewards of the asset being leased are not substantially transferred (unlike for a finance lease). In this case, this is dissimilar to the case where a user buys an asset and receives substantially all the risks and rewards incidental to ownership at inception of the lease. For this reason, the lessee should not recognise the asset. Without recognising the asset (debit), the lessee can also not recognise the amount to be paid in terms of the lease agreement (credit). The lessee therefore does not recognise the lease at inception of the lease (unless some form of lease-related payment is made).

11.5.2.2 Subsequent measurement

Subsequent to initial recognition, the lessee has to recognise the lease payments made (credit), but cannot debit a lease liability as no lease liability was recognised at initial recognition. Therefore, the lessee has to recognise a lease expense (debit). Often, the lease payments are not the same each period. For instance, the lease payments could increase (escalate) over the lease term. If the lease payments change for factors other than an increase in expected general inflation, the operating lease payments should be recognised as expenses on a straight-line basis unless another system is more representative of the time pattern of the user's benefit (s20.15). Any difference between the amount recognised as an expense and the amount paid shall be recognised as a prepaid lease expense (asset where the lease expense is lower than the lease payment) or accrued lease expense (liability where the lease payment is lower than the lease expense).

Illustrative Example 11.3: Lessee operating lease – subsequent measurement

A manufacturer leases equipment, with a fair value of R120,000 and a minimum lease payment of R100,000 at inception, from a supplier from 1 January 20X6. The lease is correctly classified as an operating lease at inception. The equipment has an estimated remaining useful life of 12 years and a zero estimated residual value. The lease term is for a period of 4 years. The lessee has to return the asset to the lessor after the lease term and there is no option to renew. The lease payments are R12,000 increasing annually by 10% per annum (assume that this does not equate to the increase in general inflation).

You are required to:
Prepare the journal entries necessary to account for the lease for the year ended 31 December 20X9 in the financial statements of the lessee.

Suggested solution:

INITIAL RECOGNITION
1 January 20X9: no journal entry recognised.

CALCULATION OF LEASE EXPENSE	
31 December 20X6 [given]	12,000
31 December 20X7 [12,000 × 110%]	13,200
31 December 20X8 [13,200 ×110%]	14,520
31 December 20X9 [14,520 × 110%]	15,972
Total lease expense [12,000 + 13,200 + 14,520 + 15,972]	55,692
Annual lease expense straight-lined (equalised) [55,692/4]	13,923

SUBSEQUENT MEASUREMENT		
31 December 20X6	**Debit**	**Credit**
	CU	CU
Lease expense [P/L]	13,923	
Accrued lease expense [SFP]		1,923
Bank [SFP]		12,000

[Recognising the lease payment, related lease expense and accrued lease expense]

11.6 LESSOR

11.6.1 Lessor – Finance lease

11.6.1.1 Initial recognition

Under a finance lease agreement, the lessor leases the asset to the lessee and the substantial risk and rewards associated with that asset are considered to transfer to the lessee from inception of the lease. As such, the lessor derecognises the carrying amount of the asset (credit) in exchange for the recognition of the present value of the amounts received and receivable under the lease (debit) (s20.17). The amount thus recognised as a lease receivable represents the net investment in the lease (defined as the gross investment in the lease discounted at the interest rate implicit in the lease). Any difference between the net credit and the debit entries above is recognised as profit or loss on disposal of the related asset.

The following illustration shows the recognition of a transaction as it would appear in the general journal:

LESSOR – FINANCE LEASE		
	Debit	**Credit**
	CU	CU
Lease receivable [SFP]	90,000	
Accumulated depreciation – eg property [SFP]	25,000	
Asset – eg property [SFP]		100,000
Profit on disposal of asset [P/L]		15,000
[Recognising the payment under an arrangement recognised as a finance lease]		

11.6.1.2 Subsequent measurement

The related lease receivable recognised at initial recognition shall be accounted for using the amortised cost method. This implies that interest will be charged on the lease liability at the effective interest rate and any lease payments (excluding costs for services) made will be used to reduce the lease liability (s20.19).

Illustrative Example 11.4: Lessor finance lease – subsequent measurement

A manufacturer leases equipment, with a fair value of R120,000 and a minimum lease payment of R100,000 at inception, to a lessee from 1 January 20X6. The equipment had an original cost of R100,000 to the lessor when initially recognised and accumulated depreciation of R25,000 has been accounted for since initial recognition until the asset was leased to the lessee. The lease is correctly classified as a finance lease at inception. The equipment has an estimated remaining useful life of 12 years and a zero estimated residual value. The lease term is for a period of 10 years. The lessee has to return the asset to the lessor after the lease term and there is no option to renew. The effective rate implicit in the lease is 8% per annum compounded annually. The lease payments are R14,903.

You are required to:

Prepare the journal entries necessary to account for the lease for the year ended 31 December 20X6 in the financial statements of the lessor.

Suggested solution:

INITIAL RECOGNITION		
	Debit	**Credit**
	CU	**CU**
Lease receivable [SFP]	90,000	
Accumulated depreciation – eg property [SFP]	25,000	
Asset – eg property [SFP]		100,000
Profit on disposal of asset [P/L]		15,000
[Recognising the payment under an arrangement recognised as a finance lease]		

SUBSEQUENT MEASUREMENT		
31 December 20X6	**Debit**	**Credit**
	CU	**CU**
Lease receivable [SFP]	8,000	
Interest income [P/L]		8,000
[Recognising the interest expense related to the lease]		

SUBSEQUENT MEASUREMENT		
31 December 20X6	**Debit**	**Credit**
	CU	**CU**
Lease liability [SFP]	14,903	
Bank [SFP]		14,903
[Recognising the lease payment at year end]		

The last two journal entries can be consolidated into one comprehensive journal entry as shown in Illustrative Example 11.2.)

11.6.2 Lessor – Operating lease

11.6.2.1 Initial recognition
An operating lease is one in which the risks and rewards incidental to ownership do not transfer from the lessor to the lessee. As such, the lessor does not derecognise the asset from its accounting records. A consequence of not recognising a credit to derecognise the asset is that the lessor can also not recognise the lease payments to be received as a receivable (debit).

11.6.2.2 Subsequent measurement
As explained above, the lessor does not derecognise the asset which is the subject of the lease. As such, the asset remains in the accounting records of the lessor. The lessor continues to account for the asset being leased to the lessor in terms of the relevant section of IFRS for SMEs in which scope the asset fits (s20.24). For instance, if the asset being leased to the lessee is within the scope of s17 – *Property, plant & equipment*, the asset should be accounted for under the cost or revaluation models, depreciated and tested for indications of impairment.

As the lessor did not recognise the lease payments as a lease receivable asset on initial recognition, the lessor recognises the payments received (cash or bank) or receivable (both resulting in debit entries) and related income (credit), with any difference between the amount of the asset and income recognised as prepaid rent or rent accrued. If the lease payments received or receivable change for factors other than an increase in expected general inflation, the operating lease receipts should be recognised as income on a straight-line basis unless another system is more representative of the time pattern of the user's benefit (s20.25).

Illustrative Example 11.5: Lessor operating lease – subsequent measurement

A manufacturer leases equipment, with a fair value of R120,000 and a minimum lease payment of R100,000 at inception, to a lessee from 1 January 20X6. The lease is correctly classified as an operating lease at inception. The equipment has an estimated useful life of 12 years and a zero estimated residual value. The lease term is for a period of 4 years. The lessee has to return the asset to the lessor after the lease term and there is no option to renew. The lease payments are R12,000 increasing annually by 10% per annum (assume that this does not equate to the increase in general inflation).

You are required to:
Prepare the journal entries necessary to account for the lease for the year ended 31 December 20X6 in the financial statements of the lessor.

Suggested solution:

INITIAL RECOGNITION
1 January 20X6: no journal entry recognised.

CALCULATION OF LEASE EXPENSE	
31 December 20X6 [given]	12,000
31 December 20X7 [12 000 × 110%]	13,200
31 December 20X8 [13 200 ×110%]	14,520
31 December 20X9 [14 520 × 110%]	15,972
Total lease expense [12,000 + 13,200 + 14,520 + 15,972]	55,692
Annual lease expense straight-line [55,692/4]	13,923

SUBSEQUENT MEASUREMENT		
31 December 20X6	**Debit**	**Credit**
	CU	**CU**
Bank [SFP]	12,000	
Accrued rental income [SFP]	1,923	
Lease income [P/L]		13,293
[Recognising the lease payment, related lease income and accrued lease income]		

11.7 MANUFACTURER OR DEALER LESSORS

The difference between the total amount receivable (the total payments received and/or receivable) and the carrying amount of the asset derecognised by the manufacturer or dealer lessor, can be split between an interest component and a profit component (s20.20). The profit component of the sale is recognised immediately, while the interest income is recognised over the lease term. It is possible (in absence of the requirements of the standard) for the manufacturer or dealer lessor to manipulate the amount of profit to be recognised immediately and, consequently, the interest income to be recognised over the lease term, by manipulating the stated interest rate for the lease. However, to mitigate this risk, the standard requires manufacturer or dealer lessors to recognise the revenue to be recognised immediately by discounting the cash receivable by a market-related discount rate and not the stated interest rate.

Illustrative Example 11.6: Maufacturer or dealer lessors

Company A manufactures equipment A at a total cost of CU90,000. Company A sells equipment A to a customer, who agrees to pay company A CU115,000 in one year from the date of sale. The financial manager of company A instructed the sales manager to conclude the sales agreement at an interest rate of 4,454%, while a market-related interest rate is 15%.

You are required to:
Discuss how the revenue from the lease of Equipment A should be recognized in the financial statements of Company A.

Suggested solution:
If the amount receivable in one year's time is discounted by the stated interest rate of 4,545%, the present value of the future cash flow and therefore the selling price will be determined to be CU110,000 (CU115,000/1,04545). This would result in a profit of CU20,000 (CU110,000 – CU90,000) on the date of sale and interest income of CU5,000 over the lease term.
You will notice that the total amount above the cost of the asset given up is CU25 000 (CU115 000 – CU90 000).

However, as the standard requires the revenue to be recognised on the date of sale to be determined by discounting the amount receivable by the market interest rate at the date of sale, the selling price should be determined as CU100 000 (CU115 000/1.15). This results in a profit of CU10,000 on the date of sale and interest of CU15,000 over the lease term.
You will notice here also that the total amount above the cost of the asset given up is CU25 000 (CU115 000 – CU90 000), but the split between the profit component and interest component is different depending on which interest rate you use. The standard is clear that the market interest rate (s20.21) (in this case 15%) must be used. It should be evident how, in the absence of this guidance, the manufacturer or dealer lessor could manipulate the amount of revenue that they want to recognise on initial recognition of the sale.

11.8   SALE AND LEASEBACK

A sale and leaseback arrangement is one in which one party sells an asset and then leases it back from the buyer. The main reason for the seller engaging in such an activity is to increase its cash flow and liquidity while still having access to the use of the asset. For instance, if company A sells equipment to a third party for CU100 000 and leases that equipment back from the third party for CU25 000 for five years, then company A will be able to increase its available cash by CU75 000 (CU100 000 – CU25 000) during year one while still ensuring its ability to use the equipment (selling the asset without leasing it back will increase company A's cash in year one, but company A would then no longer have the ability to use the equipment to produce more income).

Where the entity sells the asset and leases it back, there are essentially two transactions which may or may not be considered to be interrelated. The first transaction is the sale of the asset to the buyer, and the second transaction is the lease of the same asset from the buyer. It is clear that the second transaction, the lease of the asset, is a lease agreement and should be accounted for in terms of s20 – *Leases*. As such and in accordance with requirements for any lease agreement, the lessee should identify whether the second transaction, the leaseback of the asset, should be classified as an operating lease or a finance lease (s20.32).

You will notice that the IFRS for SMEs only provides guidance for accounting for sale and leasebacks to lessees. This is because the primary issue at hand is whether to recognise or defer the profit on the sale of the asset (only the seller-lessee makes a profit on the sale of the equipment).

11.8.1 Lessee sale and leaseback – Operating lease

If the leaseback is classified as an operating lease, the following guidance will be relevant (s20.34):

(a)   if the sale is at fair value, the seller-lessee should recognise any profit or loss immediately. This is because there does not appear to be any interdependence between the two transactions, the sale of the asset and the leaseback. This would be no different to the lessee selling the asset to one party for its fair value and leasing a similar asset from another party;

(b)   if the sale price is below fair value, the seller-lessee should sany profit or loss immediately, unless the loss is compensated for by future lease payments at below market price. In that case, the seller-lessee must amortise the loss in proportion to the lease payments over the period for which the asset is expected to be used. Where future lease payments compensate for a loss on the sale of an asset, it implies that the two transactions, the sale and the leaseback, are interdependent. In other words, it appears as if the financial structure of the sale and leaseback is that the asset is initially sold for less than could be received in the market only because the lessee will get relief in the form of reduced lease payments in the future; and

(c)   if the sale price is above fair value, the seller-lessee shall defer the excess over fair value and amortise it over the period for which the asset is expected to be used.

	SP = FV (SP equal to FV)	SP < FV (SP lower than FV)	SP > FV (SP greater than FV)
Compensated for in lease payment	Recognise profit or loss immediately	Defer and amortise	Defer and amortise
Not compensated for in lease payment	Recognise profit or loss immediately	Recognise profit or loss immediately	Defer and amortise

Illustrative Example 11.7: Sale and leaseback – operating lease

On 1 January 20X9, company A sells an erf of land to an independent third party and leases its back under an operating lease. The land had a carrying amount of CU100,000 and a fair value of CU150,000 on the date of sale. Company A immediately enters into a lease for the same erf of land in terms of which company A has to pay the buyer-lessor CU10,000 per annum for the next five years, with the first payment being on 31 December 20X9.

Consider the following scenarios related to above information:

Scenario 1:	Scenario 2:	Scenario 3:
The land was sold by company A for CU150,000.	The land was sold by company A for CU120,000 and the lease payment of CU10,000 is lower than market-related lease payments in order to compensate for the sale price being lower than the fair value.	The land was sold by company A for CU180,000.

You are required to:

Provide the journal entries necessary to account for the sale and leaseback transaction in the financial statements of Company A for the year ended 31 December 20X9.

Suggested solution:

Scenario 1:	Scenario 2:	Scenario 3:
1 January 20X9: Dr: Bank 150,000 Cr: Land 100,000 Cr: Profit 50,000 [Recording sale of land]	1 January 20X9: Dr: Bank 20,000 Cr: Land 100,000 Cr: Deferred profit 20,000 [Recording sale of land]	1 January 20X9: Dr: Bank 180,000 Cr: Land 100,000 Cr: Profit 50,000 Cr: Deferred profit 30,000 [Recording sale of land]
31 December 20X9: Dr: Rent expense 10,000 Cr: Bank 10,000 [Recording payment of rent]	31 December 20X9: Dr: Rent expense 10 000 Cr: Bank 10 000 [Recording payment of rent]	31 December 20X9: Dr: Rent expense 10,000 Cr: Bank 10,000 [Recording payment of rent]
	31 December 20X9: Dr: Deferred rent 4,000 Cr: Rent expense 4,000 [Recognising the profit previously deferred]	31 December 20X9: Dr: Deferred rent 6,000 Cr: Rent expense 6,000 [Recognising the profit previously deferred]

The deferred profit account above is presented in the statement of financial position

11.8.2 Lessee sale and leaseback – Finance lease

If a sale and leaseback is classified as a finance lease, none of the profit should be recognised on the date of the sale. The profit (amount above the asset's carrying amount) should be deferred. The profit should then be amortised over the term of the lease (s20.33).

Illustrative Example 11.8: Sale and leaseback – finance leases

On 1 January 20X9, company A sells an erf of land to an independent third party for CU120,000 and leases its back under an operating lease. The land had a carrying amount of CU100,000 and a fair value of CU150,000 on the date of sale. Company A immediately enters into a lease for the same erf of land in terms of which company A has to pay the buyer-lessor CU35,000 per annum for the next five years, with the first payment being on 31 December 20X9. Ownership of the land automatically passes back to company A at the end of the lease term. The interest rate implicit in the lease is 14.1%.

You are required to:
Prepare the journal entries necessary to account for the sale and leaseback transaction in the financial statements of Company A for the year ended 31 December 20X9.

Suggested solution:

1 January 20X9:

Dr: Bank	120,000	
Cr: Land	100,000	
Cr: Deferred profit		20,000
[Recording sale of land]		

Dr: Land	120,000	
Cr: Lease liability		120,000
[Recognising the lease liability]		

31 December 20X9:

Dr: Interest expense [P/L] [120 000 × 14,1%]	16,920	
Cr: Lease liability		16,920
[Recognising interest expense]		

Dr: Lease liability	35,000	
Cr: Bank		35,000
[Recording payment of lease]		

Dr: Deferred profit	4,000	
Cr: Profit sale of land [P/L]	4,000	
[Recognising the profit previously deferred]		

11.9 PRESENTATION AND DISCLOSURE

11.9.1 Lessee – Finance lease

S20.13: A lessee shall disclose the following information relating to its finance leases:
(a)   for each class of asset, the net carrying amount at the end of the reporting period;
(b)   the total of future minimum lease payments at the end of the reporting period, for each of the following periods:
(i)   not later than one year;
(ii)   later than one year and not later than five years; and
(iii)   later than five years,
(c)   a general description of the lessees significant leasing arrangements including, for example, information about contingent rent, renewal or purchase options and escalation clauses, subleases and restrictions imposed by lease arrangements.

In addition, the lessee has to disclose any other information required by the relevant section of the IFRS for SMEs in which the asset being leased is classified, for example s17 – *Property, plant & equipment.*

11.9.2 Lessee – Operating lease

S20.16: A lessee shall disclose the following information relating to its operating leases:
(a)   the total of future minimum lease payments under non-cancellable operating leases for each of the following periods:
(i)   not later than one year;
(ii)   later than one year and not later than five years; and
(iii)   later than five years;
(b)   lease payments recognised as an expense; and
(c)   a general description of the lessee's significant leasing arrangements including, for example, information about contingent rent, renewal or purchase options and escalation clauses, subleases, and restrictions imposed by lease agreements.

11.9.3 Lessor – Finance lease

S20.23: A lessor shall disclose the following information relating to its finance leases:
(a)   a reconciliation of the gross investment in the lease at the end of the reporting period and the present value of minimum lease payments at the end of the reporting period for each of the following periods and in total:
(i)   not later than one year;

(ii)   later than one year and not later than five years; and

(iii)   later than five years;

Gross investment reconciled to present value of minimum lease payments for finance leases			
	0-1	**2-5**	**5+**
	CU	**CU**	**CU**
Gross investment	100,000	400,000	100,000
Unearned finance income	9,091	111,830	43,553
Present value of minimum lease payments	90,909	288,170	56,447

(b)   unearned finance income;

(c)   the unguaranteed residual values accruing to the benefit of the lessor;

(d)   the cumulative allowance for uncollectable minimum lease payments receivable;

(e)   contingent rents recognised as income during the period; and

(f)   a general description of the lessor's general leasing arrangements including, for example, information about contingent rent, renewal or purchase options and escalation clauses, subleases and restrictions imposed by lease arrangements.

11.9.4 Lessor – Operating lease

S20.30: A lessor shall disclose the following for operating leases:

(a)   the future minimum lease payments under non-cancellable operating leases for each of the following periods:

(i)   not later than one year;

(ii)   later than one year and not later than five years; and

(iii)   later than five years.

Minimum lease payments under non-cancellable operating leases			
	0–1	**2–5**	**5+**
	CU	**CU**	**CU**
Minimum lease payments	100,000	400,000	100,000

(b)   total contingent rents recognised as income; and

(c)   a general description of the lessor's significant leasing arrangements, including, for example, information about contingent rent, renewal or purchase options and escalation clauses and restrictions imposed by lease arrangements.

SELF-ASSESSMENT
Multiple choice questions: Testing principles of accounting for leases

1.   A lease is defined as:

(a) an agreement whereby the lessor conveys to the lessee in return for a payment or a series of payments the right to use an asset for an agreed period of time	
(b) an agreement whereby the lessee conveys to the lessor in return for a payment or a series of payments the right to use an asset for an agreed period of time	
(c) an agreement whereby the lessor conveys to the lessee in return for a payment or a series of payments the ownership of an asset for an agreed period of time	
(d) an agreement whereby the lessor conveys to the lessee, for free, the right to use an asset for an agreed period of time	

2.   A finance lease is one which:

(a) transfers minimal risks and rewards of ownership of an asset from the lessor to the lessee	
(b) transfers ownership of an asset from the lessor to the lessee	
(c) transfers significant risks and rewards of ownership of an asset from the lessor to the lessee	
(d) none of the above	

3. An operating lease expense is recognised by:

(a) recognising the payment for the lease as an expense in that period	
(b) recognising the lease expense by systematically allocating the total lease payments over the lease term (eg straight-line method of lease payments)	
(c) recognising all of the payments to be made in terms of the lease as an expense at the beginning of the lease term	
(d) recognising all of the payments to be made in terms of the lease as an expense at the end of the lease term	

4. A lessor accounts for a finance lease by:

(a) derecognising the asset being leased to the lessee and recognising a lease receivable	
(b) derecognising the asset being leased to the lessee and recognising a lease payable	
(c) continuing to recognise the asset leased to the lessee and recognising the lease receipts as income	
(d) continuing to recognise the asset leased to the lessee and recognising the lease receipts as an expense	

5. A lessee recognises a finance lease by:

(a) not recognising the asset being leased and only recognising the lease payments as an expense	
(b) not recognising the asset being leased and only recognising the lease payments as income	
(c) recognising the asset being leased and the lease payments as an expense	
(d) recognising the asset being leased and a related lease liability	

6. A lessee should disclose the minimum lease payments related to an operating lease into the following time periods:

(a) 0 to 5 years	
(b) 0 to 2 years	
(c) 0 to 1 year; 1 to 5 years and greater than 5 years	
(d) 0 to 2 years and greater than 5 years	

7. The lessee agrees to make the following lease payments in terms of an operating lease – year 1: CU100,000; year 2: CU250,000; year 3: CU150,000. The expense to be recognized for year 2 is:

(a) CU200,000	
(b) CU300,000	
(c) CU250,000	
(d) CU100,000	

8. A lease includes that ownership of the leased asset transfers to the lessee at the end of the lease term once the lessee makes a payment equivalent to the fair value of the asset on the date of transfer. Based only on the information provided, the agreement is most likely:

(a) a finance lease	
(b) an operating lease	
(c) not a lease	
(d) both (a) and (b)	

9. An asset with a cash cost of CU174 is rented to a lessee for two lease payments of CU100 per annum payable on the anniversary of the lease. The lease is for a period of 2 years and bears a rate implicit in the lease of 10% per annum. The asset does not transfer to the lessee at the end of the lease term. Based only on the information provided, the agreement is most likely:

(a) a finance lease	
(b) an operating lease	
(c) not a lease	
(d) both (a) and (b)	

10. A lease agreement includes the following payments: year 1: CU100,000; year 2: CU200,000. A lessor records the following journal entries for year 1, assuming that the lease is an operating lease:

(a) Dr: Bank CU100,000; Cr: Accrued rental income CU150,000; Cr: Lease income [P/L] CU50,000	
(b) Dr: Bank CU100,000; Dr: Accrued rental income CU50,000; CR: Lease income [P/L] CU150,000	
(c) Dr: Bank CU100,000; Cr: Accrued rental income CU50,000; Cr: Lease income [P/L] CU150,000	
(d) none of the above	

Practical questions:
Application of principles to business scenarios

QUESTION 1

]JKJ (Pty) Ltd, an entity engaged in the manufacture metal products, leases a factory space in an industrial area in terms of an operating lease for a period of 5 years. The following schedule is an extract of the lease agreement:

Lease period			5 years	
Commencement date			01 July 20X6	
Rental payment			Half-yearly payable in advance	
Annual payment schedule:				
Year 1	Year 2	Year 3	Year 4	Year 5
CU60,000	CU90,000	CU150,000	CU175,000	CU175,000

You are required to:
Record the journal entries in respect of the above lease agreement for the reporting period ended 28 February 20X7 in compliance with the accounting standards.

QUESTION 2

Lessor (Pty) Ltd entered into a lease agreement with Lessee (Pty) Ltd. The lease is classified as a finance lease of machinery which had a carrying amount of CU250,000 (cost CU400,000 and accumulated depreciation of CU150,000) in the records of Lessor (Pty) Ltd before being leased out.

The lease agreement includes the following terms:

Lease commencement date	1 January 20X1
Lease period	5 years
Interest rate implicit in the lease	8%
Lease payments (annually in arrears)	CU100,000

You are required to:
Record the journal entries to be recognised in the accounting records of Lessor (Pty) Ltd at 31 December20X1 in respect of the lease agreement.

QUESTION 3

Squash (Pty) Ltd entered into a lease agreement with Property (Pty) Ltd. The lease is classified as a finance lease of equipment. The equipment has an expected useful life of 4 years and no residual value.

The lease agreement includes the following terms:

Lease commencement date	1 January 20X1
Lease period	4 years
Interest rate implicit in the lease	8%
Lease payments (annually in advance)	CU50,000

You are required to:
Record the journal entries to be recognised in the accounting records of Squash (Pty) Ltd at 31 December20X1 in respect of the lease agreement, assuming that it is:
(a)   an operating lease; and
(b)   a finance lease.

CHAPTER 12
REVENUE

I consider each business investment based on concept and revenue – Daymond John

ILLUSTRATIVE DISCLOSURE [EXTRACT]

IFRS ref			Notes	20X2	20X1
				CU'000	CU'000
S5.5(a)	Revenue		10	100,000	81,000

IFRS ref				20X2	20X1
				CU'000	CU'000
	10	REVENUE CONSISTS OF THE FOLLOWING			
		Revenue		100,000	81,000
S23.30(b)		Revenue from the sale of goods		40,000	34,000
		Revenue from rendering of services		35,000	27,000
		Revenue from royalties		15,000	12,000
		Revenue from commissions earned		10,000	8,000
S23.31		Contract revenue			
		Included in revenue from the rendering of services is an amount related to contract revenue of 20X2: CU27,000 (20X1: CU21,000). The contract revenue recognised is based on the stage of completion of the related contract. The stage of completion of the contract is calculated with reference to the costs incurred to date in relation to the estimated total expected costs to complete the contract. There are no amounts outstanding from nor owing to contract customers.			

12.1   INTRODUCTION

Revenue forms the backbone of income in an organisation. Revenue is the amount of income that is derived from the entity engaging in its ordinary activities and therefore should represent the most sustainable form of income for the business. Because of this, revenue is a significant performance indicator and is required to be presented separately from other forms of income and on a gross basis (as opposed to the costs of sales or other expenses being set off against revenue).

The requirements for accounting for revenue differ fundamentally between IFRS for SMEs and IFRS. The focus of this chapter is on the accounting for revenue in terms of IFRS for SMEs.

12.2   LEARNING OUTCOMES

Upon completion of this unit you should know the financial reporting requirements for accounting for the revenue of a business in accordance with the IFRS for SMEs. In particular, you should be able to:
(a)   identify transactions that result in increases or decreases to revenue for the period;
(b)   explain the nature and economic substance of revenue transactions;
(c)   distinguish between transactions resulting in revenue and other items of income;
(d)   recognise and measure revenue transactions at the appropriate recognition dates; and
(e)   present and disclose revenue in the financial statements of the entity.

12.3   DEFINITIONS

The definitions for the important concepts and terms used in IFRS for SMEs are found in Appendix B – *Glossary of terms* in IFRS for SMEs. Some important definitions relating to revenue include the following:

- **Revenue:** The gross inflow of economic benefits during the period arising in the course of the ordinary activities of an entity when those inflows result in increases in equity, other than increases relating to contributions from equity participants

- **Effective interest rate:** The rate that exactly discounts estimated future cash payments or receipts through the expected life of the financial instrument or, when appropriate, a shorter period to the net carrying amount of the financial asset of financial liability

12.4   SCOPE AND OBJECTIVES

This section is applicable to accounting for revenue arising from the following transactions [s23.1]:
(a)   the sale of goods;
(b)   the rendering of services;
(c)   construction contracts; and
(d)   use of assets:
      (i)   royalties;
      (ii)   interest; and
      (iii)   dividends.

Revenue and income arising from other transactions are dealt with in the applicable standards governing those transactions, such as (s23.2):
(a)   leases (s20);
(b)   dividends arising from investments accounted for using the equity method (s14 and s15);
(c)   changes in the fair value of financial assets and financial liabilities (s11 and s12);
(d)   changes in the fair value of investment property (s16);
(e)   initial recognition and fair value of biological assets related to agricultural activities (s4); and
(f)   initial recognition of agricultural produce (s34).

12.5   RECOGNITION

An entity should *measure* revenue at the fair value of the consideration received or receivable net of any discounts that the entity expects to allow (s23.3). The entity should only include revenue collected on its own behalf (s23.4) so, for instance, if the entity collects value added tax (VAT) on behalf of a government agency, the VAT portion of the sale is excluded from the revenue recognised and the revenue is recognised net of VAT. Similarly, as the revenue is to be measured at the fair value of the consideration received or receivable, where the entity allows for deferred payment terms beyond the credit terms it normally grants, the fair value of the deferred payment should be the present value of the future cash flows. Therefore, s23.5 requires that revenue should be recognised at the present value of the future cash flows, using an imputed rate of interest where the payments related to the revenue transaction are deferred beyond the normal credit terms. The imputed rate of interest is the more clearly determinable of either:
(a)   the prevailing rate for a similar instrument of an issuer with a similar credit rating; or

(b)   a rate of interest that discounts a nominal amount of the instrument to the current cash sales price of the goods or services.

Illustrative Example 12.1: Initial recognition

An entity sells inventory to a customer for CU110,000 on 01 January 20X8. The normal credit terms for similar sales are 6 months, but the entity grants the customer credit for a period of 12 months. The imputed rate of interest related to the sale is 10%.

You are required to:

Prepare the journal entries necessary to account for the effects of the transaction in the financial statements of the selling entity for the year ended 31 December 20X8.

Suggested solution:

01 January 20X8:

Dr:	Accounts receivable	100,000	
Cr:	Revenue [CU110,000/110%]		100,000
[Recognising revenue at the present value of the future cash flow]			

31 December 20X8:

Dr:	Accounts receivable	10,000	
Cr:	Interest income [P/L] [CU100,000 × 10%]		10,000
[Recognising the interest income at the imputed interest rate]			

31 December 20X8:

Dr:	Bank	110,000	
Cr:	Accounts receivable [CU100,000 + CU10,000]		110,000
[Recognising the settlement of the amount due from the customer]			

The requirements for the *timing* of the recognition of revenue are dependent on what kind of revenue is being recognised. As indicated in the scope, the standard is applicable for the recognition of revenue from different transactions as follows:
(a)   the sale of goods;
(b)   the rendering of services;
(c)   construction contracts; and
(d)   use of assets:
      (i)   royalties;
      (ii)   interest; and
      (iii)   dividends.

12.5.1 Sale of goods

Revenue from the sale of goods must be recognised when the following conditions are all satisfied (s23.10):

(a)   the entity has transferred to the buyer the significant risks and rewards of ownership of the goods;

(b)   the entity retains neither continuing managerial involvement to the degree usually associated with ownership nor effective control over the goods sold;

(c)   the amount of revenue can be measured reliably;

(d)   it is **probable** that the economic benefits associated with the transaction will flow to the entity; and

(e)   the costs incurred or to be incurred in respect of the transaction can be measured reliably.

Illustrative Example 12.2: Revenue sale of goods

On 01 January 20X8, a customer orders inventory from the entity amounting to CU100,000. The entity delivers the inventory to the customer on 01 February 20X8. The inventory was purchased by the entity for CU70,000. The amount is payable by the customer on 15 March 20X8, which is the entity's normal credit terms. The customer is a returning customer with a good credit record. The accountant is uncertain about which date to recognise the inventory.

You are required to:

Discuss the date at which the entity can recognize the revenue from the sale of the inventory mentioned above.

Suggested solution:

The revenue results from the sale of goods and therefore all of the following criteria should be met:

(a) The entity has transferred to the buyer the significant risks and rewards of ownership of the goods.	The entity transfers the significant risks and rewards of ownership of the goods to the customer on delivery being 01 February 20X8. From this date, the customer is responsible for insuring or safekeeping the goods and can sell or use the goods for its own benefit.

(b) The entity retains neither continuing managerial involvement to the degree usually associated with ownership nor effective control over the goods sold.	Once the entity has transferred the specific goods to the customer, the entity no longer controls the goods nor retains continuing managerial involvement to the degree associated with ownership. Therefore, control transfers to the goods on the date of delivery being, 1 February 20X8.
(c) The amount of revenue can be measured reliably.	The amount of revenue is clearly identified and measurable at CU100,000.
(d) It is probable that the economic benefits associated with the transaction will flow to the entity.	The scenario indicates that the customer is a returning customer with a good credit rating and therefore it is assumed that it is probable that the customer will pay the amount due.
(e) The costs incurred or to be incurred in respect of the transaction can be measured reliably.	The scenario indicates that the cost of the inventory was CU70,000. The only other costs to consider might be the cost of delivery to the customer (if the customer did not collect the inventory themselves). It is therefore safe to assume that the costs related to the transaction are measurable.

12.5.2 Rendering of services and construction contracts

Revenue related to the rendering of services and construction contracts should be recognised based on the stage of completion of the service at year-end, if the outcome of the transaction can be estimated reliably (s23.14 and s23.17). Services, including those for construction, are usually rendered over extended periods of time. Sometimes it is not certain whether the entity will receive any form of compensation. In that case, the entity will recognise revenue based on the amount of the expenses that it thinks it will recover (s23.16, s23.24 and s23.25).

Illustrative Example 12.3: Rendering of services

An entity renders services to a customer. Consider the following three independent scenarios:

(a)   the entity is uncertain whether it will receive any form of remuneration from the customer;

(b)   the entity is uncertain as to how much of the revenue it will receive from the customer, but considers it probable that the customer will at least compensate the entity for the costs incurred; and

(c)   the entity is certain that the customer will pay the full amount of revenue due.

You are required to:

Discuss how the entity should recognize the revenue from the rendering of services in each of the three independent scenarios mentioned above.

Suggested solution:

(a) The entity has incurred costs, but is uncertain as to whether the customer will pay anything (ie the entity will make a loss on the agreement as it will incur costs with no revenue).	The entity should only recognise revenue up to the extent that it thinks it probable that the customer will cover some of the costs. If the entity does not think it probable that the customer will pay any of the costs, it should not recognise any of the revenue.
(b) The entity has incurred costs and is uncertain that the customer will pay the full amount of revenue, but is certain that the customer will pay at least an amount equal to the costs incurred (in other words, the entity will make no profit or loss on the agreement).	The entity should recognise revenue up to the extent that it thinks it probable that the customer will cover the costs. If the entity thinks that it is probable that the customer will reimburse all of the costs incurred, then the entity should recognise revenue based on the costs incurred to date.
(c) The entity has incurred costs and considers it probable that the customer will pay the revenue (costs plus a profit)	If the entity considers it probable that the entity will pay the full amount of revenue, the entity recognises the revenue with reference to the stage of completion.

If the outcome of the transaction involving the rendering of services and construction contracts can be estimated reliably, the entity recognises revenue based on the stage of completion if the following conditions are met (s23.14):
(a)   the amount of revenue can be measured reliably;
(b)   it is probable that the economic benefits associated with the transaction will flow to the entity;
(c)   the stage of completion of the transaction at the end of the reporting period can be measured reliably; and
(d)   the costs for the transaction and the costs to complete the transaction can be measured reliably.

In terms of s23.14, a requirement for the recognition of revenue from services is that the stage of completion must be able to be measured reliably. The stage of completion can be measured with reference to, for example (s23.22):
(a)   the proportion that costs incurred to date relate to the total estimated costs;
(b)   surveys of work performed; or
(c)   completion of a physical proportion of the service.

Illustrative Example 12.4: Rendering of services

An entity renders services to a customer over a period of two years starting on the first day of the financial year being 01 January 20X8. The expected revenue related to the contract amounts to CU200,000. The entity has incurred costs of CU75,000 at 31 December 20X8. The total expected cost of the contract amounts to CU125,000. The entity determines the stage of completion of the services rendered with reference to the relationship between the costs incurred to date and the total estimated costs of the contract. The customer is a returning customer who has an excellent credit record. The entity therefore expects to recover the full contract revenue from the customer.

You are required to:
(i)   Discuss and quantify what the amount of revenue is that the entity can recognize for the year ended 31 December 20x8; and
(ii)   Calculate the gross profit earned by the entity for the year ended 31 December 20x8 as a result of the transaction mentioned above.

Suggested solution:
As the outcome of the transaction can be estimated reliably, the entity recognises revenue based on the stage of completion of the services (in this scenario, it is explicitly stated that the entity measures the stage of completion with reference to the relationship between the costs incurred to date and the total estimated costs of the contract).

Therefore, the revenue to be recognised for the period ended 31 December 20X8 is: CU75,000/CU125,000 × CU200,000 = CU120,000.

The gross profit earned for the year ended 31 December 20X8 is therefore:

	20X8
	CU
Revenue	120,000
Cost of sales	(75,000)
Gross profit	**45,000**

12.5.3 Revenue from the use of entity assets

Revenue from the use of the entity's assets by others must be recognised based on the requirements set out in the sections below and on condition that (s23.28):
(a)   it is probable that the economic benefits associated with the transaction will flow to the entity; and
(b)   the amount of the revenue can be measured reliably.

12.5.3.1 Interest

Interest is to be recognised using the effective interest rate method (s23.29). The effective interest rate method is described in detail in the chapter on financial instruments, but effectively involves:
(a)   determining the interest rate that will reconcile the cash flows to the amount initially recognised for the asset; and then
(b)   applying the interest rate determined in (a) to the balance of the asset.

Illustrative Example 12.5: Interest revenue

An entity regularly engages in lending money as part of its normal operations and considers any income that it earns from the lending as revenue. The entity lent CU100,000 to a customer on 01 July 20X8. The customer is obligated to repay the entity CU110,000 on 30 June 20X9. The entity's year end is 31 December 20x8.

You are required to:
Explain how and calculate the interest for the year ended 31 December 20x8.

Suggested solution:

The amount of revenue to be recognised in the form of interest is determined as follows:

(a)   determine the effective interest rate as the amount that discounts the cash flows to the initial amount of CU100,000, ie 10% per annum; and

(b)   calculate interest based on the effective interest rate calculated in (a): CU100,000 × 10% = CU10,000/2 = CU5,000 (for the half year starting 01 July 20X8 and ending on 31 December 20X8).

12.5.3.2 Royalties

Revenue from royalties should be recognised on an accrual basis based on the details of the agreement (s23.29(b)).

Illustrative Example 12.6: Royalty revenue

An entity earns royalty revenue of CU15 per book sold by its publisher. The publisher informed the entity that 100 copies of the book had been sold during the financial year ended 31 December 20X8.

You are required to:

Calculate the amount of revenue that the entity can recognize for the year ended 31 December 20x8, related to the royalties earned from the sale of its books.

Suggested solution:

As the entity has established the right to receive royalties and accrues CU1,500 (100 books × CU15) in terms of this, the entity can recognise the CU1,500 as revenue for the year ended 31 December 20X8.

12.5.3.3 Dividends

Dividends should be recognised when the shareholder's right to receive the dividend has been established.

12.6   GENERAL

12.6.1 Revenue in a compound transaction

We have discussed the revenue earned from individual transactions in the sections above. Revenue should be recognised for each individual transaction (each separately identifiable component) even if those transactions are grouped into one bigger compound transaction (s23.8).

Illustrative Example 12.7: Compound revenue transactions

An entity sells a motor vehicle together with a service plan for a total amount of CU120,000 on 01 January 20X8. The service plan allows the customer five free services over the life of the vehicle. The entity usually sells motor vehicles such as the one sold to the customer for CU100,000 and service plans such as the one included in the agreement separately for CU20,000. The customer serviced the vehicle once during the year ended 31 December 20X8. The entity evaluates the stage of completion for the service component within the contract with reference to the number of services incurred to date in relation to the total number of services allowed under the contract.

You are required to:

(i)   Discuss how the transaction mentioned above should be accounted for in the financial statements of the entity; and

(ii)   Prepare the journal entries necessary to account for the above mentioned transaction in the financial statements of the entity for the year entity for the year ended 31 December 20x8.

Suggested solution:

As the sale of the vehicle and the service plan are two distinct and separate components of the transaction of CU120,000, each component must be separately classified as being for the sale of goods, rendering of services or revenue from the use of assets of the entity. As the sale of the motor vehicle represents revenue from the sale of goods, all of the requirements for the recognition of revenue from the sale of goods must be met before revenue from the transaction can be recognised. As the service plan represents revenue to be recognised from the rendering of services, all of the requirements for the recognition of revenue from the rendering of services must be met before the revenue from the service plan can be recognised.

Assuming these requirements are met, the entity will recognise the following journal entries to account for revenue from the compound transaction for the year ended 31 December 20X8:

01 January 20X8:

Dr	Bank	120,000	
Cr	Revenue [CU110,000/110%]		100,000
Cr	Revenue received in advance [SFP]		20,000
[Recognising revenue for the sale of the motor vehicle and the liability for services to be performed]			

31 December 20X8:

Dr	Revenue received in advance [SFP] [CU20,000/5]	4,000	
Cr	Revenue		4,000
[Recognising revenue from services rendered]			

From the discussion above, it follows that when an entity sells goods or services with loyalty awards, the compound transaction can be separated into two distinct components as follows:

(a)   sale of goods or rendering of services currently being consumed; and

(b)   the obligation to deliver goods or services in the future when the customer redeems the loyalty awards.

The customer measures the revenue for the current goods sold or services produced as the balance calculated by deducting the fair value of the loyalty awards from the (compound) transaction price.

Illustrative Example 12.8: Compound revenue transactions

An entity sells inventory to a customer for CU20,000 on 01 January 20X8. The customer earns 10 loyalty points which allows the customer to purchase goods in future at a discount of CU1,000. The loyalty points expire after six months. There is a 90% probability associated with the customer redeeming the loyalty points within the six-month period.

You are required to:
Prepare the journal entries necessary to account for the above mentioned transaction in the financial statements of the entity on 1 January 20x8.

Suggested solution:
As the sale of the inventory and loyalty awards are two distinct and separate components of the transaction of CU20,000, each component must be separately classified and recognised. The following journal entries account for revenue from the compound transaction at 01 January 20X8:

01 January 20X8:

Dr	Bank	20,000	
Cr	Revenue [CU20,000 – CU900]		19,100
Cr	Loyalty award liability [SFP] [CU1,000 × 90%]		900
[Recognising revenue for the sale of inventory and the liability for the loyalty awards]			

12.6.2 Lay-away (lay-bye) sales

Lay-away sales refer to the sale of goods where the goods are delivered after the final payment in a series of instalments (s23A.8). The revenue from these sales are recognised when the goods are delivered, but where the entity has a history of such sales being completed, revenue may be recognised when a significant deposit is received, on condition that the goods:
(a)   are on hand;
(b)   identified; and
(c)   ready to be delivered to the buyer.

Illustrative Example 12.9: Royalty revenue

An entity sells inventory to a customer for CU50,000 on a lay-away sale basis. The customer pays the entity CU10,000 per week for five weeks. The entity's history of such sales shows that when customers pay more than half of the money due (considered by the entity to be a significant deposit), that the sale is almost always completed. The items of inventory are on hand, identified and available for delivery to the customer from the date that the lay-away agreement is concluded.

You are required to:
Prepare the journal entries that should be prepared each week, necessary to account for the above transaction in the financial statements of the entity.

Suggested solution
The entity records the following journal entries related to the sale:
Week 1:

Dr	Bank	10,000	
Cr	Revenue received in advance [SFP]		10,000
[Recognising the first payment related to a lay-away sale]			

Week 2:

Dr	Bank	10,000	
Cr	Revenue received in advance [SFP]		10,000
[Recognising the second payment related to a lay-away sale]			

Week 3:

Dr	Bank	10,000	
Dr	Revenue received in advance [SFP]	20,000	
Dr	Accounts receivable [50,000 – 30,000]	20,000	
Cr	Revenue		50,000
[Recognising revenue from the lay-away sale as more than half of the money has been received [CU30,000 received > CU25,000 (CU50,000 × 50%)]]			

Week 4:

Dr	Bank	10,000	
Cr	Accounts receivable		10,000
[Recognising the fourth payment related to a lay-away sale]			

Week 5:

Dr	Bank	10,000	
Cr	Accounts receivable		10,000
[Recognising the fifth payment related to a lay-away sale]			

12.6.3 Bill-and-hold sale

A bill-and-hold sale is where the seller has invoiced the customer for the goods and is ready to deliver the goods to the customer, but the customer requests that delivery is delayed (maybe for logistical reasons). The revenue related to a bill-and-hold sale is recognised when (s23A.3):

(a) it is probable that delivery will be made;

(b) the item is on hand, identified and ready for deliver to the buyer at the time the sale is recognised;

(c) the buyer specifically acknowledges the deferred delivery instructions; and

(d) the usual payment terms apply.

12.6.4 Exchange of goods or services

The primary evaluation in deciding whether to recognise revenue from the exchange of goods or services is to evaluate whether the goods or services exchanged are similar in nature and value and whether the transaction has commercial substance (s23.6).

When the exchange transaction has commercial substance and involves the exchange of goods or services that are dissimilar, the entity should measure the revenue as follow (s23.7):

(a) at the fair value of the goods or services received adjusted by the amount of any cash or cash equivalents transferred;

(b) if the fair value of the goods or services received cannot be reliably estimated, at the fair value of the goods or services given up, adjusted by the amount of any cash or cash equivalents transferred; or

(c) if the fair value of neither the goods or services received or transferred can be measured reliably, then at the amount of the goods or services given up, adjusted by the amount of any cash or cash equivalents transferred.

Illustrative Example 12.10: Compound revenue transactions

An entity transfers inventory with a carrying amount of CU10,000 and a fair value of CU12,000 to an advertising company for advertising services which the advertising company rendered. The fair value of the services rendered amounts to CU15,000.

You are required to:

Discuss how the revenue from the above transaction should be recognized in the financial statements of the entity.

Suggested solution:

As the goods (inventory) and services exchanged are dissimilar in nature and it is apparent that the transaction has commercial substance, the entity should recognise revenue from the transaction. The revenue should be recognised at the fair value of the services received, in this case being CU15,000. The entity will recognise the carrying amount of the inventory given up as cost of sales.

12.7   PRESENTATION AND DISCLOSURE

12.7.1 Presentation

An entity has to present revenue as a line item in its statement of comprehensive income (s5.5(a)). When the revenue is earned as a result of inventories being sold, the entity should recognise the carrying amount of the inventories sold as cost of sales in the period in which it recognises the related revenue from the sale (s13.20).

12.7.2 Disclosure

12.7.2.1 General disclosures

The entity should disclose the accounting policies that are adopted for the recognition of revenue, including which methods were used to determine the stage of completion of revenue from services and construction contracts (s23.30(a)). In addition, the entity should disclose the amount of revenue recognised from the following categories (s23.30(b)):

(a)   sale of goods;
(b)   rendering of services;
(c)   interest;
(d)   royalties;
(e)   dividends;
(f)   commissions;
(g)   government grants; and
(h)   any other significant types of revenue.

12.7.2.2 Disclosures relating to revenue from construction contracts

An entity should disclose (s23.31):

(a)   the amount of contract revenue recognised as revenue in the period;
(b)   the methods used to determine the contract revenue recognised during the period; and
(c)   the methods used to determine the stage of completion of contracts in progress.

An entity should also disclose: (s23.32)

(a)   the gross amount due from customers for contract work, as an asset; and
(b)   the gross amount due to customers for contract work, as a liability.

SELF-ASSESSMENT
Multiple choice questions: Testing for principles of accounting for revenue

1. Revenue is defined as:

(a) the gross inflow of economic benefits during the period arising in the course of the ordinary activities of an entity when those inflows result in increases in equity, other than increases relating to contributions from equity participants	
(b) the gross inflow of economic benefits during the period arising when those inflows result in increases in equity, other than increases relating to contributions from equity participants	
(c) the inflow of economic benefits during the period arising in the course of the ordinary activities of an entity when those inflows result in increases in equity, other than increases relating to contributions from equity participants	
(d) the gross inflow of economic benefits arising in the course of the ordinary activities of an entity when those inflows result in increases in equity, other than increases relating to contributions from equity participants	

2. The following income is excluded from s23 – *Revenue* of IFRS for SMEs:

(a) income from the sale of inventory	
(b) revenue from the rendering of services	
(c) income from the sale of property, plant and equipment	
(d) revenue from royalties	

3. Revenue from a lay-away sale is normally recognised when:

(a) the lay-away agreement is entered into	
(b) the first payment is made	
(c) a significant deposit has been received	
(d) the VAT (or similar tax) related to the sale has been paid	

4. An entity sells inventory to a customer for CU121,000, payable in two years' time. The agreement includes that the sale is interest free, but the entity establishes that the imputed rate of interest related to the sale is 10% per annum compounded annually. The revenue from the sale is measured at:

(a) CU121,000	
(b) CU110,000	
(c) CU133,100	
(d) CU100,000	

5. An entity sells inventory to a customer for CU57,500 (including VAT). The VAT rate has remained unchanged at 15%. The amount of revenue to be recognised is:

(a) CU57,500	
(b) CU7,500	
(c) CU65,000	
(d) CU50,000	

6. Which of the following is not a requirement for an entity to recognise revenue from services rendered:

(a) the amount of revenue can be measured reliably	
(b) it is probable that the economic benefits associated with the transaction will flow to the entity	
(c) the inventory must have been transferred to the customer	
(d) the stage of completion of the transaction at the end of the reporting period can be measured reliably	

7. An entity renders a service to a customer over a period of three years. The revenue related to the three-year period is CU100,000. The stage of completion is measured with reference to the costs incurred to date in relation to the total estimated costs of the project. The total costs of the project are estimated at CU40,000, while the costs incurred by the end of the first year amount to CU10,000. The amount of revenue that the entity can recognise at the end of the first year is:

(a) CU25,000	
(b) CU10,000	
(c) CU40,000	
(d) CU20,000	

8. The following is not a requirement for a bill-and-hold sale to be recognised as revenue:

(a) the item is on hand, identified and ready for delivery to the buyer at the time the sale is recognised	
(b) it is probable that delivery will be made	
(c) the usual payment terms apply	
(d) the contract is for the rendering of services	

9. Revenue from dividend income should be recognised when:

(a) the shareholder's right to the dividend has been established	
(b) the dividend has been proposed	
(c) the dividend has been paid	
(d) none of the above	

10. Unredeemed loyalty awards represent:

(a) a liability to the entity	
(b) revenue to the entity	
(c) an asset to the entity	
(d) none of the above	

Practical questions:
Application of principles to business scenarios

QUESTION 1

WMR (Pty) Ltd sold inventory to a long-standing customer for CU287,500 (inclusive of VAT) on 01 January 20X8. The inventory was delivered to the customer on 15 January 20X8, at which date the significant risks and rewards of ownership of the goods were considered to be transferred. The inventory cost the WMR (Pty) Ltd CU115,000 (including VAT). The customer is only required to pay the amount related to the sale after 30 days, which is in accordance with the normal credit terms granted by WMR (Pty) Ltd. The customer has a good credit rating. The VAT rate has remained unchanged at 15%.

You are required to:
Discuss the date on which WMR (Pty) Ltd should recognise the revenue related to the above transaction.

QUESTION 2

Construct (Pty) Ltd entered into an agreement, on 01 January 20xX7, to construct a building for a customer over three years for a total consideration of CU900,000 (excluding VAT). The customer will provide all of the material and Construct (Pty) Ltd will only be responsible for providing building services. The total estimated cost of construction is considered to be CU500,000 (mostly made up of salaries paid to employees). The entity had incurred costs of CU100,000 at 31 December 20X7 and total costs (cumulative costs to date over the life of the project) of CU250,000 at 31 December 20X8. Construct (Pty) Ltd evaluates the stage of completion with reference to the costs incurred to date in relation to the total estimated costs of construction. The customer pays the portion of the revenue recognised by Construct (Pty) Ltd in any particular year.

You are required to:
Record the journal entries to account for the revenue to be recognised for the construction for the year ended 31 December 20X8.

QUESTION 3

Car (Pty) Ltd sold a vehicle to a customer on 01 January 20X8 for CU200,000 (excluding VAT) together with a maintenance plan which allows the customer to receive six free services over the life of the motor vehicle. Car (Pty) Ltd normally charges a mark-up of 20% on the cost of the maintenance services. Each maintenance service costs Car (Pty) Ltd CU4,000. The customer serviced the vehicle twice during the year ended 31 December 20X8. The stage of completion for the recognition of revenue from the maintenance services rendered is measured with reference to the number of free maintenance services conducted in relation to the six free maintenance services as per the contract.

You are required to:
Record the journal entries related to the revenue transactions to be recognised in the accounting records of Car (Pty) Ltd at 31 December20X8.

CHAPTER 13
GOVERNMENT GRANTS

ILLUSTRATIVE DISCLOSURE [EXTRACT]

IFRS ref		Notes	20X2	20X1
			R'000	R'000
S24 IAS 20	Income from government grants	18	10	4

IFRS ref		Notes	20X2	20X1
			R'000	R'000
	Non-current liabilities			
S24 IAS 20	Long-term portion of government grants	18	25	24
	Current liabilities			
S24 IAS 20	Current portion of government grants	18	15	-

IFRS ref		GOVERNMENT GRANTS	20X2	20X1
			R'000	R'000
S24.6 IAS 20 p.39	18	**At beginning of the year**	24	30
		Received during the year	16	14
		Released to the statement of profit or loss	0	(19)
		At the end of the year	40	25
		Current	15	0
		Non-current	25	25

		Government grants relate to the construction of qualifying assets. These government grants recognised in the statement of financial position represent amounts received in cash, but which still have unfulfilled conditions. When the related conditions are fulfilled, these amounts will be recognised as income in the statement of profit or loss.

13.1   INTRODUCTION

Government often incentivises entities to undertake particular actions by offering to cover some of their costs through allocating resources to them. The conditions often encourage behaviour that will benefit the public or the local community in the area in which the entities operate. Sometimes, government requires the entities to pay for the cost of acquiring an asset or incurring an expense, while other times, entities are not required to acquire the asset (and get refunded), but are given the asset directly.

13.2   LEARNING OUTCOMES

- Upon completion of this unit you should know the financial reporting requirements for government grants in accordance with the accounting standards. In particular, you should be able to:
- distinguish between government grants and other forms of government assistance;
- identify and recognise government grants for presentation in financial statements;
- measure the amounts to be recognised in the different components of the financial statements in relation to government grants; and
- present and disclose the effects of government grant transactions in the financial statements.

13.3   DEFINITIONS

The definitions for the important concepts and terms used in IFRS for SMEs are found in Appendix B – *Glossary of terms* in IFRS for SMEs. The following is an important definition relating to government grants:

- **Government grant:** Assistance by government in the form of transfers of resources to an entity in return for past or future compliance with certain conditions relating to the operating activities of the entity

13.4   SCOPE AND OBJECTIVES

A government grant is assistance by government in the form of transfers of resources to an entity in return for past or future compliance with certain conditions relating to the operating activities of the entity. It excludes (ss24.1–3 and IAS 20 pp.1–2):

(a)   government assistance that cannot reasonably have a value placed upon it;

(b)   transactions with government that cannot be distinguished from the normal trading transactions of the entity; and

(c)   assistance that is available in determining taxable profit (tax loss) or is determined or limited on the basis of income tax liability.

In addition, full IFRS excludes the following transactions with government (IAS 20 p.2):

(a)   special problems arising in accounting for government grants in financial statements reflecting the effects of changing prices or in supplementary information of a similar nature;

(b)   government participation in the ownership of the entity; and

(c)   government grants covered by IAS 41 – Agriculture.

Illustrative Example 13.1: Classification of transaction as government grant

An entity received the following from government:

(a)   government paid the entity for goods which the entity supplied;

(b)   government gives the company CU5,000 per month for each employee that it employs from the surrounding area; and

(c)   government allows the company to deduct wear and tear calculated on 200% of the cost of the asset.

You are required to:

Discuss whether each of the above mentioned transactions should be classified as a government grant.

Suggested solution:

(i)   The payment for goods provided is not considered a government grant as it represents a transaction with government that cannot be distinguished from the normal trading activities of the company.

(ii)   The CU5,000 monthly payment constitutes a government grant as it represents government assistance to the entity in the form of transfers of resources to the entity for compliance with certain conditions relating to the operating activities of the entity.

(iii)	The allowance for wear and tear calculated on 200% of the cost of the asset is not considered a government grant as it is assistance that is available in determining taxable profits.

13.5 RECOGNITION & MEASUREMENT

Government grants are recognised as follows (s24.4):

(a)	a grant that does not require future performance conditions is recognised in income when the grant proceeds are receivable;
(b)	a grant that requires specified future performance conditions is recognised when the performance conditions are met; and
(c)	a grant received before the revenue recognition principle criteria are satisfied is recognised as a liability.

Illustrative example 13.2: Recognition and measurement

The entity received the following three amounts from government relating to three separate government grants:

(a)	government transferred CU5,000 per month per employee to the entity for three employees that the entity hired from the surrounding area. The grant was conditional upon the entity hiring employees from the surrounding area;
(b)	government has committed to transfer CU15,000 to the entity for exports which it made to a designated country as a condition of the government grant. All of the exports were made by year-end. Government is expected to make payment shortly after year-end; and
(c)	government transferred CU10,000 to the entity for a satellite office which it will rent from a local resident in the following year. The condition of the government grant was that the property used as the office must be rented from a local resident.

You are required to:

(i)	Discuss how the government grants in each of the above mentioned transactions should be accounted for; and
(ii)	Prepare the journal entries necessary to account for each of the above government grants in the financial statements of the entity for the current year.

Suggested solution:

(i)	The CU5,000 transferred per month per employee for the year, represents government assistance for performance conditions which are received as the performance conditions are met. The amount becomes receivable as

each performance condition is met. The following journal entry is processed related to the payments for the year:

DR Bank 180,000
CR Government grant income [P/L] 180,000
[Recognition of government grant funds – (3 × 12 × 5,000)]

(ii)   The government grant for export already made represents resources received for past and fulfilled performance conditions. The full amount related to the government grant can therefore be recognised as income. The following journal entry is processed related to the payment for the exports:

DR Bank 15,000
CR Government grant income [P/L] 15,000
[Recognition of government grant funds]

(iii)   The CU10,000 transferred to the entity for the satellite office still to be rented represents resources for unfulfilled performance conditions. The amount must therefore be recognised as a liability until the performance conditions are fulfilled. The following journal entry is processed related to the payment:

DR Bank 180,000
CR Government grant liability [SFP] 180,000
[Recognition of government grant funds]

13.6   DISCLOSURE

An entity must disclose the following (s24.6):
(a)   the nature and amounts of government grants recognised in the financial statements;
(b)   unfulfilled conditions and other contingencies attaching to government grants that have not been recognised in income; and
(c)   an indication of other forms of government assistance from which the entity has directly benefitted.

13.7   REQUIREMENTS IN FULL IFRS

It should be noted that the accounting requirements relating to the recognition and measurement of government grants in full IFRS differ to those in IFRS for SMEs. The following summarises the recognition and measurement requirements of full IFRS:

13.7.1 Grants related to assets and grants related to income

Full IFRS requires a distinction between government grants provided for the construction or acquisition of long-term assets and other government grants (considered to be related to income if not related to assets).

13.7.2 Recognition

Government grants related to assets

If resources are received in terms of a government grant related to the construction, purchase or other acquisition of a long-term asset, the entity can choose between one of two accounting policies IAS 20 p.24.

Deferred income

The entity can recognise the asset at its construction, purchase or other acquisition cost and also recognise the grant as deferred income. In this case, the grant recognised as deferred income has to be transferred to profit or loss on a systematic basis over the useful life of the asset (IAS 20 p.26). If the entity does not have a cost, purchase or other acquisition cost for the asset, the asset can be recognised at its fair value.

Reduction from the cost of the asset

The government grant can also be set-off against the amount recognised for the asset. In this way, the government grant is automatically recognised over the useful life of the asset in the form of reduced depreciation expense (IAS 20 p.27).

Government grants related to income

Government grants related to income are recognised in profit or loss either separately as 'Other Income' or as a reduction from the expense it compensates (IAS 20 p.29).

SELF-ASSESSMENT
Multiple choice questions: Testing principles of accounting for government grants

1. A cash payment of CU12,000 is received from government for advertising services that the entity performed for government. The transaction should be classified as:

(a) government assistance	
(b) a government grant	
(c) a tax incentive	
(d) none of the above	

2. The entity receives CU200,000 from government for building factory in a particular area. The transaction should be classified as:

(a) a refund	
(b) a government grant	
(c) a tax incentive	
(d) none of the above	

3. The entity receives CU10,000 as a government grant for purchasing a particular machine. In terms of IFRS for SMEs, the government grant should be:

(a) deducted from the cost of the machine	
(b) recognised as income in profit or loss	
(c) recognised as deferred income in the statement of financial position	
(d) none of the above	

4. Government agrees to transfer CU15,000 to an entity in terms of a government grant. The government grant should be recognised when:

(a) the agreement is entered into with government	
(b) the cash is received	
(c) the conditions related to the government grant are fulfilled	
(d) none of the above	

5. Government transfers CU25,000 to the entity in terms of a government grant. The conditions related to the government grant have not been fulfilled as yet. The amount received should be recognised as a(n):

(a) income	
(b) expense	
(c) equity	
(d) liability	

Practical questions:
Application of principles to business scenarios

QUESTION 1

Objective: Accounting for the cash receipt related to a government grant.

GGS (PTY) LTD received a cash payment of CU100,000 from government on 1 July 20X7 related to a government grant. The conditions attached to the receipt of money is that the entity construct or purchase a building for which they will receive CU52,000 in the form of a government grant and that the company hires staff from the surrounding community for at least its first year of operations for which the remaining CU48,000 will be allocated. GGS (PTY) LTD purchased a building and commenced operations with staff from the surrounding community on 1 October 20X7.

You are required to:
Prepare the journal entries necessary to account for the transactions relate to the government grant in the financial statements of GGS (PTY) LTD for the year ended 31 December 20X7.

QUESTION 2:

Objective: Initial and subsequent recognition of provisions

At the reporting date 28 February 20X6, the Company recognized a provision of R 500,000 in respect of a claim resulting from a dispute with a customer. The dispute was resolved, and the Company agreed to make a final payment of R 300,000 in settlement of the claim, which was paid on 30 April 20X6.

You are required to:
Record the journal entries relating to the claim by the customer for the reporting periods ended 28 February 20X6 and 20X7 in compliance with the accounting standards.

QUESTION 3:

Objective: Initial and subsequent recognition and measurement of a provision

With effect from 01 June 20X5 the company implemented a warranty policy of one year for certain of its high value products. In terms of the warranty the company took responsibility to (i) repair the products at no cost to the customer, and (ii) replace the product if it cannot be repaired. The customer relations manager estimated that only 15% of the products sold will be returned of which 90% required repairs while the remainder is replaced. The cost of repairs is estimated at R 800 per unit while the standard unit cost is R 12 500. The company maintains a mark-up of 50% on repairs and 25% on goods sold. The company sold 1 200 of the products during the year of which 10 were returned and repaired at a cost of R 8 000 and 2 were replaced at the standard cost by 31 December 20X5.

You are required to:
Record the journal entries relating to the warranty agreements for the reporting period 31 December 20X5 in compliance with the IFRS for SMEs.

QUESTION 4:

Objective: Recognition and measurement of the re-imbursement for obligations/provisions

The goods sold by a retailer contain a manufacturer's warranty of one year, but the retailer included a further one-year warranty – the total warranty is for two years. The retailer estimated the value of the warranty on goods sold to be R 325 000 of which R 250 000 represents the manufacturer's warranty. It is virtually certain that the manufacturer will reimburse the retailer for fulfilling the obligations of the warranty.

You are required to:
Record the journal entries relating to the warranty agreements for the reporting period 28 February 20X7 in compliance with IFRS for SMEs in the accounting records of the retailer.

CHAPTER 14
ACCOUNTING POLICIES, ESTIMATES AND ERRORS, AND EVENTS AFTER THE END OF THE REPORTING PERIOD

ILLUSTRATIVE DISCLOSURE [EXTRACT]

Statement of Financial Position at				
IFRS ref		**Notes**	**20X7**	**20X6**
			CU'000	**CU'000**
S6.5 IAS 1 p.106	Retained earnings opening balance		488,000	348,000
	Correction of prior period error/effect of change in accounting policy		(42,000)	(35,000)
	Correction of period error		60,000	45,000
	Restated retained earnings opening balance		**506,000**	**358,000**
	Profit for the year as previously presented		185,000	140,000
	Change in accounting policy		(8,000)	(7,000)
	Effect of correction of prior period error		15,000	15,000
	Restated profit for the year		**192,000**	**148,000**
	Retained earnings closing balance		573,000	488,000
	Correction of prior period error		(50,000)	(42,000)
	Effect of change in accounting policy		75,000	60,000
	Restated retained earnings closing balance		**698,000**	**506,000**
Notes to the financial statements for the period ended				

IFRS ref	Change in accounting policy			
S10.14 IAS 8 p.29	During the current year, the entity changed its method for inventory valuation from the FIFO to the weighted average method. Management is of the opinion that the change will result in more reliable and relevant information for its users, given the nature of the inventory. The inventory consists of identical items, which are stored together and issued irrespective of their purchase date. The entity does not track whether the first items purchased are the first items sold and therefore the weighted average method is more reflective of how the inventory is managed.			

The effect of the change in accounting policy for inventory valuation is as follows:

	20X7	20X6	Before 20X6
	CU	CU	CU
Decrease to closing inventory	50,000	42,000	35,000
Increase to cost of sales	8,000	7,000	35,000
Decrease to closing balance of retained earnings	50,000	42,000	35,000

IFRS ref	
S10.23 IAS 8 p.49	**Correction of prior period error**

It came to the attention of management during the current year that certain items of administration costs were erroneously capitalised to the cost of constructing a building classified as property, plant and equipment. The effect of the error was corrected for retrospectively.

The effect of the correction of the prior period error is as follows:

	20X7	20X6	Before 20X6
	CU	CU	CU
Decrease to depreciation expense	15,000	15,000	45,000
Decrease to accumulated depreciation	15,000	15,000	45,000
Increase to closing balance of retained earnings	15,000	15,000	45,000

IFRS ref	
S10.18 IAS 8 p.39	**Change in accounting estimate**

The entity changed the useful life of its buildings from 45 years to 50 years. The following items in the financial statements are affected as a result:

	20X9	20X8	20X7
	CU	CU	CU
Decrease in depreciation expense	10,000	10,000	10,000
Effect of increase in carrying amount of property	10,000	10,000	10,000

14.1 INTRODUCTION

Accounting policies, changes in estimates and errors affect financial statements in different ways. Accounting policies refer to *how* companies account for different transactions and the method of accounting can affect the resultant reported financial performance and position of the entity. For this reason, and to ensure comparability, accounting policies should be applied consistently over time. Estimates are integral to the measurement of transactions and balances in the financial statements. They differ from accounting policies as estimates do not refer to how we account for transactions, but how we measure them and the related balances. On the other hand, errors refer to mistakes, either deliberate or unintentional, that are reflected in the financial statements.

This section only gives guidance for accounting for prior period errors because any error found in the current period should be corrected for, anyway, and not reflected in the financial statements.

Financial statements are designed to show the performance and financial position of an entity over time and at a point in time respectively. A significant amount of judgement is used to compile financial statements. Sometimes, this judgement is confirmed or refuted by information obtained after the financial year-end. This section guides the accounting for such information obtained after year-end.

14.2 LEARNING OUTCOMES

Upon completion of this unit you should know the financial reporting requirements for accounting for accounting policies, changes in estimates, correction of errors and disclosing related party transactions in accordance with the IFRS for SMEs. In particular, you should be able to:
(a)   identify and select appropriate accounting policies to reflect transactions and balances in the financial statements;
(b)   identify which information obtained after year-end should be reflected in the current period financial statements;
(c)   recognise and measure the effect of changes in accounting policies, changes in estimates and correction of prior period errors as well as the effects of information obtained after year-end; and
(d)   present and disclose the effects of changes in accounting policies, changes in estimates and correction of prior period errors as well as disclose information obtained after year-end related to transactions or balances of the entity.

14.3   DEFINITIONS

The definitions for the important concepts and terms used in IFRS for SMEs are found in Appendix B – *Glossary of terms* in IFRS for SMEs. Some important definitions relating to changes in accounting policies, changes in estimates and correction of prior period errors as well as the disclosure of related party transactions are as follows:

- **Accounting policies:** The specific principles, bases, conventions, rules and practices applied by an entity in preparing and presenting financial statements

- **Change in accounting estimate:** An adjustment of the carrying amount of an asset or liability, or the amount of the periodic consumption of an asset, that results from the assessment of the present status of, and expected future benefits and obligations associated with, assets and liabilities. Changes in accounting estimates result from new information and new developments and, accordingly, are not corrections of errors.

- **Errors:** Omissions from, and misstatements in, the entity's financial statements for one or more prior periods arising from a failure to use, or misuse of, reliable information that:
  - (a)   was available when financial statements for those periods were authorised for issue; and
  - (b)   could reasonably be expected to have been obtained and taken into account in the preparation and presentation of those financial statements.

14.4   SCOPE AND OBJECTIVES

Section 10 (IAS 8) provides guidance for selecting and applying the accounting policies used in preparing the financial statements. It also addresses how to account for changes in accounting estimates and correction of errors in prior period financial statements (s10.1 & IAS 8 p.3).

Section 32 defines events after the end of the reporting period and sets out the principles for recognising, measuring and disclosing those events (s32.1 & IAS 8 p.1).

14.5   ACCOUNTING POLICIES

14.5.1 Selecting accounting policies

In terms of s1.6 (IAS 1 p.16), an entity's financial statements that are described as conforming to IFRS for SMEs (IFRS) have to comply with all of the provisions of the IFRS for SMEs standard (IFRS). The entity does not need to follow a requirement of the IFRS for SMEs standard if the effect of doing so would be immaterial.

If a transaction, event or condition is not addressed by the IFRS for SMEs standard, the entity has to develop an accounting policy that delivers information that is (s10.4 & IAS 8 p.10):

(a)   relevant; and
(b)   reliable, so that it:
  (i)   faithfully represents the financial position, performance and cash flows of the entity;
  (ii)   reflects the substance of transactions over its legal form;
  (iii)   is neutral and free from bias;
  (iv)   is prudent; and
  (v)   is complete in all material respects.

The entity should apply the following hierarchy when IFRS for SMEs does not prescribe the accounting for a particular transaction or event (s10.5 & IAS 8 p.11):

(a)   the guidance in IFRS for SMEs (IFRS) for similar transactions and events;
(b)   the concepts contained in Section 2 – *Concepts and pervasive principles* (Conceptual Framework); and
(c)   the requirements in full IFRS dealing with similar and related issues (s10.6).

Full IFRS states in IAS 8 p.12 that the entity may also consider pronouncements of other standard-setting bodies that use a similar conceptual framework to develop accounting standards, other accounting literature and accepted industry practices, to the extent that these do not conflict with the sources above.

Once an entity has selected an accounting policy, it should apply that accounting policy consistently for similar items or transactions (s10.7).

14.5.2 Changes in accounting policies

The choice of accounting policy can affect the profit of the company. The risk for users is that the preparers of financial statements do not consistently apply accounting policies over time and for similar transactions and events. This leaves room for preparers to manipulate profits. For instance, in the example above, the entity could be incentivised to keep its profits above CU1,000 (possibly due to debt covenants). You will notice that changing the accounting policy from weighted average to FIFO will achieve that result. For this reason, IFRS for SMEs has strict guidance around changing accounting policies and accounting for those changes.

Accounting policies should only be changed if (s10.8 & IAS 8 p.14):
(a)   it is required by changes to this standard; and
(b)   it results in the financial statements being more relevant and reliable.

It is evident that an entity might have to recognise the effects of a change in accounting policy either because:
(a)   there is a new section in IFRS for SMEs (or a change in how transactions were accounted for in terms of IFRS for SMEs); or
(b)   the entity decides to change the manner in which it accounts for certain transactions or events (for instance, in accounting for inventory from the weighted average to FIFO policy).

If the change in policy is due to a transition to new IFRS for SME requirements, then the entity must account for that change in accordance with the transition requirements of the applicable section (s10.11(a) and (b) & IAS 8 p.19). If the change in accounting policy is because the entity decides to change the manner in which it accounts for transactions and events, the entity must apply the change in accounting policy retrospectively. Retrospective application means that the entity has to restate all of its information of the past as if the new accounting policy had always been the policy applied.

Illustrative Example 14.1: Retrospective application

Company A has historically applied the weighted average method to account for its inventory. Management is of the opinion that the FIFO method will provide more relevant and reliable information to the users of its financial statements, and therefore decides to change the accounting policy for accounting for inventory to the FIFO method in 20X7. The revenue for 20X7: CU2,000 (20X6: CU1,800). Company A purchased CU750 inventory in 20X7 and CU580 inventory in 20X6.

The following additional information is relevant:

	CU 20X7	CU 20X6	CU 20X5
Closing inventory:			
Weighted average	427	390	245
FIFO	480	440	275
Retained earnings			10,000

You are required to:
Calculate the following:
(a) What was the gross profit for 20X6 and 20X7 using the weighted average accounting policy before the change to FIFO?
(b) What is the gross profit for 20x6 and 20x7 after the change in accounting policy7?

Suggested solution:

	20X7 CU	20X6 CU
Revenue	2,000	1,800
Cost of sales^{W1}	(1,213)	(735)
Gross profit	787	1,065

Working 1: W1	20X7 CU	20X6 CU
Opening inventory	390	245
Purchases	1,250	880
Cost of goods available for sale	**1,640**	**1,125**
Closing inventory	(427)	(390)
Cost of sales	**1,213**	**735**

	20X7 CU	20X6 CU
Revenue	2,000	1,800
Cost of sales^{W2}	(1,210)	(715)
Gross profit	790	1,085

Working 2: W2	20X7	20X6
	CU	CU
Opening inventory	440	275
Purchases	1,250	880
Cost of goods available for sale	1,690	1,155
Closing inventory	(480)	(440)
Cost of sales	1,210	715

Retained earnings:	20X6
	CU
Opening balance	10,000
Restatement of opening balance [CU275 – CU245]	30
Restated opening balance	10,030

NB: The opening balance of inventory will be the same as the closing balance of inventory for the prior periods. If the new accounting policy makes the closing balance of inventory for the prior period increase, it means that the combined cost of sales for the prior periods decreases (remember that we subtract the closing balance to calculate cost of sales – refer to working 1 and working 2 above). The resultant decrease in cost of sales means that profit (retained earnings in this case) for the prior period increases.

The following highlights the impact of the treatment of deferred tax on the change in accounting policy for inventory. This is provided as additional information here as Chapter 3 set out the requirements of accounting for tax and deferred tax.

The impact of taxes on the change in accounting policies depends on how the relevant tax authority treats the change in accounting policy. The tax authority has two options:

(a) to accept the updated inventory balances for prior periods and adjust the same numbers for inventory for tax purposes; or

(b) not to accept the changes in inventory balances for prior reporting periods.

You may assume that the relevant company tax rate is 28%.

1. The tax authority accepts the updated inventory balances for prior years and adjusts the tax for those periods:

Working 1: W2	20X7	20X6	20X5
	CU	CU	CU
Current tax expense before adjustment	[2](220.36)	[1](298.2)	
(Increase)/decrease in current tax for the period	[5](0.84)	[4](5.6)	[3](8.4)

[1] Profit CU1,065 × 28% = CU298.2
[2] Profit CU787 × 28% = CU220.36
[3] Closing balance: CU275 – CU245 = CU30 × 28% = CU8.4
[4] Closing balance: CU440 – CU390 = CU50
   Opening balance: CU245 – CU275 = (CU30)
   Increase in profit: CU50 – CU30 = CU20
   Tax increase: CU20 × 28% = CU5.6
[5] Opening balance: CU390 – CU440 = (CU50)
   Increase in profit: CU53 – CU50 = CU3
   Tax increase: CU3 × 28% = CU0.84

No adjustment is needed for deferred tax in this case.

2.   The tax authority does not accept the adjustment to the prior period inventory balances:

Working 1: W2	20X7	20X6	20X5
	CU	CU	CU
Current tax expense before adjustment	[2](220.36)		
(Increase)/decrease in current tax for the period	[3](14.84)	0	0
(Increase)/decrease in deferred tax for the period	[6]14	[5](5.6)	[4](8.4)

[1] Profit (weighted average 20X6): CU1,065 × 28% = CU298.2
[2] Profit (weighted average 20X7): CU787 × 28% = CU220.36
[3] Change in closing balance: CU480 – CU427 = CU53
   Increase in current tax: CU53 × 28% = CU14.84
[4] Closing balance: CU275 – CU245 = CU30 × 28% = CU8.4
[5] Closing balance: CU440 – CU390 = CU50
   Opening balance: CU245 – CU275 = (CU30)
   Increase in profit: CU50 – CU30 = CU20
   Tax increase: CU20 × 28% = CU5.6
[6] Opening balance: CU440 – CU390 = CU50
   Tax decrease: CU50 × 28% = CU14

14.5.3 Changes in accounting estimates

Changes in accounting estimates differ from changes in accounting policies in that changes in accounting policies reflect a change in **how** an entity accounts for a transaction or event, whereas a change in accounting estimate reflects a change in how an entity measures an item or transaction. For instance, an entity's policy might be to account for equipment under the cost less accumulated depreciation and impairment model in s17 (IAS 16). This reflects a chosen method of accounting for equipment (this is **how** the entity accounts for equipment, ie its accounting policy). Quantifying the residual value of the equipment in order to depreciate it might involve the use of an estimate which can change over time. However, this change in the residual value does not change **how** the entity accounts for the equipment (under the cost less accumulated depreciation and impairment model used in this example) (s10.15 & IAS 8 p.35).

A change in accounting estimate is accounted for prospectively (s10.16 & IAS 8 p.36). This means that the effect of the change must be reflected against the asset in the period of the change (s10.17 & IAS 8 p.37) and/or in profit or loss (s10.16 & IAS 8 p.36):

(a)   in the period of the change, if the change affects that period only; or
(b)   in the period of the change and future periods, if the change affects both.

Illustrative Example 14.2: Basic financial instruments

Company A purchased machinery at a cost of CU100,000 on 01 January 20X6. Company A depreciates the machinery on the straight-line method over an estimated useful life of 10 years, to a nil residual value. On 01 January 20X7, company A revises the residual value to CU9,000 and does not consider its useful life to change.

You are required to:
Calculate the carrying amount of the machine at 31 December 20x7 and 20x6.

Suggested solution:

	20X7	20X6
	CU	CU
Carrying amount	90,000	100,000
Residual value	(9,000)	0
Depreciable amount	**81,000**	**100,000**
Useful life	9 years	10 years
Depreciation expense	**9,000**	**10,000**
Carrying amount	**81,000**	**90,000**
[CU90,000 – CU9,000]; [CU100,000 – CU10,000]		

An acceptable alternative method of accounting for the change in accounting estimate is the *cumulative catchup* method. Under this approach, the entire impact of the change in estimate is accounted for in the current period as follows (use the same information as above):

	20X7	20X6	20X6
	CU	**CU**	**CU**
Carrying amount	90,000	100,000	100,000
Adjustment for 20X6 depreciation [CU10,000 – CU9,100]	(900)	0	0
Adjusted carrying amount	**89,100**	**100,000**	**100,000**
Residual value	(9,000)	(9,000)	0
Depreciable amount	**80,100**	**91,000**	**100,000**
Useful life	9 years	10 years	10 years
Depreciation expense (without the adjustment)	**8,900**	**9,100**	**10,000**
Total P/L impact [CU8,900 – CU900]	**8,000**		
Carrying amount	**82,000**		**90,000**

14.6 CORRECTIONS OF PRIOR PERIOD ERRORS

Prior period errors result from a failure to use or the misuse of information that (s10.19 & IAS 8 p.5):

(a)   was available when financial statements for those periods were authorised for issue; or

(b)   could reasonably have been expected to have been obtained and taken into account in the preparation and presentation of those financial statements.

The errors to which we refer are prior period errors. There should be no known errors in the current financial reporting period, as they should all have been corrected in the current period on discovery.

An entity should correct a prior period error retrospectively in the first financial statements authorised for issue after its discovery by (s10.21 & IAS 8 p.42):

(a)   restating the comparative amounts for the prior period(s) presented in which the error occurred; or

(b)   if the error occurred before the first prior period presented, restating the opening balances of assets, liabilities and equity for the earliest prior period presented.

Illustrative Example 14.3: Correction of prior period error

Company A purchased equipment with a cost of CU100,000 on 01 January 20X5. However, the initial recognition of the equipment was at a cost of CU120,000 in error. The equipment is depreciated on a straight-line basis over an estimated useful life of 10 years to a nil residual value. The error was discovered when preparing the financial statements for the year ended 31 December 20X7, but before the depreciation for the current year was calculated. The opening balance of retained earnings was 20X7: CU320,000 (20X6: CU250,000) and the profit was 20X7: CU85,000 (20X6: CU70,000) before the correction of the prior period error.

You are required to:

Prepare an extract of the statement of changes in equity, reconciling the opening and closing balance of retained earning, for the year ended 31 December 20x7 (comparatives are required).

Suggested solution:
31 December 20X7:

	20X7	20X6
	CU	CU
Opening balance of retained earnings	320,000	250,000
Correction of prior period error	4,000	2,000
Restated opening balance of retained earnings	**324,000**	**252,000**
Profit for the year restated [CU85,000 + CU2,000]; [CU70,000 + 2,000]	87,000	72,000
Closing balance of retained earnings	405,000	320,000
Correction of prior period error	6,000	4,000
Restated closing balance of retained earnings	**411,000**	**324,000**

	Correct	Incorrect	Cumulative
	CU	CU	CU
01 January 20X5 cost	100,000	120,000	
Depreciation 20X5 [CU100,000/10]; [CU120,000/10]	(10,000)	(12,000)	2,000
31 December 20X5 carrying amount	**90,000**	**108,000**	**2,000**
Depreciation 20X6 [CU100,000/10]; [CU120,000/10]	(10,000)	(12,000)	2,000
31 December 20X6 carrying amount	**80,000**	**96,000**	**4,000**
Depreciation [CU100,000/10]; [CU120,000/10]	(10,000)	(12,000)	2,000
31 December 20X7 carrying amount	**70,000**	**84,000**	**6,000**

14.7   DISCLOSURE

14.7.1 Items requiring retrospective adjustment (such as changes in accounting policies and correction of prior period errors)

When a change in accounting policy has an effect on the current or any prior period, an entity should disclose the following (s10.13 & 14 & IAS 8 p.29):
(a)   the nature of the change in accounting policy or correction of prior period error;
(b)   the reason why applying the new accounting policy will provide more reliable and relevant information (only needed for a voluntary change in accounting policy);
(c)   to the extent practicable, the amount of the adjustment for each financial statement line item affected, shown:
   (i)   for the current period;
   (ii)   for each prior period presented; and
   (iii)   in the aggregate for periods before those presented.
   Items (i) and (ii) can be combined for those changes relating to changes to the IFRS for SMEs standard;
(d)   an explanation if it is impracticable to determine the amounts above.

Financial statements of subsequent periods need not repeat this information.

Full IFRS includes additional disclosure when the change in accounting policy relates to the initial application of an IFRS (IAS 8 p.28).

14.7.2 Change in accounting estimate

An entity should disclose the following for a change in accounting estimate (s10.18 & IAS 8 p.39):
(a)   the nature of the change in accounting estimate;
(b)   the effect of the change on assets, liabilities, income and expense:
   (i)   for the current period; and
   (ii) if it is practical, for one or more future periods.

14.8   EVENTS AFTER THE END OF THE REPORTING PERIOD

14.8.1 Scope

All events after the end of the reporting period should be considered in terms of this section (s32.1 & IAS 10 P.2).

The Conceptual Framework (s2.7) lists reliability as a qualitative characteristic and describes reliable information as faithfully representing what it purports to represent. The objective of financial statements is indicated as being to provide information about the financial position, performance and cash flows for the entity (s2.2). A reading of these facts therefore implies that the entity should reflect all information relevant to the performance of the entity for and as at the end of the period. There is also a practical element to incorporating all information obtained at any time into the current period financial statements. For instance, it is difficult to update the financial statements after they have been authorised for issue and are already in the hands of millions of users. For this reason, s32 – *Events after the end of the reporting period* (IAS 10 – *Events after the reporting period*) splits the events after the reporting period into two categories:

(a)   events after the reporting period and before the financial statements are authorised for issue; and

(b)   events after the reporting period and after the financial statements are authorized for issue.

14.8.2 Events after the end of the reporting period and before the financial statements are authorised for issue

The financial statements show the performance for and the financial position at a period in time. Therefore, not all information relating to events after the end of the reporting period relate to the reporting period. For instance, a fleet of vehicles owned by the entity can be damaged after the end of the reporting period and therefore this damage does not relate to the reporting period. However, sometimes, the entity obtains information from an event occurring after the end of the reporting period, but which provides information about conditions that existed at the end of the reporting period. For example, suppose that those same vehicles were damaged before the end of the reporting period, but that the entity could not measure the extent of the damages – assume that a valuator is able to measure the extent of the damages existing at the end of the reporting period, but can only provide the information after the end of the reporting period. The provision of the information (which happens after the end of the reporting period) is an event after the reporting period and provides information about conditions that existed at the end of the reporting period (the vehicles were already damaged at the end of the reporting period).

For this reason, s32 – *Events after the end of the reporting period* (IAS 10 – *Events after the Reporting Period*) distinguishes between two types of events after the end of the reporting period and before the financial statements are authorised for issue:

• **Adjusting events:** those events which provide information related to conditions existing at the reporting period end; and

• **Non-adjusting events:** those events which provide information relating to conditions that arose after the end of the reporting period.

Illustrative Example 14.4: Adjusting vs Non-adjusting events

The following information is presented to you. You may assume in all cases that the company's year-end is 31 December 20x7 and the financial statements are not yet authorized for issue.

An entity loses a court case and is required to pay damages as a result. The damages could not quantify at the end of the reporting period and as a result, the entity recognized a contingent liability. However, the court granted the plaintiff damages of CU100,000 after reporting period end.

An entity loses a court case and is required to pay damages as a result. The damages could not quantify at the end of the reporting period and as a result, the entity recognized a contingent liability. However, the court granted the plaintiff damages of CU100,000 after reporting period end. The entity

The entity broke a municipal by-law on 5 January 20x8 and received a fine on 20 January 20x8 as a result.

The entity received an invoice on 2 January 20x8 for equipment which is to be delivered on 5 January 20x8.

You are required to:

Discuss whether each of the above mentioned transactions should be classified as adjusting or non-adjusting events.

Suggested solution:

Event	Adjusting/non-adjusting
An entity loses a court case and is required to pay damages as a result. The damages could not be quantified at the end of the reporting period and as a result, the entity recognised a contingent liability. However, the court granted the plaintiff damages of CU100,000 after reporting period end.	*Adjusting event:* The decision by the court happened after the end of the reporting period, but before the financial statements were authorised for issue and provides information about conditions existing at year-end (the liability was already established at year-end). As a result, the entity will have to adjust the classification of the contingent liability to a provision/recognised liability in the financial statements for the year ended 31 December 20X7.

The company was informed on 02 January 20X8 that a debtor who is recognised in its financial statements for the year ended 31 December 20X7 was declared insolvent on 02 January 20X8.	*Adjusting event:* The debtor was most likely insolvent at 31 December 20X7 as it is very unlikely that their financial condition only deteriorated on 01 and 02 January 20X8. This event therefore provides information about conditions that most likely already existed at the end of the reporting period. The related accounts receivable balance will have to be impaired in the financial statements for the year ended 31 December 20X7.
The entity broke a municipal by-law on 05 January 20X8 and received a fine on 20 January 20X8 as a result.	*Non-adjusting event:* The fine received on 20 January 20X7 is an event after the end of the reporting period and before the financial statements are authorised for issue, but relates to conditions that did not exist at the end of the reporting period. The event will therefore not be reflected in the financial statements for the year ended 31 December 20X7.
The entity received an invoice on 02 January 20X8 for equipment which is to be delivered on 05 January 20X8.	*Non-adjusting event:* The receipt of the invoice and the delivery of the equipment is an event after the end of the reporting period and before the financial statements are authorised for issue, but does not relate to conditions existing at the end of the reporting period. The event will therefore not be reflected in the financial statements for the year ended 31 December 20X7.

14.8.2.1 Adjusting events

An entity should adjust the amounts recognised and disclosed in the financial statements for adjusting events (s32.4 & IAS 10 p.8).

Illustrative Example 14.5: Adjusting events

Company A purchases inventory on 28 December 20X7 for CU100,000. On 01 January 20X8, the staff open the sealed boxes housing the inventory and discover that all of the inventory was damaged and that the damage seemed to have occurred before receipt of the inventory. The inventory cannot be returned to the supplier as the staff who received the inventory signed for receipt of the goods before checking their condition. The damaged inventory is considered worthless. The discovery of the goods being damaged is considered an adjusting event after the end of the reporting period.

You are required to:

Prepare the journal entry necessary to account for the above mentioned event in the financial statements of the entity for the year ended 31 December 20X7.

Suggested solution:

Dr	Cost of sales	CU100,000	
Cr	Inventory		CU100,000
[Recognising the effect of the adjusting event]			

IFRS requires specific consideration of events after the reporting period which give information about the ability of the entity to continue as a going concern. IAS 10 p.14 requires a fundamental change in the basis of preparation of the financials when the entity determines after reporting date that it intends (or has no realistic option but to) liquidate the entity or cease trading.

14.8.2.2 Non-adjusting event

Because non-adjusting events provide information related to conditions that did not exist at year-end, these events should not be adjusted for and recognised in the financial statements under consideration (s32.6 & IAS 10 p.10). These events will instead be recognised in the financial statements of the period in which the event occurred.

14.8.3 Disclosure

Adjusting events are those events which:

(a)   occur after the end of the reporting period and before the financial statements are authorised for issue; and

(b)   provide information about conditions that exist at the end of the reporting period.

It is therefore important for users to know what date the financial statements are authorised for issue because it gives the user an idea of the period during which adjusting events could have occurred, among other relevant information. For this reason, s32.9 (IAS 10 p.17) requires an entity to disclose:
(a)   the date when the financial statements were authorised for issue;
(b)   who gave the authorisation; and
(c)   whether anybody has the power to amend the financial statements after issue.

The effects of adjusting events are recognised and disclosed in the financial statements under consideration and therefore no additional disclosure guidance is given in s32 – *Events after the end of the reporting period* (IAS 10 – *Events after the reporting period*).

The effects of non-adjusting events are not recognised in the financial statements under review and therefore s32.10 (IAS 10 p.21) requires the following information to be disclosed for non-adjusting events:
(a)   the nature of the event; and
(b)   an estimate of its financial effect or a statement that such an estimate cannot be made.

SELF-ASSESSMENT
Multiple choice questions: Testing principles of accounting for accounting policies, esitmates and errors and events after the reporting period

1.   The following definition refers to accounting policies:

(a) omissions or misstatements of information used in the financial statements	
(b) the classification of assets and liabilities	
(c) the measurement attributed to an asset	
(d) the specific bases, conventions, rules and practices applied by an entity in preparing and presenting financial statements	

2.   Prior period errors result from a failure to use or the misuse of reliable information that:

(a) was available when the financial statements were authorised for issue	
(b) was available after the financial statements were authorised for issue	
(c) was private information held by third parties	
(d) could *not* reasonably be expected to be obtained	

3. A change from the cost less accumulated depreciation to the revaluation model for accounting for property is considered:

(a) a correction of a prior period error	
(b) a change in accounting policy	
(c) a change in estimate	
(d) none of the above	

4. A change in the residual value of equipment is considered:

(a) a correction of a prior period error	
(b) a change in accounting policy	
(c) a change in estimate	
(d) none of the above	

5. The following event is an adjusting event:

(a) an event that occurs after the financial statements are authorised for issue that relates to conditions existing at year-end	
(b) an event that occurs before the financial statements are authorised for issue that relates to conditions existing at year-end	
(c) an event that occurs after the financial statements are authorised for issue that does not relate to conditions existing at year-end	
(d) an event that occurs before the financial statements are authoriaed for issue that relates to conditions existing at year-end	

6. Company A uses IFRS for SMEs to prepare its financial statements and has capitalised borrowing costs to the cost of an asset (which is not allowed in terms of IFRS for SMEs) in a prior period. This represents:

(a) a prior period error	
(b) a change in accounting policy	
(c) a change in estimate	
(d) none of the above	

7. Flooding which occurred two days after year-end causes significant damage to property owned by the entity. The financial statements have not been authorised for issue at the date of the flood. The following is required:

(a) recognise and disclose the effect of the flood in the financial statements	
(b) do not recognise or disclose anything related to the flood in the financial statements	
(c) disclose the nature and amount of damage only in the financial statements	
(d) recognise the effect of the flood, but do not provide any disclosure related to the flood in the financial statements	

8. A correction of a prior period error:

(a) must be made prospectively	
(b) must be made retrospectively	
(c) should not be corrected	
(d) must be made prospectively or retrospectively at the choice of the entity	

9. A change in estimate:

(a) must be adjusted for retrospectively	
(b) should be ignored	
(c) must be adjusted for in any period	
(d) must be adjusted for prospectively	

10. The entity obtains information that indicates that assets which it owns but which are situated overseas were damaged before year-end. The information is obtained before the financial statements are authorised for issue. The entity should:

(a) adjust the financial statements if it does not result in the entity incurring an overall net loss in its income statement	
(b) not adjust the financial statements, but should disclose the effect of the damage	
(c) not adjust or disclose any information related to the damage	
(d) adjust the financial statements	

Practical questions:
Application of principles to business scenarios

QUESTION 1

KLC (Pty) Ltd is a company engaged in the sale of household commercial products. The company changed its accounting policy from the FIFO method of accounting for inventory to the weighted average method. The following information is provided:

	20X7	20X6	20X5
	CU	CU	CU
Closing balance:			
FIFO	123,000	80,000	68,000
Weighted average	135,000	87,000	72,000

You are required to:
(a)   Record the journal entries to account for the change in accounting policy for the year ended 31 December 20X7.

Optional additional required incorporating the effects of tax:
(b)   Record the journal entries relating to the deferred tax to account for the change in accounting policy for the year ended 31 December 20X7. You may assume that the tax authority will not reopen and update any prior period assessments. You may assume a company tax rate of 28%.

QUESTION 2

Borrower (Pty) Ltd constructed a building and capitalised all of the borrowing cost incurred on the loan it took out specifically to finance the construction. The building had a total cost of CU120,000 (including capitalised borrowing cost of CU20,000, incurred in the year ended 31 December 20X6) which was available for use from 01 January 20X7. Borrower (Pty) Ltd depreciates buildings on the straight-line method over an estimated useful life of 10 years. The opening retained earnings were CU500,000 on 01 January 20X7, while the profit was 20X8: CU75,000 (20X7: CU70,000) (all calculated before the correction of the prior period error).

You are required to:
Prepare the retained earnings column in the statement of changes in equity for Borrower (Pty) Ltd for the year ended 31 December 20X8. Comparatives are required.

QUESTION 3

Scaffold (Pty) Ltd manufactures scaffolding and other equipment for the building industry. On 1 January 20X4, Scaffold (Pty) Ltd purchased machinery for CU250,000. The machinery was depreciated on the straight-line method over an estimated useful life of 10 years to an estimated nil residual value. On 31 December 20X7, Scaffold (Pty) Ltd revised the remaining useful life to five years while the residual value was revised to CU25,000.

You are required to:
Prepare the journal entries necessary to account for the depreciation expense related to the equipment for the financial year ended 31 December 20X7. You may assume that no depreciation expense related to the equipment has been accounted for as yet.

CHAPTER 15
FOREIGN CURRENCY TRANSLATION

ILLUSTRATIVE DISCLOSURE [EXTRACT]

IFRS ref		Notes	20X7	20X6
			CU	CU
S30.10 & IAS 21 p.28	Foreign exchange gain	14	20,000	15,000
IFRS ref	**14. Foreign exchange gains and losses**			
S30.25 & IAS 21 p.52	Foreign exchange gains and losses are included in a separate line item in profit or loss. The total amount of foreign exchange gains recognised in profit for the period amounts to 20X7: CU20,000 (20X6: CU15,000). There were no foreign exchange gains or losses recognised outside of profit or loss.			

15.1   INTRODUCTION

Given the trends in globalisation, entities often engage in transactions in various currencies. However, each currency has its own value. Each entity, therefore, needs one 'base' currency in which it accounts for its transactions so that different transactions and account balances remain comparable. While section 30 – *Foreign currency translation* prescribes the accounting treatment to include foreign operations in the financial statements of an entity and how to translate financial statements into a presentation currency, this will not be covered in this chapter as those situations normally arise in group and its related scenarios, which is not the focus of this text.

15.2   LEARNING OUTCOMES

This chapter is designed to explain the accounting principles and practices for accounting for foreign currency transactions. Upon completion of this chapter you should be able to:

(a)   identify and classify currencies into the functional and foreign currencies of an entity;

(b)   recognise foreign currency transactions in the functional currency of the entity;

(c)   translate the various elements of the statement of financial position into the functional currency of the entity; and

(d)   measure the various elements of the financial statements in the separate and group financial statements.

15.3   DEFINITIONS

The definitions for the important concepts and terms used in IFRS for SMEs are found in Appendix B – *Glossary of terms* in IFRS for SMEs. Some important definitions relating to foreign currency translation include the following:

- **Functional currency:** The currency of the primary economic environment in which the entity operates

- **Monetary items:** Units of currency held and assets and liabilities to be received or paid in a fixed or determinable number of units of currency

15.4   SCOPE AND OBJECTIVES

Section 30 – *Foreign currency translation* provides guidance for the inclusion of the following into the financial statements of an entity (s30.1 and IAS 21 p.3):

(a)   foreign currency transactions (covered in this chapter);

(b)   foreign operations (not covered in this chapter); and

(c)   how to translate financial statements into a presentation currency (not covered in this chapter).

15.5   IDENTIFYING THE FUNCTIONAL CURRENCY OF THE ENTITY

An entity has to identify what is functional currency is (s). All other currencies are then considered to be foreign currencies for the entity. Each transaction entered into by the entity and all balances for the statement of financial position accounts must be translated into the entity's functional currency.

The functional currency for the entity is the currency of the primary economic environment in which the entity operates (s30.2 and IAS 21 p.8). Factors that an entity should consider in determining its functional currency include (s30.3 and IAS 21 p.9):

(a)   the currency:

        (i)   that mainly influences sales prices for goods and services (this will often be the currency in which sales prices for its goods and services are denominated and settled); and

        (ii)   of the country whose competitive forces and regulations mainly determine the sales prices of its goods and services.

(b)   the currency that mainly influences labour, material and other costs of providing goods or services (this will often be the currency in which such costs are denominated and settled).

Additional factors that may also assist in determining an entity's functional currency are (s30.5 and IAS 21 p.10):

(a)   the currency in which funds from financing activities (issuing debt and equity instruments) are generated; and

(b)   the currency in which the receipts from operating activities are usually retained.

Illustrative Example 15.1: Determining the functional currency of an entity

Company A produces product A which it sells both locally and internationally. It agrees to sell its products in foreign currency units (FCU) when dealing with international customers. However, it agrees to the FCU after translating its price in local currency units (LCU) at an appropriate exchange rate (based on the spot exchange rate between LCU and FCU at the contract date). It determines the price in FCU by considering the cost to make the product, which consists of material (sourced from a local supplier), labour (all sourced from local labour markets), overheads (all paid and denominated in LCU) and a desired profit (determined in LCU). It also translates any FCU received into LCU and retains its receipts from operating activities in LCU. On the rare occasions where company A has sourced funds for financing capital and operating activities, it has done so in LCU.

Based on the information above, discuss whether company A's functional currency is LCU or FCU.

You are required to:

Discuss what the functional currency of the entity is.

Suggested solution:

In order to determine company A's functional currency, the following factors will be considered:

Factor	Consideration
S30.3(a)(i) The currency that mainly influences sales prices for goods and services (this will often be the currency in which sales prices for its goods and services are denominated and settled)	Although the foreign transactions are denominated in FCU, the fact that the drivers of price setting are determined by local influences (represented by LCU), company A would most likely conclude that LCU is the currency that mainly influences sales prices for goods and services.
S30.3(a)(ii) The currency of the country whose competitive forces and regulations mainly determine the sales prices of its goods and services	For the same reasons as above, it appears reasonable to conclude that as the sales prices are set based on the cost of variables, which cost is determined by the competitive forces of the country whose currency is LCU, that LCU is the currency of the country whose competitive forces and regulations mainly determine the sales prices of the goods or services of company A.
S30.3(b) The currency that mainly influences labour, material and other costs of providing goods or services (this will often be the currency in which such costs are denominated and settled)	As mentioned, the cost of providing the goods seem to be influenced primarily by LCU.
Additional factors:	
S30.5(a) The currency in which funds from financing activities (issuing debt and equity instruments) are generated	Funds from financing are generated in LCU.
S30.5(b) The currency in which the receipts from operating activities are usually retained	Receipts from operating activities are retained in LCU. Funds received in FCU are also translated into LCU in order to be retained.

Based on the arguments provided above, it is clear that the functional currency of company A is LCU.

15.6 REPORTING FOREIGN CURRENCY TRANSACTIONS IN THE FUNCTIONAL CURRENCY

15.6.1 Initial recognition

An entity should recognise a foreign currency transaction on initial recognition by translating it into the entity's functional currency by applying the spot exchange rate (between the foreign and functional currencies) at the transaction date (s30.7 and IAS 21 p.21).

Illustrative Example 15.2: Determining the functional currency of an entity

Company A purchases equipment from a foreign supplier for FCU10,000. The spot exchange rate on the date that the equipment qualifies for recognition is FCU1 = LCU2.50.

You are required to:

Prepare the journal entry necessary to recognise the equipment in the financial statements of company A.

Suggested solution:

No date given in the scenario:

		LCU	LCU
Dr	Equipment [FCU10,000 × LCU2.50]	25,000	
Cr	Bank/foreign creditor		25,000
[Recording the initial recognition of the equipment]			

Sometimes, especially in the case of services provided or received and for practical purposes, an average rate will be used instead of the actual rate. However, the average rate should approximate the actual rate and if the exchange rate fluctuates significantly and renders the average rate not indicative of the actual rate over the period, then the entity should not use the average rate (s30.8 and IAS 21 p.22).

Illustrative Example 15.3: Recognising a foreign currency transaction:

Company A pays FCU1,200 per annum for access to legal services (irrespective of whether it uses the services, access to the service is guaranteed) in a foreign country in which it conducts operations. The average exchange rate over the period is determined as the average of the opening and closing exchange rates for the year. The following table lists the opening and closing exchange rates for the year:

	FCU1 = LCU?
01 January 20X7	1.80
31 December 20X7	2.20

You are required to:
Prepare the journal entries necessary to recognise the services (access to legal fees) and the related foreign exchange gain or loss, in the financial statements of company A for the year ended 31 December 20X7.

Suggested solution:
31 December 20X7:

		LCU	LCU
Dr	Legal service expense [P/L] [FCU1,200 × LCU2 ((LCU2.20 – LCU1.80)/2]	2,400	
Cr	Bank/foreign creditor		2,400
[Recording the services received during the year]			

		LCU	LCU
Dr	Foreign exchange loss [P/L] [FCU1,200 × LCU0.20 ((LCU2.20 – LCU2)]	240	
Cr	Foreign creditor		240
[Recording the services received during the year]			

15.6.2 Measurement after initial recognition

An entity shall measure balances related to foreign currency transactions as follows at the end of each reporting period (s30.9 and IAS 21 p.23):
(a)   **monetary items:** at the closing rate at year-end;
(b)   **non-monetary items measured at historical cost:** these items are translated to local currency units on transaction date and accounted for in local currency from that date. Therefore, no further translation is necessary; and
(c)   **non-monetary items measured at fair value in a foreign currency:** the exchange rate at the date when the fair value was determined.

Any gain or loss on remeasurement should be recognised in profit or loss in the period of the remeasurement (s30.10 & 11 and IAS 21 p.28) unless the gain or loss relates to an item recognised in other comprehensive income (s30.11 and IAS 21 p.30).

Illustrative Example 15.4: Monetary item

Company A transferred FCU10,000 to a foreign third party in terms of a loan agreement on 30 November 20X7. The recipient has agreed to pay the amount due on 05 January 20X8. The effects of discounting are considered immaterial given the short period of the loan. The exchange rate on 30 November 20X7 is FCU1 = LCU2.70 and on 31 December 20X7 FCU1 = LCU2.88.

You are required to:
Prepare the journal entry necessary to account for the foreign loan receivable in the financial statements of company A for the year-ended 31 December 2017.

Suggested solution:
30 November 20X7:

		LCU	LCU
Dr	Loan receivable [FCU10,000 × LCU2.70]	27,000	
Cr	Bank		27,000
[Recording the initial recognition of the loan receivable]			

31 December 20X7:

		LCU	LCU
Dr	Loan receivable [FCU10,000 × (LCU2.88 – LCU2.70)]	1,800	
Cr	Foreign exchange gain [P/L]		1,800
[Recording the gain on the foreign loan receivable]			

Illustrative Example 15.5: Non-monetary item measured at historical cost

Company A purchases equipment from a foreign supplier for FCU10,000 on 01 January 20X7. The spot exchange rate on the date that the equipment qualifies for recognition is FCU1 = LCU2.50. The exchange rate at 31 December 20X7 is FCU1 = LCU3. Company A accounts for the equipment on the cost model in terms of section 17 – *Property, plant and equipment*. Company A depreciates the equipment over an estimated useful life of 10 years to a nil residual value.

You are required to:
Prepare the journal entry necessary to account for the equipment in the financial statements of company A for the year ended 31 December 20X7.

Suggested solution:

		LCU	LCU
Dr	Equipment [FCU10,000 × LCU2.50]	25,000	
Cr	Bank/foreign creditor		25,000
[Recording the initial recognition of the equipment]		

		LCU	LCU
Dr	Depreciation expense [P/L] [LCU25,000/10]	2,500	
Cr	Accumulated depreciation – equipment		2,500
[Recording the depreciation expense for the year]		

Illustrative Example 15.6: Non-monetary item measured at historical cost

Company A purchased an investment property for FCU100,000 on 01 January 20X7. The property is situated in a foreign country. The spot exchange rate on the date that the investment property qualifies for recognition is FCU1 = LCU2.50. The exchange rate at 31 December 20X7 is FCU1 = LCU2.50. The fair value of the investment property is FCU110,000 on 31 December 20X7 when the exchange rate is FCU1 = LCU3.10. Company A accounts for the investment property in terms of section 16 – *Investment property*.

You are required to:

Prepare the journal entry necessary to account for the equipment in the financial statements of company A for the year ended 31 December 20X7.

Suggested solution:

		LCU	LCU
Dr	Equipment [FCU100,000 × LCU2.50]	250,000	
Cr	Bank/foreign creditor		250,000
[Recording the initial recognition of the equipment]		

		LCU	LCU
Dr	Investment property [(FCU110,000 × LCU3.10) – LCU250,000]	91,000	
Cr	Gain on investment property [P/L]		91,000
[Recording the fair value adjustment to the investment property for the year]		

15.7   DISCLOSURE

An entity should disclose (s30.25 and IAS 21 p.52):

(a)   the amount of exchange gains and losses recognised in profit or loss during the period, except for those arising on financial instruments measured at fair value through profit or loss in accordance with section 11 – *Basic financial instruments* and section 12; and

(b)   the amount of exchange differences arising during the period and classified in a separate component of equity at the end of the period.

SELF-ASSESSMENT
Multiple choice questions: Testing principles of accounting for foreign currency translations

1. The entity's functional currency is defined as:

(a) the currency of the primary economic environment in which the entity operates	
(b) the currency of the country in which the entity is domiciled	
(c) the currency of the country in which the entity is registered	
(d) the currency of the country in which the entity has customers	

2. Foreign currency is:

(a) the functional currency	
(b) any currency besides the functional currency	
(c) the currency of its last transaction	
(d) the currency of its next expected transaction	

3. All transactions must be recognised in an entity's:

(a) foreign currency	
(b) presentation currency	
(c) expected currency	
(d) functional currency	

4. All transactions in foreign currency are initially recognised as follows:

(a) translated to another foreign currency using the exchange rate at transaction date	
(b) translated to the entity's presentation currency using the exchange rate at transaction date	
(c) translated to the entity's functional currency using the exchange rate at transaction date	
(d) none of the above	

5. Which circumstances render it appropriate to use the average exchange rate to translate foreign exchange transactions?

(a) high volatility in exchange rates for the period over which a transaction occurs	
(b) the average exchange rate approximates the actual exchange rate over the period and the transaction occurs at a point in time	
(c) high volatility in exchange rates over the period of a point in time a transaction occurs	
(d) the average exchange rate approximates the actual exchange rate over the period and the transaction(s) occurs over the period.	

6. The following treatment is prescribed to account for balances of monetary items in the statement of financial position at year-end:

(a) leave unadjusted from initial recognition	
(b) translate at the closing exchange rate at year-end	
(c) translate at the average exchange rate for the year	
(d) translate at the opening exchange rate for the year	

7. The following treatment is prescribed to account for balances of non-monetary items accounted for under the cost model in the statement of financial position at year-end

(a) leave unadjusted from initial recognition	
(b) translate at the closing exchange rate at year-end	
(c) translate at the average exchange rate for the year	
(d) translate at the opening exchange rate for the year	

8. The following treatment is prescribed to account for balances of non-monetary items carried at fair value, in a foreign currency in the statement of financial position at year-end:

(a) leave unadjusted from initial recognition	
(b) translate at the exchange rate at year-end	
(c) translate at the exchange rate on the date that the fair value was determined	
(d) translate at the average exchange rate for the year	

9. Gains or losses on translating monetary items from the foreign currency to the functional currency should be recognised:

(a) in profit or loss	
(b) in other comprehensive income	
(c) in the statement of changes in equity	
(d) as a deferred liability (if a gain) or an asset (if a loss)	

10. Gains or losses or translating non-monetary items from the foreign currency to the functional currency, related to an item for which gains and losses are measured in other comprehensive income, should be recognised:

(a) in profit or loss	
(b) in other comprehensive income	
(c) in the statement of changes in equity	
(d) as a deferred liability (if a gain) or an asset (if a loss)	

Practical questions:
Application of principles to business scenarios

QUESTION 1

LR (Pty) Ltd transferred FCU250,000 to Loan (Pty) Ltd on 21 December 20X7. Loan (Pty) Ltd agreed to repay the amount which it borrowed on 12 January 20X7. The exchange rate was FCU1 = LCU0.40 on 21 December 20X7 and FCU1 = LCU0.42 on 31 December 20X7. You may ignore any time value of money related to the transaction.

You are required to:
Prepare the journal entries necessary to account for the loan in the financial statements of LR (Pty) Ltd for the year ended 31 December 20X7.

QUESTION 2

CF (Pty) Ltd purchased machinery for FCU50,000 in cash on 01 January 20X7. CF (Pty) Ltd accounts for the machinery at cost less accumulated depreciation and impairment. CF (Pty) Ltd depreciates the machinery over a useful life of eight years to a residual value of LCU15,000. The exchange rate on 01 January 20X7 was FCU1 = LCU1.50, while the exchange rate on 31 December 20X7 was FCU1 = LCU1.60.

You are required to:
Prepare the journal entries necessary to account for the machinery in the financial statements of CF (Pty) Ltd for the year-ended 31 December 20X7.

QUESTION 3

AGJ (Pty) Ltd purchased investment property for FCU180,000, which it accounts for in terms of section 16 – *Investment property*, on 01 June 20X7. The fair value of the property was FCU200,000 at 31 December 20X7. The exchange rate was FCU1 = LCU1.30 on 01 June 20X7 and FCU1 = LCU1.20 on 31 December 20X7.

You are required to:
Prepare the journal entries necessary to account for the investment property in the financial statements of AGJ (Pty) Ltd for the year ended 31 December 20X7.

CHAPTER 16
STATEMENT OF CASH FLOWS

ILLUSTRATIVE DISCLOSURE [EXTRACT]

IFRS ref		Notes	20X2	20X1
			CU'000	CU'000
S7.4 & IAS 7 p.13	**Cash flows from operating activities**			
S7.7(b) & IAS 7 p.18(a)	Cash received from customers	14	125,000	100,000
S7.7(b) & IAS 7 p.18(a)	Cash paid to customers and employees		(48,000)	(39,000)
	Cash flow from operations		**77,000**	**61,000**
S7.14 & IAS 7 p.31	Interest paid		(5,000)	(4,200)
S7.14 & IAS 7 p.31	Interest received		1,350	950
S7.14 & IAS 7 p.31	Dividends received		500	420
S7.14 & IAS 7 p.31	Dividends paid		(1,800)	(1,400)
S7.17 & IAS 7 p.35	Tax paid		(30,000)	(24,000)
S7.4 & IAS 7 p.13	**Cash flow from operating activities**		**42,050**	**32,770**
S7.5 & IAS 7 p.16	**Cash flows from investing activities**			
S7.5(b) & IAS 7 p.16(b)	Proceeds from sale of property		70,000	55,000
S7.5(a) & IAS 7 p.16(a)	Payment on purchase of property		(40,000)	(37,000)
S7.5(b) & IAS 7 p.16(b)	Proceeds on disposal of equipment		15,000	10,000
S7.5(a) & IAS 7 p.16(a)	Payment on purchase of machinery		(7,000)	(4,000)

S7.5 & IAS 7 p.16	Cash flows from investing activities	38,000	24,000
S7.6 & IAS 7 p.17	**Cash flows from financing activities**		
S7.6(a) & IAS 7 p.17(a)	Proceeds on issue of ordinary shares	1,000	900
S7.6(c) & IAS 7 p.17(c)	Proceeds received from loan provider	800	700
S7.6(d) & IAS 7 p.17(d)	Repayment of loan	(200)	(140)
S7.6 & IAS 7 p.17	**Cash flows from financing activities**	1,600	1,460
S7.1 & IAS 7 p.10	**Net in(out)flow of cash and cash equivalents**	81,650	58,230
S7.1 & IAS 7 p.10	**Balance of cash and cash equivalents 01 January 20X2**	208,230	150,000
S7.1 & IAS 7 p.10	**Balance of cash and cash equivalents 31 December 20X2**	289,880	208,230

16.1 INTRODUCTION

While the accrual basis of accounting provides important information which enables users to evaluate the future cash flows of an entity, users also need information on how well management has managed their cash and cash equivalents in the past. For this reason, the statement of cash flows provides useful information to users relating to its movement in cash and cash equivalents for the period. The cash flows for the period are classified into three broad activities undertaken by the entity and used to reconcile the opening and closing balances of cash and cash equivalents.

16.2 LEARNING OUTCOMES

Upon completion of this unit, you should know the financial reporting requirements for preparing the statement of cash flows in accordance with IFRS for SMEs. In particular, you should be able to:

(a)   identify cash and cash equivalents;

(b)   classify cash flows into either operating activities, investing activities or financing activities; and

(c)   prepare the statement of cash flows.

16.3   DEFINITIONS

The definitions for the important concepts and terms used in IFRS for SMEs are found in Appendix B – *Glossary of terms* in IFRS for SMEs. Some important definitions relating to the statement of cash flows include the following:

- **Cash:** Cash on hand and demand deposits

- **Cash equivalent:** Short-term, highly liquid investments that are readily convertible to known amounts of cash and that are subject to an insignificant risk of changes in value

- **Financing activities:** Activities that result in changes in the size and composition of the contributed equity and borrowings of the entity

- **Investing activities:** The acquisition and disposal of long-term assets and other investments not included in cash equivalents

- **Operating activities:** The principle revenue-producing activities of the entity and other activities that are not investing or financing activities

16.4   SCOPE AND OBJECTIVES

Section 7 – *Statement of cash flows* sets out the information to be presented in a statement of cash flows and provides guidance on how to present such information (s7.1 and IAS 7 p.1).

16.5   CLASSIFICATION

In order to provide users with useful information related to changes in the entity's cash flow for the period, the entity first has to identify which items meet the definitions of cash and cash equivalents (s7.2 and IAS 7 p.7). Thereafter, the entity needs to classify the cash flows into one of the following three categories of activities (s7.3 and IAS 7 p.10):
(a)   operating activities;
(b)   investing activities; or
(c)   financing activities.

16.5.1 Cash and cash equivalents

Cash and cash equivalents are held to meet short-term cash flow needs rather than strategic investment needs (s7.2 and IAS 7 p.7). Therefore, normally an investment will only be classified as a cash equivalent if it has a short period to maturity (IFRS for SMEs s7.2 and IAS 7 p.7 deems a short period to be three months or less). Bank overdrafts, like other lending arrangements, are considered financing activities unless they are repayable on demand and form an integral part of the entity's cash management, in which case they are also considered to be cash equivalents (s7.2 and IAS 7 p.7).

Illustrative Example 16.1: Classification of cash equivalents

The entity has the following balances in its trial balance: long-term loan receivable; 32-day notice deposit; five years, fixed term, investment with a local bank; long-term loan payable; lease payable.

You are required to:
Use the template below to indicate whether or not each item is a cash equivalent.

Item:	Cash equivalent?
Long-term loan receivable	
32-day notice deposit	
Five years, fixed term, investment with a local bank	
Long-term loan payable	
Lease payable	

Suggested solution:

Item:	Cash equivalent?
Long-term loan receivable	No – longer than three months to maturity
32-day notice deposit	Yes – shorter than three months to maturity
Five years, fixed term, investment with a local bank	No – longer than three months to maturity
Long-term loan payable	No – longer than three months to maturity, unlikely to be payable on demand and unlikely to be an integral part of entity's cash management
Lease payable	No – unlikely to be payable on demand and unlikely to be an integral part of entity's cash management

16.5.2 Operating activities

Operating cash flows relate to revenue-producing activities of the entity such as cash received from customers (s7.4 and IAS 7 p.13). Cash flows from operating activities include cash paid to suppliers and employees, payments of tax or tax refunds (unless it can be linked with investing or financing activities) and interest/dividend payments and receipts (interest/dividend payments can also be classified as financing activities, while interest/dividend receipts can also be classified as investing activities).

16.5.3 Investing activities

Investing activities include those cash flows to acquire or dispose of long-term assets (s7.5 and IAS 7 p.16). Cash flows from investing activities include the cash flows relating to the purchase or sale of property, plant and equipment and intangible assets, investments in the shares of other entities, cash loans made to other parties, and other investments not classified as cash and cash equivalents.

16.5.4 Financing activities

Financing activities include those cash flows related to the financing (equity and borrowings) of the entity (s7.6 and IAS 7 p.17). Cash flows from financing activities include cash flows relating to the issue or redemption of equity, loans, and the repayment of liabilities relating to finance leases.

Illustrative Example 16.2: Classification of cash flows

The entity has the following cash flows for the period: revenue received in cash; settlement of accounts payable; payment of dividend to shareholders; proceeds from the sale of machinery; payment of loan instalment; proceeds from the issue of ordinary shares; payment of capital portion of lease instalment.

You are required to:
Use the template below to indicate whether each item is a cash flow from operating activities, investing activities or financing activities.

Item:	Classification of cash flow?
Revenue received in cash	
Settlement of accounts payable	
Payment of dividend to shareholders	
Proceeds from the sale of machinery	
Payment of loan instalment	
Proceeds from the issue of ordinary shares	
Payment of capital portion of lease instalment	

Suggested solution:

Item:	Classification of cash flow?
Revenue received in cash	Operating activities
Settlement of accounts payable	Operating activities
Payment of dividend to shareholders	Operating activities/financing activities
Proceeds from the sale of machinery	Investing activities
Payment of loan instalment	Financing activities
Proceeds from the issue of ordinary shares	Financing activities
Payment of capital portion of lease instalment	Financing activities

16.6   REPORTING

16.6.1 Cash flows from operating activities

Cash flows from operating activities are split into two sections:
(a)   cash flows from operations; and
(b)   Cash flows from separately disclosed items.

16.6.1.1 Cash flows from operations

Cash flows from operations are reported using one of two approaches (s7.7 and IAS 7 p.18):
(a)   the direct method; or
(b)   the indirect method.

Cash flows from operating activities – the direct method:

Under the direct method of reporting cash flows from operating activities, the entity reports cash flows typically as (s7.9 and IAS 7 p.18(a)):
(a)   cash received from customers; and
(b)   cash paid to suppliers and employees.

Illustrative Example 16.3: Cash flows from operations – direct method

The following information is presented to you:

COMPANY A	
Statement of profit or loss for the year ended 31 December 20X8	
	20X8
	CU'000
Revenue	2,500
Cost of sales	(500)
Gross profit	**2,000**
Other income	250
Other expenses	(750)
Administrative expenses	(500)
Profit before interest and tax	**1,000**
Interest expense	(200)
Profit before tax	**800**
Tax expense	(224)
Profit for the year	**576**

	20X8	**20X7**
	CU'000	**CU'000**
Accounts receivable	80,000	68,000
Inventory	14,000	11,000
Accounts payable	7,200	6,200

Additional information:

1. included in other expenses is depreciation expense of CU100,000; and
2. the carrying amount of accounts receivable is provided after the allowance for credit loss of 20X8: CU20,000 (20X7: CU15,000) and bad debts expense of 20X8: CU3,000 (20X7: 2,000).

You are required to:

Prepare the extract of the statement of cash flows of Company A showing the cash flows from operating activities (cash flows from operations only) for the year ended 31 December 20x8.

Suggested solution:

COMPANY A	
Statement of cash flows for the year ended 31 December 20X8	
	20X8
	CU'000
Cash flows from operating activities	
Cash received from customers **W1**	2,480
Cash paid to suppliers and employees **W2**	(1,394)
Cash flow from operations	**1,086**

Working 1 (W1):	**CU'000**
Revenue	2,500
Adjusted for changes in working capital:	
Movement in accounts receivable [80,000 – 68,000]	(12)
Adjusted for non-cash items:	
Movement in allowance for credit losses [20,000 – 15,000]	(5)
Bad debts expense [given]	(3)
Cash received from customers	**2,480**

Working 2 (W2):	**CU'000**
Expenses [2,500 – 576]$^{\#}$	(1,924)
Adjusted for items to be disclosed elsewhere:	
Interest expense	200
Tax expense	224
Adjusted for changes in working capital:	
Movement in accounts payable [7,200 – 6,200]	1
Movement in inventory [14,000 – 11,000]	(3)
Adjusted for non-cash items:	
Depreciation expense	100
Movement in allowance for credit losses [20,000 – 15,000]	5
Bad debts expense [given]	3
Cash received from customers	**1,394**

$^{\#}$We could start with profit before interest and tax and then not reduce the items to be disclosed elsewhere.

NB: It is imperative that you consider what sign you used to indicate your expenses when you start your calculation as this will determine the signs of all adjustments.

Cash flows from operating activities – the indirect method:

Under the indirect method of reporting cash flows from operating activities, the entity starts with and then adjusts the profit for the period (s7.8 and IAS 7 p.18(b)).

Illustrative Example 16.4: Cash flows from operations – indirect method

Use the same information as in Illustrative Example 16.3.

You are required to:

Using the same information as in illustrative example 3, prepare the cash flows from operating activities section (only up to the cash flow from operations) of the statement of cash flows for Company A using the indirect method.

Suggested solution:

COMPANY A	
Statement of cash flows for the year ended 31 December 20X8	
	20X8
	CU'000
Cash flows from operating activities	
Profit for the year#	576
Adjusted for non-cash items:	
Depreciation expense	100
Movement in allowance for credit losses [20,000 – 15,000]	5
Bad debts expense [given]	3
Adjusted for changes in working capital:	
Movement in accounts receivable [80,000 + 20,000 + 7,000 – 68,000 – 15,000 – 4,000]	(20)
Movement in accounts payable [7,200 – 6,200]	1
Movement in inventory [14,000 – 11,000]	(3)
Adjusted for items to be disclosed elsewhere:	
Interest expense	200
Tax expense	224
Cash flow from operations	**1,086**

#We could start with profit before interest and tax and then not reduce the items to be disclosed elsewhere.

Cash flows from items which are separately disclosable

In addition to the items included in cash flows from operations, some items are separately disclosable in the cash flows from operating activities (usually after cash flows from operations). These items can also be presented under investing or financing activities as appropriate, but are also separately disclosable under those sections. The following items are separately disclosable (s7.7.14–7.17 and IAS 7 p.31–36):

(a)   dividends received;
(b)   dividends paid;
(c)   interest received;
(d)   interest paid; and
(e)   tax paid.

Illustrative Example 16.5: Cash flows from operating activities – separately disclosable items

Use the same information as in Illustrative Example 16.3.

You are required to:

Prepare the cash flows from operating activities section of the statement of cash flows using the indirect method.

Suggested solution:

COMPANY A	
Statement of cash flows for the year ended 31 December 20X8	
	20X8
	CU'000
Cash flows from operating activities	
Cash received from customers **W1**	2,480
Cash paid to suppliers and employees **W2**	(1,394)
Cash flows from operations	**1,086**
Interest paid (assumed all cash for illustrative purposes)	(200)
Dividends paid (assumed for illustrative purposes as no information given in the scenario)	(150)
Tax paid (assumed all cash for illustrative purposes)	(224)
Cash flows from operating activities	**512**

16.6.2 Cash flows from investing activities

Cash flows from investing activities show all of the cash flows related to the acquisition and disposal of long-term assets (s7.5 and IAS 7 p.16).

Illustrative Example 16.6: Cash flows from investing activities

Company A has the following information related to its cash flows from investing activities for the year ended 31 December 20X8:

(a)   it purchased 1,000 shares in an independent third party company for CU10 per share;

(b)   it purchased land for a total cost of CU100,000; and

(c)   it sold vehicles with an original cost of CU200,000 at a profit of CU45,000 on 31 December 20X8. The vehicles were originally purchased by company A on 01 January 20X6 as new vehicles. The vehicles are depreciated based on the units of production method with reference to the number of kilometres driven as a proportion of the total kilometres expected to be driven. Company A assesses the total average that each vehicle will be driven as being 500,000 km. The vehicles had been driven for an average of 300,000 km each at 31 December 20X8.

You are required to:

Prepare the statement of cash flows from investing activities for company A for the year ended 31 December 20X8.

Suggested solution:

COMPANY A	
Statement of cash flows for the year ended 31 December 20X8	
	20X8
	CU'000
Cash flows from investing activities	
Cash paid to acquire shares [1,000 × CU10]	(10)
Cash paid to acquire land	(100)
Proceeds on sale of vehicles	125
Cash flows from investing activities	**15**

Working 1 (W1):	**CU'000**
Cost	200,000
Accumulated depreciation [200,000/500,000 × 300,000]	(120,000)
Carrying amount	**80,000**
Profit on disposal	45,000
Proceeds on sale of vehicles	**125,000**

16.6.3 Cash flows from financing activities

Cash flows from financing activities show all of the cash flows from the issue and payment of borrowings and equity (37.6 and IAS 7 p.17).

Illustrative Example 16.7: Cash flows from investing activities

Company A has the following information related to its cash flows from investing activities for the year ended 31 December 20X8:

(a)   it issued 1,000 shares to an independent third party company for CU25 per share;

(b)   it received the proceeds from a loan of CU58,000; and

(c)   it repaid a lease instalment of CU100,000 during the year ended 31 December 20X8.

You are required to:

Prepare the statement of cash flows from investing activities for company A for the year ended 31 December 20X8.

Suggested solution:

COMPANY A	
Statement of cash flows for the year ended 31 December 20X8	
	20X8
	CU'000
Cash flows from financing activities	
Proceeds from the issue of shares [1,000 × CU25]	25
Proceeds from the incurrence of a loan	58
Cash paid on lease instalments	(100)
Cash flows from investing activities	**(17)**

16.7   PRESENTATION AND DISCLOSURE

The complete statement of cash flows based on the above examples would be as follows.

16.7.1 Presentation

16.7.1.1 Direct method

Illustrative Example 16.8: Cash flows from operations – direct method

COMPANY A	
Statement of cash flows for the year ended 31 December 20X8	
	20X8
	CU'000
Cash flows from operating activities	
Cash received from customers	2,480
Cash paid to suppliers and employees	(1,394)
Cash flows from operations	**1,086**
Interest paid (assumed all cash for illustrative purposes)	(200)
Dividends paid (assumed for illustrative purposes as no information given in the scenario)	(150)
Tax paid (assumed all cash for illustrative purposes)	(224)
Cash flows from operating activities	**512**
Cash flows from investing activities	
Cash paid to acquire shares [1,000 × CU10]	(10)
Cash paid to acquire land	(100)
Proceeds on sale of vehicles	125
Cash flows from investing activities	**15**
Cash flows from financing activities	
Proceeds from the issue of shares [1,000 × CU25]	25
Proceeds from the incurrence of a loan	58
Cash paid on lease instalments	(100)
Cash flows from investing activities	**(17)**
Net cash flow for the year	**510**
Balance of cash and cash equivalents at 01 January 20X8	1,000
Balance of cash and cash equivalents at 31 December 20X8	**1,510**

16.7.1.2 Indirect method

Illustrative Example 16.9: Cash flows from operations – direct method

COMPANY A	
Statement of cash flows for the year ended 31 December 20X8	
	20X8
	CU'000
Cash flows from operating activities	
Profit for the year	576
Adjusted for non-cash items:	
Depreciation expense	100
Movement in allowance for credit losses [20,000 – 15,000]	5
Bad debts expense [given]	3
Adjusted for changes in working capital:	
Movement in accounts receivable [80,000 + 20,000 + 7,000 – 68,000 – 15,000 – 4,000]	(20)
Movement in accounts payable [7,200 – 6,200]	1
Movement in inventory [14,000 – 11,000]	(3)
Adjusted for items to be disclosed elsewhere:	
Interest expense	200
Tax expense	224
Cash flow from operations	**1,086**
Interest paid (assumed all cash for illustrative purposes)	(200)
Dividends paid (assumed for illustrative purposes as no information given in the scenario)	(150)
Tax paid (assumed all cash for illustrative purposes)	(224)
Cash flows from operating activities	**512**
Cash flows from investing activities	
Cash paid to acquire shares [1,000 × CU10]	(10)
Cash paid to acquire land	(100)
Proceeds on sale of vehicles	125
Cash flows from investing activities	**15**

Cash flows from financing activities	
Proceeds from the issue of shares [1,000 × CU25]	25
Proceeds from the incurrence of a loan	58
Cash paid on lease instalments	(100)
Cash flows from investing activities	**(17)**
Net cash flow for the year	**510**
Balance of cash and cash equivalents at 01 January 20X8	1,000
Balance of cash and cash equivalents at 31 December 20X8	**1,510**

16.7.2 Disclosure

An entity must disclose the amount, reason and fact that the entity has cash and cash equivalents that are not available for use by the entity (eg cash and cash equivalents that a foreign currency has placed restrictions on accessing by the entity) (s7.21 and IAS 7 p.48).

SELF-ASSESSMENT
Multiple choice questions: Testing principles of accounting for statement of cash flow

1. The following describes one of the activities that cash flows are classified as according to the statement of cash flows:

(a) non-current	
(b) ordinary	
(c) operating	
(d) none of the above	

2. The statement of cash flows:

(a) converts the accrual basis of accounting to the cash basis	
(b) shows the financial position at a point in time	
(c) shows the financial performance on the accrual basis over time	
(d) all of the above	

3. The cash flows from operating activities can be prepared on the:

(a) FIFO method	
(b) indirect method	
(c) accrual basis	
(d) revaluation method	

4.   The following items are separately disclosable:

(a) interest paid	
(b) dividends paid	
(c) tax paid	
(d) all of the above	

5.   The indirect method of presenting the cash flows from operating activities starts with:

(a) profit for the year	
(b) cash received from customers	
(c) cash paid to suppliers and employee	
(d) cash paid on loan instalment	

6.   Cash paid on the capital portion of a lease payment is classified as:

(a) cash flow from operations	
(b) cash flow from operating activities	
(c) cash flow from investing activities	
(d) cash flow from financing activities	

7.   What information will appear in the statement of cash flows relating to an item of property which is sold?

(a) the carrying amount of the property	
(b) the proceeds on disposal of the property	
(c) the cost of the property	
(d) the profit on disposal of the property	

8. Changes in working capital are considered when preparing the:

(a) cash flow from investing activities	
(b) cash flow from financing activities	
(c) cash flow from operating activities	
(d) cash and cash equivalents at the end of the period	

9. Cash flow from the issue of ordinary shares is classified in the statement of cash flows as:

(a) cash flow from investing activities	
(b) cash flow from financing activities	
(c) cash flow from operating activities	
(d) cash and cash equivalents at the end of the period	

10. Cash paid on the acquisition of land is classified in the statement of cash flows as:

(a) cash flow from investing activities	
(b) cash flow from financing activities	
(c) cash flow from operating activities	
(d) cash and cash equivalents at the end of the period	

Practical questions:
Application of principles to business scenarios

QUESTION 1

Spando (Pty) Ltd included the following extracts from its financial statement in a pack forwarded to you, to assist it in preparing the operating activities of the statement of cash flows:

SPANDO (PTY) LTD	
Extract of the statement of profit or loss for the year ended 31 December 20X8	
	20X8
	CU
Revenue	1,000,000
Cost of sale	(200,000)
Gross profit	**800,000**
Profit before interest and tax	**500,000**
Interest expense	(100,000)
Profit before tax	**400,000**
Tax expense	(112,000)
Profit for the year	**288,000**

SPANDO (PTY) LTD		
Extract of the statement of financial position for the year ended 31 December 20X8		
	20X8	**20X7**
	CU	**CU**
Accounts receivable	120,000	100,000
Inventory	57,000	50,000
Accounts payable	(102,000)	(95,000)
Interest payable	(18,000)	(12,000)

Additional information:
1. The carrying amount of accounts receivable is reflected after considering the allowance for credit losses of 20X8: CU12,000 (20X7: CU10,000) and bad debts expense of 20X8: CU5,000 (20X7: CU4,000).

378

2. The interest payable reflects the interest on a loan that was recognised separately as interest payable instead of being capitalised to the loan account. The interest expense for the year is calculated as 10% of the opening balance of the loan for the year of CU500,000.

You are required to:
Prepare the operating activities section of the statement of cash flows for the year ended 31 December 20X8 for Spando (Pty) Ltd using the direct method.
Comparatives are not required.

QUESTION 2

Unigrad (Pty) Ltd provided you with the following extracts from its financial statements for the 31 December 20X8 year:

	Note	20X8 CU	20X7 CU
Property, plant & equipment	1	5,000,000	3,800,000
Intangible assets	2	1,750,000	1,000,000
Other non-current assets	3	2,000,000	1,300,000

Notes:
1. Property, plant and equipment with a carrying amount of CU1 million was sold during the year ended 31 December 2018. The total amount of depreciation expensed during the year related to property, plant and equipment amounted to CU500,000.
2. The total amortisation expense related to intangible assets amounted to CU400,000 for the year ended 31 December 2018. Included in the closing balance of intangible assets is an amount of CU1.5 million related to the acquisition of software licences.
3. The movement in other non-current assets relates entirely to additions.

All additions and disposals were settled in cash at transaction date. Any items disposed of were sold for their carrying amounts.

You are required to:
Prepare the cash flows from investing activities section of the statement of cash flows of Unigrad (Pty) Ltd for the year ended 31 December 20X8.

QUESTION 3

Sterling (Pty) Ltd presented the following statement of financial position, statement of profit or loss and additional information to you:

STERLING (PTY) LTD		
Statement of financial position as at 31 December 20X8		
	20X8	**20X7**
	CU	**CU**
ASSETS		
Non-current assets:		
Property, plant & equipment	2,500,000	1,700,000
Intangible assets	1,000,000	800,000
Current assets:		
Inventory	140,000	90,000
Accounts receivable	100,000	75,000
Bank	250,000	150,000
TOTAL ASSETS	**3,990,000**	**2,815,000**
Equity:		
Ordinary shares	2,000,000	2,000,000
Retained earnings	1,000,000	500,000
Non-current liabilities:		
Loan payable	890,000	200,000
Current liabilities:		
Accounts payable	100,000	115,000
TOTAL EQUITY & LIABILITIES	**3,990,000**	**2,815,000**

STERLING (PTY) LTD		
Statement of profit or loss for the year ended 31 December 20X8		
	20X8	20X7
	CU	CU
Revenue	1,800,000	1,500,000
Cost of sales	(860,000)	(720,000)
Gross profit	**940,000**	**780,000**
Other income	600,000	500,000
Other expenses	(340,000)	(280,000)
Administration expenses	(250,000)	(200,000)
Selling and distribution expenses	(150,000)	(150,000)
Profit before interest and tax	**800,000**	**650,000**
Interest expense	(105,000)	(95,000)
Profit before tax	**695,000**	**555,000**
Tax expense	(195,000)	(155,000)
Profit for the year	**500,000**	**400,000**

Additional information:
1. A building with an original cost of CU1 million was sold by Sterling (Pty) Ltd on 30 June 20X8. The building was originally purchased on 01 January 20X4. The building was always considered to have an estimated useful life of 20 years and a nil residual value. The proceeds from the sale of the building were received in cash on the date of sale. Profit of CU100,000 related to the disposal of the building was recognised in other income.
2. Intangible assets with a carrying amount of CU300,000 were purchased on 01 May 20X8.
3. Accounts receivable is stated after taking into account the allowance for credit losses of 20X8: CU14,000 (20X7: CU11,000) and bad debts expense of 20X8: CU5,000 (20X7: CU4,000).
4. Other expenses include depreciation on property, plant and equipment of CU350,000, amortisation on intangible assets of CU80,000 and profit on disposal of intangible assets of CU15,000.
5. Except for items in the additional information, all other income and expense items are earned and incurred in cash.

You are required to:
Prepare the statement of cash flows for Sterling (Pty) Ltd for the year ended 31 December 20X8. You may assume that Sterling (Pty) Ltd presents its cash flows from operating activities using the direct method in its statement of cash flows. *Comparatives are not required.*

CHAPTER 17
EMPLOYEE BENEFITS AND RELATED PARTY DISCLOSURES

ILLUSTRATIVE DISCLOSURE [EXTRACT]

Statement of profit or Loss and Other Comprehensive Income for the year ended				
IFRS ref		**Notes**	**20X7**	**20X6**
			CU'000	**CU'000**
S28.39 - 44 IAS 19 p.25, 53, 135 & 158	Employee-related costs	16	145,000	132,000
	Other comprehensive income			
	Items that will not subsequently be reclassified to profit or loss:			
S28.24(b) IAS 19 p.57(d)	Actuarial gains or losses		10,000	8,500
S29.35 IAS 12 p.58	Tax expense		(2,800)	(2,380)

Statement of financial position as at......................				
		Notes	**20X7**	**20X6**
	Non-current liabilities			
S28	Post-employment defined benefit plan obligation		400,000	350,000

Notes to the financial statements for the period ended					
IFRS ref	1	**Accounting policy**			
		The entity has one defined contribution plan and one defined benefit plan related to its post-employment benefits. Staff members who joined the employ of the entity after 01 April 20X4 were automatically included on the defined contribution plan. The entity took the decision no longer to include new staff members on the defined benefit plan in order to manage its exposure to the related risks. Defined benefit plan: The entity's defined benefit plan includes 100 staff members and			

		pays out an amount of five times the employee's salary earned just before retirement. The entity has invested in plan assets which are used to satisfy the defined benefit obligations. The entity measures the defined benefit obligation using the projected unit credit method. The entity recognises actuarial gains or losses related to its defined benefit plan in other comprehensive income. The latest actuarial valuation was received on 31 December 20X7.			
	16	**Post-employment defined benefit plan**			
S28.41(e) & (f) IAS 19 p.140 & 141			**Defined benefit obligation**	**Plan asset**	
		Opening balance	97 000	90 000	
		Current service cost	40 000		
		Past service cost	10 000		
		Interest expense	12 840		
		Actuarial loss	5 160		
		Contributions/(payments)	-20 000	10 000	
		Interest income		12 000	
		Other income		3 000	
		Closing balance	**145 000**	**115 000**	
S28.41(k) IAS 19 p.144		The following estimates were used and incorporated in calculating the actuarial gains or losses on the post-employment defined benefit obligation (asset). The discount rate used to determine the present value of the defined benefit obligation was referenced to high-quality corporate bonds and determined to be 12% per annum compounded annually. The interest rate used to calculate the interest income on the plan assets was 10%. Salary increases were estimated at 6.5% per annum. There were no other material actuarial assumptions used.			

| S33.5 & 8 | | The entity is wholly owned by Parent (Pty) Ltd. The entity has not entered into any transactions with Parent (Pty) Ltd during the current financial reporting period.

The entity was party to an operating lease (as lessee) with Rent (Pty) Ltd, which is a fellow subsidiary of Parent (Pty) Ltd (the parent of the entity). The rent includes monthly arrear payments of CU4,000 per month over the lease term of two years. As the payments are evenly spread over the lease term, no additional straight-line adjustments are needed for recognition in the financial statements. There are no outstanding balances related to the lease.

The following amounts have been paid to key management personnel: |

	Salary	Share-based compensation	Total
	CU	CU	CU
V Bloom	75,000	12,000	**87,000**
Q Brown	57,000	10,000	**67,000**
S Mase	43,000	8,000	**51,000**
Total	**175,000**	**30,000**	**205,000**

17.1   INTRODUCTION

Entities enter into sophisticated transactions to pay their employees. They enter into these sophisticated transactions for a number of reasons, including goal congruence between the employee and the entity, and sometimes also as a means of tax structuring. However, the accounting principle of substance over form should always prevail with entities faithfully representing the economic reality of transactions and balances. For this reason, section 28 – *Employee benefits* (IAS 19 – *Employee benefits*) gives guidance for the accounting for employee benefits.

Similarly, transactions entered into with related parties might be structured in such a way that limits the users' ability to evaluate the potential impact of assets, liabilities and cash flows to an entity. For instance, an entity might purchase an asset recognised at cost from a related party. However, the cost of the asset might be significantly lower than it would have been if it was purchased from an independent third party. This lower carrying amount might materially impact the decision of a user elicited to lend money to the entity. For this reason, related party transactions (and certain related party relationships regardless of whether there were transactions with the entity) are disclosed as prescribed by section 33 – *Related party disclosures* (IAS 24 – *Related party disclosures*). Related parties for SMEs often centre around the key shareholder (owner) and its key management personnel.

17.2 LEARNING OUTCOMES

Upon completion of this chapter you should know the financial reporting requirements for accounting for employee benefits and disclosing related party transactions in accordance with the IFRS for SMEs. In particular, you should be able to:

(a)   identify and classify consideration appropriately as employee benefits, and relationships with other entities correctly as related parties;

(b)   identify and classify employee benefits into each of the four types;

(c)   identify and classify relationships between the entity and others as involving related parties;

(d)   recognise and measure the effect of employee benefits in the financial statements of an entity;

(e)   present and disclose the effects of employee benefits and relationships, the effects of transactions, and balances with related parties on the transaction totals and/or balances of the entity; and

(f)   disclose the effects of transactions, events and balances with related parties of the entity.

17.3 DEFINITIONS

The definitions for the important concepts and terms used in IFRS for SMEs are found in Appendix B – *Glossary of terms* of IFRS for SMEs. Some important definitions related to employee benefits include the following:

- **Employee benefits:** All forms of consideration given by an entity in exchange for service rendered by employees

- **Short-employee benefits:** Employee benefits (other than termination benefits) that are wholly due within 12 months after the end of the period in which the employees render the related service

- **Post-employment benefits:** Employee benefits (other than termination benefits) that are payable after the completion of employment

- **Other long-term employee benefits:** Employee benefits (other than post-employment benefits and termination benefits) that are not wholly due within 12 months after the end of the period in which the employees render the related service

- **Termination benefits:** Employee benefits payable as a result of either:
  - (a) an entity's decision to terminate an employee's employment before the normal retirement date; or
  - (b) an employee's decision to accept voluntary redundancy in exchange for those benefits.

17.4   SCOPE AND OBJECTIVES

Section 28 (IAS 19) provides guidance for accounting and disclosure for employee benefits except for those within the scope of section 26 (IFRS 2) – *Share-based payments*, in which case the entity shall apply section 26 (IFRS 2) instead (s28.2 and IAS 19 p.2).

17.5   EMPLOYEE BENEFITS

17.5.1 Introduction

Employee benefits involve all consideration given by the entity to an employee in exchange for consideration. The standard classifies employee benefits into four types (s28.1 and IAS 19 p.5):
- (a) short-term employee benefits;
- (b) post-employment benefits;
- (c) other long-term employee benefits; and
- (d) termination benefits.

17.5.2 General recognition

The entity should recognise the employee benefits expense as an asset or expense and a reduction in cash or the incurrence of a liability. The debit side of the transaction:
- (a) **an expense**: to the extent that the entity has benefited and consumed the benefit of the employee's services at year-end; or
- (b) **an asset:** to the extent that the entity has prepaid for services still to be received.

The credit side of the transaction:
- (a) **reduction in cash**: to the extent that the amount has been paid; or
- (b) **a liability:** to the extent that the employee is entitled to the amount related to the employee services.

Illustrative Example 17.1: General employee cost

Company A is in its first year of operation and has 100 employees who have rendered services to the company over the 20X7 financial year. Each employee earns CU1,000 per month, which company A pays on the 15th of each month.

You are required to:

Provide the journal entry for the year ended 31 December 20X7 (one journal entry for the entire year) necessary to account for employee costs in the accounting records of company A.

Suggested solution:

Dr	Employee costs [P/L] **W1**	1,200,000	
Cr	Bank **W1**		1,150,000
Cr	Liability – employee costs **W1**		50,000
[Recognising the employee costs for the year]			

Working 1:

	CU
Total employee costs [CU1,000 × 100 employees × 12 months]	1,200,000
Paid [(January CU1,000 × 100 employees × 1/2 month) + (11 months × CU1,000 × 100 employees)]	1,150,000
Cash [(CU1,200,000 – CU1,150,000) OR (December CU1,000 × 100 employees 1 × / 2 months)]	50,000

17.5.3 Short-term employee benefits

Short-term employee benefits are defined as those employee benefits which are wholly due within 12 months after the end of the period in which the employees render the related service (s28.1 and IAS 19 p.8). Examples include the following (s28.4 and IAS 19 p.9):

(a)   wages, salaries and social security contributions;
        short-term compensated absences (such as annual leave) when the absences are expected to occur within 12 months of the end of the reporting period in which employees render the related employee service;

(b)   profit-sharing and bonuses payable within 12 months after the end of the reporting period in which the employees rendered the related employee services; and non-monetary benefits (such as medical aid) for current employees.

A distinction is made between accumulating and non-accumulating short-term employee benefits. *Accumulating* short-term employee benefits are those benefits that employees can use in the next accounting period if they did not use them in the current accounting period. It is then natural for the entity to recognise the obligation to grant the employee the benefit as a liability at the end of the current financial reporting period. *Non-accumulating* short-term employee benefits are those that employees lose if they do not use it in the current reporting period (ie they do not carry forward). Therefore no liability can exist for *non-accumulating* short-term employee benefits as the entity would not owe the employee anything in relation to these benefits.

17.5.3.1 Recognition

The entity accounts for short-term employee benefits as explained in section 17.5.2 above (as an asset or expense and a reduction in cash or a liability). It is important to note that an entity should not discount the amount of settlement related to the liability component of the short-term employee benefit.

Non-accumulating short-term employee benefits are recognised as expenses when they occur.

Illustrative Example 17.2: Short-term employee benefits

Company A grants employees 20 days annual leave per annum which, if untaken during the current year, can be taken or paid out in the following year. Employees work 250 days per annum and earn CU2,300 per annum. There are 100 employees employed by company A. An average of 8 days were taken by each employee during the year-ended 31 December 20X7. The remaining leave days are all expected to be taken during the year ended 31 December 20X8. There were no leave days carried forward at 31 December 20X6.

You are required to:
Prepare the journal entries necessary to account for the leave policy for the financial year ended 31 December 20X7 in the financial statements of company A.

Suggested solution:

Dr	Employee costs [P/L]	230,000	
Cr	Bank		230,000
[Recognising the employee costs for the year]			

Dr	Employee costs [P/L]	11,040	
Cr	Provision for leave **W1**		11,040
[Recognising the employee costs for the year]			

Working 1:

	CU
Total employee costs	230,000
Rate per working day [CU230,000/250]	9.20
Provision for leave [(CU9.20 × 100 employees × (20 days – 8 days taken)]	11,040

An extra consideration is vested vs non-vested benefits. Vested benefits are those that accrue to the employee whether or not they remain employed by the entity. For instance, leave which has vested will accrue to employees irrespective of whether they leave the entity (they will not lose the benefit – it is theirs) and could, for instance, be paid out to them in lieu of them taking it.

Non-vested benefits are those benefits which employees lose if they do not use them. These benefits might also carry forward, but will expire either at some point in time or when the employee leaves the entity. In this case, the entity has to consider the probability of having to satisfy the obligation. For instance, using Illustrative Example 17.2, if the employees lose their leave if they do not take it in the year following the year in which they earned it and the entity expects 70% of the employees to use their leave, then the leave pay provision should reflect the 70% probability. The leave pay provision recognised in the example above would then be CU7,728 (CU11,040 × 70%).

17.5.3.2 Disclosure
Section 28 does not prescribe specific disclosure for short-term employee benefits (s28.39 and IAS 19 p.25).

17.5.4 Post-employment benefits

17.5.4.1 Introduction
Post-employment benefits include the following (s28.9 and IAS 19 p.26):
(a)   retirement benefits, such as pensions; and
(b)   other post-employment benefits, such as post-employment life insurance and post-employment medical care.

Post-employment benefit plans are either defined contribution or defined benefit plans (s28.10(a) and IAS 19 p.27).

17.5.4.2 Defined contribution plans
Under defined contribution plans, the entity defines and commits to what contributions it will make to a post-employment benefit plan. However, it does not commit to what benefit the employee will receive. For instance, an entity might commit to paying CU5,000 per month to a post-employment benefit plan

(such as a pension fund) for an employee. At no point does the entity commit to nor define the amount of pension that the employee will be paid post-employment. Therefore, the entity has defined the contribution to be paid (CU5,000) and not the benefit (the entity did not define the post-employment pension).

Based on the above discussion, it follows that the entity can only be liable for contributions committed to but not paid by the end of the reporting period when it comes to a defined contribution plan (s28.13 and IAS 19 p.51).

Illustrative Example 17.3: Short-term employee benefits

Company A agrees to make payments of CU4,000 for each of its 10 employees towards a pension fund which is a defined contribution plan. Six of the employees work in the production department and their employee costs are capitalised to the cost of inventory. The remaining four employees are employed in the administration department. Company A transferred CU32,000 to the pension fund during the year.

You are required to:
Prepare the journal entries necessary to account for the pension of the 10 employees for the current reporting period.

Dr	Inventory	24,000	
Dr	Employee costs [P/L]	16,000	
Cr	Bank		32,000
Cr	Pension fund liability		8,000
[Recognising the employee pension costs for the year]			

Working 1:

		CU
Pension fund contribution per employee		4,000
No. of employees	10	
Total pension fund contribution [CU4,000 × 10]		**40,000**
Paid in cash		32,000
Pension fund liability [CU40,000 – CU32,000]		**8,000**
No. of employees in production department	6	
Capitalised to inventory [CU4,000 × 6]		24,000
No. of employees in the administration department	4	
Expensed in profit or loss [CU4,000 × 4]		16,000

17.5.4.3 Defined benefit plans

Defined benefit plans are all those post-employment benefit plans other than defined contribution plans (s28.10(b) and IAS 19 p.27). Under defined benefit plans, the entity defines and commits to the post-employment benefit that the employee will receive. For instance, instead of defining and committing to contributing CU5,000 per month to a pension plan (post-employment benefit plan) for an employee, the entity defines and commits to provide the employee with a pension of CU5 million (the defined benefit) on retirement.

Entities often strategically set assets aside (or more commonly invest, often through an intermediary, in a pension or other retirement scheme) with the idea of using this investment to settle its obligation with respect to the defined benefit obligation. The entity then presents the net of its obligations and assets with respect to its post-employment defined benefit obligation in its statement of financial position. The net defined benefit obligation is measured as follows (s28.15 and IAS 19 p.57):

(a)   the *present value* of its defined benefit obligation (the liability component); minus

(b)   less the *fair value* of the plan assets.

If the present value of the defined benefit obligation is more than the fair value of the plan assets, then the entity recognises a net defined benefit obligation (s28.14(a) and IAS 19 p.57). If the present value of the defined benefit obligation is less than the fair value of the plan assets, then the entity recognises a net defined benefit plan asset to the extent that the surplus is recoverable through reduced contributions in the future or through refunds from the plan.

Any net change (after accounting for settlements and investments) in the net liability shall be recognised as its cost of the defined benefit plan during the period (s28.14). The liability is only accounted for to the extent that employees have earned the amount due for their service in the current and prior periods (s28.16 and IAS 19 p.72) and includes benefits that have not yet vested.

Post-employment benefit obligations are discounted to determine their carrying amount. The discount rate is determined by using high-quality corporate bonds failing which government bonds are used (s28.17 and IAS 19 p.83). The currency and term of the corporate bonds or government bonds must be consistent with the currency and estimated period of future payments.

In order to correctly account for and present the information above, it is advised that the entity prepare a ledger account (T-account) for the plan assets and the

defined benefit obligation separately. The following will then be accounted for in the plan assets account:
(a)   the opening balance of the plan assets;
(b)   the contributions made towards the plan assets;
(c)   payments made to retired employees;
(d)   interest income on the plan assets; and
(e)   other returns related to the plan assets.

These adjustments to the plan assets have to total the fair value of the plan assets (which is the closing balance).

Illustrative Example 17.4: Short-term employee benefits

Company A has the following information related to its plan assets in a post-employment defined benefit arrangement:
(a)   opening balance: CU90,000;
(b)   contribution made to the plan at the beginning of the year: CU30,000;
(c)   payments made to retired employees at the end of the year: CU20,000;
(d)   interest rate: 10% per annum compounded annually; and
(e)   the fair value of the plan assets at the end of the year: CU115,000.

You are required to:
Prepare the general ledger account for the plan assets.

Suggested solution:

		Plan assets			
Balance	b/d	90 000	Bank		20 000
Bank		30 000			
Interest income P/L	**W1**	12 000			
Other income P/L	**W1**	3 000			
			Balance	c/d	115 000
		135 000			135 000
Balance	b/d	115 000			

Working 1:

	CU
Interest income [(CU90,000 + CU30 000) × 10%]	12 000
Other income [CU135,000 – (CU90,000 + CU30,000 + CU12,000)]	3 000

The following will be accounted for in the defined benefit obligation account:
(a)   the opening balance of the defined benefit obligation;
(b)   current service costs (increases due to employees working in the current year);
(c)   adjustments for past service costs (adjustments due to employees working in prior years);
(d)   interest on the unwinding of the discount related to the defined benefit obligation;
(e)   payments relating to benefits; and
(f)   actuarial gains or losses (see below).

These adjustments to the defined benefit obligations have to total the present value of the defined benefit obligation at the end of the year (the closing balance).

The one new concept that the list above introduces is the actuarial gains or losses. As the defined benefit obligation is only going to be settled in the distant future (in many cases), information relating to the future needs to be estimated and this is best done using the projected unit credit method. In order to calculate the present value of the defined benefit obligation, a host of variables needs to be considered and measured. These include discount rates, expected rates of return, expected rates of salary increases, employee turnover and mortality (s28.18 and IAS 19 p.76). Actuaries, who are professionals who deal with the measurement of risk and uncertainty, are often employed to measure the variables listed above. The actuarial gain or loss is often calculated as the balancing figure between all of the other variables and the present value of the defined benefit obligation, calculated using the projected unit credit method as measured by an actuary.

Illustrative Example 17.5: Short-term employee benefits

Company A has the following information related to its defined benefit obligation in a post-employment defined benefit arrangement:
(a)   opening balance: CU97,000;
(b)   current service costs charged at the end of the year: CU40,000;
(c)   past service costs: CU10,000
(d)   payments made to retired employees at the end of the year: CU20,000;
(e)   interest rate: 12% per annum compounded annually; and
(f)   the present value of the defined benefit obligation at the end of the year: CU145,000.

You are required to:
Prepare the general ledger account for the defined benefit obligation.

Suggested solution:

Defined benefit obligation (liability)					
Bank		20 000	Balance	b/d	97 000
			Current service costs P/L		40 000
			Past service costs P/L		10 000
			Interest expense P/L		12 840
			Actuarial loss P/L or OCI		360
Balance	c/d	145 000			
		165 000			165 000
			Balance	b/d	145 000

Working 1:

	CU
Interest expense [(CU97,000 + CU40 000 + CU10,000) × 12%]	17 640
Actuarial loss [CU165,000 – (CU97,000 + CU40,000 + CU10,000 + CU17,640)]	360

It should be noted that the authors labelled the applicable statement affected by the actuarial gains and losses as either the statement of profit or loss (P/L) or the statement of comprehensive income (OCI) (alternatively the other comprehensive income section of the statement of comprehensive income if one statement is used). This is because in terms of section 28.24, the entity may choose between a policy of recognising actuarial gains and losses in profit or loss, or an accounting policy of recognising actuarial gains and losses in other comprehensive income. This accounting policy choice has to be applied consistently for all defined benefit plans and all of their related actuarial gains and losses.

It should be noted that full IFRS has additional principles and rules regarding the amounts that can be recognised in relation to a post-employment defined benefit plan such as the use of an asset ceiling and the fact that all actuarial gains or losses must be recognised in other comprehensive income.

17.5.4.4 Presentation and disclosure
Presentation
In terms of section 28.14(a) (IAS 19 p.57), an entity should present the net defined benefit obligation (or asset) in its statement of financial position. In addition, section 28.14(b) requires an entity to present the net change in the net liability (or asset) as the cost of its defined benefit plans. The following will, therefore, be presented in each of the statements (note that Illustrative Example

17.6 shows more than what is presented in the statements as it attempts to reconcile the amounts presented to the detailed workings underpinning the presentations).

Illustrative Example 17.6: Short-term employee benefits

You are required to:
Use the same information as in illustrative examples 4 and 5. You may assume that company A's accounting policy is to recognise actuarial gains and losses on its defined benefit plans in other comprehensive income.

	Defined benefit obligation[1]	Plan asset[1]	Statement of financial position	Statement of profit or loss[2]	Statement of comprehensive income
Opening balance	97 000	90 000	7 000		
Current service cost	40 000			−40 000	
Past service cost	10 000			−10 000	
Interest expense	12 840			−12 840	
Actuarial loss	5 160				−5 160
Bank	−0 000	10 000	−30 000		
Interest income		12 000		12 000	
Other income		3 000		3 000	
Closing balance	145 000	115 000	30 000		

[1][et1] The greyed-out area shows the working.
[2] The amounts shown in profit or loss will be presented as a single line item.

It should be noted that the standard does make provision for the case where an entity is not able to use the projected unit credit method without undue cost or effort. In this case, the entity can make the following simplifications in measuring its defined benefit obligation with respect to current employees, including its vested and unvested benefits (s28.19):
(a)   ignore estimated future salary increases (ie assume current salaries continue until current employees are expected to begin receiving post-employment benefits)
(b)   ignore future service of current employees (ie assume closure of the plan for existing as well as any new employees)

(c)   ignore possible in-service mortality of current employees between the reporting date and the date employees are expected to begin receiving post-employment benefits (ie assume all current employees will receive the post-employment benefits). However, mortality after service (ie life expectancy) will still need to be considered.

The entity needs to engage an independent actuary to perform the actuarial valuation each year. If the principal actuarial assumptions have not changed significantly during the periods between the comprehensive actuarial valuations, the defined benefit obligation can be measured by adjusting the prior period measurement for changes in employee demographics such as the number of employees and salary levels (s28.20).

Disclosure
Defined contribution plans
The entity should disclose the amount recognised in profit or loss as an expense for defined contribution plans (s28.40 and IAS 19 p.53).

Defined benefit plans
In terms of section 28.41 (IAS 19 p.135), an entity shall disclose the following information about defined benefit plans (except for any defined multi-employer benefit plans that are accounted for as a defined contribution plan in accordance with paragraph 28.11, for which the disclosures in paragraph 28.40 apply instead). If an entity has more than one defined benefit plan, these disclosures may be made in total, separately for each plan, or in such groupings as are considered to be the most useful:

(a)   a general description of the type of plan, including **funding** policy;

(b)   the entity's accounting policy for recognising actuarial gains and losses (either in profit or loss or as an item of other comprehensive income) and the amount of actuarial gains and losses recognised during the period;

(c)   if the entity uses any of the simplifications in paragraph 28.19 in measuring its defined benefit obligation, it shall disclose that fact and the reasons why using the projected unit credit method to measure its obligation and cost under defined benefit plans would involve undue cost or effort;

(d)   the date of the most recent comprehensive actuarial valuation and, if it was not as of the reporting date, a description of the adjustments that were made to measure the defined benefit obligation at the reporting date;

(e)   a reconciliation of opening and closing balances of the defined benefit obligation showing separately benefits paid and all other changes;

(f)   a reconciliation of the opening and closing balances of the fair value of plan assets and of the opening and closing balances of any reimbursement right recognised as an asset. showing separately, if applicable:
    (i)   contributions;
    (ii)   benefits paid; and
    (iii)   other changes in plan assets;

(g)   the total cost relating to defined benefit plans for the period, disclosing separately the amounts:
    (i)   recognised in profit or loss as an expense; and
    (ii)   included in the cost of an asset;

(h)   for each major class of plan assets, which shall include, but is not limited to, equity instruments, debt instruments, property, and all other assets, the percentage or amount that each major class constitutes of the fair value of the total plan assets at the reporting date;

(i)   the amounts included in the fair value of plan assets for:
    (i)   each class of the entity's own **financial instruments**; and
    (ii)   any property occupied by, or other assets used by, the entity.

(j)   the actual return on plan assets; and

(k)   the principal actuarial assumptions used, including, when applicable:
    (i)   the discount rates;
    (ii)   the expected rates of return on any plan assets for the periods presented in the **financial statements**;
    (iii)   the expected rates of salary increases;
    (iv)   medical cost trend rates; and
    (v)   any other **material** actuarial assumptions used.

The reconciliations in (e) and (f) need not be presented for prior periods. A subsidiary that recognises and measures employee benefit expense on the basis of a reasonable allocation of the expense recognised for the group (see paragraph 28.38) shall, in its separate financial statements, describe its policy for making the allocation and shall make the disclosures in (a)–(k) for the plan as a whole.

It should be noted that IAS 19 – Employee benefits *requires substantially more disclosure than required in section 28 –* Employee benefits.

17.5.5 Other long-term employee benefits

Other long-term employee benefits include those benefits that are due 12 months or more after the reporting date (but exclude, for instance, post-employment benefits). These benefits include:

(a)   long-term compensated absences such as long-service or sabbatical leave;

(b)   long-service benefits;

(c)   long-term disability benefits;

(d)   profit sharing and bonuses payable 12 months or more after the end of the period in which the employees render the related service; and

(e)   deferred compensation paid 12 months or more after the end of the period in which it is earned.

17.5.5.1 Recognition and measurement

Similarly to the post-employment benefits, the entity must recognise the present value of the other long-term employee benefits obligation net of the fair value of plan assets out of which the obligations are to be settled directly (s28.30 and IAS 19 p.57). Unlike post-employment benefits, the entity need not incorporate actuarial assumptions. Any net change in that net liability for the period (except for benefits paid to employees or contributions from the employer) must be recognised in profit or loss (unless it qualifies to be capitalised to the cost of an asset) (s28.30 and IAS 19 p.156).

Illustrative Example 17.7: Retrospective application

Company A grants its senior employee leave of one month for every year of service worked. The leave can be taken after three years of service. Company A pays its employee CU12,100 per month. An appropriate discount rate is 10% per annum compounded annually.

You are required to:

Prepare the journal entries necessary to account for the senior employee's leave at the end of her first year of employment.

Suggested solution

		Rand	Rand
Dr	Employee costs P/L **(W1)**	10,000	
Cr	Other long-term employee benefit obligations **(W1)**		10,000
[Recognising the long-term employee benefit]		

Working 1: W1	**CU**
Future cost (gross)	12,100
Factor for 2 years* (1/1.1/1.1 = 0.82645)	
Present value (12,100 × 0.82645)	**10,000**

*The settlement is expected at the end of year 3. As it is the end of year 1, the settlement is expected in two years' time.

17.5.5.2 Disclosure

The entity must disclose the nature and amount of its obligation, and the extent of funding of each category of other long-term benefits (s28.42).

IAS 19 p.158 does not require any specific disclosure related to other long-term employee benefits.

17.5.6 Termination benefits

Termination benefits refers to payments that an entity is committed to make to an employee when it terminates his/her employment (s28.31 and IAS 19 p.159).

17.5.6.1 Recognition and measurement

Due to the fact that they will yield no future economic benefits, the termination benefits should be recognised as an expense when and a related liability (if not paid immediately) when the entity has demonstrably committed either (s28.32 & 34):

(a)   to terminate the employment of an employee or group of employees before the normal retirement date; or

(b)   to provide termination benefits as a result of an offer made in order to encourage voluntary redundancy.

An entity is demonstrably committed to a termination when it has a formal plan for the termination and is without realistic possibility of withdrawal from the plan (s28.36). If the termination benefits are due later than 12 months after the end of the reporting period, the amount should be discounted (s28.37).

IAS 19 p.165 requires that termination benefits only be recognised at the earlier of the following:
(a)   when the entity can no longer withdraw the offer of those benefits; and
(b)   when the entity recognises costs for a restructuring that is within the scope of IAS 37 and involves the payment of termination benefits.

Illustrative Example 17.8: Basic financial instruments

Company A has been experiencing financial difficulties and has decided to offer 10 of its employees' voluntary redundancy packages. The employees can take the offer before the following financial year-end. The employees are all expected to accept the offer, which amounts to a cash payment of CU15,000 each.

You are required to:
Prepare the journal entries necessary to account for the voluntary redundancy packages for the current reporting period.

Suggested solution:

		Rand	Rand
Dr	Employee costs P/L **(W1)**	150,000	
Cr	Other long-term employee benefit obligations **(W1)**		150,000
[Recognising the long-term employee benefit]			

Working 1: W1	CU
Amount payable per employee	15,000
No. of employees: 10	
Employee cost (CU15,000 × 10)	**150,000**

*The settlement is expected within twelve months and therefore does not have to be discounted.

17.5.6.2 Disclosure

The entity must disclose the nature and amount of its obligation, and the extent of funding of each category of other long-term benefits (s28.43 and IAS 19 p.).

IAS 19 p.171 does not require any specific disclosure related to other long-term employee benefits.

17.6   RELATED PARTY DISCLOSURES

17.6.1 Classifying another as a related party

The following are related parties to the entity (s33.2 and IAS 19 p.):
(a)   a person or a close member of that person's family is related to a reporting entity if that person:
 (i)   is a member of the key management personnel of the reporting entity or a parent of the reporting entity;
 (ii)   has control or joint control over the reporting entity; or
 (iii)   has significant influence over the reporting entity;
(b)   an entity is related to a reporting entity if any of the following conditions apply:
 (i)   the entity and the reporting entity are members of the same group (so all parents, subsidiaries and fellow subsidiaries are related to each other);
 (ii)   one entity is an associate or joint venture of the other entity (or an associate or joint venture of a member of a group of which the other entity is a member);
 (iii)   both entities are joint ventures of the same third entity;
 (iv)   one entity is a joint venture of a third entity and the other is an associate of the third entity;

(v)   the entity is a post-employment benefit plan for the benefit of employees of either the reporting entity or an entity related to the reporting entity. If the reporting entity is itself such a plan, the sponsoring employers are also related to the reporting entity;

(vi) the entity is controlled or jointly controlled by a person identified in (a);

(vii) the entity or any member of a group of which it is a part provides key management personnel services to the reporting entity or to the parent of the reporting entity; and

(viii) a person identified in (a)(ii) has significant influence over the entity or is a member of the key management personnel of the entity (or a parent of the entity).

Key management personnel: Persons having authority and responsibility for planning, directing and controlling the activities of the entity, directly or indirectly, including any director (whether executive or otherwise) of that entity (s33.6).

Illustrative Example 17.9: Basic financial instruments

Company A is part of a large group of companies. Company A is controlled by Parent (Pty) Ltd (which has a 65% shareholding in company A) and is also an associate of Investor (Pty) Ltd, who has a 35% shareholding in company A. Investor (Pty) Ltd has another company, Associate (Pty) Ltd which it has also classified as an associate. Mr Charlie is the CEO of Parent (Pty) Ltd and is married to Mrs Charlie.

You are required to:
Discuss which of the parties in the group are related parties of Company A.

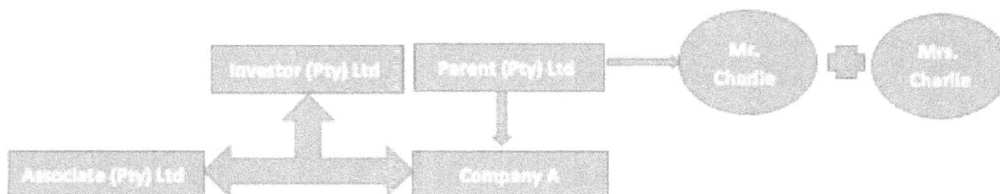

Suggested solution:

The following parties are/(are not) related to company A:
(i)   Parent (Pty) Ltd and Company A are related parties (s33.2(b)(i));

(ii)   Mr Charlie, as CEO of Parent (Pty) Ltd, is part of the key management personnel of company A's parent and is therefore related to company A (s33.2(a)(i)); and

(iii)   Mrs Charlie, as a close family member of the CEO of Parent (Pty) Ltd, is related to company A (s33.2(a)(i)).

The following parties are/(are not) related to company A:

(a)   Associate is not related to company A (not mentioned in s33.2); and

(b)   company A and Investor (Pty) Ltd are related parties (s33.2(a)(iii)).

17.6.2 Disclosure

17.6.2.1 Parent-subsidiary relationship

A relationship between a parent and its subsidiaries should be disclosed irrespective of whether there are any transactions between the parties. In doing so, an entity should disclose the name of its parent and if different, the name of the ultimate controlling party. The entity must disclose the name of its next most senior parent that produces financial statements for public use in the event that its parent or the ultimate controlling party does not produce such financial statements (s33.5 and IAS 24 p.13).

17.6.2.2 Key management personnel compensation

The entity should disclose all key management personnel compensation in total (s33.7 and IAS 24 p.17), which includes all employee benefits (defined in terms of section 28 – *Employee benefits* and IAS 19 – *Employee benefits* (see 4 above)) and any consideration paid by the parent of the entity for goods or services provided to the entity (s33.6 and IAS 24 p.9).

IAS 24 p.17 requires specific additional disclosure related to compensation to key management personnel such as that the compensation is split into the following categories:

(a)   *short-term employee benefits;*

(b)   *post-employment benefits;*

(c)   *other long-term benefits;*

(d)   *termination benefits; and*

(e)   *share-based payment.*

17.6.2.3 Related party transactions

An entity should disclose the following for related party transactions (s33.9 and IAS 24 p.18):

(a)   the nature of the related party relationship;

(b)   information about the transactions, outstanding balances and commitments necessary for an understanding of the potential effect of the relationship on the financial statements;

(c)   the amount of the transactions;

(d)   the amount of outstanding balances:

    (i)   their terms and conditions, including whether they are secured and the nature of the consideration to be provided in settlement; and

    (ii)   details of any guarantees given or received;

(e)   provision for uncollectable receivables related to the amount of outstanding balances; and

(f)   the expenses recognised during the period in respect of bad or doubtful debts due from related parties.

An entity has to make the disclosure separately for each of the following categories of related party relationships (s33.10 and IAS 24 p.19):

(a)   entities with control, joint control and significant influence over the entity;

(b)   entities over which the entity has control, joint control or significant influence;

(c)   key management personnel of the entity or its parent (in the aggregate); and

(d)   other related parties.

An entity does not have to make the disclosures in s33.9 (IAS 24 p.18), but must still disclose the parent–subsidiary relationship in s33.5 for the following related parties (s33.11 and IAS 24 p.25):

(a)   a state that has control, joint control or significant influence over the reporting entity; and

(b)   another party that is a related party because the same state has control, joint control or significant influence over both the reporting entity and the other entity.

However, IAS 24 p.26 still mandates certain additional disclosure not required by IFRS for SMEs in relation to the above.

Illustrative Example 17.10: Basic financial instruments

Company A is a wholly owned subsidiary of Parent (Pty) Ltd but has not transacted with Parent (Pty) Ltd during the course of the year. It has five staff members with only its CEO classified as key management personnel. The CEO earned a salary of CU100,000 for the year, of which CU50,000 was paid in cash, CU30,000 paid in share options and CU20,000 is still outstanding. There were no other related party relationships or transactions during the financial year.

You are required to:

Prepare the note to the financial statements with respect to company A's related party relationships and transactions.

Suggested solution:

Company A has the following related party relationships:

(i)   Parent (Pty) Ltd is the sole shareholder and parent of company A. Company A did not enter into any related party transaction during, nor has any outstanding balances with Parent (Pty) Ltd at the end of, the current financial year; and

(ii)   company A has one member of key management personnel, its CEO Mr Brown. Details of key management personnel compensation paid to Mr Brown and related outstanding balances are included below.

Executive compensation: CEO Mr Brown	CU
Salary in total	**100,000**
- Paid in cash	50,000
- Share based payments	30,000
- Included in other payables	20,000

SELF-ASSESSMENT
Multiple choice questions: Testing principles of accounting employee benefits and related party disclosures

1. The following definition refers to employee benefits:

(a) all forms of consideration to employees in their capacity as shareholders	
(b) all forms of consideration given by an entity in exchange for service rendered by employees	
(c) all forms of consideration given to stakeholders	
(d) all forms of consideration given to employees in their capacity as customers	

2. The following refers to short-term employee benefits:

(a) employee benefits (other than termination benefits) that are wholly due within 12 months after the end of the period in which the employees render the related service	
(b) employee benefits (other than termination benefits) that are wholly due 12 months after the end of the period in which the employees render the related service	
(c) employee benefits (including termination benefits) that are wholly due within 12 months after the end of the period in which the employees render the related service	
(d) none of the above	

3.   The following are not related parties:

(a) parent and subsidiary	
(b) two joint ventures of the same third entity	
(c) two associates of the same investor	
(d) two subsidiaries of the same parent	

4.   Other long-term employee benefits are:

(a) employee benefits (other than termination benefits) that are wholly due within 12 months after the end of the period in which the employees render the related service	
(b) employee benefits (other than termination benefits) that are payable after the completion of employment	
(c) employee benefits that are due within the next year	
(d) employee benefits (other than post-employment benefits and termination benefits) that are not wholly due within 12 months after the end of the period in which the employees render the related service	

5.   The following refers to termination benefits:

(a) employee benefits (other than termination benefits) that are wholly due within 12 months after the end of the period in which the employees render the related service	
(b) employee benefits payable as a result of either: (i) an entity's decision to terminate an employee's employment before the normal retirement date; or (ii) an employee's decision to accept voluntary redundancy in exchange for those benefits	

(c) employee benefits (other than termination benefits) that are payable after the completion of employment	
(d) Employee benefits that are due within the next year	

6.   Short-term employee benefits are recognised at:

(a) fair value	
(b) present value	
(c) undiscounted amount due	
(d) net realisable value	

7.   Post-employment defined benefit net assets are recognised only if:

(a) it is probable that the surplus will be recoverable through reduced contributions in the future or through refunds from the plan	
(b) they are due to the defined benefit obligation being reduced	
(c) they relate to an overpayment of contributions	
(d) none of the above as they may never be recognised	

8.   A post-employment defined benefit obligation is recognised at:

(a) fair value	
(b) net realisable value	
(c) undiscounted amount due	
(d) present value	

9. The plan assets in a post-employment defined benefit plan are recognised at:

(a) fair value	
(b) net realisable value	
(c) undiscounted amount due	
(d) present value	

10. An entity should disclose the following relationship irrespective of whether the parties have entered into any transactions during the period:

(a) two subsidiaries in the same group	
(b) two associates of the same investor	
(c) an associate and subsidiary of the same third party	
(d) parent–subsidiary relationship	

Practical questions:
Application of principles to business scenarios

QUESTION 1

GAS (Pty) Ltd grants its 10 employees 15 days of leave per annum. Employees are allowed to take the leave in the year in which it is earned or the following year. Leave that is not taken by the end of the following financial year is paid out to the employee. Each employee earns CU100,000 per annum and works 250 days per annum. The 10 employees each took an average of 10 days of their annual leave during the current financial year.

You are required to:
Record the journal entries to account for the obligation related to the employees' leave in the current financial year.

QUESTION 2

Long-Term (Pty) Ltd grants its eight employees leave of three months for every three years of service worked. The leave can be taken after the three years of service. Long-Term (Pty) Ltd pays each of its employees CU129,600 per annum. An appropriate discount rate is 8% per annum compounded annually.

You are required to:
Prepare the journal entries necessary to account for the employees' leave at the end of their second year of employment.

QUESTION 3

BMJ (PTY) LTD contributes to a post-employment defined benefit plan. The following information relates to its defined benefit plan assets and liabilities:

Plan assets:
(a)   opening balance: CU110,000;
(b)   contribution made to the plan at the beginning of the year: CU50,000;
(c)   payments made to retired employees at the end of the year: CU30,000;
(d)   interest rate: 10% per annum compounded annually; and
(e)   the fair value of the plan assets at the end of the year: CU135,000.

Plan obligations
(a)   opening balance: CU118,000;
(b)   current service costs charged at the end of the year: CU60,000;
(c)   past service costs: CU18,000
(d)   payments made to retired employees at the end of the year: CU30,000;
(e)   interest rate: 12% per annum compounded annually; and
(f)   the present value of the defined benefit obligation at the end of the year: CU190,000.

You are required to:
Prepare the general ledger accounts for each of the following related to the post-employment defined benefit plan:
(a)   the plan assets; and
(b)   the plan obligations.

CHAPTER 18
OTHER FINANCIAL INSTRUMENT ISSUES

ILLUSTRATIVE DISCLOSURE [EXTRACT]

IFRS ref		Notes	20X2	20X1
			CU'000	CU'000
	Non-current assets			
S4.2(c)	Financial assets		100,000	80,000
	Current assets			
S4.2(c)	Financial assets		50,000	58,000
	Non-current liabilities			
S4.2(m)	Financial liabilities		25,000	20,000
	Current liabilities			
S4.2(m)	Financial liabilities		12,000	10,000
IFRS ref			**20X2**	**20X1**
			CU'000	**CU'000**
S5.11(b)	**Other income**		**4,500**	**3,000**
S5.5(b)	**Finance costs**		**5,000**	**4,000**
	Accounting policies			
S11.40	The entity has chosen to account for financial instruments using sections 11 and 12 of IFRS for SMEs. Basic financial instruments are initially measured at cost (including transaction costs), while complex financial instruments are initially measured at fair value.			
	Basic financial instruments are subsequently measured at amortised cost using the effective interest rate method. Complex financial instruments are measured at fair value with fair value gains recognised in profit or loss except for equity instruments not publicly traded and which fair value cannot be obtained without undue cost or effort, in which case these financial instruments are measured at cost less accumulated impairment.			

S11.41		12. Categories of financial instruments	Fair value through profit or loss	Amortised cost	Cost less impairment
			CU	CU	CU
		Financial assets	90,000	40,000	20,000
		Financial liabilities	20,000	17,000	0
S11.48		Financial asset gains/(losses)	3,000	1,500	0
		Financial liability gains/(losses)	(2,000)	(3,000)	
		All financial assets and liabilities, which are measured at fair value, have fair value determined with reference to quoted prices in active markets.			
S12.27		The entity has entered into positions in hedging relationships to protect itself from certain financial risks. These hedges have all met the hedge accounting criteria and are accounted for as such in these financial statements.			
		The entity entered into a number of foreign exchange contracts, as hedging instruments, to hedge against the foreign exchange risk exposure in highly anticipated forecast transactions, the hedged items. The fair value of the hedging instruments at 31 December 20X7 is CU10,000 (31 December 20x6: CU7,500).			

18.1 INTRODUCTION

IFRS for SMEs split the accounting for financial instruments into two sections, section 11 – *Basic financial instruments* and section 12 – *Other financial instruments*. Basic financial instruments are relevant to all entities. Entities that only have basic financial instruments do not have to be concerned about the accounting for other financial instruments, although they have to consider the scope of this section to ensure that they are exempt (s12.1). The term 'other financial instruments' used in the remainder of the chapter refers to financial instruments other than basic financial instruments and which are included in the scope of section 12 of the IFRS for SMEs standard.

18.2   LEARNING OUTCOMES

Upon completion of this unit, you should know the financial reporting requirements for accounting for financial instruments other than basic financial instruments in accordance with the IFRS for SMEs. In particular, you should be able to:

(a)   identify other financial instruments that qualify for recognition under this section;

(b)   recognise and measure other financial instruments at initial recognition;

(c)   account for the subsequent measurement of other financial instruments;

(d)   present and disclose other financial instruments in the financial statements.

18.3   DEFINITIONS

The definitions for the important concepts and terms used in IFRS for SMEs, are found in Appendix B – *Glossary of terms* in IFRS for SMEs. Some important definitions relating to financial instruments include the following:

- **Financial instrument:** A contract that gives rise to a financial asset of one entity and a financial liability or equity instrument of another entity

- **Financial asset:** Any asset that is:
  (a)   cash;
  (b)   an equity instrument of another entity;
  (c)   a contractual right:
      (i)   to receive cash or another financial asset from another entity; or
      (ii)   to exchange financial assets or financial liabilities with another entity under conditions that are potentially favourable to the entity; or
  (d)   a contract that will or may be settled in the entity's own equity instruments and:
      (i)   under which the entity is or may be obliged to receive a variable number of the entity's own equity instruments; or
      (ii)   that will or may be settled other than by the exchange of a fixed amount of cash or another financial asset for a fixed number of the entity's own equity instruments. For this purpose, the entity's own equity instruments do not include instruments that are themselves contracts for the future receipt or delivery of the entity's own equity instruments.

413

- **Financial liability:** Any liability that is:
  (a) a contractual obligation:
    (i) to deliver cash or another financial asset to another entity; or
    (ii) to exchange financial assets or financial liabilities with another entity under conditions that are potentially unfavourable to the entity; or
  (b) a contract that will or may be settled in the entity's own equity instruments and:
    (i) under which the entity is or may be obliged to deliver a variable number of the entity's own equity instruments, or
    (ii) will or may be settled other than by the exchange of a fixed amount of cash or another financial asset for a fixed number of the entity's own equity instruments. For this purpose, the entity's own equity instruments do not include instruments that are themselves contracts for the future receipt or delivery of the entity's own equity instruments.

18.4   SCOPE AND OBJECTIVES

Sections 11 and 12 together deal with the accounting for all financial instruments. Section 11 applies to basic financial instruments only, while section 12 applies to financial instruments other than basic financial instruments (s11.1). Entities applying IFRS for SMEs have to make a policy choice to determine whether they will apply the requirement of both sections 11 and 12 or IFRS 9 – *Financial instruments* of full IFRS in accounting for all financial instruments (s11.2 and s12.2).

18.5   CLASSIFICATION

As other financial instruments refer to financial instruments other than basic financial instruments, it is important for us to identify what basic financial instruments are.

Basic financial instruments are those financial instruments, which are (s11.8):
(a)   cash;
(b)   a debt instrument that meets the conditions below;*
(c)   a commitment to receive a loan that:
    (i)   cannot be settled net in cash; and
    (ii)   when the commitment is executed, are expected to meet the conditions explained below;*
    (iii)   an investment in non-convertible preference shares and non-puttable ordinary shares or preference shares.

*A financial instrument that satisfies all of the criteria in (a)–(d) shall be accounted for in accordance with section 11 – *Basic financial instruments* (s11.9):

(d) returns to the holder assessed in the currency in which the debt instrument is denominated is either:
    (i) a fixed amount;
    (ii) a fixed rate of return over the life of the instrument;
    (iii) a variable return that, throughout the life of the instrument, is equal to a single referenced quoted or observable interest rate; or
    (iv) some combination of fixed and variable rates, provided that both the fixed and variable rates are positive.

For fixed and variable rate interest returns, interest is calculated by multiplying the rate for the applicable period by the principal amount outstanding during the period;

(e) there is no contractual provision that could, by its terms, result in the holder losing the principal amount or any interest attributable to the current period or prior periods. The fact that a debt instrument is subordinated is not an example of such a contractual provision;

(f) contractual provisions that permit or require the practitioner to prepay a debt instrument or permit or require the holder to put it back to the issuer before maturity are not contingent on future events other than to protect:
    (i) the holder against credit risk of the issuer or the instrument or a change in control of the issuer; or
    (ii) the holder or issuer against changes in relevant tax or law;

(g) there are no conditional returns or prepayment provisions except for the variable rate return described in (a) and prepayment provision described in (c).

Illustrative Example 18.1: Basic financial instruments

An entity has the following balances reflected in its statement of financial position:

	CU
Cash	100,000
(Trade) Accounts receivable	50,000
Loan receivable (interest linked to prime)	40,000
Investment in compulsorily convertible preference shares	85,000

You are required to:
Explain, giving reasons, whether each of the above mentioned items should be classified as basic financial instruments or other financial instruments.

Suggested solution:
The following items are (are not) classified as basic financial instruments with the reasons provided:

	Classification
Cash	Basic – included in s11.8 (a)
Accounts receivable	Basic – included in s11.8 (b) & 11.9 (a) (ii)
Loan receivable	Basic – included in s11.8 (b) & 11.9 (a) (iii)
Preference shares	Other – excluded in s11.8 (d)

The following financial instruments are specifically excluded from section 11– *Basic financial instruments* (s11.7) and section 12 – *Other financial instruments* (s12.3):
(a)   investments in subsidiaries, associates and joint ventures;
(b)   compound financial instruments;
(c)   leases;
(d)   employee benefits;
(e)   share-based payment transactions;
(f)   reimbursement assets that are accounted for in terms of section 21 – *Provisions and contingencies*; and
(g)   contracts for contingent consideration in a business combination.

In addition, a very important exception listed (not included) is that section 12 – *Other financial instruments* excludes all financial instruments within the scope of section 11 – *Basic financial instruments* from its scope.

Contracts to buy non-financial assets such as property, plant and equipment or inventory, are excluded from the scope of section 1 – *Other financial instruments* unless the contract can be settled net in cash, or by another financial instrument, or by exchanging financial instruments as if the contracts were financial instruments. This is so, unless the contracts were entered into and continue to be held with the objective of receipt or delivery of the non-financial item.

18.6   INITIAL RECOGNITION

An entity recognises a financial asset or liability when the entity becomes a party to the contractual provisions of the instrument.

The entity should initially recognise and measure other financial instruments at fair value which is often their transaction price (s12.7).

To determine fair value, s12.10 refers us to s11.27, which states that the following hierarchy should be used:

(a)   a quoted price or an identical asset in an active market;

(b)   if quoted prices are unavailable, the price in a binding sale agreement or recent transaction for an identical asset (or similar asset), adjusted if the entity can demonstrate that the last transaction price is not a good estimate of fair value; and

(c)   failing the above, the use of a valuation technique which should:

     (i)   reasonably reflecting how the market could be expected to price the asset; and

     (ii)   have inputs that reasonably represent market expectations and measures of the risk return factors inherent in the asset.

An entity should not capitalise transaction costs on initial recognition of a financial instrument subsequently measured as at fair value through profit or loss (s12.12).

In terms of s12.11, a financial liability payable on demand is carried at an amount not less than the amount payable on demand, discounted from the first date that the amount could be required to be paid.

Illustrative Example 18.2: Initial recognition of other financial instruments

An entity purchases equity shares for CU100,000, which is their fair value, on 01 January 20X7. The entity incurs transactions costs of CU10,000. The fair value of the equity shares is CU125,000 at the year-end of the entity, which is 31 December 20X7.

You are required to:

Prepare the journal entries necessary to account for equity shares in the financial statements of the entity on 1 January 20x7.

Suggested solution:

01 January 20X7:

Dr	Financial asset	100,000	
Cr	Bank		100,000
[Recognising the acquisition of a financial asset at fair value at initial recognition]			

Dr	Transaction costs [P/L]	10,000	
Cr	Bank		10,000
[Recognising the transaction costs related to the financial asset at initial recognition]			

18.7   SUBSEQUENT MEASUREMENT

Financial instruments within the scope of section 12 – *Other financial instruments* should be accounted for at fair value, with gains and losses recognised in profit or loss subsequent to initial recognition. This does not apply to the following:

(a)   certain financial instruments accounted for in terms of hedge accounting; and

(b)   equity instruments that are not publicly traded and where the fair value cannot be determined without undue cost or effort, in which case their last fair value measured without undue cost or effort becomes their cost and they are subsequently measured at cost less impairment until the entity can measure their fair value without undue cost and effort.

Illustrative Example 18.3: Subsequent measurement

Use the information from Illustrative Example 18.2.

You are required to:

Using the same information as in Illustrative Example 2, Prepare the journal entries necessary to account for the loan will be accounted in the financial statements of the entity for the year ended 31 December 20x7. You may assume that the correct journal entry has already been prepared at initial recognition.

Suggested solution:

31 December 20X7:

Dr	Financial asset [CU125,000 – CU100,000]	25,000	
Cr	Fair value gain on financial asset [P/L]		25,000
	[Recognising the fair value gain on the financial asset at year-end]		

Illustrative Example 18.4: Subsequent measurement

Assuming that the fair value of the equity instrument cannot be determined at 31 December 20x8 without undue cost or effort.

You are required to:

Using the same information as in Illustrative Example 2, Prepare the journal entries necessary to account for the loan will be accounted in the financial statements of the entity for the year ended 31 December 20x7. You may assume that the correct journal entry has already been prepared at initial recognition.

Suggested solution:

No journal entry as the last fair value determined without undue cost or effort becomes its cost and carrying amount (subject to any adjustments related to its impairment).

18.8 IMPAIRMENT AND REVERSAL OF IMPAIRMENT OF A FINANCIAL ASSET MEASURED AT COST LESS IMPAIRMENT

Any other financial asset carried at cost less impairment shall be subject to the impairment requirements of section 11 – *Basic financial instruments* (12.13). Refer to Chapter 9 for further guidance.

18.9 HEDGE ACCOUNTING

18.9.1 Introduction

Hedging involves an entity strategically entering into a transaction or taking a position that will protect itself from particular risk. The idea is that there are often two positions taken:

(a)   the position or transaction that gives rise to risk (the hedged item); and

(b)   a counteracting position or transaction that protects the entity against the risk in (a) (the hedging instrument).

It might therefore be more useful to conceptualise the two positions taken as one net position. However, applying the guidance for accounting for financial instruments often results in the gain or loss on the hedged item and hedging instrument being recognised in profit or loss in different periods, thereby not reflecting the concept of the net position. As a result, if the hedging relationship meets certain criteria, the entity may apply hedge accounting to account for the hedged item and hedging instrument.

The following definitions related to hedge accounting are important.

- **Hedged item:** For the purpose of special hedge accounting by SMEs under section 12 of this standard, a hedged item is (s12.17):
  (a) interest rate risk of a debt instrument measured at amortised cost;
  (b) foreign exchange or interest rate risk in a firm commitment or a highly probable forecast transaction;
  (c) price risk of a commodity that it holds or in a firm commitment or highly probable forecast transaction to purchase or sell a commodity; or
  (d) foreign exchange risk in a net investment in a foreign operation.
- **Hedging instrument:** For the purpose of special hedge accounting by SMEs under section 12 of this standard, a hedging instrument is a financial instrument that meets all of the following terms and conditions (s12.17):
  (a) it is an interest rate swap, a foreign currency swap, a foreign currency forward exchange contract or a commodity forward exchange contract that is expected to be highly effective in offsetting a risk identified in paragraph section 12.17 that is designated as the hedged risk;

(b) it involves a party external to the reporting entity (ie external to the group, segment or individual entity being reported on);

(c) its notional amount is equal to the designated amount of the principal or notional amount of the hedged item;

(d) it has a specified maturity date not later than:

(i) the maturity of the financial instrument being hedged;

(ii) the expected settlement of the commodity purchase or sale commitment; or

(iii) the occurrence of the highly probable forecast foreign currency or commodity transaction being hedged;

(iv) it has no prepayment, early termination or extension features.

The following criteria need to be met in order for an entity to apply hedge accounting to a hedging relationship (s12.16):

(a) the entity designates and documents the hedging relationship so that the risk being hedged, the hedged item and the hedging instrument are clearly identified and the risk in the hedged item is the risk being hedged with the hedging instrument;

(b) the hedged risk is one of the risks specified above;

(c) the hedging instrument is as specified in paragraph 12.18; and

(d) the entity expects the hedging instrument to be highly effective in offsetting the designated hedged risk. The effectiveness of a hedge is the degree to which changes in the fair value or cash flows of the hedged item that are attributable to the hedged risk are offset by changes in the fair value or cash flows of the hedging instrument.

- **Highly probable:** Significantly more likely than probable
- **Forecast transaction:** An uncommitted but anticipated future transaction
- **Firm commitment:** A binding agreement for the exchange of a specified quantity of resources at a specified price on a specified future date or dates

18.9.2 Hedge accounting

18.9.2.1 Hedge of a fixed interest rate risk of a recognised financial instrument

A fixed rate financial instrument, which is a debt instrument, will have fixed cash flows. However, as the cash flows are fixed (based on the quoted interest rate), movements in the market interest rate will change the fair value of the financial asset.

Illustrative Example 18.5: Risk – Fair value movements in a financial instrument which is a debt instrument

The entity issues a loan on 01 January 20X7 for CU100,000, payable in full two years in arrears. The loan bears fixed interest of 10% per annum compounded annually. At 31 December 20X7, a market related interest rate is 8% per annum compounded annually.

You are required to:
Calculate the carrying amount of the loan at 31 December 20x7 using the:
(i)   contractual interest rate of 10%; and
(ii)   market related interest rate of 8%.

Suggested solution:
The carrying amount of the loan on 31 December 20X7 is:

	CU
CU100,000 × 1.1^2	121,000
CU121,000/1.1	**110,000**

The fair value of the loan based on market related interest rates is:

	CU
CU121,000/1.08	**112,037**

Therefore, the fair value of the liabilities are higher due to the change in the discount rate.

In order to protect itself against such adverse fair value movements caused by a change in interest rate, an entity can enter into an interest rate swap with a counterparty. The interest rate swap will swap the cash flows under the fixed rate loan for the cash flows that would have existed if the loan was a variable rate loan.

Illustrative Example 18.6: Interest swap to protect fair value risk

The entity enters into a loan, as the borrower, for CU100,000 on 01 January 20X7. The loan is payable in full at the end of three years (ie the capital and the interest incurred over the life of the loan is payable at the end of three years). The loan bears fixed interest of 10% per annum compounded annually. At the 31 December 20X7, the market-related interest rate is changed to 8% per annum compounded annually.

The entity anticipates the movement in the interest rate and enters into an interest rate swap with an independent third party on 01 January 20X8. The swap includes that the entity will pay the counterparty variable interest on the principal amount outstanding at the market interest rate and receive a payment based on a fixed interest rate of 10% on the principal amount outstanding. Both reference interest rates are compounded annually.

The fair value of the interest rate swap is CU2,200 favourable at 31 December 20X8.

You are required to:
Prepare the journal entries necessary to account for the loan and interest rate swap in the financial statements of the entity for the year ended 31 December 20x7.

Suggested solution:
31 December 20X7:

Dr	Interest expense [P/L] [CU100,000 x 10%]	10,000	
Cr	Loan payable		10,000
[Recognising the interest expense related to the loan payable]			

31 December 20X8:

Dr	Interest expense [P/L] [(CU100,000 + CU10,000) × 10%]	11,000	
Cr	Loan payable		11,000
[Recognising the interest expense related to the loan payable]			
Dr	Bank [CU110 000 × (10% − 8%)]	2,200	
Cr	Interest income [P/L]		2,200
[Recognising the net cash flow on the interest rate swap]			

Dr	Fair value loss on the loan [P/L]^{W1}	2,241	
Cr	Loan payable		2,241
[Recognising the net cash flow on the interest rate swap]			

Dr	Interest rate swap	2,200	
Cr	Fair value gain on interest rate swap [P/L]		2,200
[Recognising the net cash flow on the interest rate swap]			

Working 1: (W1)	CU
CU100,000 × 1.1^3	133,100
CU133,100/1.08	**123,241**
Amortised cost carrying amount [CU110,000 + CU11,000]	121,000
Fair value gain [P/L]	**2,241**

You will notice that the gain on the interest rate swap of CU2,200 largely offsets the loss on the loan payable of CU2,241, thus protecting the entity against the fair value movement in the loan payable.

18.9.2.2 Hedge of a variable interest rate risk of a recognised financial instrument, foreign exchange risk or commodity price risk in a firm commitment or highly probable forecast transaction

The entity must account for the hedging relationship for the following items as described below:

(a)   the variable interest rate in a debt instrument measured at amortised cost;

(b)   the foreign exchange risk in a firm commitment or a highly probable forecast transaction;

(c)   the commodity price risk in a firm commitment or highly probable forecast transaction; and

(d)   the foreign exchange risk in a net investment in a foreign operation.

For these hedges, the entity must recognise the fair value gain on the hedging instrument that was effective in hedging the expected change in the fair value or expected cash flow of the hedged item in other comprehensive income. The entity must then reclassify the gain in other comprehensive income to profit or loss when the hedged item is recognised in profit or loss (s12.23).

Illustrative Example 18.7: Interest swap to protect variable interest rate risk

The entity enters into a loan, as the borrower, for CU100,000 on 01 January 20X7. The loan is payable in full at the end of three years (ie the capital and the interest incurred over the life of the loan is payable at the end of three years). The loan bears variable interest at the opening prime interest rate for that year, compounded annually. The prime interest rate is 6% per annum compounded annually at the 01 January 20X7. At the 31 December 20X7, the prime interest rate is 7% per annum compounded annually.

The entity anticipated the movement in the interest rate and enters into an interest rate swap with an independent third party on 02 January 20X7. The swap includes that the entity will pay the counterparty fixed interest on the principal amount outstanding at 6% per annum and receive a payment based on the prime interest rate. Both reference interest rates are compounded annually.

The fair value of the interest rate swap is CU2,200 favourable at 31 December 20X7 (before settlement), which reflects the change in the fair value or expected cash flows of the hedged item. The entity meets all of the requirements to account for the transactions as a hedge.

You are required to:
Prepare the journal entries necessary to account for the loan and the interest rate swap in the financial statements of the entity for the year ended 31 December 20x7. You do not have to prepare the journal entry at initial recognition of the loan.

Suggested solution:
31 December 20X7:

Dr	Interest expense [P/L] [CU100,000 × 7%]	7,000	
Cr	Loan payable		7,000
[Recognising the interest expense related to the loan payable]			

Dr	Bank	1,000	
Cr	Swap asset [CU100,000 × (7% − 6%)]		1,000
[Recognising the net cash flow on the interest rate swap]			

Dr	Swap asset	2,200	
Cr	Fair value gain on swap asset [OCI]		2,200
[Recognising the fair value gain on the interest rate swap]			

Dr	Fair value gain on swap asset [OCI]	1,000	
Cr	Interest expense [P/L]		1,000
[Recognising the reclassification of the gain in OCI to P/L]			

You will notice that the interest expense for the year is CU1,000 = CU7,000 − CU6,000 (equivalent to the CU100,000 × 6% that the entity locked itself into paying the independent third party through the interest rate swap).

Illustrative Example 18.8: Hedging foreign exchange risk in a firm commitment or a highly probable forecast transaction

The entity highly anticipated purchasing (or placed the order for = firm commitment) inventory from a foreign supplier for FC50,000. In anticipation of the acquisition, the entity entered into a foreign exchange contract (FEC) with Bank Ltd on 01 December 20X7, to purchase FC50,000 on 30 June 20X8 when the foreign creditor was expected to be paid. The inventory was expected to be delivered to the entity on 01 March 20X8. The creditor was settled as planned on 30 June 20X8, which is in compliance with the supplier's normal credit terms. The entity has a 31 December year-end. All of the inventory was sold at 31 December 20X8. The entity met all of the requirements to account for the arrangement as a hedge.

The following exchange rates are applicable:

Date	Spot rate	FEC rate expiring on 1 March 20X8
	FC1:CU	**FC1:CU**
1 December 20X7	5.00	5.25
31 December 20X7	5.10	5.35
1 March 20X8	5.32	5.57
30 June 20X8	5.40	

You are required to:

Prepare the journal entries necessary to account for the arrangement in the financial statements of the entity for the year ended 31 December 20x7 and 20x8.

Suggested solution:

01 December 20X7:

No journal entry as FEC has no value in itself as at 01 December 20X7.

31 December 20X7:

Dr	FEC asset [CU50,000 × (CU5.35 – CU5.25)]	5,000	
Cr	Fair value gain on FEC asset [OCI]		5,000
[Recognising the fair value gain on the FEC asset]			

1 March 20X8:

Dr	FEC asset [CU50,000 × (CU5.57 – CU5.35)]	11,000	
Cr	Fair value gain on FEC asset [OCI]		11,000
[Recognising the fair value gain on the FEC asset]			

Dr	Inventory	266,000	
Cr	Foreign creditor [CU50,000 × CU5.32]		266,000
[Recognising the inventory delivered and the foreign creditor]			

30 June 20X8:

Dr	Fair value loss on foreign creditor [P/L]	1,000	
Cr	Foreign creditor		1,000
[Recognising the fair value loss on the foreign creditor]			

Dr	Fair value loss on FEC [P/L]	8,500	
Cr	FEC asset		8,500
[Recognising the fair value loss on the FEC asset]			

31 December 20X8:

Dr	Cost of sale [P/L]	266,000	
Cr	Inventory		266,000
[Recognising the derecognition of the inventory on sale]			

Dr	Fair value gain on FEC asset [OCI]	16,000	
Cr	Fair value gain on FEC asset [P/L]		16,000
[Recognising the reclassification of the gain in OCI to P/L]			

18.10 PRESENTATION AND DISCLOSURE

18.10.1 Presentation

Section 11 does not have specific presentation requirements for basic financial instruments. The related requirements are included in section 3, such as that the statement of financial position should have a separate line item for financial assets (s4.2(c)) and financial liabilities (s4.2(m)) and should classify financial instruments as either current or non-current in terms of sections 4.5 to 4.8. Entities should present the resultant dividend income, interest income, interest expense, impairment losses and reversals in profit or loss as appropriate in terms of section 5 (including s5.5(b)). Interest and dividend received may be presented as either operating or investing activities, and interest paid may be presented as either operating or financing activities in the statement of cash flows (s7.14 to 7.16).

18.10.2 Disclosure

18.10.2.1 General disclosures

In terms of section 12.26, an entity should refer back to the disclosure requirements in section 11 – *Basic financial instruments* and include financial instruments within the scope of section 12 – *Complex financial instruments* in those disclosures. A reference to section 11 will show the following disclosure requirements.

The entity should disclose the significant accounting policies relating to financial instruments (s11.40) together with any other information that would be useful for users to evaluate the significance of financial instruments for its financial position and performance (s11.42). An entity should disclose the carrying amounts of each of the following categories in the statement of financial position or in the notes (s11.41):

(a)   financial assets measured at fair value through profit or loss;
(b)   financial assets that are debt instruments measured at amortised cost;
(c)   financial assets that are equity instruments measured at cost less accumulated impairment;
(d)   financial liabilities measured at fair value through profit or loss;
(e)   financial liabilities measured at amortised cost; and
(f)   loan commitments measured at cost less impairment.

The entity should disclose the following for financial assets pledged as collateral or security (s11.46):

(a)   the carrying amount of financial instruments pledged as collateral; and
(b)   the terms and conditions relating to its pledge.

The entity should also disclose the following relating to any breaches of loans payable which are not remedied by reporting date:

(a)   details of the breach or default;
(b)   the carrying amount of the related loans payable at the reporting date; and
(c)   whether the breach was remedied, or the terms renegotiated before the financial statements were authorised for issue.

The entity should disclose the following relating to income, expense, gains or losses:

(a)   all income, expense, gains and losses (including fair value gains and losses) for:
    (i)   financial assets measured at fair value through profit or loss;
    (ii)   financial liabilities measured at fair value through profit or loss;
    (iii)   financial assets measured at amortised cost; and
    (iv)   financial liabilities measured at amortised cost;
    (v)   the total interest income.

The entity should disclose the following specifically related to hedge accounting.

For each of the four types of risk described in the hedge accounting section, the entity shall disclose the following related to the hedge of those risks (s12.27):

(a)   a description of the hedge;

(b)   a description of the financial instruments used as the hedging instruments and their fair values at reporting date; and

(c)   the nature of the risks being hedged, including a description of the hedged item.

The following disclosures are required if the hedge accounting is for a hedge of fixed interest rate risk or commodity price risk of a commodity held (s12.28):

(a)   the amount of the change in fair value of the hedging instrument recognised in profit or loss for the period; and

(b)   the amount in the change in fair value of the hedged item recognised in profit or loss for the period.

The entity must disclose the following if the entity uses hedge accounting for a hedge of variable interest rate risk, foreign exchange risk, commodity price risk in a firm commitment or highly probable forecast transaction, or a net investment in a foreign operation (s12.29):

(a)   the periods where the cash flows are expected to occur and when they are expected to affect profit or loss;

(b)   a description of any forecast transaction for which hedge accounting had previously been used, but which is no longer expected to occur;

(c)   the amount of the change in fair value of the hedging instrument that was recognised in other comprehensive income during the period;

(d)   the amount that was reclassified to profit or loss for the period; and

(e)   the amount of any excess of the cumulative change in fair value of the hedging instrument over the cumulative change in the fair value of the expected cash flows that was recognised in profit or loss for the period.

SELF-ASSESSMENT
Multiple choice questions: Testing principles of accounting for other financial instrument issues

1. An entity preparing its financial statements in compliance with IFRS for SMEs may choose to account for financial instruments in terms of:

(a) section 11 – *Basic financial instruments* of IFRS for SMEs and IFRS 9 – Financial instruments	
(b) sections 11 and 12 of IFRS for SMEs **OR** IFRS 9	
(c) section 12 – *Compound financial instruments* AND IFRS 9 – Financial instruments	
(d) sections 11 and 12 of IFRS for SMEs only	

2. The following financial instruments are excluded from section 12 – *Compound financial instruments*:

(a) those covered by section 11	
(b) investments in subsidiaries	
(c) investments in associates	
(d) all of the above	

3. The following financial instrument is included in the scope of section 12 – *Compound financial instruments*:

(a) a contract to buy a commodity where the intention is to take delivery of the commodity	
(b) a contract to buy a non-financial asset that can be settled net in cash	
(c) a contract to purchase property	
(d) none of the above	

4. The following financial instrument is included in the scope of section 12 – *Compound financial instruments*:

(a) share-based payment transactions issued by the entity	
(b) lease agreements.	
(c) investments in joint ventures	
(d) hedging instruments which are accounted for in terms of the hedge accounting rules IFRS for SMEs	

5. Financial instruments in the scope of section 12 – *Compound financial instruments* are initially recognised at:

(a) historical cost excluding transaction costs	
(b) historical cost including transaction costs	
(c) fair value	
(d) sunk cost	

6. Financial instruments included within the scope of section 12 – *Compound financial instruments* are subsequently accounted for at:

(a) cost (ignoring impairment)	
(b) amortised cost	
(c) fair value	
(d) net realisable value	

7. Equity instruments which are not traded on a public exchange and which fair value cannot be obtained without undue cost or effort must be accounted for at:

(a) cost (ignoring impairment)	
(b) cost less impairment	
(c) fair value	
(d) amortised cost	

8. The following risks can be accounted for under the hedge accounting requirements of section 12 – *Compound financial instruments*:

(a) interest rate risk of a debt instrument measured at amortised cost	
(b) risk of salaries increasing at higher than inflation.	
(c) political risk	
(d) credit risk	

9. A gain on the hedging instrument in a hedge of the fixed interest rate risk of a recognised financial instrument is recognised in:

(a) profit or loss	
(b) other comprehensive income	
(c) the statement of changes in equity directly	
(d) none of the above	

10. The gain on the hedging instrument in a hedge of a firm commitment is recognised in:

(a) profit or loss	
(b) the statement of changes in equity directly	
(c) the statement of financial position only	
(d) other comprehensive income	

Practical questions:
Application of principles to business scenarios

QUESTION 1

DPJ (Pty) Ltd invested CU100,000, which was the fair value of the shares on the purchase date of 01 January 20X7, in the equity shares of Boomerang (Pty) Ltd. The shares have a fair value of CU120,000 on 31 December 20X7. Boomerang (Pty) Ltd paid a dividend of CU5,000 to DPJ (Pty) Ltd on 31 December 20X7.

You are required to:
Record the journal entries to account for the equity shares in the financial statements of DPJ (Pty) Ltd for the year ended 31 December 20X7.

QUESTION 2

Brick (Pty) Ltd invested CU150,000, which is the fair value of the shares on the purchase date of 01 January 20X7, in the equity shares of Cinder (Pty) Ltd. The fair value of the shares cannot be determined without undue cost or effort at 31 December 20X7. The shares are impaired by CU10,000 on 31 December 20X7.

You are required to:
Record the journal entries to account for the equity shares in the financial statements of Brick (Pty) Ltd for the year ended 31 December 20X7.

QUESTION 3

Brujen (Pty) Ltd placed an order for machinery on 01 November 20X7 from a foreign supplier for FC100,000. The order was considered to be a firm commitment. In anticipation of the acquisition, the entity entered into a foreign exchange contract (FEC) with Globe Bank Ltd on 01 November 20X7, to purchase FC100,000 on 30 June 20X8, when the foreign creditor was expected to be paid. The machinery was delivered to the entity on 01 May 20X8 and was immediately available for use. The creditor was settled on 30 June 20X8, which is in compliance with the supplier's normal credit terms. The entity has a 31 December year-end. The machinery has always had a total estimated useful life of 10 years with nil residual value.

The following exchange rates are applicable:

Date	Spot rate	FEC rate expiring on 30 June 20X8
	FC1:CU	FC1:CU
01 November 20X7	3.00	3.07
31 December 20X7	3.05	3.12
01 May 20X8	3.20	3.25
30 June 20X8	3.40	

You are required to:
Record the journal entries to account for the receipt of the inventory and the related payable for the year ended 31 December 20X7.

CHAPTER 19
INVESTMENTS IN ASSOCIATES

IFRS ref		Notes	20X7	20X6	
			CU	CU	
S14.14 & IAS 1 p.82(c)	Share of profit or associate		140,000	90,000	

		Notes	20X7	20X6	
	Non-current Assets				
S14.11 & IAS 1 p.54(e)	Investment in associate	12	250,000	200,000	

IFRS ref	12. Investments in associates			
S14.12	The entity accounts for all of its investments in associates by applying the equity method. The cumulative carrying amount of its investments in associates is 20x7: CU250,000 (20x6: CU200,000). None of the investments in associates to which the equity method of accounting is applied has fair values which can be referenced to published price quotations.			

19.1   INTRODUCTION

Entities often invest in the ordinary shares of other entities. Depending on the degree of control (or lack thereof) associated with the shareholding, different accounting practices and principles apply. One of the shareholding positions could be a relationship in which an investor has a significant influence, but not control or joint control over an investee. If the investor does not control the investee, it should not include the assets and liabilities of the investee in its consolidated financial statements (as one economic entity). However, because of the significant influence, the investor would want to show its share of the equity of the investee in its financial statements. This is achieved through a method of accounting known as equity accounting.

This chapter is designed to introduce the accounting principles and practices for separate and group financial statements where an investor–associate relationship exists.

19.2 LEARNING OUTCOMES
Upon completion of this chapter you should be able to:
(a) identify and classify relationships into investor–associate relationships;
(b) recognise the various elements of the financial statements in the separate and group financial statements;
(c) measure the various elements of the financial statements in the separate and group financial statements; and
(d) present and disclose the various elements associated with the investor–associate relationship in the separate and group financial statements.

19.3 DEFINITIONS
The definitions for the important concepts and terms used in IFRS for SMEs are found in Appendix B – *Glossary of terms* in IFRS for SMEs. The following important definitions related to investment in associates are applicable:

•   **Associate:** An entity, including an unincorporated entity such as a partnership, over which the investor has significant influence and that is neither a subsidiary nor an interest in a joint venture.

19.4 SCOPE AND OBJECTIVES
Section 14 (IAS 28, IFRS 7 and IAS 27) provides guidance for accounting and disclosure for all investor–associate relationships.

19.5 CLASSIFICATION AS INVESTOR–ASSOCIATE RELATIONSHIP
An investor–associate relationship exists when one entity has significant influence over another entity. Significant influence is the power to participate in the operating and policy decisions of the associate, but is not control or joint control over those policies (s14.3 and IAS 28 p.3). Significant influence can be obtained in various ways, but there is a presumption that where an entity has more than 20% of the voting power of another entity, that the investor has significant influence over the investee (s14.3 and IAS 28 p.5).

Full IFRS also includes the following as examples for when significant influence might exist (these examples are not included in IFRS for SMEs IAS 28 p.6):
(a) representation on the board of directors or equivalent governing body of the investee;

(b) *participation in policy-making processes, including participation in decisions about dividends or other distributions;*

(c) *material transactions between the entity and its investee;*

(d) *interchange of managerial personnel; or*

(e) *provision of essential technical information.*

In terms of s14.4, an entity has an accounting policy choice when accounting for investments in associates. The entity may choose to account for the investment in associate at:

(a) cost;

(b) equity accounting; or

(c) fair value.

19.6 INITIAL RECOGNITION

Measurement at initial recognition will depend on the model adopted by the entity as its accounting policy.

19.6.1 Cost model

The investment in associate will initially be measured at cost (s14.5). While it is not specifically stated, it may be assumed that the cost includes transaction costs, as it does in most other sections in IFRS for SMEs (eg sections 13 – *Inventories*, 16 – *Investment in associates*, 17 – *Property, plant & equipment* and 18 – *Intangible assets*, among others).

Illustrative Example 19.1: Cost model

Company A purchases 35% of the equity shares and voting rights in company B for CU100,000 in cash. It pays CU10,000 transaction costs to its attorney to complete the transaction (the legal fees are considered to be transaction costs). Company A applies the cost model of accounting for its investment in associate in its group financial statements.

You are required to:

Prepare the journal entries necessary to account for the investment in the associate.

Suggested solution:

		CU	CU
Dr	Investment in associate [CU100,000 + CU10,000]	110,000	
Cr	Bank		110,000
[Recording the initial recognition of the investment in associate]			

19.6.2 Equity method

In terms of the equity method, the investment in associate is recognised at transaction price (***including*** transaction costs) (s14.8 and IAS 28 p.10). Therefore, the initial recognition of the investment in associate will be the same under the equity method as under the cost model (assuming that transaction costs are included – refer to the example above).

19.6.3 Fair value model

Under the fair value model, the investment in the associate shall initially be recognised at transaction price (***excluding*** transaction costs) (s14.9).

Illustrative Example 19.2: Fair value model

Company A purchases 35% of the equity shares and voting rights in company B for CU100,000 in cash. It pays CU10,000 transaction costs to its attorney to complete the transaction (the legal fees are considered to be transaction costs). Company A applies the fair value model of accounting for its investment in associate in its group financial statements.

You are required to:
Prepare the journal entries necessary to account for the investment in the associate.

Suggested solution:

		CU	CU
Dr	Investment in associate [CU100,000 transaction price only]	100,000	
Dr	Transaction costs [P/L]	10,000	
Cr	Bank		110,000
[Recording the initial recognition of the investment in associate]			

19.7 MEASUREMENT SUBSEQUENT TO INITIAL RECOGNITION

Depending on the model adopted as its accounting policy, the following will be the measurement subsequent to initial recognition (*it should be noted that full IFRS does not give these options to account for investments in associates in its group financial statements as it mandates entities to apply the equity method when accounting for its investments in associates; it should also be noted that full IFRS allows an exemption to apply the equity method under specific circumstances*):

19.7.1 Cost model

The investment in associate is accounted for at cost less accumulated impairment losses unless there is a public quoted price for the investment, in which case the investment should be accounted for at fair value (s14.5).

Illustrative Example 19.3: Cost model

Company A purchases 35% of the equity shares and voting rights in company B for CU100,000 in cash on 01 January 20X7. It pays CU10,000 transaction costs to its attorney to complete the transaction (the legal fees are considered to be transaction costs). Company A applies the cost model of accounting for its investment in associate in its group financial statements.

There is no quoted share price for the investment and company B's net profit after tax is CU40,000 for the year ended 31 December 20X7. Company B has no items classified as other comprehensive income for the financial year.

You are required to*:*
Prepare the journal entries necessary to account for the investment in the associate in the group financial statements of company A.

Suggested solution:
01 January 20X7:

		CU	CU
Dr	Investment in associate [CU100,000 transaction price only]	110,000	
Cr	Bank		110,000
[Recording the initial recognition of the investment in associate]			

31 December 20X7:
No journal entries required.

Any distributions received from the associate should be recognised as income even if they relate to accumulated profits which arose before the date of acquisition (s14.6).

Illustrative Example 19.4: Equity accounting

Company A purchases 35% of the equity shares and voting rights in company B for CU100,000 in cash on 01 January 20X7. The shares are sold cum-div (inclusive of the right to the dividend) because a dividend equivalent to CU15,000 for a 35% shareholding was declared before the purchase of the shares, but will be paid to company A (as the last date to register was after the purchase of the shares). It pays CU10,000 transaction costs to its attorney to complete the transaction (the legal fees are considered to be transaction costs). Company A applies the cost model of accounting for its investment in associate in its separate financial statements.

There is no quoted share price for the investment and company B's net profit after tax is CU40,000 for the year ended 31 December 20X7. Company B has no items classified as other comprehensive income for the financial year. Company B paid a dividend of CU15,000 to company A (in respect of the dividend declared before the purchase of the shares) on 30 April 20X7.

You are required to:
Prepare the journal entries necessary to account for the investment in the associate in the group financial statements of company A.

Suggested solution:
01 January 20X7:

		CU	CU
Dr	Investment in associate [CU100,000 transaction price only]	110,000	
Cr	Bank		110,000
[Recording the initial recognition of the investment in associate]		

30 April 20X7:

		CU	CU
Dr	Bank	15,000	
Cr	Dividend income [P/L]		15,000
[Recording the receipt of the dividend by the investor]		

31 December 20X7:
No journal entries required.

19.7.2 Equity method

Under the equity method, the amount initially recognised is adjusted (subsequent to initial recognition) for the investor's share of the profit or loss and other comprehensive income of the associate (s14.8 and IAS 28 p.10).

Illustrative Example 19.5: Equity method

Company A purchases 35% of the equity shares and voting rights in company B for CU100,000 in cash on 01 January 20X7. The shares are sold cum-div because a dividend equivalent to CU15,000 for a 35% shareholding was declared before the purchase of the shares, but will be paid to company A (as the last date to register was after the purchase of the shares). It pays CU10,000 transaction costs to its attorney to complete the transaction (the legal fees are considered to be transaction costs). Company A applies the equity method of accounting for its investment in associate in its group financial statements.

The quoted share price for the investment is CU125,000 at 31 December 20X7. Company B's net profit after tax is CU40,000 for the year-ended 31 December 20X7. Company B has no items classified as other comprehensive income for the financial year. The fair value of the 35% investment in the associate is CU125,000 on 31 December 20X7.

You are required to:
Prepare the journal entries necessary to account for the investment in the associate in the group financial statements of the Company A for the financial year ended 31 December 20x7.

Suggested solution:
1 January 20X7:

		CU	CU
Dr	Investment in associate	100,000	
Cr	Bank		100,000
[Recording the initial recognition of the investment in associate]			

31 December 20X7:

		CU	CU
Dr	Investment in associate [CU40,000 × 35%]	14,000	
Cr	Share of profit of associate [P/L][1]		14,000
[Recording the share of profit of associate for the year]			

Note:
[1]You will notice that a new line item is introduced in the statement of profit or loss (a similar line would be introduced in other comprehensive income if the associate had any items included in other comprehensive income). This new line item includes the summary of the investor's share of profit or loss of the associate. Therefore, the investor does not include the components of profit or loss of the associate on a line-by-line item basis, but only in one line summarising its share of the associate's profit or loss.

The concept behind the equity method is that the investor's share of the associate's statement of financial position is summarised in one line item, being the investment in associate. Similarly, the investor's share of the associate's entire statement of profit or loss is summarised in one line item, this being share of profit of associate, and the investor's share of the entire section of the associate's other comprehensive income is summarised in one line item, this being share of associate's other comprehensive income. Consider the following:

Illustrative Example 19.6: Equity method

Company A purchased 40% of the equity shares and voting rights of company B on 01 January 20X7 for CU48,000 and was able to exercise significant influence over company B from the date of purchase. The following trial balance is presented for companies A and B for the financial year ended 31 December 20X7:

	Company A CU	Company B CU
Investment in associate	48,000	0
Property, plant & equipment	780,000	100,000
Intangible assets	650,000	80,000
Investment property	500,000	0
Accounts receivable	50,000	25,000
Cash	40,000	15,000
Ordinary shares	(500,000)	(50,000)
Retained earnings	(400,000)	(70,000)
Revenue	(200,000)	(150,000)
Cost of sales	62,000	100,000
Long-term liability	(1,000,000)	(40,000)
Accounts payable	(30,000)	(10,000)

You are required to:
(i)   Using a table, prepare the trial balances before and after as well as the adjustments for the effects of equity accounting the investment in the associate of the Company A Group for the year-ended 31 December 20x7; and
(ii)   Prepare the journal entries necessary to equity account the profit from the associate in the financial statements of the Company A Group for the year ended 31 December 20x7

Suggested solution:

(i)   Extracts of the trial balances before and after as well as the adjustments for the investment in the associate and

	Company A (separate)		Company A (group)
	CU		CU
Investment in associate	48,000	20,000	68,000
Property, plant & equipment	780,000		780,000
Intangible assets	650,000		650,000
Investment property	500,000		500,000
Accounts receivable	50,000		50,000
Cash	40,000		40,000
Ordinary shares	(500,000)		(500,000)
Retained earnings	(400,000)		(400,000)
Revenue	(200,000)		(200,000)
Cost of sales	62,000		62,000
Share of profit of associate	0	(20,000)	(20,000)
Long-term liability	(1,000,000)		(1,000,000)
Accounts payable	(30,000)		(30,000)

(ii)   The pro forma journal entries would be as follows:

		CU	CU
Dr	Investment in associate [SFP]	20,000	
Cr	Share of profit of associate [P/L]		20,000
Recording the share of profit of associate for the year.			

As the investor includes its entire share of the associate's profit or loss (both the distributed and undistributed profit) and includes this in the investment in the associate, any distribution from the investor reduces the carrying amount of the investment in the associate (s14.8(a) and IAS 28 p.10).

Illustrative Example 19.7: Equity method

Company A purchases 35% of the equity shares and voting rights in company B for CU100,000 in cash on 01 January 20X7. The shares are sold cum-div because a dividend equivalent to CU15,000 for a 35% shareholding was declared before the purchase of the shares, but will be paid to company A (as the last date to register was after the purchase of the shares). It pays CU10,000 transaction costs to its attorney to complete the transaction (the legal fees are considered to be transaction costs). Company A applies the equity method of accounting for its investment in associate in its group financial statements.

The quoted share price for the investment reflects a fair value of CU125,000 at 31 December 20X7. Company B's net profit after tax is CU40,000 for the year ended 31 December 20X7. Company B has no items classified as other comprehensive income for the financial year. The fair value of the 35% investment in the associate is CU125,000 on 31 December 20X7.

Company B paid a dividend of CU15,000 to company A (in respect of the dividend declared before the purchase of the shares) on 30 April 20X7.

You are required to:
Prepare the journal entries necessary to account for the investor's share of profit for of the associate for the year and the dividend received.

Suggested solution:
The following journal entry reflects the expected net effect of accounting for the investment in the associate. The specific pro-forma journal entries will depend on how the investment in the associate is accounted for in the separate financial statements of the investor.

30 April 20X7:

		CU	CU
Dr	Bank	15,000	
Cr	Investment in associate [SFP]		15,000
[Recording the receipt of the dividend by the investor]			

31 December 20X7:

		CU	CU
Dr	Investment in associate	14,000	
Cr	Share of profit of associate [P/L]		14,000
[Recording the investor's share of the profit of the associate for the year]			

It should be noted that any excess of the cost of the investment over the investor's share of the fair value of the net identifiable assets (goodwill) is already included in the measurement of the initial recognition of the investment in the associate. Therefore, no additional line item needs to be recognised for goodwill. The implicit goodwill, however, still needs to be amortised over its expected useful life (s14.8(c)).

Illustrative Example 19.1: Equity method

Company A purchases 35% of the equity shares and voting rights in company B for CU100,000 in cash on 01 January 20X7. The fair value of the net identifiable assets of company B as represented by its equity, at 01 January 20X7, are as follows:

	CU
Ordinary shares	160,000
Retained earnings	70,000
Total	**230,000**

Company A applies the equity method of accounting for its investment in associate in its group financial statements.

The quoted share price for the investment reflects a fair value of CU125,000 at 31 December 20X7. Company B's net profit after tax is CU40,000 for the year ended 31 December 20X7. Company B has no items classified as other comprehensive income for the financial year. Company A amortises any goodwill over a useful life of 10 years to a nil residual value.

You are required to:
Prepare the journal entries necessary to account for the investment in associate for the year ended 31 December 20X7.

Suggested solution:
01 January 20X7:

		CU	CU
Dr	Investment in associate	100,000	
Cr	Bank		100,000
[Recording the investment in associate at initial recognition]			

Note:
[1]It should be noted that goodwill is not recognised separately, but does exist. The fair value of the identifiable net assets is CU230,000 and the investor invested in 35% of these net assets totalling CU80,500 (CU230,000 × 35%). However, the investor paid a total of CU100,000 for the CU80,500 identifiable net assets. Therefore, implicit goodwill of

CU19,500 exists, but is already recognised in the CU100,000 investment in associate and is therefore not recognised separately.

31 December 20X7:

		CU	CU
Dr	Investment in associate	12,050	
Cr	Share of profit of associate [P/L]		12,050
[Recording the investor's share of the profit of the associate for the year]			

Note:

[2]The share of profit of associate is accounted for after adjusting for the amortisation of goodwill. It should be borne in mind that the CU40,000 net profit recognised in the separate financial statements of the investee would not include the amortisation of goodwill (because the goodwill was included in the investor's consideration payable, it is not included in the separate financial statements of the associate). Therefore, the investor's share of the profit of the associate is calculated as CU12,050 [(CU40,000 × 35%) − (CU19,500 goodwill/10-year useful life)].

19.7.3 Fair value model

Under the fair value model, the amount initially recognised excludes the transaction costs (which are expenses as incurred) and is adjusted (subsequent to initial recognition) to the fair value of the investment in associate at each reporting date (s14.9).

Illustrative Example 19.9: Fair value model

Company A purchases 35% of the equity shares and voting rights in company B for CU100,000 in cash on 01 January 20X7. The shares are sold cum-div because a dividend equivalent to CU15,000 for a 35% shareholding was declared before the purchase of the shares, but will be paid to company A (as the last date to register was after the purchase of the shares). It pays CU10,000 transaction costs to its attorney to complete the transaction (the legal fees are considered to be transaction costs). Company A applies the equity method of accounting for its investment in associate in its group financial statements.

The quoted share price for the investment is CU125,000 at 31 December 20X7. Company B's net profit after tax is CU40,000 for the year ended 31 December 20X7. Company B has no items classified as other comprehensive income for the financial year. The fair value of the 35% investment in the associate is CU125,000 on 31 December 20X7.

You are required to:
Prepare the journal entries necessary to account for the investment in the associate.

Suggested solution:

01 January 20X7:

		CU	CU
Dr	Investment in associate	100,000	
Cr	Bank		100,000
[Recording the initial recognition of the investment in associate]			

31 December 20X7:

		CU	CU
Dr	Investment in associate	25,000	
	[CU125,000 – CU100,000]		
Cr	Share of profit of associate [P/L]		25,000
[Recording the share of profit of associate for the year]			

It is important to note that where an investor using the fair value model to account for its investment in an associate cannot reliably measure the fair value of its investment in the associate without undue cost or effort, it has to apply the cost model to account for the investment in the associate.

19.7.4 Separate financial statements

The investment in the equity of the associate is an asset in the separate financial statements of the investor. The investment is initially accounted for at cost. Subsequently, the investment is accounted for in accordance with one of the following accounting policies, which it has to apply consistently to all investments in the same class (subsidiaries, associates or jointly controlled entities) (s9.26 and IAS 27 p.10):
(a) at cost less impairment;
(b) at fair value with changes in fair value recognised in profit or loss; or
(c) using the equity method.

Therefore, the pro forma journal entries required will depend on how the investor accounts for the investment in associate in the separate and group financial statements. For instance, assuming that the investor accounts for the investment in associate at cost in its separate financial statements and applies the equity method to account for the investment in associate in the group financial statements, the pro forma journal entries will need to transition the group financial statements from the cost model to the equity method. Similarly, if the entity applies the fair value model in the separate financial statements and applies the equity method to account for the investment in associate in the group financial statements, the pro forma journal entries will need to transition the group financial statements from the fair value model to the equity methods. The same would be true for an entity which accounts for the investment in associate by applying the equity method in the separate financial statements and the cost or fair value model in the group financial statements. However, if the entity applies the equity method in both the separate and group financial statements, no adjustment will need to be effected via pro forma journal entries.

Illustrative Example 19.10: Separate financials

Use the information from illustrative example 19.6.

Company A purchases 35% of the equity shares and voting rights in company B for CU100,000 in cash on 1 January 20X7. The shares are sold cum-div because a dividend equivalent to CU15,000 for a 35% shareholding was declared before the purchase of the shares, but will be paid to company A (as the last date to register was after the purchase of the shares). It pays CU10,000 transaction costs to its attorney to complete the transaction (the legal fees are considered to be transaction costs). Company A accounts for the investment in associate at cost in its separate financial statements and applies the equity method of accounting for its investment in associate in its group financial statements.

The quoted share price for the investment reflects a fair value of CU125,000 at 31 December 20X7. Company B's net profit after tax is CU40,000 for the year ended 31 December 20X7. Company B has no items classified as other comprehensive income for the financial year. The fair value of the 35% investment in associate is CU125,000 on 31 December 20X7.

Company B paid a dividend of CU15,000 to company A (in respect of the dividend declared before the purchase of the shares) on 30 April 20X7.

You are required to:
Prepare the journal entries necessary to account for the investor's share of profit for of the associate for the year and the dividend received.

Suggested solution:
The following journal entry reflects the expected *net* effect of accounting for the investment in associate. The specific pro forma journal entries will depend on how the investment in associate is accounted for in the separate financial statements of the investor.

30 April 20X7:

		CU	CU
Dr	Bank	15,000	
Cr	Investment in associate [SFP]		15,000
[Recording the receipt of the dividend by the investor]			

31 December 20X7:

		CU	CU
Dr	Investment in associate	14,000	
Cr	Share of profit of associate [P/L]		14,000
[Recording the investor's share of the profit of the associate for the year]			

Note: The pro forma journal entries needed to reach the above final position (the *net* position) are explained in detail below.

The investor and investee's financial separate financial statements would have been completed before any pro forma journal entries are processed. So the question would be: what journal entries has the investor already processed in its separate financial statements?

30 April 20X7:

		CU	CU
Dr	Bank	15,000	
Cr	Dividend income [P/L]		15,000
[Recording the receipt of the dividend by the investor]			

31 December 20X7:
No journal entries, as the investment in associate is accounted for at cost.

Therefore, the following balances table shows the carrying amount and transaction total of the investment in associate, share of profit of associate and dividend income respectively in the separate financial statements (included in the column titled 'cost model') and the desired carrying amounts and transaction totals in the group financial statements (included in the column titled 'equity method').

	Cost model	Equity method
	CU	CU
Investment in associate	100,000	99,000[1]
Share of profit of associate	0	14,000
Dividend income	15,000	0

Note:
[1][100,000 cost – 15,000 dividend + 14,000 share of profit of associate]

The following pro forma journal entries are therefore required to adjust the cost model (separate financial statements) to the equity model (group financial statements):

		CU	CU
Dr	Dividend income [P/L]	15,000	
Cr	Investment in associate		15,000
[Recording the dividend received from company B]			

		CU	CU
Dr	Investment in associate	14,000	
Cr	Share of profit of associate [P/L]		14,000
[Recording the share of profit of company B]			

19.8 PRESENTATION AND DISCLOSURE
19.8.1 Presentation
Investors should present investments in associates as a non-current asset in its statement of financial position (s14.11).

19.8.2 Disclosure
An entity should disclose (s14.12):
(a)   its **accounting policy** for investments in associates;
(b)   the carrying amount of investments in associates (see paragraph 4.2(j)); and
(c)   the fair value of investments in associates accounted for using the equity method for which there are published price quotations.

For investments in associates accounted for at cost, an investor must disclose the amounts of dividends and other distributions recognised as income (s14.13). For investments accounted for using the equity method, an entity must disclose separately its share of the profit or loss of such associates and its share of any discontinued operations of such associated. For investment in associates carried at fair value, an investor must make the disclosures required for basic financial instruments. Where the entity applies the exemption relating to not accounting for investments in associates at fair value because it requires undue cost or effort to determine its fair value, the entity must disclose this fact, the reasons for its conclusion and the carrying amount of investments in associates accounted for under the cost model (s14.15).

SELF-ASSESSMENT
Multiple choice questions: Testing principles of accounting for investments in associates

1. Which of the following reflects an investor–associate relationship:

(a) an investor has control over an investee	
(b) an investor has joint control over an investee	
(c) an investor has no control, joint control or significant influence over an investee	
(d) an investor has significant influence over an investee	

2. Significant influence is presumed to exist if an investor owns more than:

(a) 10% of the equity shares of the investee	
(b) 20% of the equity shares of the investee	
(c) 40% of the equity shares of the investee	
(d) 50% of the equity shares of the investee	

3. An investor may account for the investment in associate using which of the measurement bases below in its group financial statements:

(a) cost model	
(b) equity method	
(c) fair value model	
(d) all of the above	

4. An investor may account for the investment in associate using which of the measurement bases below in its group financial statements:

(a) cost model	
(b) equity method	
(c) fair value model	
(d) all of the above	

5. Which of the following models initially recognise the investment in associate at transaction price (including transaction costs):

(a) fair value model	
(b) equity method	
(c) both of the above	
(d) none of the above	

6. The following gives guidance as to how dividends received from the associate should be treated by the investor applying the equity method of accounting for the investment in associate:

(a) reduce the investment in associate	
(b) increase in profit or loss	
(c) increase directly in equity	
(d) increase liabilities	

7. The following gives guidance as to how dividends received from the associate should be treated by the investor accounting for the investment in associate using the cost model:

(a) reduce the investment in associate	
(b) increase in profit or loss	
(c) increase directly in equity	
(d) increase liabilities	

8. The investment in associate should always be presented as follows in the statement of financial position:

(a) current assets	
(b) non-current liabilities	
(c) non-current asset	
(d) current liabilities	

9. An investment in associate accounted for under the cost model should be subjected to the following at each reporting date:

(a) tested for impairment indicators	
(b) fair valued with any gain or loss recognised in profit or loss	
(c) fair valued with any gain or loss recognised in other comprehensive income	
(d) increased (decreased) with the share of associate's profit	

10. The cost model cannot be applied if:

(a) the associate makes above market-related profits	
(b) The fair value of the investment cannot be determined from a published quoted price	
(c) the fair value of the investment can be determined from a published quoted price	
(d) the associate incurs a loss during the current financial year	

Practical questions:
Application of principles to business scenarios

QUESTION 1

FB (Pty) Ltd purchased 40% of the equity shares and voting rights of Buyme (Pty) Ltd on 01 January 20X7 for CU40,000 in cash. The acquisition of the equity shares allowed FB (Pty) Ltd to exercise significant influence over Buyme (Pty) Ltd. FB (Pty) Ltd accounts for the investment in Buyme (Pty) Ltd at cost in its separate financial statements.

At the date of purchase of the equity shares, Buyme (Pty) Ltd's identifiable net assets' carrying amounts equated their fair values and were represented by their equity of:

	CU
Equity shares	50,000
Retained earnings	40,000

You are required to:
Prepare the journal entries necessary to prepare the separate financial statements for the FB (Pty) Ltd at 01 January 20X7.

QUESTION 2

GO (Pty) Ltd purchased 30% of the equity shares and voting right of STOP (Pty) Ltd for CU35,000 in cash on 01 January 20X7, allowing GO (Pty) Ltd to exercise significant influence over STOP (Pty) Ltd. There was no adjustment to bring the carrying amounts of the net assets to their fair values. The net assets were represented by the following equity:

	CU
Ordinary shares	70,000
Retained earnings	30,000

GO (Pty) Ltd paid extra for the shares (included in the CU35,000 purchase price) because the shares were issued cum-div with a dividend of CU2,000 (meaning that dividends of CU2,000, declared before the purchase of the share, which relates to the shares will only be paid after the shares transfer to GO (Pty) Ltd. The dividend of CU2,000 was declared on 15 January 20X7. The associate earned no profit (incurred no loss) or other comprehensive income (expense) during the year. GO (Pty) Ltd accounts for the investment in associate at cost in its separate financial statements and applies the equity method to account for the investment in associate in its group financial statements.

You are required to:
Prepare the pro forma journal entries necessary to prepare financial statements for the GO (Pty) Ltd Group at 31 December 20X7.

QUESTION 3

PROFIT (Pty) Ltd purchased 24% of the equity shares and voting rights of LOSS (Pty) Ltd for CU25,000 on 1 January 20X7. The purchase of the equity shares allowed PROFIT (Pty) Ltd to exercise significant influence over LOSS (Pty) Ltd from 1 January 20X7. The carrying amounts of the net identifiable assets equated their fair values at 1 January 20X7. PROFIT (Pty) Ltd accounts for its investment in associate at cost in its separate financial statements. The net assets of LOSS (Pty) Ltd were represented by the following equity:

	CU
Ordinary shares	80,000
Retained earnings	20,000

LOSS (Pty) Ltd earned a profit of CU35,000 during the year ended 31 December 20X7.

You are required to:
Prepare the pro forma journal entries necessary to prepare the financial statements of the Profit (Pty) Ltd Group at 31 December 20X7.

CHAPTER 20
CONSOLIDATED AND SEPARATE FINANCIAL STATEMENTS

ILLUSTRATIVE DISCLOSURE [EXTRACT]

IFRS ref		Notes	20X7	20X6
			CU	CU
	Profit after tax	3	250,000	200,000
S9.21 & IFRS 10 Pb94	- Attributed to parent entity		180,000	150,000
	- Attributed to non-controlling interest		70,000	50,000
	Total comprehensive income		350,000	275,000
S9.22 & IFRS 10 Pb94	- Attributed to parent entity		230,000	210,000
	- Attributed to non-controlling interest		120,000	65,000
		Notes	20X7	20X6
	Non-current assets			
	Goodwill		10,800	12,000
	Equity			
	Ordinary shares		100,000	50,000
	Retained earnings		400,000	300,000
S9.20 & IFRS 10 p.22	Non-controlling interest		195,000	75,000
Notes to the consolidated financial statements for the period ended				

IFRS ref		Business combinations during the period
S19.25 IFRS 3 p.59		Parent (Pty) Ltd purchased 80% of the equity shares and voting rights of Subsidiary (Pty) Ltd on 01 January 20X8, for CU100,000 in cash, which resulted in Parent (Pty) Ltd exercising control over Subsidiary (Pty) Ltd. No goodwill was recognised at acquisition. The following table lists the recognised identifiable assets and liabilities at the acquisition date:

	Subsidiary (Pty) Ltd
	DR/(CR)
	CU
Investment in subsidiary	
Property, plant & equipment	140,000
Intangible assets	30,000
Inventory	25,000
Accounts receivable	12,000
Cash	5,000
Long-term loan	(82,000)
Deferred tax liability	(20,000)
Accounts payable	(10,000)

IFRS ref		
S19.24 & IFRS 3 p.B67		**Goodwill**
		Goodwill is amortised over a useful life of 10 years to a nil residual value. The following table provides a reconciliation of goodwill from the beginning to the end of the financial year:

	CU
Balance 01 January 20X8	12,000
Amortisation	(1,200)
Balance 31 December 20X8	**10,800**

20.1 INTRODUCTION

Entities often invest in the ordinary shares of other entities. Depending on the degree of control (or lack thereof) associated with the shareholding, different accounting practices and principles apply. One of the shareholding positions could be a relationship in which an investor controls an investee. Although the definitions of control for an asset and an entity differ, it is easy to think of the accounting requirements in the consolidated financial statements as follows. Suppose that entity A controls the decision-making of entity B, it would seem logical that it also controls entity B's assets. If it controls entity B's assets, it would make sense that it incorporates entity B's assets into its financial statements as part of the other assets that it controls. This is the basic principle of preparing consolidated financial statements.

20.2 LEARNING OUTCOMES

This chapter is designed to *introduce* the accounting principles and practices for separate and consolidated financial statements where a parent–subsidiary relationship exists. Upon completion of this chapter you should be able to:
(a)   identify and classify relationships into parent–subsidiary relationships;
(b)   recognise the various elements of the financial statements in the separate and consolidated financial statements;
(c)   measure the various elements of the financial statements in the separate and consolidated financial statements; and
(d)   present and disclose the various elements associated with the parent–subsidiary relationship in the separate and consolidated financial statements.

20.3 DEFINITIONS

The definitions for the important concepts and terms used in IFRS for SMEs are found in Appendix B – *Glossary of terms* in IFRS for SMEs. The following important definitions related to separate and consolidated financial statements are applicable:

- **Consolidated financial statements:** The financial statements of a parent and its subsidiaries presented as those of a single economic entity

- **Control (of an entity):** The power to govern the operating and financial policies of an entity so as to obtain benefits from its activities

- **Goodwill:** Future economic benefits arising from assets that are not capable of being individually identified and separately recognised

- **Non-controlling interest:** The equity in a subsidiary not attributable, directly or indirectly, to a parent

- **Separate financial statements:** Those presented by an entity, in which the entity could elect, in accordance with paragraphs s9.25 – 26, to account for its investments in subsidiaries, jointly controlled entities and associates either at cost less impairment, at fair value with changes in fair value recognised in profit or loss, or using the equity method following the procedures in paragraph s14.8.

20.4 SCOPE AND OBJECTIVES
Section 9 (IFRS 3, IFRS 7, IFRS 10 and IAS 27) provides guidance for accounting and disclosure for all parent–subsidiary relationships.

20.5 CLASSIFICATION AS A PARENT–SUBSIDIARY RELATIONSHIP
A parent–subsidiary relationship exists when one entity has control over another entity. Control can be gained in various ways, but there is a presumption that it exists where an entity has more than half of the voting power of another entity (s9.25). Control also exists where the parent does not own more than half of the voting power of an entity, but it has (s9.25):
(a)   power over more than half of the voting rights by virtue of an agreement with other investors;
(b)   power to govern the financial and operating policies of the entity under a statute or an agreement;
(c)   power to appoint or remove the majority of the members of the board of directors or equivalent governing body and control of the entity is by that board or body; or
(d)   power to cast the majority of votes at meetings of the board of directors or equivalent governing body and control of the entity is by that board or body.

One also has to consider whether the entity holds currently exercisable options, for instance to acquire additional shares which can give it control (s9.26).

Illustrative Example 20.1: Determining control
Company A has the following investments and relationships:
(a)   60% of the equity shares and voting rights of company B. Control over company B is by a majority of shareholder voting rights;
(b)   40% of the equity shares and voting rights of company C. Company A can also appoint six of the eight directors on the board of directors of company C. Control over company C is by the board of directors; and

(c)   70% of the equity shares and voting rights of company D. Company A has contracted with a third party in which company A receives certain benefits from the third party in exchange for control of company D. Control over company D is by a majority of shareholder voting rights.

You are required to:
Discuss which of the above relationships are between a parent (company A) and its subsidiary.

Suggested solution:

Relationship	Discussion
Company A and company B	Control over company B is through shareholder voting rights. As company A has a majority of the voting rights, company A controls company B and a parent–subsidiary relationship exists (s9.5).
Company A and company C	Control over company C is through the board of directors. As company A can appoint a majority of the directors to the board, it controls the board and company C. As such, a parent–subsidiary relationship exists (s9.5(c)). It should be noted that even though company A does not have the majority of the equity shares and shareholder voting rights, it still controls company C, as control is not established through shareholder voting rights for company C.
Company A and company D	A majority of shareholder voting rights establishes control over company D. Company A has transferred its right to control company A via an agreement with a third party. Therefore, company A does not control company D and no parent–subsidiary relationship exists.

20.6   PREPARING THE FINANCIAL STATEMENTS

A parent should prepare consolidated financial statements for all of its subsidiaries except as follows:

(a)   when the parent is itself a subsidiary; and

(b)   when its ultimate parent (or any intermediate parent) produces consolidated general purpose financial statements that comply with full IFRS or IFRS for SMEs.

Also, if a subsidiary is acquired with the intention of selling or disposing of it within one year from its acquisition date, then its parent does not have to consolidate the subsidiary (s9.3A).

The entity prepares separate and consolidated financial statements if it has a subsidiary during the year. In other words, a parent produces two figures (and possibly additional line items) – one set for the separate financial statements and one set for the consolidated financial statements. We will begin our discussion with the separate financial statements.

20.6.1 Separate financial statements

In most instances, the parent making an equity investment in the subsidiary achieves control. This investment is an asset in the separate financial statements of the entity. The investment is initially accounted for at cost. Subsequently, the investment is accounted for in accordance with one of the following accounting policies, which it has to apply consistently to all investments in the same class (subsidiaries, associates or jointly controlled entities) (s9.26 and IAS 27 p.10):

(a)   at cost less impairment;

(b)   at fair value with changes in fair value recognised in profit or loss; or

(c)   using the equity method (which is the method used to account for investments in associates –this method is covered in depth in Chapter 5, so we will not focus on it here).

Illustrative Example 20.2: Separate financial statements

Company A purchases 100% of the equity shares and voting rights of company B for CU100,000 on 01 January 20X7. The fair value of the equity shares was CU110,000 on 31 December 20X7.

You are required to:

Prepare an extract of the separate statement of financial position of company A as at 31 December 20X7. Company A has elected a policy of accounting for its investments in subsidiaries at (two separate scenarios):

(a)   cost less impairment; and

(b)   fair value.

Suggested solution:

(i) Cost:

Company A Statement of financial position as at 31 December 20X7	
	CU
ASSETS	
Non-current assets	
Investment in subsidiary	100,000

(ii) Fair value:

Company A Statement of financial position as at 31 December 20X7	
	CU
ASSETS	
Non-current assets	
Investment in subsidiary	110,000

20.6.2 Consolidated financial statements
20.6.2.1 The consolidation process

The basic principle when presenting consolidated financial statement is to present the financial information of the group as those of a single economic entity (s9.13 and IFRS 10 p.). The following consolidation procedures are followed (s9.13 and IFRS 10 p.B86):

(a) combine the **financial statements** of the parent and its subsidiaries line by line by adding together like items of assets, **liabilities**, **equity**, **income** and **expenses**;

(b) eliminate the **carrying amount** of the parent's investment in each subsidiary and the parent's portion of equity of each subsidiary;

(c) measure and present **non-controlling interest** in the **profit or loss** of consolidated subsidiaries for the **reporting period** separately from the interest of the **owners** of the parent; and

(d) measure and present non-controlling interest in the net assets of consolidated subsidiaries separately from the parent shareholders' equity in them. Non-controlling interest in the net assets consists of:

   (i) the amount of the non-controlling interest at the date of the original combination calculated in accordance with section 19 – *Business combinations and goodwill*; and

   (ii) the non-controlling interest's share of changes in equity since the date of the combination.

Illustrative Example 20.3: Consolidated financial statements

Company A purchases 100% of the equity shares and voting rights of company B for CU100,000 on 01 January 20X7. At the date of acquisition, the net identifiable assets of Company B had carrying amounts which equated their fair values. The following trial balance of Company A and Company B are provided at the date of acquisition:

	Company A	Company B
	DR/(CR)	DR/(CR)
Account:	CU	CU
Investment in subsidiary	100,000	0
Property, plant & equipment	1,000,000	140,000
Intangible assets	700,000	30,000
Inventory	200,000	25,000
Accounts receivable	20,000	12,000
Cash	15,000	5,000
Ordinary shares	(1,000,000)	(70,000)
Retained earnings	(700,000)	(30,000)
Long-term loan	(241,000)	(82,000)
Deferred tax liability	(80,000)	(20,000)
Accounts payable	(14,000)	(10,000)

You are required to:

Prepare the trial balance (TB) for the consolidated entity Company A Group.

Suggested solution:

	Company A	Company B	s9.13(a)	s9.13(b)	TB
	DR/(CR)	DR/(CR)	DR/(CR)	DR/(CR)	DR/(CR)
Account:	CU	CU	CU	CU	CU
Investment in subsidiary	100,000	0	100,000	(100,000)	**0**
Property, plant & equipment	1,000,000	140,000	1,140,000		**1,140,000**
Intangible assets	700,000	30,000	730,000		**730,000**
Inventory	200,000	25,000	225,000		**225,000**
Accounts receivable	20,000	12,000	32,000		**32,000**

Cash	15,000	5,000	20,000		**20,000**
Ordinary shares	(1,000,000)	(70,000)	(1,070,000)	70,000	**(1,000,000)**
Retained earnings	(700,000)	(30,000)	(730,000)	30,000	**(700,000)**
Long-term loan	(241,000)	(82,000)	(323,000)		**(323,000)**
Deferred tax liability	(80,000)	(20,000)	(100,000)		**(100,000)**
Accounts payable	(14,000)	(10,000)	(24,000)		**(24,000)**

Notes:
1. You will notice in the column headed s9.13(a) that the trial balances of the two entities (parent and subsidiary) are merely added together. However, the new combined trial balance, which would ideally have been that of the combined entity, shows the combined entity having an investment in itself, as it includes the ordinary shares of the subsidiary which are held by the parent (so intragroup) and the retained earnings which were acquired (not earned).
2. Therefore, the column headed s9.13(b) eliminates these amounts from the final group trial balance (the bold amounts in the column headed TB).

Any income and expenses are allocated to the owners of the subsidiary. Therefore, when the shares in the subsidiary are wholly owned by the parent, all of the profit or loss will be attributed to the parent.

Illustrative Example 20.4: Consolidated financial statements

Company A purchases 100% of the equity shares and voting rights of Company B for CU100,000 on 01 January 20X7. At the date of acquisition, the net identifiable assets of Company B had carrying amounts which equated their fair values. The following trial balances of Company A and Company B are provided at the date of acquisition:

	Company A DR/(CR)	Company B DR/(CR)
Account:	CU	CU
Investment in subsidiary	100,000	0
Property, plant & equipment	1,000,000	140,000
Intangible assets	700,000	30,000
Inventory	200,000	25,000
Accounts receivable	20,000	12,000
Cash	165,000	45,000
Ordinary shares	(1,000,000)	(70,000)
Retained earnings	(700,000)	(30,000)
Revenue	(215,000)	(54,000)

Cost of sales	65,000	14,000
Long-term loan	(241,000)	(82,000)
Deferred tax liability	(80,000)	(20,000)
Accounts payable	(14,000)	(10,000)

You are required to:

Prepare the trial balance for the consolidated entity Company A Group.

Suggested solution:

Account:	Company A	Company B	s9.13(a)	s9.13(b)	TB
	DR/(CR)	DR/(CR)	DR/(CR)	DR/(CR)	DR/(CR)
	CU	CU	CU	CU	CU
Investment in subsidiary	100,000	0	100,000	(100,000)	**0**
Property, plant & equipment	1,000,000	140,000	1,140,000		**1,140,000**
Intangible assets	700,000	30,000	730,000		**730,000**
Inventory	200,000	25,000	225,000		**225,000**
Accounts receivable	20,000	12,000	32,000		**32,000**
Cash	165,000	45,000	210,000		**210,000**
Ordinary shares	(1,000,000)	(70,000)	(1,070,000)	70,000	**(1,000,000)**
Retained earnings	(700,000)	(30,000)	(730,000)	30,000	**(700,000)**
Revenue[3]	(215,000)	(54,000)	(269,000)		**(269,000)**
Cost of sales[3]	65,000	14,000	79,000		**79,000**
Long-term loan	(241,000)	(82,000)	(323,000)		**(323,000)**
Deferred tax liability	(80,000)	(20,000)	(100,000)		**(100,000)**
Accounts payable	(14,000)	(10,000)	(24,000)		**(24,000)**

Notes:
1. You will notice in the column headed s9.13(a) that the trial balances of the two entities (parent and subsidiary) are merely added together. However, the new combined trial balance, which would ideally have been that of the combined entity, shows the combined entity having an investment in itself, as it includes the ordinary shares of the subsidiary which are held by the parent (so intragroup) and the retained earnings which were acquired (not earned).
2. Therefore, the column headed s9.13(b) eliminates these amounts from the final group trial balance (the bold amounts in the column headed TB).
3. This example assumes that the profit or loss consists only of revenue and cost of sales and that there are no other items of other comprehensive income.

20.6.2.2 Goodwill and the excess of net asset over cost

Although the objective of this chapter is not to cover section 9 – *Consolidated and separate financial statements* and section 19 – *Business combinations and goodwill* in depth, an understanding of goodwill (and the excess of the net identifiable assets recognised over the cost of the investment) is imperative to an understanding of consolidated financial statements.

Goodwill represents the excess consideration over the net identifiable assets recognised. No purchaser would pay for value that does not exist; the goodwill arises because the accounting principles do not allow all value-producing resources to be recognised. For instance, some assets are not recognised because they are not separately identifiable from a business, because it is not probable that they will result in future economic benefits or because they do not have a cost or value that can be measured with sufficient reliability. Just because they are not recognised for accounting purposes, does not mean that their value does not exist or that a willing buyer and seller will not be willing to pay or demand a price for the resource. Goodwill can also arise from a shareholder being willing to pay a premium for obtaining control over the business. However, this premium also has value in that it allows the controlling party to direct the relevant activities of the entity and hopefully create more value for the controlling party.

Illustrative Example 20.5: Consolidated financial statements

Assume the same information as in Illustrative Example 20.3, except that Company A purchased 100% of the equity shares and voting rights of Company B for CU120,000 on 01 January 20X7. At the date of acquisition, the net identifiable assets of Company B had carrying amounts which equated their fair values. The following trial balances of Company A and Company B are provided at the date of acquisition:

	Company A	Company B
	DR/(CR)	DR/(CR)
Account:	CU	CU
Investment in subsidiary	120,000	0
Property, plant & equipment	1,000,000	140,000
Intangible assets	700,000	30,000
Inventory	200,000	25,000
Accounts receivable	20,000	12,000
Cash	15,000	5,000
Ordinary shares	(1,000,000)	(70,000)
Retained earnings	(720,000)	(30,000)
Long-term loan	(241,000)	(82,000)
Deferred tax liability	(80,000)	(20,000)
Accounts payable	(14,000)	(10,000)

You are required to:

Prepare the trial balance for the consolidated entity Company A Group.

Suggested solution:

Account:	Company A DR/(CR) CU	Company B DR/(CR) CU	s9.13(a) DR/(CR) CU	s9.13(b) DR/(CR) CU	TB DR/(CR) CU
Investment in subsidiary	120,000	0	120,000	(120,000)	**0**
Goodwill	0	0	0	20,000[3]	**20,000**
Property, plant & equipment	1,000,000	140,000	1,140,000		**1,140,000**
Intangible assets	700,000	30,000	730,000		**730,000**
Inventory	200,000	25,000	225,000		**225,000**
Accounts receivable	20,000	12,000	32,000		**32,000**
Cash	15,000	5,000	20,000		**20,000**
Ordinary shares	(1,000,000)	(70,000)	(1,070,000)	70,000	**(1,000,000)**
Retained earnings	(720,000)	(30,000)	(750,000)	30,000	**(720,000)**
Long-term loan	(241,000)	(82,000)	(323,000)		**(323,000)**
Deferred tax liability	(80,000)	(20,000)	(100,000)		**(100,000)**
Accounts payable	(14,000)	(10,000)	(24,000)		**(24,000)**

Notes:

1. You will notice in the column headed s9.13(a) that the trial balances of the two entities (parent and subsidiary) are merely added together. However, the new combined trial balance, which would ideally have been that of the combined entity, shows the combined entity having an investment in itself, with no goodwill, as it includes the ordinary shares of the subsidiary which are held by the parent (so intragroup) and the retained earnings which were acquired (not earned).
2. Therefore, the column headed s9.13(b) eliminates these amounts from the final group trial balance (the bold amounts in the column headed TB).
3. The goodwill is calculated as the difference between the consideration of CU120,000 and the recognised identifiable net assets (equal to the equity) CU100,000 (CU70,000 of ordinary shares plus CU30,000 retained earnings).

When an entity pays consideration which is less than the fair value of the net identifiable assets, the entity recognises a bargain purchase in profit or loss (s19.24 and IFRS 3 p.34) after reassessing whether it has correctly identified all of the assets acquired and liabilities assumed (s19.24 and IFRS 3 p.36).

Illustrative Example 20.6: Consolidated financial statements

Assume the same information as in Illustrative Example 20.3, except that Company A purchased 100% of the equity shares and voting rights of Company B for CU90,000 on 01 January 20X7. At the date of acquisition, the net identifiable assets of Company B had carrying amounts which equated their fair values. The following trial balances of Company A and Company B are provided at the date of acquisition:

	Company A DR/(CR)	Company B DR/(CR)
Account:	CU	CU
Investment in subsidiary	90,000	0
Property, plant & equipment	1,000,000	140,000
Intangible assets	700,000	30,000
Inventory	200,000	25,000
Accounts receivable	20,000	12,000
Cash	15,000	5,000
Ordinary shares	(1,000,000)	(70,000)
Retained earnings	(690,000)	(30,000)
Long-term loan	(241,000)	(82,000)
Deferred tax liability	(80,000)	(20,000)
Accounts payable	(14,000)	(10,000)

You are required to:
Prepare the trial balance for the consolidated entity Company A Group.

Suggested solution:

	Company A DR/(CR)	Company B DR/(CR)	s9.13(a) DR/(CR)	s9.13(b) DR/(CR)	TB DR/(CR)
Account:	CU	CU	CU	CU	CU
Investment in subsidiary	90,000	0	90,000	(90,000)	0
Property, plant & equipment	1,000,000	140,000	1,140,000		1,140,000
Intangible assets	700,000	30,000	730,000		730,000

Inventory	200,000	25,000	225,000		**225,000**
Accounts receivable	20,000	12,000	32,000		**32,000**
Cash	15,000	5,000	20,000		**20,000**
Ordinary shares	(1,000,000)	(70,000)	(1,070,000)	70,000	**(1,000,000)**
Retained earnings	(690,000)	(30,000)	(720,000)	30,000	**(690,000)**
Profit for the year	0	0	0	(10,000)[3]	**(10,000)**
Long-term loan	(241,000)	(82,000)	(323,000)		**(323,000)**
Deferred tax liability	(80,000)	(20,000)	(100,000)		**(100,000)**
Accounts payable	(14,000)	(10,000)	(24,000)		**(24,000)**

Notes:

1. You will notice in the column headed s9.13(a) that the trial balances of the two entities (parent and subsidiary) are merely added together. However, the new combined trial balance, which would ideally have been that of the combined entity, shows the combined entity having an investment in itself, with no goodwill, as it includes the ordinary shares of the subsidiary which are held by the parent (so intragroup) and the retained earnings which were acquired (not earned).

2. Therefore, the column headed s9.13(b) eliminates these amounts from the final group trial balance (the bold amounts in the column headed TB).

3. The surplus recognised in profit or loss is calculated as the difference between the consideration of CU90,000 and the recognised identifiable net assets (equal to the equity) CU100,000 (CU70,000 of ordinary shares plus CU30,000 retained earnings).

20.6.2.3 Non-controlling interest

The examples above all assume that the parent purchased the entire shareholding and voting rights in the subsidiary. This may not necessarily always be the case. When the parent invests in the equity of a subsidiary but does not purchase the entire shareholding, the other shareholders are referred to as the non-controlling interest (s9.13(d) and IFRS 3 p.10). Any non-controlling interest is recognised at the proportionate share of the recognised identifiable net assets of the subsidiary (s19.14 and IFRS 3 p.19).

Note that IFRS 3 p.19(a) allows the entity the choice of recognising the non-controlling interest at fair value at acquisition.

Illustrative Example 20.7: Consolidated financial statements

Assume the same information as in Illustrative Example 20.3, except that Company A purchases 80% of the equity shares and voting rights of Company B for CU80,000 on 01 January 20X7. At the date of acquisition, the net identifiable assets of Company B had carrying amounts which equated their fair values. The following trial balances of Company A and Company B are provided at the date of acquisition:

	Company A DR/(CR)	Company B DR/(CR)
Account:	CU	CU
Investment in subsidiary	80,000	0
Property, plant & equipment	1,000,000	140,000
Intangible assets	700,000	30,000
Inventory	200,000	25,000
Accounts receivable	20,000	12,000
Cash	15,000	5,000
Ordinary shares	(1,000,000)	(70,000)
Retained earnings	(680,000)	(30,000)
Long-term loan	(241,000)	(82,000)
Deferred tax liability	(80,000)	(20,000)
Accounts payable	(14,000)	(10,000)

You are required to:

Prepare the trial balance for the consolidated entity Company A Group.

	Company A DR/(CR)	Company B DR/(CR)	s9.13(a) DR/(CR)	s9.13(b) DR/(CR)	TB DR/(CR)
Account:	CU	CU	CU	CU	CU
Investment in subsidiary	80,000	0	80,000	(80,000)	0
Property, plant & equipment	1,000,000	140,000	1,140,000		**1,140,000**
Intangible assets	700,000	30,000	730,000		**730,000**
Inventory	200,000	25,000	225,000		**225,000**
Accounts receivable	20,000	12,000	32,000		**32,000**
Cash	15,000	5,000	20,000		**20,000**
Ordinary shares	(1,000,000)	(70,000)	(1,070,000)	70,000	**(1,000,000)**
Retained earnings	(680,000)	(30,000)	(710,000)	30,000	**(680,000)**

Non-controlling interest	0	0	0	$(20,000)^3$	**(20,000)**
Long-term loan	(241,000)	(82,000)	(323,000)		**(323,000)**
Deferred tax liability	(80,000)	(20,000)	(100,000)		**(100,000)**
Accounts payable	(14,000)	(10,000)	(24,000)		**(24,000)**

Notes:
1. You will notice in the column headed s9.13(a) that the trial balances of the two entities (parent and subsidiary) are merely added together. However, the new combined trial balance, which would ideally have been that of the combined entity, shows the combined entity having an investment in itself, as it includes the ordinary shares of the subsidiary which are held by the parent (so intragroup) and the retained earnings which were acquired (not earned).
2. Therefore, the column headed s9.13(b) eliminates these amounts from the final group trial balance (the bold amounts in the column headed TB).
3. The non-controlling interest is calculated as being 20% (the parent, Company A, only purchased 80% of the equity shares of Company B) × CU100,000 (the recognised identifiable net assets of Company B which are equal to the equity of CU70,000 ordinary shares plus CU30,000 retained earnings).

As all items of income and expense must be attributed to the owners of the subsidiary, any non-controlling interest will share in these items of income and expense in proportion to their ownership interests (s9.14 and IFRS 10 p.B94). Therefore, 100% of the profit or loss and other comprehensive income is recognised in the relevant statement and once the non-controlling interest is allocated its proportion, the remaining portion is automatically allocated to the parent and will total its share in the ownership of the subsidiary.

Illustrative Example 20.8: Consolidated financial statements

Assume the same information as in Illustrative Example 20.3, except that Company A purchases 80% of the equity shares and voting rights of Company B for CU80,000 on 01 January 20X7. At the date of acquisition, the net identifiable assets of Company B had carrying amounts which equated their fair values. The following trial balances of Company A and Company B are provided at the date of acquisition:

	Company A DR/(CR)	Company B DR/(CR)
Account:	**CU**	**CU**
Investment in subsidiary	80,000	0
Property, plant & equipment	1,000,000	140,000

Intangible assets	700,000	30,000
Inventory	200,000	25,000
Accounts receivable	20,000	12,000
Cash	165,000	45,000
Ordinary shares	(1,000,000)	(70,000)
Retained earnings	(680,000)	(30,000)
Revenue	(215,000)	(54,000)
Cost of sales	65,000	14,000
Long-term loan	(241,000)	(82,000)
Deferred tax liability	(80,000)	(20,000)
Accounts payable	(14,000)	(10,000)

You are required to:
Prepare the trial balance for the consolidated entity Company A Group.

Suggested solution:

	Company A	Company B	s9.13(a)	s9.13(b)	TB
	DR/(CR)	DR/(CR)	DR/(CR)	DR/(CR)	DR/(CR)
Account:	CU	CU	CU	CU	CU
Investment in subsidiary	80,000	0	80,000	(80,000)	0
Property, plant & equipment	1,000,000	140,000	1,140,000		**1,140,000**
Intangible assets	700,000	30,000	730,000		**730,000**
Inventory	200,000	25,000	225,000		**225,000**
Accounts receivable	20,000	12,000	32,000		**32,000**
Cash	165,000	45,000	210,000		**210,000**
Ordinary shares	(1,000,000)	(70,000)	(1,070,000)	70,000	**(1,000,000)**
Retained earnings	(680,000)	(30,000)	(710,000)	30,000	**(680,000)**
Revenue	(215,000)	(54,000)	(269,000)		**(269,000)**
Cost of sales	65,000	14,000	79,000		**79,000**

Profit attributed to non-controlling interest[3]	0	0	0	8,000	**8,000**
Non-controlling interest	0	0	0	$(28,000)^3$	**(28,000)**
Long-term loan	(241,000)	(82,000)	(323,000)		**(323,000)**
Deferred tax liability	(80,000)	(20,000)	(100,000)		**(100,000)**
Accounts payable	(14,000)	(10,000)	(24,000)		**(24,000)**

Notes:
1. You will notice in the column headed s9.13(a) that the trial balances of the two entities (parent and subsidiary) are merely added together. However, the new combined trial balance, which would ideally have been that of the combined entity, shows the combined entity having an investment in itself, as it includes the ordinary shares of the subsidiary which are held by the parent (so intragroup) and the retained earnings which were acquired (not earned).
2. Therefore, the column headed s9.13(b) eliminates these amounts from the final group trial balance (the bold amounts in the column headed TB).
3. The non-controlling interest consists of two adjustments: (i) to create the at-acquisition non-controlling interest of CU20,000 which is calculated as being 20% (the parent, Company A, only purchased 80% of the equity shares of Company B) × CU100,000 (the recognised identifiable net assets of Company B which are equal to the equity of CU70,000 ordinary shares plus CU30,000 retained earnings), and (ii) to attribute the non-controlling interest share in the profits of the subsidiary of CU8,000 (profit of CU40,000 (made up of revenue of CU54,000 – cost of sales of CU14,000) × 20% ownership interest).
4. The profit attributed to the non-controlling interest line item is not recognised in any of the components of the financial statements, but is presented on the face of the statement of profit or loss and other comprehensive income.

20.6.2.4 The role of pro forma journal entries

The financial statements used to prepare the consolidated financial statements are the complete and final separate financial statements of the parent and the subsidiary. Therefore, the adjustments made to effect the consolidation in the column titled 's9.13(b)' in the illustrative examples above cannot be made to the separate financial statements of either the parent or the subsidiary, as this would adjust their final separate financial statements. Because of this, the adjustments, which are required, are processed in what is called pro forma journal entries. These pro forma journal entries are made outside the individual companies' financial statements and have to be made every year. The pro-forma journal entries are therefore only made for purposes of effecting the consolidation.

Illustrative Example 20.9: Consolidated financial statements

Company A purchases 100% of the equity shares and voting rights of Company B for CU100,000 on 01 January 20X7. At the date of acquisition, the net identifiable assets of Company B had carrying amounts which equated their fair values. The following trial balances of Company A and Company B are provided at the date of acquisition:

	Company A DR/(CR)	Company B DR/(CR)
Account:	CU	CU
Investment in subsidiary	100,000	0
Property, plant & equipment	1,000,000	140,000
Intangible assets	700,000	30,000
Inventory	200,000	25,000
Accounts receivable	20,000	12,000
Cash	· 15,000	5,000
Ordinary shares	(1,000,000)	(70,000)
Retained earnings	(700,000)	(30,000)
Long-term loan	(241,000)	(82,000)
Deferred tax liability	(80,000)	(20,000)
Accounts payable	(14,000)	(10,000)

You are required to:
(a)   Prepare the trial balance for the consolidated entity Company A Group.
(b)   Prepare the pro forma journal entries necessary to consolidate Companies A and B.

Suggested solution:
(i)   Trial balance

	Company A DR/(CR)	Company B DR/(CR)	s9.13(a) DR/(CR)	s9.13(b) DR/(CR)	TB DR/(CR)
Account:	CU	CU	CU	CU	CU
Investment in subsidiary	100,000	0	100,000	(100,000)	**0**
Property, plant & equipment	1,000,000	140,000	1,140,000		**1,140,000**
Intangible assets	700,000	30,000	730,000		**730,000**
Inventory	200,000	25,000	225,000		**225,000**

Accounts receivable	20,000	12,000	32,000		**32,000**
Cash	15,000	5,000	20,000		**20,000**
Ordinary shares	(1,000,000)	(70,000)	(1,070,000)	70,000	**(1,000,000)**
Retained earnings	(700,000)	(30,000)	(730,000)	30,000	**(700,000)**
Long-term loan	(241,000)	(82,000)	(323,000)		**(323,000)**
Deferred tax liability	(80,000)	(20,000)	(100,000)		**(100,000)**
Accounts payable	(14,000)	(10,000)	(24,000)		**(24,000)**

Notes:
1. You will notice in the column headed s9.13(a) that the trial balances of the two entities (parent and subsidiary) are merely added together. However, the new combined trial balance, which would ideally have been that of the combined entity, shows the combined entity having an investment in itself, as it includes the ordinary shares of the subsidiary which are held by the parent (so intragroup) and the retained earnings which were acquired (not earned).
2. Therefore, the column headed s9 13(b) eliminates these amounts from the final group trial balance (the bold amounts in the column headed TB).

(ii)   Pro forma journal entries

		CU	CU
Dr	Ordinary shares (Company B)	70,000	
Dr	Retained earnings (Company B)	30,000	
Cr	Investment in subsidiary (Company A)		100,000
[Eliminating the equity of and the related investment in Company B]			

20.7   DISCLOSURE
The following disclosures should be made in consolidated financial statements (s9.23):
(a)   the fact that the statements are consolidated financial statements;
(b)   the basis for concluding that control exists when the parent does not own, directly or indirectly through subsidiaries, more than half of the voting power;
(c)   any difference in the reporting date of the financial statements of the parent and its subsidiaries used in the preparation of the consolidated financial statements; and
(d)   the nature and extent of any significant restrictions (eg resulting from borrowing arrangements or regulatory requirements) on the ability of subsidiaries to transfer funds to the parent in the form of cash dividends or to repay loans.

In terms of section 9.23A, a parent entity shall disclose the carrying amount of investments in subsidiaries that are not consolidated at the reporting date, in total, either in the statement of financial position or in the notes.

For each business combination during the period, the acquirer shall disclose the following (s19.25):
(a)   the names and descriptions of the combining entities or businesses;
(b)   the acquisition date;
(c)   the percentage of voting equity instruments acquired;
(d)   the cost of the combination and a description of the components of that cost (such as cash, equity instruments and debt instruments);
(e)   the amounts recognised at the acquisition date for each class of the acquiree's assets, liabilities and contingent liabilities, including goodwill;
(f)   the amount of any excess recognised in profit or loss in accordance with paragraph 19.24 and the line item in the statement of comprehensive income (and in the **income statement**, if presented) in which the excess is recognised; and
(g)   a qualitative description of the factors that make up the goodwill recognised, such as expected synergies from combining operations of the acquiree and the acquirer, or intangible assets or other items not recognised in accordance with paragraph 19.15.

An acquirer shall disclose the following for all business combinations (s19.26): the useful lives used for goodwill and a reconciliation of the **carrying amount** of goodwill at the beginning and end of the reporting period, showing separately:
(a)   changes arising from new business combinations;
(b)   impairment losses;
(c)   disposals of previously acquired businesses; and
(d)   other changes.

This reconciliation need not be presented for prior periods.

Note that the primary disclosure requirements for interests in subsidiaries, accounted for in terms of full IFRS, are contained in IFRS 12 – Disclosure of interests in other entities. The disclosure requirements in full IFRS are a lot more onerous than in IFRS for SMEs. As the focus of this text is on IFRS for SMEs, the authors do not cover the requirements of IFRS 12.

SELF-ASSESSMENT
Multiple choice questions: Testing principles of accounting for consolidated and separate financial statements

1. The parent in a parent–subsidiary relationship is the entity that:

(a) is controlled by the investor	
(b) controls the investee	
(c) jointly controls the investee	
(d) exercises significant influence over the investee	

2. Goodwill represents the:

(a) amount paid for the investment in the subsidiary	
(b) amount attributed to those parties who do not control the investee	
(c) excess of the consideration over the recognised identifiable net assets of the subsidiary	
(d) adjustment necessary to adjust individual assets to fair value	

3. The excess of the recognised identifiable net assets of the subsidiary over the consideration transferred is recognised in:

(a) the statement of financial position	
(b) other comprehensive income	
(c) the statement of cash flows	
(d) the statement of profit or loss	

4. Control is defined as:

(a) the power to govern the operating policies of an entity so as to obtain benefits from its activities	
(b) the power to govern the financial policies of an entity so as to obtain benefits from its activities	
(c) the power to influence the operating and financial policies of an entity so as to obtain benefits from its activities	
(d) the power to govern the operating and financial policies of an entity so as to obtain benefits from its activities	

5. The following is not given as an example of when control might exist in IFRS for SMEs:

(a) a significant amount of transactions between the two entities	
(b) power over more than half of the voting rights by virtue of an agreement with other investors	
(c) power to govern the financial and operating policies of the entity under a statute or an agreement	
(d) power to cast the majority of votes at meetings of the board of directors or equivalent governing body and control of the entity is by that board or body	

6. The following is not an option when accounting for an investment in a subsidiary in the separate financial statements of the parent:

(a) equity accounting	
(b) cost	
(c) net realisable value	
(d) fair value	

7. Non-controlling interest should be measured as follows at acquisition date in terms of IFRS for SMEs:

(a) fair value	
(b) proportionate share of the recognised net identifiable assets	
(c) fair value less costs to sell	
(d) none of the above	

8. The following is the first step in the consolidation process:

(a) combine the financial statements of parent and subsidiary line item by line item	
(b) create goodwill	
(c) create non-controlling interest	
(d) eliminate intercompany transactions	

9. Pro forma journal entries are recognised:

(a) in the financial statements of the parent	
(b) in the financial statements of the subsidiary	
(c) outside of the financial statements of either the parent or the subsidiary	
(d) in the financial statements of the parent and the subsidiary	

10. Profit or loss is attributable to:

(a) only the parent	
(b) the parent and subsidiary in proportion to their ownership interest	
(c) only the subsidiary	
(d) loan providers of the group	

Practical questions:
Application of principles to business scenarios

QUESTION 1

MRB (Pty) Ltd purchased 75% of the equity shares and voting rights of Subsi (Pty) Ltd on 01 January 20X7 for CU150,000 in cash. The acquisition of the equity shares allowed MRB (Pty) Ltd to exercise control over Subsi (Pty) Ltd. MRB (Pty) Ltd accounts for the investment in Subsi (Pty) Ltd at cost in its separate financial statements. The following trial balances are presented for each company on 01 January 20X7:

| | MRB (Pty) Ltd | Subsi (Pty) Ltd |
| | DR/(CR) | DR/(CR) |
Account:	CU	CU
Investment in subsidiary	150,000	0
Property, plant & equipment	900,000	230,000
Intangible assets	800,000	80,000
Inventory	250,000	27,000
Accounts receivable	40,000	15,000
Cash	28,000	7,000
Ordinary shares	(986,000)	(175,000)
Retained earnings	(600,000)	(25,000)
Long-term loan	(268,000)	(102,000)
Deferred tax liability	(280,000)	(45,000)
Accounts payable	(34,000)	(12,000)

You are required to:
(a)   Prepare the consolidated trial balance for the MRB (Pty) Ltd Group.
(b)   Prepare the pro forma journal entries necessary to account for the consolidated financial statements for the MRB (Pty) Ltd Group at 01 January 20X7.

QUESTION 2

Investor (Pty) Ltd purchased 90% of the equity shares and voting rights of Investee (Pty) Ltd for CU230,000 on 01 January 20X7. The acquisition of equity shares allowed Investor (Pty) Ltd to exercise control over Investee (Pty) Ltd from 01 January 20X7. Investor (Pty) Ltd accounts for its investment in Investee (Pty) Ltd at cost in its separate financial statements. The following trial balances are presented for each company on 01 January 20X7:

Account:	Investor (Pty) Ltd DR/(CR) CU	Investee (Pty) Ltd DR/(CR) CU
Investment in subsidiary	230,000	0
Property, plant & equipment	1,200,000	250,000
Intangible assets	500,000	70,000
Inventory	300,000	45,000
Accounts receivable	70,000	30,000
Cash	82,000	20,000
Ordinary shares	(1,000,000)	(150,000)
Retained earnings	(860,000)	(100,000)
Long-term loan	(350,000)	(80,000)
Deferred tax liability	(82,000)	(45,000)
Accounts payable	(90,000)	(40,000)

You are required to:
(a)   Prepare the consolidated trial balance for the Investor (Pty) Ltd Group.
(b)   Prepare the pro forma journal entries necessary to account for the consolidated financial statements for the Investor (Pty) Ltd Group at 01 January 20X7.

QUESTION 3

Acquirer (Pty) Ltd purchased 65% of the equity shares and voting rights of Acquiree (Pty) Ltd for CU197,000 on 01 January 20X7. The acquisition of equity shares allowed Acquirer (Pty) Ltd to exercise control over Acquiree (Pty) Ltd from 01 January 20X7. Investor (Pty) Ltd accounts for its investment in Acquiree (Pty) Ltd at cost in its separate financial statements. The following trial balances are presented for each company on 31 December 20X7:

Account:	Acquirer (Pty) Ltd DR/(CR) CU	Acquiree (Pty) Ltd DR/(CR) CU
Investment in subsidiary	197,000	0
Property, plant & equipment	850,000	550,000
Intangible assets	600,000	100,000
Inventory	350,000	25,000
Accounts receivable	50,000	20,000
Cash	42,000	10,000
Ordinary shares	(1,000,000)	(180,000)

Retained earnings 01 January 20X7	(400,000)	(120,000)
Revenue	(140,000)	(120,000)
Cost of sales	40,000	70,000
Long-term loan	(300,000)	(250,000)
Deferred tax liability	(250,000)	(88,000)
Accounts payable	(39,000)	(17,000)

You are required to:
(a)   Prepare the consolidated trial balance for the Acquirer (Pty) Ltd Group.
(b)   Prepare the pro forma journal entries necessary to account for the consolidated financial statements for the Acquirer (Pty) Ltd Group at 31 December 20X7.

CHAPTER 21
SHARE-BASED PAYMENTS

ILLUSTRATIVE DISCLOSURE [EXTRACT]

Statement of profit or loss and other comprehensive income for the year ended …				
IFRS ref		**Notes**	**20X7**	**20X6**
			CU	CU
S26.23 & IFRS 2 p.50	Profit from operations	3	100,000	50,000

Statement of financial position as at………………….				
		Notes	**20X7**	**20X6**
	Equity			
	Share-based payment reserve		1,500	0
	Non-current liabilities			
S26.3 & IFRS 2 p.7	Share-based payment liability		1,200	0

Notes to the financial statements for the period ended ……….				
IFRS ref				
	20	**Share-based payment arrangements**		
S26.18(a) & IFRS 2 p.46		The entity entered into two share-based payment transactions during the course of the year as detailed below:		
		1. The entity entered into an equity-settled share-based payment transaction with its CEO, Mr E Adams, in which Mr Adams was granted 5,000 share options that vest only if he remains in the employ of the entity for a period of five years from grant date. The fair equity-settled share-based payment transaction was measured with reference to the fair value of the equity instruments granted as the entity was unable to determine the fair value of the services received. The fair value of the equity instruments granted was determined with reference to an independent fair valuation of the entity performed on 20 December 20X7.		
S26.19 & IFRS 2 p.46				

S26.20 & IFRS 2 p.46 S26.23 & IFRS 2 p.50 S26.18(b) & IFRS 2 p.45		2. The entity entered into a cash-settled share-based payment transaction with its key supplier of equipment, Supplier (Pty) Ltd. The terms of the arrangement include that the entity received equipment and offered the supplier cash-settled share appreciation rights, which entitle the supplier to a cash payment based on the increase of the entity's shares between the grant date and 01 December 20X7, the date of settlement. The fair value of the liability was determined with reference to an independent valuation conducted on 15 December 20X7 as part of the valuation of the entity. The carrying amount of liabilities arising from share-based payment transactions at 31 December 20X7 is CU1,200 (20X6: CU0).

Information related to share options for the year ended 31 December 20X7:	Number	Average exercise price CU
Outstanding 01 January	0	0
Granted	5 000	15
Outstanding 31 December	**5,000**	**15**

21.1 INTRODUCTION

Entities have increasingly embarked on incentivising their staff to achieve their strategic objectives by compensating them with shares, share options or other share-based payments. Employees can often work in their own interest, which may conflict with the strategic interest of the entity and shareholders. In order to achieve goal congruency, entities align the goals of employees (or certain employees) with those of the shareholders by making them shareholders through share-based payments. Employees are not the only parties to whom entities make share-based payments. Other parties might include suppliers and other stakeholders.

21.2 LEARNING OUTCOMES

This chapter is designed to introduce accounting for share-based payment transactions. Upon completion of this chapter, you should know the financial reporting requirements for accounting for share-based payments in accordance with the IFRS for SMEs. In particular, you should be able to:

(a) identify and classify share-based payments;

(b)   identify and classify share-based payments into being equity-settled and cash-settled;

(c)   recognise and measure the effect of and balances related to share-based payments in the financial statements of an entity; and

(d)   present and disclose the effects of share-based payments.

21.3   DEFINITIONS

The definitions for the important concepts and terms used in IFRS for SMEs are found in Appendix B – *Glossary of terms* of IFRS for SMEs. Some important definitions related to share-based payment arrangements include the following:

- **Share-based payment arrangement:** An agreement between the entity (or another group entity or any shareholder of any group entity) and another party (including an employee) that entitles the other party to receive:
  - (a)   cash or other assets of the entity for amounts that are based on the price (or value) of equity instruments (including shares or share options) of the entity or another group entity; or
  - (b)   equity instruments (including shares or share options) of the entity or another group entity provided the specified vesting conditions, if any, are met

- **Share-based payment transaction:** A transaction in which the entity:
  - (a)   receives goods or services from the supplier of those goods or services (including an employee) in a share-based payment arrangement; or
  - (b)   incurs an obligation to settle the transaction with the supplier in a share-based payment arrangement when another group entity receives those goods or services

- **Cash-settled share-based payment transaction:** A share-based payment transaction in which the entity acquires goods or services by incurring a liability to transfer cash or other assets to the supplier of those goods or services for amounts that are based on the price (or value) of equity instruments (including shares or share options) of the entity or another group entity

- **Equity-settled share-based payment transaction:** A share-based payment transaction in which the entity:
  - (a)   receives goods or services as consideration for its own equity instruments (including shares or share options); or
  - (b)   receives goods or services but has no obligation to settle the transaction with the supplier

21.4   SCOPE AND OBJECTIVES

Section 26 (IFRS 2) provides guidance for accounting and disclosure for all share-based payment transactions.

21.5   CLASSIFICATION AS EQUITY SETTLED OR CASH SETTLED

Equity-settled share-based payment transactions are those that typically involve the entity issuing its own equity instruments or those that do not place an obligation on the entity to settle the transaction with the supplier. In other words, the entity receives goods or services and issues shares (for instance) in lieu of paying in cash for the goods or services.

21.5.1 Recognition

Recognition principles for equity-settled and cash-settled share-based payments are the same. The entity should recognise the goods or services (the debit entry) and the corresponding increase in equity (the credit entry) when the goods or services are received (s26.3 and IFRS 2 p.7).

Illustrative Example 21.1: Share-based payment transaction with a supplier

Company A receives furniture from a key supplier. Company A issues ordinary shares to its supplier. The transaction amounts to CU100,000.

You are required to:
Prepare the journal entries necessary to account for the share-based payment transaction.

Suggested solution:

		Debit	Credit
		CU	CU
Dr	Property, plant & equipment – furniture	100,000	
Cr	Ordinary shares		100,000
[Recognising the share-based payment and the furniture received for the year]			

What happens, however, when the goods or services are not received at a point in time, but rather over time? The recognition of the transaction (recognition of an asset or expense and a related increase in equity) is still recognised as the goods or services are received (ie this time it is over time) (s26.6 and IFRS 2 p.15).

Illustrative Example 21.2: Share-based payment transaction over time

Company A enters into a share-based payment transaction with its CEO. The transaction is measured at CU100,000. The CEO will only receive the shares offered in the share-based payment transaction if he/she works for the entity for five years from the date that the arrangement is entered into.

You are required to:

Prepare the journal entries necessary to account for the share-based payment transaction for year 1.

Suggested solution:

Dr	Employee cost [P/L] [CU100,000/5]	20,000	
Cr	Share-based payment reserve [SOCE]		20,000
[Recognising the employee costs and related increase in equity for the year]			

Illustrative Example 21.2 shows vesting conditions, namely that even though the services are received over the period of five years, the shares only vest with the employee if they complete the five years of service. Sometimes, shares are issued to employees without any further vesting conditions, meaning that they do not have to do anything more for them to earn the rights to the shares. In this case, the total expense (in Illustrative Example 21.2, CU100,000) and the related equity are recognised in the current year (s26.5 and IFRS 2 p.9).

21.5.2 Measurement

The measurement principles for equity-settled and cash-settled share-based payment transactions differ significantly.

21.5.2.1 Equity-settled share-based payment transactions

We used the measurement of CU100,000 in Illustrative Example 21.2, but how do we know that this is correct? In other words, how do we measure equity-settled share-based payment transactions?

Equity-settled share-based payment transactions are measured in the following order (s26.6 and IFRS 2 p.16–18):
(a) at the fair value of the goods or services received; and
(b) if the entity cannot measure the fair value of the goods or services received, at the fair value of the equity instruments granted.

In Illustrative Example 21.1, if the fair value of the furniture can be measured, then the CU100,000 measurement would have been made with reference to the fair value of the furniture and not the equity instruments granted. It is often difficult for an entity to estimate the fair value of the service that it receives from its employees. For this reason, section 26.7 (IFRS 2 p.11) states that transactions with employees are measured with reference to the equity instruments granted. So, in Illustrative Example 21.2, the CU100,000 would be referenced to the fair value of the equity instruments granted as it would be unlikely that company A would be able to estimate the fair value of the services from the CEO.

The fair value of the equity instruments granted can differ over time, so which fair value should the entity use? For instance, should the entity use the fair value at each year-end over the period that it recognises share-based payments, when those share-based payments are recognised over a number of years? In terms of section 26.8 (IFRS 2 p.11), the fair value of the equity instruments granted should be measured once, at grant date. The grant date fair value does not include all variables relating to vesting conditions. For instance, an employee might be entitled to certain forms of equity dependent on the employee satisfying certain service or performance conditions or the entity meets certain market conditions (such as a target share price). These vesting conditions can be market or non-market related. The grant date fair value is adjusted for all market conditions and therefore does not need to be taken into account when considering the number of shares or share options expected to vest (s26.9(a) and IFRS 2 p.19). The non-market conditions (such as the employee's performance) are not taken into account in the grant date fair value and therefore are taken into account when considering the number of shares or share options expected to vest (s26.9(b) and IFRS 2 p.19).

Illustrative Example 21.3: Share-based payment transaction with vesting conditions

Company A enters into a share-based payment transaction with its CEO on 01 January 20X7, the grant date. The CEO will only receive the 1,000 shares offered in the share-based payment transaction, if he/she works for the entity for five years from the date that the arrangement is entered into and if the share price of company A increases by 80% using the current year as a base. Company A is uncertain whether it will meet the share price target at the end of year 5, but considers it probable that the CEO will still be employed by the entity at the end of the five years.

The following information is provided:

	Fair value including share price target probability and probability that CEO will work for five years	Fair value including share price target probability only
	CU	CU
01 January 20X7	90	100
31 December 20X7	110	115

You are required to:
Prepare the journal entries necessary to account for the share-based payment transaction for the year ended 31 December 20X7.

Suggested solution:

Dr	Employee cost [P/L] [CU100,000*/5]	20,000	
Cr	Share-based payment reserve [SOCE]		20,000
[Recognising the employee costs and related increase in equity for the year]			

*The entity uses the CU100 fair value × 1,000 shares as it includes the effect of the market condition (s26.9(b) and IFRS 2 p.), but not the non-market performance condition (s26.9(a) and IFRS 2 p.). Because the market condition is factored into the grant date fair value, its probability is not considered in the recognition of the transaction at the end of the year. However, because the non-market vesting performance condition is not factored into the grant date fair value, its probability is considered (if it were unlikely that the CEO would complete the five-year service, no expense would be recognised)

When measuring the grant date fair value of the equity instruments granted, the following three-tier hierarchy should be followed (s26.10 and IFRS 2 p.16–18):
(a)   an observable market price for the equity instrument;
(b)   if an observable market price is not available, use entity-specific observable market data such as:
  (i)   a recent transaction in the entity's shares;
  (ii)   a recent independent fair valuation of the entity or its principal assets;
(c)   if an observable market price is not available and the use of entity-specific observable market data is impracticable, then use a valuation method that uses market data to the greatest extent practicable (for equity-settled share appreciation rights and share options, the entity should use an acceptable option pricing model).

21.5.2.2 Cash-settled share-based payment transactions

An entity should recognise the goods or services acquired (the debit entry) and the liability incurred (the credit entry) at the fair value of the liability (s26.14 and IFRS 2 p.30).

Illustrative Example 21.4: Share-based payment transaction with a supplier

Company A receives furniture from a key supplier. Company A issues its supplier 100 share appreciation rights. Each share appreciation right entitles the supplier to the cash equivalent to the increase in one ordinary share at 31 December 20X7, the date of settlement. The transaction amounts to CU100,000.

You are required to:

Prepare the journal entries necessary to account for the share-based payment transaction.

Suggested solution:

Dr	Property, plant & equipment – furniture	100,000	
Cr	Share-based payment liability		100,000
[Recognising the share-based payment and the furniture received for the year]			

The goods or services received are accounted for in terms of the relevant standard such as section 16 – *Investment property* (IAS 40 – *Investment property*), section 17 – *Property, plant and equipment* (IAS 16 – *Property, plant and equipment*), etc. The share-based payment liability is remeasured each reporting date and at the settlement date with changes recognized in profit or loss (s26.14 and IFRS 2 p.30).

Illustrative Example 21.5: Share-based payment transaction with a supplier – cash-settled

Company A receives furniture from a key supplier. Company A issues its supplier 100 share appreciation rights. Each share appreciation right entitles the supplier to the cash equivalent to the increase in one ordinary share at 31 December 20X7, the date of settlement. The total fair value of the share-based payment liability at transaction date is CU10,000. The total fair value of the share-based payment liability at 30 November 20X7 (year-end) is CU12,000.

You are required to:

Prepare the journal entries necessary to account for the share-based payment transaction at initial recognition and year-end.

Suggested solution:

Dr	Property, plant & equipment – furniture	10,000	
Cr	Share-based payment liability		10,000
[Recognising the share-based payment and the furniture at initial recognition]			

Dr	Fair value loss on share-based payment liability [P/L]	2,000	
Cr	Share-based payment liability		2,000
[Recognising the share-based payment at year-end]			

21.5.3 Disclosure

An entity must disclose the following about the nature and extent of a share-based payment arrangement that existed during the period (s26.18 and IFRS 2 p.44):
(a)   a description of each type of share-based payment arrangement that existed during the period;
(b)   the number and weighted average exercise prices of share options for each of the following groups of options:
    (i)   outstanding at the beginning of the period;
    (ii)   granted during the period;
    (iii)   forfeited during the period;
    (iv)   exercised during the period;
    (v)   expired during the period;
    (vi)   outstanding at the end of the period; and
    (vii)   exercisable at the end of the period.

For equity-settled share-based payment arrangements, disclose information about how the entity measured the fair value of the goods or services received or the value of the equity instruments granted. If a valuation methodology was used, an entity needs to disclose the method and the reason for using it (s26.19 and IFRS 2 p.46).

For cash-settled share-based payment arrangements, disclose information about how the liability was measured (s26.20 and IFRS 2 p.46).

Disclose the following about the impact of share-based payment transactions on the profit or loss and financial position:
(a)   the total expense recognised in profit or loss for the period; and
(b)   the total carrying amount at the end of the period for liabilities arising from share-based payment transactions (s26.23 and IFRS 2 p.50).

Note 3: Profit from operations
Included in profit from operations is the following expenses:
equity-settled share-based payment arrangement   CU1,500
cash-settled share-based payment arrangement   CU1,200

Note 20: Share-based payment arrangements
The entity entered into two share-based payment transactions during the course of the year as detailed below:

1. The entity entered into an equity-settled share-based payment transaction with its CEO, Mr. E Adams, in which Mr. Adams was granted 5 000 share options that vest only if he remains in the employ of the entity for a period of five years from grant date; and

2. The entity entered into a cash-settled share-based payment transaction with its key supplier of equipment, Supplier (Pty) Ltd. The terms of the arrangement include that the entity received equipment and offered the supplier cash-settled share appreciation rights, which entitle the supplier to a cash payment based on the increase of the entity's shares between the grant date and 1 December 20x7, the date of settlement.

The carrying amount of liabilities arising from share-based payment transactions at 31 December 20x7 is CU1,200 (20x6: CU0).

Information related to share options for the year ended 31 December 20X7:	Number	Average exercise price CU
Outstanding 1 January	0	0
Granted	5 000	15
Outstanding 31 December	**5,000**	**15**

SELF-ASSESSMENT
Multiple choice questions: Testing principles of accounting for share-based payments

1. The following transactions are not within the scope of the standard on share-based payments:

(a) payment of employees with shares	
(b) payment of suppliers with share appreciation rights	
(c) payment of employees based on an increase in net income	
(d) payment of suppliers with share options	

2. The following transaction refers to an equity-settled share-based payment:

(a) payment of employees in cash based on the current share price	
(b) payment of employees in cash based on the increase in the share price over a certain period of time	
(c) payment of employees in cash based on the increase in net income	
(d) payment of employees in share options	

3. A transaction related to an equity-settled share-based payment for goods or services, where the fair value of both the goods and the equity being issued can be measured reliably, is:

(a) fair value of the goods or services received	
(b) fair value of the equity instruments granted	
(c) net realisable value of the goods or services received	
(d) fair value less costs of disposal of the goods or services received	

4. The grant date fair value of equity instruments granted excludes:

(a) all vesting conditions	
(b) vesting conditions based on non-market performance	
(c) vesting conditions based on market performance	
(d) none of the above	

5. The following share-based payment balances get remeasured to fair value at each reporting date and on settlement date:

(a) cash-settled liabilities related to share-based payments	
(b) equity balances related to equity settled share-based payments	
(c) all balances related to share-based payments	
(d) none of the balances related to share-based payments	

6. Share-based payment transactions are recognised on:

(a) the date that the equity instruments are granted	
(b) the date that cash payments are made	
(c) the date that the related goods or services are received	
(d) the date that the share-based payment contract is entered into	

7. Share-based payment transactions related to services received from employees are usually measured at:

(a) fair value of the equity instruments granted	
(b) fair value of the services received	
(c) net realisable value of the services received	
(d) none of the above	

8. Share-based payments made to employees which have no further vesting conditions are recognised:

(a) retrospectively	
(b) over the employee's remaining contract period	
(c) in the following financial period	
(d) in full at grant date	

9. The following basis should be used as the first measure of share-based payments involving the issue of shares:

(a) a valuation technique like discounted cash flows	
(b) recent fair valuation of the assets of the entity	
(c) observable market price for the equity instruments granted	
(d) none of the above	

10. An entity should disclose the following information regarding share-based payment arrangements entered into during the year:

(a) to whom the shares were issued	
(b) the expected future price of the shares being issued	
(c) the historical price of the shares being issued	
(d) none of the above	

Practical questions:
Application of principles to business scenarios

QUESTION 1

GECR (Pty) Ltd purchased equipment from a key supplier, which was delivered on 01 June 20X7. GECR (Pty) Ltd issued 100 shares to its supplier on the date of delivery. The shares have a fair value of CU250 each. The equipment has a fair value of CU26,000.

You are required to:
Record the journal entries to account for the purchase of the equipment and issue of the shares on 01 June 20X7.

QUESTION 2

Equity-Settled (Pty) Ltd grants its eight employees 100 share options each on 01 January 20X6. Each share option allows the employee to convert the share options into one ordinary share on 31 December 20X8 on condition that the employee is still employed by Equity-Settled (Pty) Ltd at that date. Equity-Settled (Pty) Ltd estimates that six of the employees who received share options will still be employed by the entity at 31 December 20X7, and five at 31 December 20X8. The grant date fair value of each share option is CU50 on 01 January 20X6.

You are required to:
Prepare the journal entries necessary to account for the share-based payment transaction at 31 December 20X7.

QUESTION 3

Cash-Settled (Pty) Ltd offered to pay its supplier using share appreciation rights in settlement for furniture which it purchased. It granted its CEO 1,000 share appreciation rights in terms of which Cash-Settled (Pty) Ltd offered to pay its supplier the equivalent of the increase in the price of one share, from 01 January 20X7 to 31 December 20X8, for each right it held. The following fair values relating to each share appreciation right are relevant:

	CU
01 January 20X7	30
31 December 20X7	37

You are required to:

Prepare the journal entries necessary to account for the share appreciation rights for the year ended 31 December 20X7.

CHAPTER 22
ANALYSIS AND INTERPRETATION OF FINANCIAL STATEMENTS

ILLUSTRATIVE DISCLOSURE [EXTRACT]

		20X2	20X1
		CU'000	CU'000
Liquidity ratios:			
Current ratio		2.5:1	2.3:1
Quick/acid-test ratio		1:1	1.14:1

A review of the liquidity ratios shows an improvement of current assets to current liabilities, but also a relatively lower quick/acid-test ratio. This is indicative of the fact that the entity has significant investment in current assets in its inventory which increases:
(a)   holding cost;
(b)   risk for stock obsolescence due to ageing inventory; and
(c)   increased liquidity risk if the inventory cannot be sold for at least its cost.

Working capital ratios:			
Inventory turnover		5	8
Days inventory on hand		73	47
Accounts receivable collection period		18	23
Accounts payable days outstanding		47	41

The working capital ratios show that inventory appears to have a longer holding period or greater investment in inventory (refer to the inventory turnover and days inventory on hand ratios), which aligns to the comment regarding inventory under the liquidity ratios above. As such, the risk as identified under the liquidity ratios are listed here again:
(a)   holding cost;
(b)   risk for stock obsolescence due to ageing inventory; and
(c)   increased liquidity risk if the inventory cannot be sold for at least its cost.

The accounts receivable collection period has improved and all else remaining the same, coupled with the accounts payable days outstanding, means an improvement in cash flow management given that accounts receivable is collected far in advance of the period in which accounts payable is settled, although the combination of the inventory days on hand and accounts receivable collection period shows that the supplier of the inventory is paid before the cash from the inventory is received. The entity should consider the agreements with its suppliers to ensure that it manages the risk of tarnishing its relationship with its clients if the entity is unduly delaying payment to the supplier.

Debt management ratios:		
Debt ratio	45%	60%
Debt to equity ratio	82%	152%
Times interest earned	7	5
EBITDA coverage ratio	10	11

It is evident from the debt management ratios that the reliance on third-party liability funding has decreased when compared to the prior year (evidenced by the debt and debt to equity ratios). This is also evidenced by the times interest earned ratio. Finally, depreciation and amortisation must have increased as evidenced by the fact that the EBITDA ratio is lower than in the prior year although the times interest earned has increased.

Profitability ratios:		
Gross profit margin	59%	48%
Net profit margin	15%	12%
Return on assets	23%	18%
Return on capital employed	31%	25%
Return on equity	42%	45%

The gross and net profit margins show that the company is in a profitable position and on a year-on-year positive trajectory with respect to profitability. Return on assets and capital employed reflects an increasingly positive trend, however the return on equity decreased, which is symptomatic of the decrease in the debt to equity ratio, whereby the entity now uses more expensive (equity) to finance operations than in the prior year, when it used a lot cheaper finance (debt).

22.1   INTRODUCTION

The objective of financial reporting is to provide information about the entity to users that is useful for economic decision-making (s2.2 and CF p.x). Therefore, the sole purpose for producing financial statements is to provide information that can be used as inputs to decision-making. Because financial statements prepared in terms of IFRS for SMEs (and IFRS) are general purpose (s1.2(b) and CF p.x) financial statements, they do not meet all needs of all users as they are prepared. For this reason, users often have subjected the information to further analysis to answer their specific questions. This chapter considers some of the more common analyses done on the information provided by financial statements to answer the frequently asked questions that users have. We refer to this as financial statement analysis.

22.2   LEARNING OUTCOMES

Upon completion of this chapter you should know the commonly used financial ratios. In particular, you should be able to apply and interpret ratios related to an entity's:
(a)   liquidity;
(b)   working capital;
(c)   debt management; and
(d)   profitability.

In order to achieve the learning outcomes, the following selected information from an illustrative set of financial statements will be consistently used in the illustrative examples which follow:

Extract of the financial statements for the year ended 31 December 20X8

The entity has the following balances in its trial balance.

You are required to:
Using the information provided, calculate the debt ratio.

	CU
Property, plant & equipment	450,000
Intangible assets	200,000
Other non-current assets	150,000
Non-current assets	**800,000**

Inventory	123,000
Accounts receivable	74,000
Cash	3,000
Current assets	**200,000**
Total assets	**1,000,000**
Ordinary share capital	100,000
Retained earnings	450,000
Total equity	**550,000**
Long-term loan	370,000
Non-current liabilities	**370,000**
Trade payables	80,000
Current liabilities	**80,000**
Total liabilities	**450,000**
Total equity & liabilities	**1,000,000**

	CU
Revenue	1,500,000
Cost of sales	(612,000)
Gross profit	**888,000**
Other expenses	(50,000)
Administrative expenses	(250,000)
Selling and distribution expenses	(88,000)
Profit before interest and tax	**500,000**
Interest expense	(72,000)
Profit before tax	**428,000**
Tax expense	(196,000)
Profit after tax	**232,000**

Extract of the notes to the financial statements for the year ended 31 December 20X8:

Note 7:

Profit before interest and tax includes depreciation and amortisation expense totalling 20X8: CU220,000 (20X7: CU300,000).

22.3   LIQUIDITY RATIOS

Liquidity ratios help us to analyse the financial information in a way that gives us insight into the entity's ability to convert current assets into cash in time to settle our current liabilities. As such, we will focus on the following two ratios:
(a)   current ratio; and
(b)   quick/acid-test ratio.

22.3.1 Current ratio

Current ratio = $\dfrac{\text{Current assets}}{\text{Current liabilities}}$

The current ratio identifies the entity's ability to cover its current liabilities using its current assets. A rule of thumb is that a healthy current ratio is reflected by a ratio of 2:1 (ie the entity has two currency units of current assets to fund every one currency unit of current liabilities).

Illustrative Example 22.1: Current ratio

You are required to:
Using the same information provided in Illustrative Example 1, calculate the current ratio.

Current ratio	$\dfrac{\text{Current assets}}{\text{Current liabilities}}$
	$\dfrac{200,000}{80,000}$
	2.5:1

22.3.2 Quick/acid-test ratio

Current ratio = $\dfrac{\text{Current assets} - \text{Inventory}}{\text{Current liabilities}}$

The quick/acid-test ratio is similar to the current ratio in that it tests the entity's ability to cover its current liabilities using its current assets, but differs in that it ignores any future economic benefits expected from the sale of inventory. It takes the worst-case scenario approach, looking at the liquidity position of the entity should the entity experience difficulty in selling its inventory and only recovers the future economic benefits embodied in its remaining current assets. A rule of thumb is that a healthy current ratio is reflected by a ratio of 1:1 (ie the entity has one currency unit of current assets to fund every one currency unit of current liabilities).

Illustrative Example 22.2: Quick/acid-test ratio

You are required to:

Using the same information as in Illustrative Example 22.1, calculate the current ratio.

Current ratio	$\dfrac{\text{Current assets} - \text{inventory}}{\text{Current liabilities}}$
	$\dfrac{\text{CU200,000} - \text{CU123,000}}{\text{CU80,000}}$
	1:1

22.4   WORKING CAPITAL RATIOS

Working capital ratios analyse information around how well the entity manages its working capital, ie how long the entity holds and settles the assets and liabilities included in working capital. The following working ratios will be discussed:

(a)   inventory turnover;
(b)   inventory days on hand;
(c)   accounts receivable collection period; and
(d)   accounts payable days outstanding.

22.4.1 Inventory turnover

Inventory turnover = $\dfrac{\text{Cost of sales}}{\text{Inventory}}$

The inventory turnover ratio lets us know how many times an amount of inventory, equivalent to the amount of inventory currently on hand, was sold during the year. It is indicative of:

(a)   how quickly the entity sells its inventory; and relatedly
(b)   helps the entity assess whether it has sufficient inventory on hand to satisfy its sales demand.

Illustrative Example 22.3: Inventory turnover

You are required to:

Using the information provided, calculate the inventory turnover ratio.

Inventory turnover	$\dfrac{\text{Cost of sales}}{\text{Inventory}}$
	$\dfrac{\text{CU612,000}}{\text{CU123,000}}$
	5

22.4.2 Inventory days on hand

$$\text{Inventory days on hand} = \frac{\text{Inventory}}{\text{Cost of sales}} \times 365 \text{ days}$$

The inventory days on hand ratio assists us in predicting how many days' inventory we have in our inventory balance, assuming that we continue selling inventory at the average rate reflected by our cost of sales.

Illustrative Example 22.4: Inventory days on hand

You are required to:

Using the same information as in Illustrative Example 22.3, calculate the inventory days on hand ratio.

Inventory days on hand	$\dfrac{\text{Inventory} \times 365}{\text{Cost of sales}}$
	$\dfrac{\text{CU123,000}}{\text{CU612,000}} \times 365$
	73 days

22.4.3 Accounts receivable collection period

$$\text{Accounts receivable collection period} = \frac{\text{Accounts receivable}}{\text{Revenue}} \times 365 \text{ days}$$

The accounts receivable collection period determines how long it would take on average to collect the accounts receivable balance in the financial statements. It should be referenced to revenue from credit transactions, but for the remainder of the chapter, we assume that all revenue is from credit transactions.

Illustrative Example 22.5: Accounts receivable collection period

You are required to:
Using the information provided in Illustrative Example 1, calculate the accounts receivable collection period ratio.

Accounts receivable collection period	$\dfrac{\text{Accounts receivable} \times 365}{\text{Revenue}}$
	$\dfrac{\text{CU74,000} \times 365}{\text{CU1,500,000}}$
	18

22.4.4 Accounts payable days outstanding

$$\text{Accounts payable days outstanding} = \frac{\text{Accounts payable}}{\text{Cost of sales}} \times 365 \text{ days}$$

Accounts payable days outstanding identifies how long it will take on average for the entity to settle the balance of accounts payable in the financial statements. It should be referenced to cost of sales from credit transactions, but for the remainder of the chapter, we will assume that all purchases are made on credit.

Illustrative Example 22.6: Accounts payable days outstanding

Using the information provided in Illustrative Example 1, calculate the accounts payable days outstanding ratio.

Accounts payable days outstanding	$\dfrac{\text{Accounts payable}}{\text{Cost of sales}} \times 365 \text{ days}$
	$\dfrac{\text{CU80,000}}{\text{CU612,000}} \times 365$
	47

22.5 DEBT MANAGEMENT RATIOS

The debt management ratios analyse how the entity funds its assets, its mix between equity and liabilities, and how well it can pay the cost of the capital employed (in the form of interest etc.). The following debt management ratios will be focused on:
(a)   debt ratio;
(b)   debt to equity ratio;

(c) times interest earned; and

(d) Earnings before interest, tax, depreciation and amortisation (EBITDA) coverage ratio.

22.5.1 Debt ratio

Debt ratio = $\dfrac{\text{Debt}}{\text{Total assets}}$

The debt ratio analyses the proportion of assets funded by debt financing. It is the ratio of total debt (including current and non-current liabilities) to total assets (including current and non-current assets).

Illustrative Example 22.7: Debt ratio

You are required to:

Using the information provided in Illustrative Example 1, calculate the debt ratio.

Debt ratio	$\dfrac{\text{Debt}}{\text{Total assets}}$ × 100
	$\dfrac{\text{CU450,000}}{\text{CU1,000,000}}$ × 100
	45%

22.5.2 Debt to equity ratio

Debt to equity = $\dfrac{\text{Total debt}}{\text{Total equity}}$

The debt to equity ratio analyses the relationship between debt financing and equity financing to ascertain how the entity leverages its sources of finance. Debt finance is normally cheaper than equity finance, due to the relative risk exposure to financiers and possible tax savings available when satisfying debt finance as opposed to equity finance. However, increasing the proportion of debt to equity exposes the entity to significantly more risk and so each entity will have an ideal balance of debt to equity.

Illustrative Example 22.8: Debt to equity ratio

Using the information provided in Illustrative Example 1, calculate the debt to equity ratio.

Debt to equity ratio	$\dfrac{\text{Total debt} \times 100}{\text{Total equity}}$
	$\dfrac{\text{CU450,000} \times 100}{\text{CU550,000}}$
	82%

22.5.3 Times interest earned

$$\text{Times interest earned} = \frac{\text{EBIT*}}{\text{Interest expense}}$$

The times interest earned ratio analyses the margin of safety, measured as a multiple, of the profit before interest (*EBIT = *earnings before interest and tax*) available to pay for the cost of debt (ie interest expense).

Illustrative Example 22.9: Debt to equity ratio

You are required to:

Using the information provided in Illustrative Example 1, calculate the times interest earned ratio.

Times interest earned ratio	$\dfrac{\text{EBIT}}{\text{Interest expense}}$
	$\dfrac{\text{CU500,000}}{\text{CU72,000}}$
	7

22.5.4 EBITDA coverage ratio

$$\text{EBITDA coverage ratio} = \frac{\text{EBITDA}}{\text{Interest expense}}$$

Depreciation and amortisation are often the largest non-cash expenses recognised in the statement of profit or loss. Therefore, analysing the amount of profit that the entity has available (that most closely represents a cash profit) to settle the cost of debt will probably best be calculated using this ratio.

You are required to:
Using the information as provided in Illustrative Example 1, calculate the EBITDA coverage ratio.

EBITDA coverage ratio	EBITDA
	Interest expense
	CU500,000 + CU220,000
	CU72,000
	10

22.6 PROFITABILITY RATIOS

Profitability ratios analyse the margins earned as well as the return on the capital employed in the entity. In particular, the following profitability ratios will form the focus of this chapter:
(a)   gross profit margin;
(b)   net profit margin;
(c)   return on assets;
(d)   return on capital employed; and
(e)   return on equity.

22.6.1 Gross profit margin

Gross profit margin = $\frac{\text{Gross profit}}{\text{Revenue}} \times 100$

The gross profit margin informs the entity about the return that it earns from selling its inventory, but only considers the direct cost of the inventory. The gross profit margin is calculated as a percentage of revenue, unlike the gross profit markup, which is calculated as a percentage markup on cost.

Illustrative Example 22.10: Debt to equity ratio

You are required to:
Using the information provided in Illustrative Example 1, calculate the gross profit margin ratio.

Gross profit margin ratio	$\frac{\text{Gross profit} \times 100}{\text{Revenue}}$
	$\frac{\text{CU888,000} \times 100}{\text{CU1,500,000}}$
	59%

22.6.2 Net profit margin

Net profit margin = $\dfrac{\text{Net profit}}{\text{Revenue}} \times 100$

The net profit margin informs the entity about the return that it earns from all of the amounts that it expended during the year. The net profit margin is calculated as a percentage of revenue.

Illustrative Example 22.11: Debt to equity ratio

You are required to:

Using the information as provided in Illustrative Example 1, calculate the net profit margin ratio.

Net profit margin ratio	$\dfrac{\text{Net profit}}{\text{Revenue}} \times 100$
	$\dfrac{\text{CU232,000}}{\text{CU1,500,000}} \times 100$
	15%

22.6.3 Return on assets

Return on assets = $\dfrac{\text{Net profit}}{\text{Total assets}} \times 100$

The return on assets ratio analyses the return during the period earned per currency unit of assets.

Illustrative Example 22.12: Return on assets ratio

You are required to:

Using the information as provided in Illustrative Example 1, calculate the gross return on assets ratio.

Return on assets ratio	$\dfrac{\text{Net profit}}{\text{Total assets}} \times 100$
	$\dfrac{\text{CU232,000}}{\text{CU1,000,000}} \times 100$
	23%

22.6.4 Return on capital employed

Return on capital employed = $\dfrac{\text{NOPAT*}}{\text{Net operating assets}}$

The return on capital employed ratio analyses the *net operating profit after tax* (NOPAT), as a return of on the net operating assets (total assets less accounts payable) used to earn the related profit.

Illustrative Example 22.13: Return on capital employed

You are required to:

Using the information as provided in Illustrative Example 1, calculate the return on capital employed ratio.

Return on capital employed ratio	$\dfrac{\text{NOPAT} \times 100}{\text{Net operating assets}}$
	$\dfrac{\text{CU232,000} + (\text{CU72,000} \times 72\%) \times 100}{\text{CU1,000,000} - \text{CU80,000}}$
	$\dfrac{\text{CU283,840} \times 100}{\text{CU920,000}}$
	31%

22.6.5 Return on equity

Return on equity = $\dfrac{\text{Net profit} \times 100}{\text{Equity}}$

The return on equity ratio analyses the net profit earned for every currency unit of equity investment.

Illustrative Example 22.14: Return on equity

You are required to:

Using the information as provided in Illustrative Example 1, calculate the return on equity ratio.

Return on equity ratio	$\dfrac{\text{Net profit} \times 100}{\text{Equity}}$
	$\dfrac{\text{CU232,000} \times 100}{\text{CU550,000}}$
	42%

SELF-ASSESSMENT
Multiple choice questions: Testing principles of analysis and interpretation of financial statements

1. The following formula represents the calculation to determine the current ratio:

(a) (current assets – inventory)/current liabilities	
(b) (current assets – accounts receivable)/current liabilities	
(c) current liabilities/current assets	
(d) current assets/current liabilities	

2. The following formula represents the calculation to determine the quick/acid-test ratio:

(a) (current assets – inventory)/current liabilities	
(b) (current assets – accounts receivable)/current liabilities	
(c) current liabilities/current assets	
(d) current assets/current liabilities	

3. The liquidity ratios analyse information to determine:

(a) the solvency of the entity	
(b) whether the entity will have sufficient cash to satisfy its longer-term obligations	
(c) whether the entity will have sufficient cash to satisfy its shorter-term obligations	
(d) how much cash the entity has	

4.   The inventory days on hand ratio determines:

(a) how much inventory the entity has on hand	
(b) how long the inventory will still be on hand	
(c) when to sell the inventory	
(d) none of the above	

5.   The accounts receivable collection period ratio is calculated as follows:

(a) accounts receivable/days	
(b) accounts receivable/revenue $\times$ 365	
(c) revenue/accounts receivable $\times$ 365	
(d) accounts receivable $\times$ 365	

6.   The accounts payable days outstanding ratio determines:

(a) when the entity should purchase from its supplier again	
(b) what the balance of accounts payable is	
(c) how much of the accounts payable is represented by debit balances	
(d) how long it would take to settle the current accounts payable balance	

7.   The debt ratio is calculated using the following formula:

(a) debt/total assets	
(b) debt/equity	
(c) debt/current assets	
(d) current liabilities/total debt	

8. The debt to equity ratio is calculated using the following formula:

(a) debt/total assets	
(b) debt/current assets	
(c) debt/equity	
(d) current liabilities/total debt	

9. Return on capital employed aims to identify the relationship between net operating assets and:

(a) net operating profit after tax	
(b) net operating profit	
(c) EBIT	
(d) earning after tax	

10. The interest coverage ratio identifies:

(a) whether the entity has interest expense	
(b) the level/margin of safety, in the form of a multiple, that the entity has to pay its cost of debt	
(c) the level/margin applied to markup its inventory	
(d) whether the entity has debt	

Practical questions:
Application of principles to business scenarios

QUESTION 1

Ballet (Pty) Ltd requested for you to assist them in evaluating their liquidity position. The entity presented the following information which is extracted from its trial balance to you:

BALLET (PTY) LTD		
Extract from the trial balance for the year ended 31 December 20X8		
	DR	CR
	CU	CU
Inventory	100,000	
Accounts receivable	80,000	
Cash	20,000	
Accounts payable		120,000

Note:
The information extracted from the trial balance above is the only information classified as current assets and liabilities.

You are required to:
Calculate the two liquidity ratios discussed in this chapter for Ballet (Pty) Ltd using the information provided above and provide a critique of the entities liquidity position as at 31 December 20X8.

QUESTION 2

Pristine (Pty) Ltd provided you with the following information and requested you to assist in evaluating their working capital position:

PRISTINE (PTY) LTD		
Extract from the trial balance for the year ended 31 December 20X8		
	DR	CR
	CU	CU
Revenue		1,000,000
Cost of sales	750,000	
Inventory	100,000	
Accounts receivable	80,000	

Cash	20,000	
Accounts payable		120,000

Additional information
1. 80% of the revenue and cost of sales consists of revenue earned from credit sales purchases made on credit respectively.
2. You may assume that the entity works for 365 days per annum.

You are required to:
Calculate the following ratios for Pristine (Pty) Ltd using the information provided above and provide a critique of the entities liquidity position as at 31 December 20X8:
(a) inventory days on hand;
(b) accounts receivable collection period; and
(c) accounts payable days outstanding.

QUESTION 3

Diamond (Pty) Ltd presented the following statement of profit or loss, statement of financial position and additional information to you:

DIAMOND (PTY) LTD		
Statement of profit or loss for the year ended 31 December 20X8		
	20X8	**20X7**
	CU	**CU**
Revenue	2,500,000	2,000,000
Cost of sales	(980,000)	(900,000)
Gross profit	**1,520,000**	**1,100,000**
Other expenses	(320,000)	(300,000)
Administrative expenses	(210,000)	(200,000)
Selling and distribution expenses	(120,000)	(100,000)
Profit before interest and tax	**870,000**	**500,000**
Interest expense	(40,000)	(25,000)
Profit before tax	**830,000**	**475,000**
Taxation expense	(196,000)	(133,000)
Profit for the year	**634,000**	**342,000**

DIAMOND (PTY) LTD		
Statement of financial position as at 31 December 20X8		
	20X8	**20X7**
	CU	**CU**
Non-current assets		
Property, plant & equipment	1,100,000	500,000
Intangible assets	220,000	200,000
Other non-current assets	150,000	150,000
Total non-current assets	**1,470,000**	**850,000**
Current assets		
Inventory	115,000	100,000
Accounts receivable	85,000	80,000
Cash	30,000	20,000
Total current assets	**230,000**	**200,000**
TOTAL ASSETS	**1,700,000**	**1,050,000**
Equity		
Ordinary share capital	200,000	200,000
Retained earnings	1,134,000	500,000
Total equity	**1,334,000**	**700,000**
Non-current liabilities		
Long-term loan	286,000	300,000
Total non-current liabilities	**286,000**	**300,000**
Current liabilities		
Accounts payable	80,000	50,000
Total current liabilities	**80,000**	**50,000**
Total liabilities	**366,000**	**350,000**
TOTAL EQUITY & LIABILITIES	**1,700,000**	**1,050,000**

Additional information:

The total depreciation and amortisation expense included in the profit before interest and tax amounts to 20X8: CU300,000 (20X7: CU100,000).

You are required to:

Using all of the ratios covered in the chapter, analyse the information provided to you above and discuss each of the following for and as at the year ended 31 December 20X8:

(a)   the liquidity position of the entity;

(b)   the working capital of the entity;

(c)   the debt management of the entity; and

(d)   the profitability of the entity.

www.ingramcontent.com/pod-product-compliance
Lightning Source LLC
Chambersburg PA
CBHW051114200326
41518CB00016B/2501